THE REBELLION
-OF-
RONALD REAGAN

THE REBELLION
-OF-
RONALD REAGAN

A HISTORY OF THE END OF THE COLD WAR

JAMES MANN

VIKING

VIKING
Published by the Penguin Group
Penguin Group (USA) Inc., 375 Hudson Street,
New York, New York 10014, U.S.A.
Penguin Group (Canada), 90 Eglinton Avenue East, Suite 700,
Toronto, Ontario, Canada M4P 2Y3
(a division of Pearson Penguin Canada Inc.)
Penguin Books Ltd, 80 Strand, London WC2R 0RL, England
Penguin Ireland, 25 St. Stephen's Green, Dublin 2, Ireland
(a division of Penguin Books Ltd)
Penguin Books Australia Ltd, 250 Camberwell Road, Camberwell,
Victoria 3124, Australia
(a division of Pearson Australia Group Pty Ltd)
Penguin Books India Pvt Ltd, 11 Community Centre, Panchsheel Park,
New Delhi – 110 017, India
Penguin Group (NZ), 67 Apollo Drive, Rosedale, North Shore 0632,
New Zealand (a division of Pearson New Zealand Ltd)
Penguin Books (South Africa) (Pty) Ltd, 24 Sturdee Avenue,
Rosebank, Johannesburg 2196, South Africa

Penguin Books Ltd, Registered Offices:
80 Strand, London WC2R 0RL, England

First published in 2009 by Viking Penguin,
a member of Penguin Group (USA) Inc.

10 9 8 7 6 5 4 3 2 1

Copyright © James Mann, 2009
All rights reserved

LIBRARY OF CONGRESS CATALOGING-IN-PUBLICATION DATA

Mann, Jim, 1946–
   The rebellion of Ronald Reagan : a history of the end of the Cold War / James Mann.
      p.   cm.
   Includes bibliographical references and index.
   ISBN 978-0-670-02054-6
   1. Reagan, Ronald—Political and social views.   2. United States—Foreign relations—1981–1989.
3. Cold War.   4. Political leadership—United States—Case studies.   5. Presidents—United States—
Biography.   6. Nixon, Richard M. (Richard Milhous), 1913–1994—Influence.   7. Massie, Suzanne—
Influence.   8. Reagan, Ronald—Oratory.   9. United States—Foreign relations—Soviet Union.
10. Soviet Union—Foreign relations—United States.   I. Title.
   E877.2.M36 2009
   973.927092—dc22
                                                                2008029029

Printed in the United States of America
Set in Adobe Garamond
Designed by Spring Hoteling

For Elizabeth and Ted,
who will always mean more to me
than they can ever know

CONTENTS

PART II: INFORMAL ADVISER

PART III: BERLIN

CONTENTS

CHRONOLOGY

1982

November 8–10:   Soviet general secretary Leonid Brezhnev dies and is succeeded by Yuri Andropov.

1983

March 8:   Reagan, speaking to the National Association of Evangelicals, denounces the Soviet Union as an "evil empire."

March 23:   Reagan announces Strategic Defense Initiative.

September 1:   Soviet military shoots down South Korean commercial flight KAL 007, killing 269 passengers.

November 2–11:   NATO forces conduct Able Archer 83, a military exercise testing chain-of-command procedures for nuclear weapons; CIA reports that Soviet officials feared it was the start of a surprise nuclear attack.

November 20:   ABC television airs *The Day After,* dramatizing the impact of nuclear war on a single town in Kansas.

November 23:   American Pershing II missiles are deployed in West Germany.

1984

January 16–17:   Reagan delivers speech calling for renewed dialogue with the Soviet Union and mentioning opportunities for peace. Reagan meets at White House with Suzanne Massie and sends her to Moscow as intermediary seeking a new cultural agreement.

February 9–13:   Andropov dies; Konstantin Chernenko named new Soviet leader.

August 17:   At secret meeting in Moscow, Soviet leaders complain to Erich Honecker that East Germany is drawing too close to West Germany.

November 6:   Reagan wins reelection.

1985

March 10–11:   Chernenko dies; Mikhail Gorbachev becomes fourth Soviet leader in less than three years.

November 19–21: Reagan and Gorbachev meet for the first time in Geneva.

1986

January 15:   Gorbachev unveils a proposal for a nuclear-free world by 2000.

April 26:   Soviet nuclear disaster occurs at Chernobyl.

July 18:   Richard Nixon visits Gorbachev in Moscow, describes him as a leader with a "steel fist."

August 13:   Residents of West Berlin let the twenty-fifth anniversary of the Berlin Wall pass quietly by. Reagan calls for the wall to be torn down.

August 30:   Soviets detain American reporter Nicholas Daniloff in response to American arrest of a Soviet diplomat on spying charges.

September 28–30: U.S. and Soviet officials announce a deal for Daniloff's release. Shortly afterward, the White House announces that Reagan and Gorbachev will meet again soon in Reykjavik.

October 11–12:   At Reykjavik, Reagan and Gorbachev discuss dramatic cutbacks in missiles and nuclear weapons, but no agreement is reached.

November 3–4:   Iran-Contra scandal breaks.

1987

February 26:   Tower Commission finds Reagan traded arms to Iran in exchange for release of American hostages in Lebanon. Reagan fires Chief of Staff Donald Regan, names Howard Baker to succeed him.

February 28:   Gorbachev announces Soviet Union is willing to try to conclude a treaty limiting intermediate-range missiles in Europe, without insisting that it be part of a larger agreement.

April 26–27:   Richard Nixon and Henry Kissinger warn in an op-ed of the dangers of Reagan's diplomacy with Gorbachev. Reagan meets with Nixon at the White House.

May 27–28:	In East Berlin, Gorbachev persuades Eastern European leaders to approve new military doctrine in which Warsaw Pact is considered a strictly defensive alliance.
May 28:	West German teenager Matthias Rust flies Cessna plane through Soviet air defenses to Moscow; Gorbachev responds by shaking up Soviet military command.
June 12:	Reagan, in West Berlin, delivers speech calling on Gorbachev to "tear down this wall."
September 7:	With Soviet acquiescence, Erich Honecker makes first visit to West Germany.
December 8–10:	Reagan and Gorbachev hold summit in Washington, conclude INF Treaty.

1988

May 27:	Senate ratifies INF Treaty.
May 29–June 1:	Reagan visits Moscow, says his description of Soviet Union as an "evil empire" was from "another time and another era."
November 8:	Bush wins presidency.
December 7:	At United Nations Gorbachev announces troop reductions; holds brief meeting at New York's Governor's Island with Reagan and Bush.

1989

January 19:	Erich Honecker says the Berlin Wall will still exist in "100 years."
January 22:	Two days after Bush's inauguration, National Security Adviser Brent Scowcroft says, "The Cold War is not over."
May 31:	On trip to Europe, Bush repeats Reagan's exhortation to tear down the Berlin Wall; calls for a Europe "whole and free."
June 4:	In Poland, opposition Solidarity candidates triumph in parliamentary elections.
June 13:	Reagan, in Europe, urges Bush administration to be willing to take some "risks" by negotiating with Gorbachev.
September 11:	Hungary lifts controls on travel by East Germans to Austria. East Germans stream across borders to Hungary and Czechoslovakia.
October 11:	Honecker steps down as East German leader, is succeeded by Egon Krenz.
November 9:	Krenz's regime says it will ease travel restrictions; amid confusion about what the new rules mean, East Germans stream through Berlin Wall and are not stopped.

INTRODUCTION

Several competing mythologies have developed about the role of Ronald Reagan in the end of the Cold War. On one side is the view that through confrontation and pugnacity Reagan "won" America's four-decade-long conflict with the Soviet Union. Proponents of an opposing view hold that the fortieth president was merely lucky or utterly irrelevant. My aim in this book is to reach beyond these simple formulas, to challenge old stereotypes about Reagan, and, through a combination of new interviews and newly available documents, to look back at what actually happened.

I first became interested in the Reagan years while working on another project. I was examining the careers of the members of George W. Bush's foreign-policy team for a book that was later published as *Rise of the Vulcans*. During this research, I happened across a then-unknown episode: the Reagan administration had conducted elaborate, highly classified exercises designed to keep the U.S. government operating in various "undisclosed locations" outside Washington in case of a nuclear war with the Soviet Union. The details of the secret program (in which Dick Cheney and Donald Rumsfeld had been key participants) made me want to look further at the Reagan years. Where did this episode fit in? Was the president of the United States really willing to contemplate a large-scale nuclear conflict? More generally, what was Reagan himself thinking and doing? Reagan's rhetoric toward the Soviet

Union was clear enough, but what was the relationship between his rhetoric and his actual policies? That was the starting point for this book. As I had in previous books, I wanted to examine the hidden aspects of American foreign policy and to explain them in a historical narrative.

During the course of the research, I found some surprises. The archives show that in dealing with the Soviet Union, Reagan on occasion operated in much the same way as he did in the Iran-Contra affair, secretly making use of low-level private intermediaries to carry personal messages back and forth. Even some of the plans for summit meetings with Mikhail Gorbachev went not through the secretary of state but through a lowly American author, a woman who had gotten to know both Reagan in Washington and a KGB official in Moscow. The archives also show that Reagan at one point had a frosty standoff inside the White House with former president Richard Nixon, who had been secretly brought back to his old haunts for the first time since he had left after his Watergate resignation. Nixon was more skeptical than Reagan that Mikhail Gorbachev represented a significant change in Moscow. Reagan sought Nixon's support for his efforts to cut back on nuclear weapons and ballistic missiles; Nixon refused to give it.

In Reagan's second term in the White House, his views and his policies were generally at variance with his image as a truculent Cold Warrior. Indeed, during the final three years of his presidency, Reagan was usually among the doves in the often-contentious American debates about the Soviet Union. Reagan was also horrified by the possibility of nuclear war, even during his first term in the White House. The rehearsals for nuclear war of the early 1980s that I had earlier discovered were not at all representative of Reagan's overall approach to nuclear weapons. In fact, these doomsday exercises of the early 1980s may have scared Reagan into trying to change American policy; in his second term, he repeatedly prodded U.S. military and defense officials to accept cutbacks in nuclear weapons and ballistic missiles.

Increasingly, Reagan rebelled against the forces and ideas that had made the Cold War seem endless and intractable. From 1986 to 1988, the period at the heart of this book, Reagan was increasingly at odds over Soviet policy with three separate but overlapping constituencies, each of which had played a powerful role in influencing American policy during the Cold War. The first of these was the political right, that is, the same American conservatives who had supported Reagan from the beginning of his political career through his early years in the White House. Magazines such as *National Review* and columnists such as George Will despised Reagan's unfolding diplomacy with Gorbachev.

The second constituency opposing Reagan was made up of the so-called realists, the group of officials who had teamed up to run American foreign policy during the Nixon and Ford administrations, including Nixon, Henry Kissinger, and Brent Scowcroft. During the 1970s, this group had battled with conservatives (including Reagan himself) as they pursued détente with the Soviet Union. Yet in the mid-1980s, they, together with the conservatives, opposed the efforts by Reagan and his secretary of state, George P. Shultz, to reduce the arsenals of missiles and nuclear weapons that had been at the heart of America's military strategy throughout the Cold War.

Third, leading American intelligence and defense officials also disputed Reagan's view of Gorbachev. They argued that the Soviet leadership was not changing as much as Reagan and Shultz believed, and that Gorbachev represented merely a new face for the same old Soviet foreign policies.

At the end of Reagan's presidency, these constituencies were all working to slow down Reagan's diplomacy with the Soviet Union. When Reagan left office, the new George H. W. Bush administration took office convinced that Reagan had gone too far with Gorbachev. Bush froze diplomacy with Gorbachev for most of his first year in office, until just before the fall of the Berlin Wall.

Two decades later, in the aftermath of the U.S. intervention in Iraq of 2003, it is tempting to view American foreign policy as an unending struggle between, on the one hand, hawkish neoconservatives and, on the other hand, more cautious realists. And so it is all the more tempting to superimpose back onto the events of the 1980s the philosophical struggles of the post-Iraq milieu.

Yet in fact, this would be inaccurate. When one looks at what actually transpired during the final years of the Cold War, one finds that history did not play out in the way that we might imagine today. As Reagan proceeded to deal with Gorbachev and to consider cutbacks in nuclear weaponry, *both* the political right *and* the foreign-policy realists were against him. William Buckley's *National Review* published, with approval, a critique of Reagan's Soviet policy by Nixon and Kissinger. During his second term in the White House,

Reagan repeatedly forsook the advice of his old conservative friends, while also rejecting the ideas of the national-security establishment. This book is an attempt to tell the story of that era, the period leading up to the end of the Cold War.

Anyone writing about Ronald Reagan encounters a special problem: Reagan rarely chose to explain his policy shifts or his not-infrequent changes in strategy or tactics. He had shrewd political instincts but rarely if ever articulated his underlying motivations. His interviews at the time, his private meetings, his autobiography, and his diaries have little to offer on questions of political judgments, trade-offs, or his reasons for reversing course.

Reagan was content to leave everyone with the impression that he was a man of simple principles, a leader utterly without cunning. He was often taken to be merely the instrument of others: at first of the political right and in later years, of a "moderate" group of officials, including Shultz. These impressions sometimes seemed to make sense until the people thought to be controlling Reagan would unexpectedly lose a major policy battle (or occasionally, their own jobs).

Reagan's way of avoiding extended explanations was to offer a few deflecting phrases that would shut off discussion. When conservative leaders complained about his courtship of Gorbachev, Reagan would dismiss their arguments by saying, "I just think they're wrong," without specifying how or why. Like any politician, Reagan had an ego, but in his particular case, the ego wasn't at all in the words or justifications he uttered. It was, rather, in his public performances. He proudly took note of the size of the crowds at his speeches or how much they cheered or how many letters or calls he received after he appeared on television. When his actions sometimes didn't seem to fit with the principles he had laid out, Reagan simply restated those principles and left it to others to wrestle with the contradictions. Because he was so opaque, Reagan could not be understood through his words alone or through his actions alone.

I have chosen to probe Reagan's role in the Cold War's end through the use of four narrative parts. In its own way, each illuminates the way Reagan operated, the role he played, the influences on his thinking, and the underlying dynamics at work during the last years of his administration.

Part I examines the story of Reagan and Nixon, the two leading anti-Communist politicians of the Cold War. The relationship between the two men and the progress of their political careers offer some understanding of Reagan's distinctive evolution. Their differing views of the Cold War help to explain how Reagan, after campaigning against détente with the Soviet Union in the 1970s, became such a strong proponent of easing tensions with Gorbachev's Soviet Union a decade later.

Part II looks at Reagan's curious relationship with an informal adviser, Suzanne Massie, whom he welcomed to the White House again and again to talk about life in the Soviet Union, even though she was not an established scholar or expert. The Massie story offers some insight into Reagan's ideas and thinking about the Soviet Union during the mid-1980s, as he was beginning to change his approach to the regime he had called an evil empire.

Part III tells the story of Reagan's famous speech at the Berlin Wall in June 1987. The speech was vintage Reagan. In uttering the words, "Mr. Gorbachev, tear down this wall," Reagan spurned the advice of virtually his entire foreign-policy team, up to and including Shultz. They feared the reproach would alienate Gorbachev or jeopardize his position in Moscow. Reagan judged, correctly as it turned out, that Gorbachev could handle it. Reagan's speech was much less of a departure from American policy than is commonly imagined, yet it set forth a powerful idea in simple terms and dramatic fashion. The speech reaffirmed the anticommunism on which Reagan had based his career, but it also began to reckon with the idea that under Gorbachev, the Soviet system might be changing. A toughly worded speech, it also maintained support in the United States for Reagan's subsequent efforts to work with Gorbachev.

Finally, Part IV describes the easing of Cold War tensions during Reagan's final two years in office. Reagan welcomed Gorbachev to Washington and then visited Moscow, where he proclaimed that the era of the "evil empire" had passed. In between these two summits, Reagan won Senate approval for a major arms-control treaty with the Soviet Union, overcoming the opposition of conservatives from within his own party. Through these endeavors Reagan helped to foster a growing realization inside the United States that America did not need to exist in a state of permanent enmity with the Soviet Union—and that, in fact, the Cold War was coming to an end.

There have been several biographies of Reagan, but these by their very nature cannot concentrate specifically on the final years of the Cold War. Separately, there have also been several books about the Reagan-era negotiations with the Soviet Union (including Shultz's own extraordinarily detailed memoir). But these books tend to focus, understandably, on the diplomacy, not the political judgments and presidential choices involved in bringing the Cold War to a close.

My own goal was different. I wanted to find what was uniquely Reagan during this period—the personal role and views of the president himself, apart from the work of his subordinates or the diplomacy of his administration. Reagan didn't operate entirely through subordinates such as Shultz; he had his own unusual advisers and intermediaries. Members of his foreign-policy team often thought of Reagan's rhetoric as a nuisance or a hindrance; in fact, it was an integral part of his overall approach to the Soviet Union.

The role of any president is inherently more political than that of any of the officials working for him. Presidents must choose when to push initiatives and when to back off, which route to take when cabinet secretaries disagree. They must decide what the American people will support and how to win congressional approval or acquiescence. Reagan, in particular, confronted considerable resistance to his efforts to scale back America's reliance on nuclear weaponry and to his unfolding relationship with Mikhail Gorbachev.

In the middle to late 1980s, the Cold War was winding down. Gorbachev's ascent triggered a series of political and bureaucratic battles in Washington. Ronald Reagan was at the center of those conflicts. This is the story of Reagan's role.

PART I
TWO ANTI-COMMUNISTS

-1-

CLANDESTINE VISIT

In the final days of April 1987, American newspapers carried a routine photograph of Soviet soldiers drilling in Moscow's Red Square, preparing for the annual May Day parade, a wave of arms and legs lined up in parallel against the backdrop of St. Basil's Cathedral. It was what the newspapers call filler art, not meant to convey news or change but rather a sense of the world as usual.

Americans, inured to the tensions of the Cold War, were preoccupied with more mundane pursuits. That spring the Los Angeles Lakers, led by Magic Johnson and Kareem Abdul-Jabbar, dethroned Larry Bird's Boston Celtics as champions of the National Basketball Association, after the Celtics had themselves defeated the Chicago Bulls and their young star Michael Jordan. America's dominant computer company, IBM, proclaimed that it would be working with Microsoft, the upstart Seattle software firm to develop a new system that could do several tasks at once in different "windows." In music, the AIDS charity song "That's What Friends Are For," a collaboration by Stevie Wonder, Elton John, Dionne Warwick, and Gladys Knight, had just won the Grammy Award for best song of the year, while Paul Simon's *Graceland* was declared the best album. The gossip columns informed Americans that film director Woody Allen and Mia Farrow were expecting a child. *Time* magazine wrote of the increasing problem of sticker shock in college costs: Stanford University had raised its tuition to $11,880.

Late in the afternoon of April 27, 1987, a cloudy, cool spring day, a secret visitor was smuggled into the White House. Reporters and photographers would have climbed over one another to talk to him and take his picture if they had known he was there, but the attention of the press corps had been diverted. President Ronald Reagan had met with reporters two hours earlier, offering homilies on everything from AIDS to the Iran-Contra scandal, and the correspondents were busy filing their stories. A helicopter swooped low and onto the White House landing pad. Out stepped a familiar figure: Richard M. Nixon, the thirty-seventh president of the United States, who had been living in seclusion ever since being forced to resign thirteen years earlier.

At the Diplomatic Entrance to the White House, Chief of Staff Howard Baker and National Security Adviser Frank Carlucci were waiting, hands outstretched.[1] The illustrious greeters hurriedly escorted Nixon inside and up a private elevator to the second floor, the residence quarters of the White House, now occupied by Ronald and Nancy Reagan. Nixon had once lived there himself, of course, but had not returned to his old haunts since August 9, 1974, the day he later called "the nightmare end of a long dream."[2] He had been at the White House twice since, but only for formal ceremonies downstairs: in 1979, Nixon was on Jimmy Carter's guest list for a state dinner for Chinese leader Deng Xiaoping, and in 1981 he had joined Carter and Gerald Ford in a thirty-five minute stopover on the White House grounds before the three ex-presidents flew to Egypt to represent the United States at the funeral of Anwar Sadat. This time, the occasion was more intimate: Nixon had been invited inside and upstairs for a private chat with Reagan.[3]

Nixon's eyes scanned the living quarters, recording the changes with his characteristic blend of calculation and resentment. The Reagans, never known for parsimony, had given the place a sense of opulence. "I would not have recognized it because of the luxurious furnishings and decorating," wrote Nixon in a memo for his own files a few hours later. "As I looked up and down the hall, I would estimate that at least $2 million, rather than the

$1 million that has been reported in the press, had been expended for this purpose." By contrast—Nixon reflected to himself—his wife, Pat, had spent less money on redecoration, and had concentrated on the downstairs public spaces of the White House, such as the dining rooms and ballroom.[4]

Reagan, dressed in a brown suit, was waiting for him behind a desk in an upstairs study filled with pictures and mementos. Nixon remembered this particular room all too well. It had once been a bedroom, the one where Nixon had slept as president. As he sat down next to Reagan, and Baker and Carlucci settled into chairs across from them, Nixon tried to lighten the mood by launching into the story of when he had first set foot in that room. In 1966, when Nixon, out of office, was in town for the Washington press corps' annual Gridiron Dinner, President Lyndon Johnson invited him to drop by the White House afterward. To Nixon's astonishment, he was ushered upstairs to this very room, a bedroom even then. Johnson chose to chat with him from atop the bed, while Lady Bird Johnson nestled under the covers. Three years later, when the Nixons moved into the White House, he had discovered there were wires under that bed—wires, that is, to make tape recordings.

Reagan laughed at the story and its irony. The White House taping system, of course, was what had eventually led to Nixon's resignation.

Returning from his reverie to the situation at hand, Nixon took his awkward attempt at humor one final step further. He said that Carlucci could take written notes of the meeting if he wanted, and then joked: "I assume that the place isn't taped." Trying to ease the awkwardness, Reagan asked Nixon if he'd like a drink. Nixon, who'd enjoyed his share of cocktails in the White House, might have liked one, but decided that Reagan's offer seemed a bit late and perfunctory. He declined.

This was not to be a social occasion. Reagan and his top aides had invited Nixon to this clandestine White House meeting to talk about the Soviet Union. They wanted Nixon's endorsement for far-reaching new steps Reagan was preparing to take with the Soviet Communist Party secretary, Mikhail S. Gorbachev, steps that were aimed at easing the nuclear standoff of the Cold War. Nixon wasn't going to give Reagan what he wanted.

———

This was not merely a meeting of two men, or even of two presidents. Reagan and Nixon were more than that: they had been the two most successful anti-Communist politicians of the entire Cold War. Between them, their careers had spanned virtually the entire period. In the late 1940s, Nixon, as a young congressman, had led the campaign against Alger Hiss, the former State Department official who was eventually convicted of perjury after being accused of serving as an agent of the Soviet Union. In the early 1980s, Reagan, as president, had branded the Soviet Union an "evil empire."

When it came to the foreign policy of the Cold War, Harry Truman held pride of place among America's leaders; his administration had come up with both the strategy and the structure for containing the Soviet Union. For charting the paranoiac outer limits of American anticommunism, Senator Joseph McCarthy was the symbol of the age. But for sheer electoral politics, for comprehending the mood and voting habits of the nation, no other American leaders of the Cold War could compare with these two men, Nixon and Reagan. Each man had mounted a full-scale nationwide campaign for the White House three times. Each had won the presidency twice. Nixon had also been elected twice as Dwight D. Eisenhower's vice president. Of the ten presidential elections in the United States in the Cold War era from the end of World War II through 1984, there had only been two (1948 and 1964) in which neither Nixon nor Reagan had figured prominently as either a presidential candidate or as a vice presidential nominee.

The two men were, essentially, of the same generation; both had been born in the half decade before the outbreak of World War I. Reagan was two years older than Nixon. Politically, however, Nixon was the senior figure, having begun to run for office much earlier in life. In the 1940s and 1950s, while Reagan pursued an acting career, Nixon had served as congressman, senator, and vice president. For most of the time Reagan was governor of California, his first job in public life, Nixon overshadowed him as president of the United States.

Yet Reagan, once he started in politics, proved to have an unsurpassed touch with American voters, one that Nixon had sought but always failed to achieve. Nixon could never escape the accurate perception that he was a career politician; Reagan, having not campaigned for public office until age fifty-five, managed to convey the impression, an inaccurate one, that he was a reluctant candidate, one who stood outside of politics and whose career was elsewhere. Nixon's identity was built upon the fact that he suffered adversity along with the victories; he had lost the 1960 presidential election, failed when he ran for governor of California in 1962, and finally, lost the White House and support of the nation in the middle of his second term. By contrast, Reagan won virtually every election in which he ran. Even the lone exception, the time Reagan didn't win, demonstrated his popularity: in 1976, Reagan challenged an incumbent president, Gerald Ford, for the Republican nomination, winning several primaries before he was defeated.

-2-

"IT'S TIME TO STROKE RONNIE"

Reagan and Nixon had dealt with each other in a cordial if guarded fashion for more than a quarter century, since Nixon's presidential campaign in 1960. At that time, Reagan was still a Democrat, a devoted admirer of Franklin Roosevelt and Harry Truman. In 1950, Reagan had even campaigned for the Democrats against Nixon when Nixon had run for the Senate against Helen Gahagan Douglas (whose husband, the actor Melvyn Douglas, was Reagan's friend).

Reagan had grown ever more disenchanted with the Democrats through the 1950s. After first hoping Dwight Eisenhower might run for president as a Democrat, he voted for Eisenhower on the Republican ticket. Later in the decade, Reagan began speaking out against the evils of big government, high taxes, and communism while touring the country as a spokesman for General Electric. Nixon, who had noticed what Reagan was saying, asked for his support in the 1960 campaign against John F. Kennedy. Reagan gave his assent and told Nixon he planned to switch his party registration to Republican. But Nixon asked him not to do so: it would be better, Nixon said, if Reagan endorsed him and campaigned for him as a Democrat. This was, in retrospect, an episode tinged with irony. Despite Reagan's help, Nixon never succeeded in attracting many Democrats; but two decades later, Reagan himself would build a new Republican majority with his startling ability to win over formerly loyal Democratic voters.[1]

Reagan finally registered as a Republican in 1962, supporting Nixon's losing race for governor of California. Then, encouraged by wealthy conservative friends, Reagan began to move into Republican politics himself—and for a time in the 1960s he emerged as a potential rival to Nixon. The week before the 1964 election, Reagan delivered a nationwide television speech on behalf of Barry Goldwater, repeating his favorite antigovernment themes. Goldwater lost badly, but Reagan's speech transformed him from the role of actor to rising political star, the natural heir to Goldwater's conservative constituency.

After Reagan won California's gubernatorial election in 1966, some of his conservative supporters and Reagan's own staff began putting his name forward as a possible presidential candidate. The leading candidate for the 1968 Republican nomination was Nixon, who was seeking to occupy the center of the party, between Goldwater-Reagan conservatives on the right and the party's liberal wing, which supported Nelson Rockefeller, on the left.

In July 1967, Nixon and Reagan crossed paths in northern California, where both were guests at the Bohemian Grove, the annual, exclusive all-male retreat of business executives and political leaders. Delivering the main address for the gathering, Nixon revived some of his traditional anti-Soviet themes. "They [Soviet leaders] seek victory, with peace being at this time a means towards that end," Nixon asserted.

Outside the formal sessions, Nixon and Reagan sat down privately to talk presidential politics. On a bench under the lofty redwoods, Nixon probed Reagan's intentions concerning the coming presidential campaign. Nixon said he was planning to enter the presidential primaries. He would try to unite the party by campaigning only against Lyndon Johnson and the Democrats, not against other Republicans. This message was perfectly tailored to appeal to Reagan's loyalties. One of the enduring clichés of Republican politics, the Eleventh Commandment, which holds that "thou shalt not speak ill of any fellow Republican," originated during California's 1966 gubernatorial campaign, when Reagan was an untested new candidate. His political

strategists were trying to prevent attacks by his Republican primary opponent, San Francisco mayor George Christopher. "We created [the Eleventh
Commandment] for his protection," recalled Stuart Spencer, Reagan's political consultant in the 1966 campaign.[2]

During their Bohemian Grove meeting, Reagan told Nixon that he really
didn't want to run for president but would allow his name to be put forward
as a favorite-son candidate from California. He said he wanted to do so in
order to preserve party unity within the state's delegation and to smooth over
the divisions between Rockefeller and Goldwater forces that had plagued the
party in 1964.[3] Thus Reagan, like Nixon, managed to advance his own political interests while cloaking them in the guise of what was best for the Republican Party.

As he often did, Reagan was feigning modesty. As the 1968 presidential
campaign unfolded, he began touring the country to give speeches, and while
he didn't enter the primaries, neither did he forswear the nomination. Yet a
full-scale Reagan campaign never materialized that year. Nixon had managed
to lock up the endorsements of other prominent conservatives, including
Goldwater and Strom Thurmond, the leader of the newly emerging southern
Republicans. Reagan's own aides seemed to be far more enthusiastic about the
1968 campaign than Reagan himself, who had just settled into his new life as
governor. "We pushed . . . , but Reagan was not interested, really, in being
president [in 1968]," Lyn Nofziger, who served as Reagan's communications
director when he was governor of California, later ruefully concluded. "He
gave us damn little help, I must say. . . . What we did, we did pretty much on
our own."[4] As the Republican National Convention in Miami opened,
Nofziger and former California senator William Knowland persuaded Reagan to drop his status as merely a favorite-son candidate of California Republicans and declare himself a full-fledged nationwide candidate. They hoped
Reagan on the right and Rockefeller on the left could come up with enough
delegates to deny Nixon the nomination.

Reagan went along with this last-minute strategy, but it did no good. At
the convention in Miami, Nixon won easily on the first ballot. Later, William
Safire, who was working for Nixon, would observe that the potential challenge from Reagan had been "the only one that Nixon had ever been con-

cerned about." Reagan later maintained he was relieved when Nixon was nominated. "I knew I wasn't ready to be president," Reagan said.[5]

After Nixon was elected president in 1968, he and Reagan no longer saw themselves as rivals. From the White House, Nixon was cordial to Reagan—understandably so, since Reagan was the Republican governor of the largest state in the nation. In response, Reagan treated Nixon with considerable deference.

Privately, however, Nixon spoke of Reagan with disdain. Brent Scowcroft, who was working on the National Security Council (NSC) as an aide to Henry Kissinger, recalled years later that the president thought of Reagan as a lightweight politician, someone who should not be taken too seriously. "Nixon used to call me periodically, and he'd say, 'It's time to stroke Ronnie. Find somewhere for him to go, on a presidential mission,'" Scowcroft said. "So we'd send Reagan out here and there and elsewhere."[6] Reagan made four trips overseas as a presidential emissary for Nixon, meeting with eighteen heads of state. Nixon always provided him with the trappings: an Air Force plane, Secret Service protection, and other aides to pay all of Reagan's expenses. Reagan later joked that he'd once traveled to seven European countries for Nixon with a total of $5.11 in his pocket.

Although officials such as Scowcroft made light of these trips, they served a political purpose. Nixon used them in order to profit from Reagan's anti-Communist credentials. The most important mission was to Taiwan less than three months after Nixon had stunned the world by announcing that Henry Kissinger, his national security adviser, had paid a secret visit to Beijing. Chiang Kai-shek's Nationalist government was celebrating its sixtieth birthday on October 10, 1971, and Nixon sent Reagan to Taipei as his special envoy to the festivities. The trip provided some small degree of reassurance to Chiang and his aides that the United States would not abandon them. More important, Reagan's mission helped Nixon protect his political flanks at home by demonstrating that America's most prominent conservative politician was working alongside Nixon and would not oppose his new opening to China.

From Sacramento, Reagan strongly defended Nixon throughout the Watergate scandal until the very end of his presidency. On August 6, 1974, as

Nixon's support in Washington was rapidly collapsing, Reagan said he had finally changed his mind and concluded that Nixon had not told the public the truth about Watergate. Even then, Reagan said he still felt that Nixon should not step down and that instead, the "constitutional process" of impeachment should go forward.[7] Nixon resigned three days later after even Barry Goldwater told him that he had lost virtually all support in the Senate and that Goldwater himself might have to vote for impeachment.

Two months later, when Nixon—by then a depressed, shunned, and marginalized ex-president—was hospitalized in California with potentially life-threatening blood clots in his leg, an apparently distraught Reagan called to cheer him up. "Gov. Reagan called and told Tricia, 'I just hope your father knows how many people love him and are pulling for him,'" Julie Nixon Eisenhower told her father in a handwritten note. "What we want to tell you about the call is that Gov. Reagan could hardly speak because he was so emotional—really crying."[8]

Gradually, the relationship between Nixon and Reagan began to shift. In the mid-to-late 1970s, Reagan was the rising Republican star, while Nixon remained a political untouchable. The former president began to court the aspiring presidential candidate, sending him regular letters, memos, speeches, and newspaper clips, usually offering bits of advice. Reagan always responded graciously, if cautiously.

On August 20, 1976, after Reagan's challenge to President Ford failed at the Republican convention, Nixon sent him a handwritten note of consolation. "Having won a few and lost a few, I can say that winning is a lot more fun!" Nixon said. "But you can take pride that in losing you conducted yourself magnificently. . . . Keep fighting and speaking for those ideals in which you so deeply believe." Reagan's thank-you note supplied the tidbits of insider politics and anti-Rockefeller sentiments he knew Nixon would love. "Where delegates had freedom to vote, we did well," he said. "Defeat came in those three North East states where the party structure controlled the vote and I suspect 'Rocky' controlled the party structure."[9]

Reagan seemed to want to draw closer to Nixon, but his wife, Nancy, made sure that a certain distance was preserved. When the Reagans were traveling through Europe in 1978, they found themselves in Paris at the same time as Nixon, who was making his first sojourn abroad since his resignation. Richard Allen, the conservative foreign-policy expert who was traveling with the Reagans, suggested that he could call Nixon and arrange a meeting.

"That's a great idea," Reagan told Allen.

"No, Ronnie, no," said Nancy Reagan. "No, I don't want to. We shouldn't see Nixon." She won the argument.[10]

For his own part, Nixon, while solicitous of Reagan, did not take his side in intramural Republican political battles. Nixon operated within the party only behind the scenes, in private conversations with friends and with Republican politicians, because in the wake of his Watergate resignation, no candidate sought his public endorsement. He of course did not support Reagan's 1976 challenge to Ford, who after all had been Nixon's vice president and was seeking to perpetuate Nixon's foreign policies. In 1980, the year Reagan won the presidency, Nixon's first choice for the Republican presidential nomination had been John Connally, who had been Nixon's treasury secretary and since then his favorite politician.

After Reagan became the Republican nominee, Nixon began sending him practical advice about the general-election campaign. Keep the events indoors in the last, late-autumn days of the campaign so that you don't lose your voice, Nixon told him. And stick to your proven campaign speech. Reagan, a vastly more skilled speaker and performer than Nixon, did not need this advice, but he sent Nixon his thanks anyway.

Reagan's campaign staff and his new administration included a number of Republicans who had earlier worked for Nixon. Allen, who became Reagan's first national security adviser, had worked in the Nixon White House; so had Martin Anderson, a domestic policy adviser, and Ken Khachigian, a speechwriter. Moreover, behind the scenes, Nixon went to considerable lengths to try to place some of the officials he liked best from his own administration at the top levels of Reagan's new cabinet.

Two weeks after the 1980 election, Nixon sent Reagan a detailed, private memo of cabinet-level recommendations, explaining that he was writing "as one who has been there and who seeks or wants absolutely nothing except your success in office." He recommended Connally as the best candidate both for secretary of defense and also as head of the Office of Management and Budget. For CIA, he recommended William Casey, another Nixon administration alumnus, who had chaired Reagan's campaign; for deputy CIA director, he suggested Vernon Walters, who had been deputy CIA director for a time in the Nixon administration, be given the same job once again. (Casey got the job; Walters was made a roving ambassador.)

Nixon devoted the heart of his memo to persuading Reagan that the best choice for secretary of state would be Alexander Haig, Nixon's former deputy national security adviser and White House chief of staff. "He is intelligent, strong and generally shares your views on foreign policy," wrote Nixon. "He would be personally loyal to you and would not backbite you on or off the record." The former president went out of his way to warn against the appointment of George Shultz, Nixon's own former labor and treasury secretary, as Reagan's secretary of state. "George Shultz has done a superb job in every government position to which I appointed him," Nixon told the president-elect. "However, I do not believe that he has the depth of understanding of world issues generally and the Soviet Union in particular that is needed for this period."[11]

Reagan didn't take all of Nixon's suggestions; he recognized from the start, for example, that the brash, strong-willed Connally would not fit into his administration. Reagan, however, did follow Nixon's recommendation of Haig for secretary of state. Allen, who had been Reagan's leading foreign-policy adviser during the campaign, later claimed that Nixon had been the driving force behind Haig's nomination, manipulating events behind the scenes and working closely with members of Reagan's kitchen cabinet.[12]

Once Reagan occupied the White House, Nixon's private notes to him took on the nature of fan mail; they were often flattering and unctuous. "Pat and my reactions were the same: 'Thank God for Ronald Reagan,'" Nixon wrote in early 1981 when Reagan granted a pardon to Mark Felt, the former associate director of the FBI who had been convicted of approving illegal break-ins for surveillance; Nixon did not know at the time that Felt had been Deep Throat, Bob Woodward's principal source for the *Washington Post* articles about Watergate.

"Reggie Jackson used to be Mr. October. Now, you deserve that accolade," Nixon wrote on October 31, 1981, as Reagan was completing a successful month that had culminated with legislative approval of the sale of AWACS planes and other military equipment to Saudi Arabia. At the end of 1981, he wrote Reagan a note saying: "I like and admire [Lech] Walesa, but in my book, *Time* missed the boat: President Reagan should have been Man of the Year."

Interspersed with such praise were bits of inside political advice of the sort that only Richard Nixon could have given. In late 1982, Nixon sent Reagan a long letter urging the president to prepare for his 1984 reelection campaign by bringing onto his team some people who could engage in slashing attacks on the Democrats. "You need at least two or three nut cutters who will take on the opposition so that you can take the high road," wrote Nixon, the acknowledged master at this technique. Vice President Bush had been a good campaigner and a good soldier, but he did not fit the nut-cutting role, Nixon argued. "You need someone (or two) in the Cabinet and the RNC who are heavyweights and who will carry the attack to the opposition as I did for Eisenhower in 1954 and Ted Agnew did for me in 1970."[13]

-3-

TWO SCHOOLS OF THOUGHT

During the 1970s, two schools of thought emerged within the Republican Party over the Cold War, one symbolized by Nixon and the other by Reagan. The two men were friendly if not friends, a relationship reinforced by their identification with each other as politicians. Both had embraced anticommunism in the late 1940s. Both had been influenced by Whittaker Chambers, a former Communist Party member who had provided dramatic public accounts of his life in the party, describing the former State Department official Alger Hiss as a Soviet agent.

In their early careers, both men spoke of an eventual American triumph in the Cold War. For Reagan, this was an enduring theme: he once told a startled visitor, "My theory of how the Cold War ends is: We win, they lose."[1] During the 1950s and early 1960s, Nixon had sounded a similar refrain. "I know that talk of victory over Communism is not fashionable these days," he said in one 1963 speech, adding that he could not accept the idea of coexistence with the Soviet Union, because that was "another word for creeping surrender."[2]

Yet despite these superficial similarities, Nixon's and Reagan's views of the

Soviets had different origins and developed in different ways. As a result, they eventually found themselves on opposing sides in a series of philosophical and factional struggles among the Republicans.

For Nixon, politics came first: he had won election to Congress in 1946, and only subsequently, as a new member of the House Un-American Activities Committee, did he seize upon anticommunism, most notably in the Hiss case, quickly discovering the electoral appeal of the issue. His rise in Republican politics was so swift that within six years, he became vice president. Afterward, from the early 1950s onward, anticommunism was for Nixon tied primarily to questions of foreign policy and geopolitics: the problem to be addressed was how to cope with the Soviet Union. Nixon's underlying message, carefully honed from the late 1950s through the remainder of his career, was that Moscow was run by tough leaders and that he was the American official most qualified and experienced to deal with them.

One might call this the static version of American anticommunism: Nixon often suggested that American and Soviet leaders were engaged in an unending series of geopolitical challenges to one another. What America needed, he maintained, were officials in Washington who could stand up to the Soviets, as he had as vice president in the famous "kitchen debate" with Nikita Khrushchev in Moscow in 1959. Nixon rarely spoke of changing the Soviet system itself; the assumption was that it was a permanent if unpleasant fact of life. Nixon's message to the American public relied on preserving what he once privately told H. R. Haldeman was his "position as a big-league operator . . . the unusual world statesman capability."[3]

Reagan's anticommunism was rooted much more deeply in his personality and political career. He hadn't seized upon anticommunism after becoming a politician; anticommunism came first and politics, later. It was, indeed, the cause of anticommunism that had propelled Reagan into politics. As an actor and a liberal Democrat, he had joined film-industry organizations of the late 1940s, eventually rising to president of the Screen Actors Guild in the midst of a labor strike over the role of unions in constructing movie sets. In this strike and elsewhere, Reagan became embroiled in the acrimonious fights of this period over communist influence in Hollywood, skirmishing regularly with other left-wing figures such as the screenwriter Dalton Trumbo, who had for a time been a Communist Party member. Reagan and associates such as the actress Olivia de Havilland tried to win support for statements repudiating communism in the United States; opponents such as Trumbo refused.

In a 1960 letter to *Playboy* publisher Hugh Hefner, who had published an article by Trumbo and defended his right to freedom of speech, Reagan recalled how his views had been formed during that era. "I once thought exactly as you think. . . . It took seven months of meeting communists and communist-influenced people across a table in almost daily sessions while pickets rioted in front of studio gates, homes were bombed and a great industry almost ground to a halt." What bothered Reagan above all, he wrote, was the discovery that Communist Party members operated in secret and did not tell the truth. "I, like you, will defend the right of any American to openly practice and preach any political philosophy from monarchy to anarchy," he told Hefner. "But this is not the case with regard to the communist. He is bound by party discipline to *deny* he is a communist so that he can by subversion and stealth *impose* on an unwilling people the rule of the International Communist Party which is in fact the government of Soviet Russia."[4] Anticommunism for Reagan, then, was not primarily foreign policy or geopolitics; it was personal and moralistic in nature, driven by his experiences with people he considered sophisticated and devious, who did not abide by the small-town Midwestern values he had absorbed in his youth.

Stuart Spencer, who as a political consultant worked over two decades in campaigns both for and against Reagan, said he gradually learned that Reagan was a practical politician, less impassioned than his conservative public positions might indicate. There was, however, a single exception. "He was obsessed with one thing, the communist threat," Spencer said. "Everything else was second tier." When Spencer asked Reagan why he wanted to be president, he recalled, "I'd get the speech and the program on communism." Spencer concluded that communism was "the driving force behind his political participations. It was the only thing he really thought about in depth. . . . With everything else, from welfare to taxation, he went through the motions."[5]

This was an exaggeration, since it turned out Reagan did care about taxes, and Spencer's list of Reagan's concerns omitted the subject of nuclear weapons, about which Reagan also cared a great deal. But there was no doubt that anticommunism ranked at the top of Reagan's priorities, and that his outlook differed from Nixon's. Reagan's version was transformational; he was unwilling to accept the permanence of the Soviet Union. His anticommunism was based on what he perceived to be the untrustworthiness of Communist Party members, including Soviet leaders; their philosophy; and their political system. This was the other side of Reagan's generally sunny personality. "I think communism was the only thing that Reagan actually hated," said Kenneth Adelman, who worked in the Reagan administration. "It was hard to hate anybody else or anything else in his life."[6]

Reagan's personalized version of anticommunism also implied, however, that once a Soviet leader could establish that he was straightforward rather than deceitful and was trying to alter the Soviet system, then Reagan might be willing—more willing, in fact, than Richard Nixon—to give credence to that leader and to try to do business with him.

It took some time, until well into the 1970s, for these different versions of anticommunism to burst into the open. Nixon and Reagan had echoed each other in their attacks upon the Kennedy and Johnson administrations, with both arguing repeatedly that the Democrats were too accommodating toward the Soviet Union. After Nixon, as president, began to move American foreign policy toward the Soviet Union and China in startling new directions, Reagan refrained from criticizing him. He accepted the American opening to China, for example, as a stratagem that would tie down Soviet troops in Asia that might otherwise be used in Europe.

When Nixon hosted a lavish poolside party at his estate in San Clemente for Leonid Brezhnev in June 1973, introducing the Soviet leader to Bob Hope, Frank Sinatra, Gene Autry, and a flock of other Hollywood celebrities, Reagan was among the few political leaders invited to the festivities. He was apparently moved by the event and impressed with the artfulness of Nixon's diplomacy with Brezhnev. "I just think it's too bad that [Watergate] is taking people's attention away from what I think is a most brilliant accomplishment of any president of this century, and that is the steady progress towards peace and the easing of tensions," Reagan declared a few days later. From the White House, Nixon continued to shower Reagan with briefings, phone calls and official trips; Reagan stayed in Nixon's corner to the bitter end.[7]

It was only after Nixon left the White House that Reagan mounted a full-scale challenge to the foreign policy Nixon had forged. By 1975, the political dynamics had shifted. Reagan was in position to challenge Gerald Ford, Nixon's successor, for the Republican presidential nomination in 1976. Although he was president of the United States, Ford had never won an election outside his congressional district in Grand Rapids, Michigan. Reagan possessed a solid base within the Republican Party, because he was both California's leading Republican and the acknowledged leader of the party's growing conservative wing. Moreover, Ford had angered conservative Republicans, including Reagan, at the very start of his presidency by naming Nelson Rockefeller as his vice president.[8]

Reagan finished his second term as governor of California and left Sacramento in early 1975. He was sixty-three years old, no longer so coy or hesitant about running for president as he had been in 1968. Events overseas were working in his favor. In the spring of 1975, North Vietnamese troops overran South Vietnam, forcing the humiliating, chaotic American withdrawal from the country. There was an opening among Republican conservatives for a political leader who would talk both about America as a force for good in the world and also about the need to rebuild and reassert American military strength.

Reagan's campaign against Ford for the 1976 Republican nomination focused on foreign policy, particularly American policy toward the Soviet Union. Reagan took aim at two targets in particular: first, Henry Kissinger, the architect of Soviet policy as national security adviser and secretary of state under both Nixon and Ford, and second, détente, the vague word used to describe the relaxation of tension between Washington and Moscow and the several arms-control and trade agreements negotiated between the two governments. Détente dated back to Richard Nixon's summit with Brezhnev in Moscow in May 1972. During the following two years, while Reagan supported the Nixon administration, the leading challenger to détente had been Senator Henry Jackson, a Democrat, who was a determined supporter of a strong national defense.

The policy of détente seemed to incorporate several intellectual trends of the 1960s and early 1970s. Some American scholars had been arguing that the political systems of the United States and the Soviet Union were gradually converging and that both countries might evolve toward some sort of democratic socialism. Others asserted that the Soviet system no longer fit the totalitarian model, that it had become more pluralistic since Stalin's death, that the Soviet leadership now enjoyed greater popular support and legitimacy than in the past.[9]

To be sure, Nixon and Kissinger did not themselves put forward such arguments. Instead, they claimed, particularly to conservative audiences, that détente was merely a temporary tactic aimed at outflanking American liberals and counteracting the Democratic Congress, which, in reaction to the Vietnam War, was seeking to reduce America's involvements and troop deployments overseas. Kissinger later argued that the aim of détente was not to eliminate the adversarial relationship between the United States and the Soviet Union but merely to control it. In fact, Kissinger maintained, he shared the same anti-Soviet goals as the conservative and neoconservative critics of détente.

"Throughout, Nixon and I considered the Soviet Union ideologically hostile and militarily threatening," Kissinger later wrote.[10] This was not a point Nixon and Kissinger made to audiences of liberals, moderates, or independent voters, however. They believed at first that détente would prove politically popular in the United States—an assumption that had proven accurate in the 1972 campaign, when Nixon won reelection by a landslide, but was open for question four years later, after the Soviet Union had been posing new challenges to American foreign policy in the Middle East, Africa, and elsewhere.

Running against Ford in 1976, Reagan said the policy of détente had become "a one-way street that simply gives the Soviets what they want with nothing in return." In campaign speeches, he regularly promised Republican voters that if elected, "I will appoint a new secretary of state." He said Kissinger's stewardship of American foreign policy had "coincided precisely with the loss of American military supremacy." Under Kissinger's leadership, Reagan said, the United States had acted "as if we expected the Soviets to inherit the earth. . . . If you were a Russian official and you heard the American secretary of state deliver stern warnings to you for trying to dominate the situation in Angola, but all the time you knew he was packing his bags to come to

Moscow to negotiate a new arms limitation agreement, would you really take his words seriously?"[11]

Initially, Reagan's attacks had little impact. He lost the first five Republican primaries in 1976, including New Hampshire, Florida, and Illinois. By late March, there was considerable speculation in the press that he might quit. Indeed, in a hotel room on the eve of the North Carolina primary, Nancy Reagan began talking with Lyn Nofziger, Reagan's press secretary, about how to persuade her husband to withdraw. "Lyn, you know you've got to get Ronnie out of this race," she told him. "We can't embarrass him any further." Walking in upon this conversation, Reagan angrily refused to consider dropping out. "I'm going to stay in it all the way," he told them. Reagan soon won the North Carolina primary, scoring a stunning victory over an incumbent president.[12]

After North Carolina, Reagan went on to win primaries in Texas, Alabama, Georgia, and California, keeping the Republican nomination in doubt until the Republican National Convention in Kansas City that July. There, Reagan and his supporters staged a final test of strength with Ford, seeking to win over some delegates by introducing a plank to the party platform that called for "Morality in Foreign Policy." It unmistakably repudiated Kissinger's policy of détente. In 1975, the Ford administration, out of deference to the Soviet leadership, had refused to permit the exiled Soviet dissident Alexander Solzhenitsyn to visit the White House. The "Morality in Foreign Policy" plank praised Solzhenitsyn as a "beacon of human courage and morality" and for his "compelling message that we must face the world with no illusions about the nature of tyranny."[13] Ford and his advisers (including his White House chief of staff, Dick Cheney) decided that if they attempted to defeat this plank, Ford's own nomination might be in jeopardy, because some delegates might be angered enough to switch to Reagan. The Ford forces thus accepted the "Morality" plank as part of the Republican platform, and Ford went on to win the nomination. Nevertheless, on the issue of détente, Reagan had defeated Ford and Kissinger and won the support of the Republican Party.

The Democratic candidate, Jimmy Carter, won the general election that November. During the following four years, in the radio commentaries Reagan often wrote himself, he advanced the same themes he had during his 1976 campaign. "We continue to believe we can maintain a détente with the Soviet Union, and that their leaders down underneath must be pretty much like us," he complained in one 1978 radio commentary. But he said that Soviet leaders had continued to engage in treachery, deceit, destruction, and bloodshed. "Détente—isn't that what a farmer has with his turkey—before Thanksgiving?" Reagan concluded. "This is Ronald Reagan. Thanks for listening."[14]

Reagan portrayed détente in terms similar to those he had used to describe the Hollywood battles of the 1940s: America was honest, open, and virtuous; the Soviet leadership was duplicitous, secretive, and evil. Once again, his portrayal raised the question of how he might respond in the future if there were Soviet leaders who did not quite fit into this paradigm.

The result of these struggles over détente was to produce two different viewpoints within the Republican Party on foreign policy: those of the Nixon-Kissinger team and of the Reaganites. The Nixon group included not only the former president and Kissinger but others who had served in the Nixon administration, such as former Kissinger aides Brent Scowcroft and Alexander Haig. They viewed the Cold War as, above all, a geopolitical struggle. The proper goals for U.S. foreign policy, they believed, were stability and a balance of power that favored American interests. The Soviet Union, in this view, was an enduring, immutable presence; its leadership was firmly entrenched.

The Reaganites, on the other hand, viewed the Cold War not as a test of military and diplomatic strategy, but as a struggle of ideas and economic systems. In this view, America should not simply accept the Soviet Union as an unpleasant reality and attempt to deal with it; rather, it should seek to change the nature of the Soviet system, which, in Reagan's view, was neither legitimate nor well established at home. Communism, he wrote in 1975, was "a temporary aberration which will one day disappear from the earth because it is contrary to human nature."[15] While the Nixon group sought to maintain the relationship with the Soviet Union that had been worked out in the early 1970s, the Reagan Republicans did not accept the status quo and sought to challenge it.

"The concept of détente was, 'We are here, they are here, that's life, and the name of the game is peaceful coexistence and the avoidance of war,'" reflected Reagan's secretary of state, George Shultz, many years later. "Reagan rejected that concept, explicitly. Because [he believed] their system is fatally flawed, ours isn't. And ours is open, representative, democratic. And so he didn't accept the principle of détente."[16]

-4-

EVIL EMPIRE

The acrimony between the former Nixon foreign-policy team and the Reaganites was temporarily submerged during the Carter administration, when the Republicans were able to join with one another to challenge a Democratic president. The Soviet Union's foreign policy grew increasingly assertive, culminating in the invasion of Afghanistan in December 1979. By the end of the decade, Nixon himself had begun to characterize the Soviet Union in language that sounded strikingly similar to Reagan's. In Nixon's book *The Real War*, published in 1980, he noted with alarm how many countries had become communist over the previous six years. "The United States represents hope, freedom, security and peace. The Soviet Union stands for fear, tyranny, aggression and war," Nixon wrote. "If these are not poles of good and evil in human affairs, then the concepts of good and evil have no meaning."[1]

After Reagan won the Republican presidential nomination in 1980, easily defeating George Bush and several other candidates, the veterans of the Nixon administration went to great lengths to cultivate the Reagan team. Kissinger hosted a dinner at his New York apartment in honor of Nancy Reagan. Brent Scowcroft, the former Kissinger deputy who had become national security adviser in the Ford administration, made a private visit to Soviet ambassador Anatoly Dobrynin on Reagan's behalf. "He characterized Reagan as pragmatic and not as incorrigibly anti-Soviet as his public statements made him appear," Dobrynin later wrote.[2]

For their own part, Reagan and his aides were even more eager to have the support of the Nixon foreign-policy network. The Reaganites were, at the time, extremely insecure about their prospects for winning the White House. Barry Goldwater, the last conservative Republican to win a presidential nomination, had lost in a landslide. Richard Allen, Reagan's principal campaign adviser for national security, had told an interviewer in 1977 that while he favored Reagan's candidacy, he doubted that any conservative Republican could become president, at least not for many years. In 1978, Allen told Reagan in a private memo that he needed to address "the problem of how you are perceived by a wide stratum of the public: for many, you come across as a 'saber-rattler,' a 'button pusher,' or as 'too willing to send in the Marines.' This false image is happily amplified by the media. . . ." Allen advised Reagan not to retreat at all on issues, but to "soften the delivery of your message."[3]

It was this sense of fragility, and the fear of a Goldwater-style defeat, that prompted Reagan to pursue, in the days before and during the 1980 Republican convention, the idea of selecting Ford as his vice presidential running mate. Ford's aides countered with a proposal that Ford would operate as a copresident in a Reagan administration and that Kissinger would have effective control of American foreign policy. On the surface, the notion seemed preposterous: Reagan had only four years earlier promised Republican voters that he would replace Kissinger as secretary of state. Nevertheless, Reagan and his aides dithered over the idea for several days and began to negotiate with Ford's advisers, including Kissinger and Alan Greenspan, until Ford himself finally said no in the final hours before Reagan was scheduled to name his running mate.

Even after Reagan won the November election, lingering insecurities again prompted him, as president-elect, to appoint Haig as his first secretary of state. Haig not only enjoyed Nixon's strong personal endorsement, he also was a symbol of continuity with the foreign policies of the Republican administrations of the early 1970s. As they prepared for the new president, Soviet leaders hoped that Reagan would turn out to be like Nixon: an avowed anti-Communist with whom they could do business, as they had in the days of détente. They had been intensely unhappy with the Carter administration, which had responded to the Soviet invasion of Afghanistan by boycotting the 1980 Moscow Olympics and imposing a series of trade restrictions on the Soviet Union. "The mood in Moscow was, 'Anyone but Carter,' because Carter was so irritating to us at the end of his presidency . . . ," recalled Alexander Bessmertnykh, then a Soviet Foreign Ministry official. "When Reagan won the election, everyone was happy in Moscow."[4]

In seeking to deal with Reagan, the Soviets had the benefit of one well-connected American adviser: Richard Nixon. Within days after Reagan's victory over Carter, Nixon traveled to Washington for a private chat with Soviet ambassador Anatoly Dobrynin. "He had decided to talk with me about Reagan and asked me to bring his views to [Leonid] Brezhnev's notice," Dobrynin later recalled. Nixon advised the Soviets that Reagan was a pragmatic politician, but that it would take a long time to establish a relationship with him. "Nixon went on to say that he maintained private contacts with Reagan, who consulted him on various questions time and again," wrote Dobrynin many years later. Nixon hoped "to make a positive contribution by drawing on his own long experience to help Reagan get a better idea of the Soviet Union and its policies."[5]

It took barely nine days after his inauguration for Reagan to serve notice that his administration would be different from those of his predecessors and that he would not be guided or kept in check by Haig. Before Reagan's first presidential news conference, he took part in two preparatory "murder boards" in which his aides asked questions they thought might be posed by reporters. None of Reagan's answers to questions about the Soviet Union in these rehearsals was particularly distinctive. But at the news conference itself, on January 29, 1981, when asked whether he thought détente was still possible, Reagan volunteered some new phrases about Soviet perfidy, words he realized his secretary of state and other advisers would have vetoed at the prep sessions:

Well, so far détente's been a one-way street that the Soviet Union has used to pursue its own aims. I don't have to think of an answer as to what I think their intentions are; they have repeated

> *it. I know of no leader of the Soviet Union since the revolution,*
> *and including the present leadership, that has not more than*
> *once repeated in the various Communist congresses they hold*
> *their determination that their goal must be the promotion of*
> *world revolution and a one-world Socialist or Communist state,*
> *whichever word you want to use.*
>
> *Now, as long as they do that and as long as they, at the same*
> *time, have openly and publicly declared that the only morality*
> *they recognize is what will further their cause, meaning they*
> *reserve unto themselves the right to commit any crime, to lie, to*
> *cheat, in order to attain that, and that is moral, not immoral,*
> *and we operate on a different set of standards, I think when*
> *you do business with them, even at a detente, you keep that*
> *in mind.*[6]

Richard Allen, Reagan's national security adviser, noticed that as Reagan said this, Haig seemed to gasp. After the news conference ended, walking back to the Oval Office, Reagan turned to his national security adviser and said, "Say, Dick, they do lie and cheat, don't they?" Allen quickly responded: "Yes, sir."[7]

Later that day, Soviet Ambassador Dobrynin complained to Haig about Reagan's "hostile statement," which he said "will undoubtedly make a most unfavorable impression" on the Soviet leadership. "How is he going to do business with us?" Dobrynin asked. Haig explained that Reagan hadn't meant to offend anyone in Moscow, but was instead merely expressing his own deep convictions. Dobrynin countered that such an explanation only made things worse.[8]

This press conference was merely the beginning of a prolonged rhetorical campaign in which Reagan attempted to alter the language, the ideas, and the very thought processes used in American discussions about the Soviet Union. The purposes were to strip the Soviet Union of its legitimacy, to express a sense of moral condemnation toward the regime, and to characterize the Cold War as a battle of ideas and ideals. In Reagan's first speech in Europe, an address to British members of Parliament at Westminster on June 8, 1982, he spoke of "the march of freedom and democracy, which will leave Marxism-

Leninism on the ash heap of history." Reagan's aides had deliberately given him that phrase to insert into the speech as a mocking reversal of the words of Leon Trotsky, who had said in 1917 that the opponents of the Bolshevik Revolution would be consigned to the "ash heap of history."[9] Reagan also warned, somewhat abstractly, about the dangers of "a quiet, deadening accommodation with totalitarian evil." Nevertheless, the Westminster speech was also, in its own peculiar way, optimistic about the future of the Soviet Union, more optimistic than Nixon or Kissinger had been: "The Soviet Union is not immune from the reality of what is going on in the world. It has happened in the past—a small ruling elite either mistakenly attempts to ease domestic unrest through greater repression and foreign adventure, or it chooses a wiser course. It begins to allow its people a voice in their own destiny."[10]

Reagan's ideological offensive culminated with his speech to the National Association of Evangelicals in Orlando, Florida, on March 8, 1983, an event that symbolized the growing power of evangelicals in American politics. At the time, a movement for a freeze on nuclear weapons was gathering strength in both the United States and Europe. Two of America's large mainstream religious organizations, the National Council of Churches and the National Conference of Catholic Bishops, were moving toward support of the freeze. In inviting Reagan to speak at the convention in Orlando, Robert P. Dugan, Jr., director of the National Association of Evangelicals, wrote Michael Deaver at the White House to say that evangelicals "are not yet firmly positioned on the nuclear freeze issue. They are, thus, a major bloc of support for the Administration."[11]

Reagan seized upon the occasion to portray the Soviet Union as the force of darkness. The Cold War and the arms race between the United States and the Soviet Union were not the result of some "giant misunderstanding," Reagan declared; rather, they were a "struggle between right and wrong and good and evil." Choosing words that would be remembered for decades, Reagan branded the Soviet Union "an evil empire."[12] Stuart Spencer, Reagan's longtime political adviser, had opposed the use of this rhetoric, and Reagan later admitted that Nancy Reagan hadn't liked it either. Yet Reagan later acknowledged that he had given the "evil empire" speech "with malice aforethought. . . . I wanted to let [Soviet leader Yuri] Andropov know we recognized the Soviets for what they were."[13]

Thus, Reagan was recasting the American approach toward the Soviet Union to conform to his own transformational version of anticommunism. The Cold War, in Reagan's terms, was not primarily a foreign-policy struggle but a moral one; the heart of the problem was the nature of the Soviet system. During the Nixon administration, the United States had dealt with the Soviet Union primarily as a rival superpower. Now, Reagan was branding the Soviet regime as repressive and repugnant.

Reagan's rhetoric was accompanied by a startling series of policy changes aimed at reversing the course of the Cold War. During his first three years in office, Reagan approved a substantial defense buildup, a series of covert intelligence actions, a campaign to limit Soviet access to Western technology, and a series of secret national-security directives—all aimed at challenging the Soviet Union. In early 1982, before the Westminster speech relegating Marxist-Leninist doctrine to "the ash heap of history," Reagan issued NSDD-32, a national-security directive declaring that the United States would seek to undermine Soviet control of Eastern Europe. On January 17, 1983, he went considerably further by approving NSDD-75, an order that committed the Reagan administration to a policy of seeking change inside the Soviet Union itself.

NSDD-75 said that the "primary focus" of American policy would be to "contain and over time reverse Soviet expansionism" by competing with Moscow in military power and in international diplomacy. That was, in itself, a hardening of America's longstanding policies in the Cold War. Of even greater moment, the document said the Reagan administration's policies would be dedicated to another purpose as well:

> *To promote, within the narrow limits available to us, the process of change in the Soviet Union toward a more pluralistic political and economic system in which the power of the privileged elite is gradually reduced. The U.S. recognizes that Soviet aggressiveness has deep roots in the internal system, and that relations with the USSR should therefore take into account whether or not they help to strengthen this system and its capacity to engage in aggression.*[14]

Reagan approved this directive less than two months before his "evil empire" speech. The speech was, in effect, the public version of the secret policy. NSDD-75 had been drafted by one of Reagan's most hawkish aides: Richard Pipes, the Harvard historian of Soviet affairs. "As our unfortunate war in Vietnam demonstrated, it was impossible to stanch communist expansion by military means," Pipes later explained. "One had to strike at the very heart of Soviet imperialism, its system." The new Reagan policy did not call for use of military force against the Soviet Union, but it was, in the words of another Reagan aide, "a confidential declaration of economic and political war."[15]

Still, by Pipes's own subsequent account, Reagan personally emphasized during the National Security Council's final discussion of NSDD-75 that he wanted nothing in the document that would stand in the way of "compromise and quiet diplomacy" with Soviet leaders.[16] Indeed, the document also included a section that said Reagan administration policy should seek to "engage the Soviet Union in negotiations to attempt to reach agreements which protect and enhance U.S. interests." Thus, while labeling the Soviet Union an evil empire and challenging its policies around the globe, Reagan was at the same time laying the groundwork for talks with the Soviet leadership.

Two weeks after the "evil empire" speech, Reagan unveiled the final element in his array of new Soviet policies: the Strategic Defense Initiative, a proposal for a system that would shoot down incoming missiles and thus protect the United States from a nuclear attack. SDI (or "Star Wars," as opponents nicknamed it) was easily the most far-reaching and expensive of Reagan's defense programs. It was also a radical departure from past American ideas about national security. Previous American presidents had dealt with the threat of nuclear weapons through the policies of deterrence and "mutually assured destruction." They accepted the idea that there was no way to defend the United States against a Soviet nuclear attack and relied instead on having the ability to retaliate with a massive American nuclear strike against the Soviet Union; by this logic, the leaders of the two superpowers would be held back from nuclear war by the certain knowledge that it would lead to a cataclysmic response, costing millions of lives in their own countries.

By 1984, as Reagan's first term drew to a close, it had become clear that his administration was fundamentally different in nature from those of Nixon and Ford, his two Republican predecessors. While Nixon had held three summit meetings in three years with Leonid Brezhnev between 1972 and 1974, Reagan avoided summits throughout his first term. In that period, his foreign policy had been dominated by the relentlessly anti-Soviet policies of Secretary of Defense Caspar Weinberger; William Casey, CIA director; Jeane Kirkpatrick, ambassador to the United Nations; and a series of second-level officials, such as Undersecretary of Defense Richard Perle.

Haig, the Reagan appointee who symbolized continuity with the Nixon-Kissinger era, had been eased out as secretary of state in 1982 and had been replaced by George Shultz, the former treasury secretary whom Nixon had denounced in his memo to Reagan as lacking a depth of understanding in foreign policy. Jack F. Matlock, Jr., who served as a Soviet specialist on Reagan's National Security Council and later as U.S. ambassador in Moscow, described succinctly the underlying disagreement in approach between Haig and Reagan. "He [Haig] was less sanguine than Reagan and Shultz that the Soviet Union could change, and therefore posed more limited goals for U.S. policy than they eventually did," wrote Matlock. "[He] would very likely have settled for something resembling a cease-fire in place. This would have reduced pressure for internal reform in the Soviet Union. . . . The world would have seemed safer to Western publics, but the East-West divide would have remained. The Cold War would perhaps have been dormant for a time, but would not have ended as a result."[17]

The Nixon veterans reacted to Reagan's first-term Soviet policies with a peculiar blend of horror and admiration. They were taken aback by Reagan's rhetoric and by his emphasis on moral concerns and ideals, rather than geopolitics, as the basis for American foreign policy. Yet the old Nixon team also recognized that Reagan had managed to win public support for his defense buildup and anti-Soviet policies and had overcome the opposition of liberals and Democrats—goals the Nixonites had sought but failed to accomplish in the 1970s. "Reagan was succeeding at what Nixon and Ford had wanted to do," observed Peter Rodman, a former aide to Kissinger.[18]

The Nixonites sought during this period to play the role of intermediaries between the Reagan administration and the Soviet Union. Nixon and Kissinger met from time to time with Dobrynin to offer information on what the Reagan White House was thinking and to offer tips on how to cope with Reagan. In these conversations, they sometimes spoke in scathing terms about the president. "Henry Kissinger . . . stressed that the Reagan administration had no coherent program to deal with the Soviet Union because Reagan had never thought about it seriously, and the State Department was characteristically lacking in initiative and courage to suggest new ideas," recorded Dobrynin.[19] Conversely, Nixon and Kissinger also offered advice to the Reagan White House about what the Soviets were thinking and about how to deal with Moscow.

Harmony appeared to prevail. Kissinger served as head of a presidential commission appointed by Reagan to study American policy in Central America. Brent Scowcroft chaired another commission appointed to study missile deployments. In public, the Nixonites continued to line up behind Reagan throughout his first term, suppressing the disagreements that would burst into the open only a couple of years later.

-5-

NIXON DETECTS GORBACHEV'S "STEEL FIST"

On November 6, 1984, Reagan was elected for a second term, defeating Walter Mondale everywhere but Minnesota and the District of Columbia. Summarizing the campaign two weeks later, Henry Kissinger complained in his newspaper column that both Democrats and Republicans had wrongly suggested that there could be some resolution to the Cold War. The Democrats had argued peace might be attainable through negotiations, while the Republicans talked as though military power would lead to peace. Kissinger ridiculed all such suggestions. "There are no final 'happy endings,'" Kissinger wrote. "Whatever they may agree on, the United States and the Soviet Union will remain superpowers impinging globally on each other. Ideological hostility will continue. Specific, precise arrangements can, indeed must be made. But they are more likely to ameliorate tensions than to end them."[1]

It was a classic statement of the belief in the permanence of the Cold War. In this view, since the basis of the conflict between the two superpowers was geopolitical, and since neither the United States nor the Soviet Union had the military strength to defeat the other, there could be no way for the Cold War to end. Moreover, since each power had enough nuclear weapons to obliterate the other, and each side viewed its nuclear weapons as fundamental to its security, the unending nature of the Cold War was linked inextricably to the nuclear standoff. This static view failed to reckon with the possibility that the Cold War was also a battle of ideas in which the belief system of one of the two superpowers might crumble, or that it was an economic competition, in which one of the two superpowers might not last. The Kissingerian view also did not envision the possibility that an American president or a Soviet leader might consider the elimination of his nuclear arsenal.

Richard Nixon and Henry Kissinger did not see themselves as examples of Cold War inertia or as resistant to fundamental change. They were simply applying their views of the way the Cold War had worked, based on their own experiences in government. Over the next several years, however, Ronald Reagan and a new Soviet leader would gradually begin to operate in a different fashion, based on different assumptions. The Nixonites would insist all the while that this could not happen, that the possibility of far-reaching change was illusory.

The new Soviet leader, Mikhail Gorbachev, was appointed general secretary of the Communist Party of the Soviet Union on March 11, 1985. During Reagan's first term, the Soviet leadership had passed in remarkably short order from Leonid Brezhnev, who died in November 1982 after eighteen years in office, to Yuri Andropov, who spent fifteen months at the helm, to Konstantin Chernenko, who lasted only eleven months. Gorbachev thus became the fourth Soviet leader in four years. In Moscow, the progression of aging Soviet leaders from frailty to illness to death watch to funeral had became almost a ritual; the repeated deaths served as a symbol of a system in decay and a leadership unable to summon the energy to change. Gorbachev was picked above all because, at the age of fifty-four, he was relatively young, healthy, firm of voice, and unlikely to die any time soon.

Gorbachev represented a new generation of Soviet leaders. They were known as *shestidesyatnaki*, Russian for "men of the sixties." They had come of age in the early 1960s, the brief period of Nikita Khrushchev's challenge to orthodox Stalinism, between the terrifying repression of the Stalin era and the stagnation of the Brezhnev years.[2] Gorbachev and the leaders around him, such as Eduard Shevardnadze, whom he soon appointed as his foreign minister, were eager to get the Soviet Union moving again, to reinvigorate or even to change the system.

The ascension of Gorbachev thus brought to the fore old and unresolved questions in the United States about the nature of the Soviet regime and its Communist system: Could the system ever be changed? Did the nature of the regime matter to the United States? Was the Cold War primarily a conflict of tanks and missiles, or was it a contest of beliefs and economic systems?

Nixon sketched out his own vision of an everlasting Cold War a few months after Gorbachev took office. Writing both in the *New York Times* and at greater length in *Foreign Affairs* magazine, the former president warned that Gorbachev represented merely a new face for the same old Soviet policies. "We must disabuse ourselves from the start of the much too prevalent view that if only the two [American and Soviet] leaders could develop a new 'tone' or 'spirit' in their relationship, our problems would be solved," said Nixon. "Such factors are irrelevant when nations have irreconcilable differences." The extensive press coverage of Gorbachev's personal qualities—his firm handshake, sense of humor, and more fashionable dress—represented an obsession with style over substance, Nixon wrote. "Anyone who reaches the top in the Soviet hierarchy is bound to be a dedicated Communist and a strong, ruthless leader who supports the policy of extending Soviet domination into the non-Communist world."[3] Nixon's words sounded sober and prudent, but they turned out to be largely wrong. Over the next few years, Gorbachev would demonstrate that he was a dedicated Communist but not a ruthless one, and that he did not press for Soviet domination in the non-Communist world. Indeed, he even loosened the grip on the Eastern European countries already in the Soviet orbit.

Nixon formed this initial judgment of Gorbachev from a distance, at his home in Saddle River, New Jersey. The following summer, Nixon visited Moscow and met Gorbachev for the first time. The session at the Kremlin late in the afternoon of July 18, 1986, lasted for more than an hour and a half. Afterward, Nixon wrote a private memo, twenty-six pages long, and sent a copy to Reagan. Once again, he portrayed the new Soviet leader as having the same aims as his predecessors:

Gorbachev is the third General Secretary of the U.S.S.R. that I have met. He is without question the ablest. While not quite as quick, he is as smart as Khrushchev. Unlike Khrushchev, he has no inferiority complex. . . . Gorbachev is as tough as Brezhnev, but better educated, more skillful, more subtle. . . . Brezhnev used a meat axe in his negotiations, Gorbachev uses a stiletto. But beyond the velvet glove he always wears, there is a steel fist. . . . In essence, he is the most affable of all the Soviet leaders I have met, but at the same time without question the most formidable because his goals are the same as theirs and he will be more effective in attempting to achieve them.[4]

Nixon's personal impressions of Gorbachev fit the conventional American Cold War images: since the 1940s, Soviet leaders had been characterized as having steel fists (or flinty eyes or iron resolve) so often that Americans sometimes forgot that all these metallurgical allusions were merely metaphors. In fact, Gorbachev was not quite so formidable; under economic pressure, the new Soviet leader was beginning to establish more limited goals for Soviet foreign policy.

While Nixon's views of Gorbachev embodied old stereotypes, his impressions of American politics were as shrewd as ever. He offered Gorbachev some sophisticated advice about why he should try to do business with the Reagan administration. Nixon told Gorbachev it would be a mistake to try to avoid negotiations with Reagan, in hopes that Reagan's successor would take a softer line. Reagan had the ability to get whatever deal he made with the Soviet Union through the Senate, Nixon pointed out—unlike, for example, Jimmy Carter, who had negotiated a proposed treaty on strategic arms control that could not win Senate approval. Moreover, Nixon told Gorbachev, the Soviet Union should want to make sure that after Reagan left office in 1988, he would support good relations with Moscow and not stand in the way. "Failure to reach agreement while President Reagan is in office might run the risk of developing a situation where President Reagan might become a powerful critic of his successor's Soviet-American initiatives," Nixon asserted.[5]

On the question of whether to deal with Reagan or wait him out, Gorbachev needed little persuading. According to the Soviet notes of the Nixon meeting, Gorbachev himself raised this issue. Some had argued that he should postpone any hopes of an agreement with Washington until after the next presidential election, the Soviet leader said. "It would mean that we were ready to wait another three or four years," Gorbachev said. "But during this time, much could change. . . . In today's tense atmosphere, we simply cannot afford to wait."[6] That was a vague, fleeting acknowledgment of the huge problems of the Soviet economy and of the Soviet leadership's desperate need for agreements that would limit their military expenditures.

Nixon and Kissinger were hardly unique in expressing the view that the arrival of Gorbachev meant little or no change for Soviet foreign policy. In fact, they were merely expressing the conventional view at the time within the U.S. government, particularly within the Pentagon and the U.S. intelligence community.

In June 1985, William Casey, CIA director, informed Reagan that Gorbachev and his associates "are not reformers and liberalizers, either in Soviet domestic or foreign policy." Secretary of Defense Caspar Weinberger and the CIA's top Soviet specialist, Robert M. Gates, believed that Gorbachev was "simply a new and more clever and subtle proponent of Soviet global imperialism abroad and communism at home," according to Gates. They found confirmation for their beliefs in some Soviet actions overseas during Gorbachev's first two years, particularly the continuing Soviet war in Afghanistan. Yet they erred in extrapolating from these events sweeping conclusions about the nature of Gorbachev and the future direction of his policies. They were trapped in a clichéd world of steel fists and old wine in new bottles. They failed to see the dynamics that were propelling change. Reagan would come to grasp the situation better and more quickly than they did.

-6-

ABOLITION

Within months, Nixon and Kissinger came to an open break with Reagan. They were supported by quite a few others at the top of America's foreign-policy establishment who had been imbued with the geopolitics of an endless Cold War. The catalysts for this change were Reagan's summit with Gorbachev in Reykjavik in October 1986, and more generally, his willingness to move toward a world without nuclear weapons.

Reagan had arrived in the White House with a well-deserved reputation as a conservative Republican, a hawk on national defense and a proponent of openly confrontational policies toward the Soviet Union. However, after he became president, his own advisers were increasingly taken aback to discover that he also favored the abolition of nuclear weapons. "Reagan had a totally naïve view against nuclear weapons, which I saw time and again," Kenneth Adelman, a Reagan aide and for a time the director of the Arms Control and Disarmament Agency, recalled many years later. "All of us who were conservative thought that when [Jimmy] Carter said, 'I want to eliminate nuclear weapons,' that was the stupidest thing we'd ever heard. We all made fun of it, and then we have our hero [Reagan] who says things really more extreme than Carter ever does, and he's unstoppable in doing it."[1]

Some commentators have argued that one can detect evidence of anti-nuclear sentiments throughout Reagan's career. It is true that he occasionally voiced alarm about the impact of nuclear weapons. At the 1976 Republican National Convention, after President Ford had accepted the Republican nomination, he called Reagan to the podium and invited him to address the audience. Reagan, who had not prepared a speech, talked extemporaneously about the horrors of a world where the great powers have missiles and nuclear weapons "that can in minutes . . . destroy virtually the civilized world we live in." Reagan told the assembled Republicans he had just been invited to write a letter for a time capsule. "Suddenly it dawned on me: those who would read this letter a hundred years from now will know whether those missiles were fired."[2]

Those remarks stand out only in hindsight, however. More frequently, the early Reagan struck a belligerent pose. A more representative quote from the era of the 1960s and 1970s was Reagan's reaction to North Korea's seizure of the USS *Pueblo* and its American crew in 1968. Asked what he would have done, Reagan replied, "How many people were on that ship?" Told there were sixty-eight, Reagan continued, "Right, right, sixty-eight. I'll tell you what I'd do, I'd send them a cable tonight listing sixty-eight cities, and I would tell them I'm going to bomb one city an hour until I get the boys back."[3] (As president, Reagan responded very differently to the seizure of American hostages in Lebanon. There was no city-an-hour bombing; Reagan instead negotiated for the hostages' release, without acknowledging that he had done so.)

At the time Reagan arrived in the White House, there was no reason to think of him as antinuclear. He had run two extended campaigns for the governorship and two more for the presidency without letting on to voters that he favored the abolition of nuclear weapons. His address to the 1976 convention was given only after his primary challenge to Ford had ended— and even then, the speech was more an expression of anxiety about nuclear weapons than a specific call for their abolition. During his 1980 campaign, Reagan had spoken about the need for civilian defense programs to help the United States survive a nuclear exchange.

Nor were there grounds to think of Reagan as opposed to nuclear weapons during his first years in the White House. After Reagan took office, his administration not only moved to bolster civil defense, but also approved a new defense policy that included plans for a "protracted" nuclear war. The new administration also launched extensive preparations to keep the federal government running with teams of officials outside of Washington if the president and vice president were killed or incapacitated during a nuclear exchange with the Soviet Union. (Among the leading participants in this secret program for "continuity of government" were a former defense secretary, Donald Rumsfeld, and a member of Congress, Dick Cheney.) During Reagan's first term, the movement for a nuclear freeze gained in strength both in Europe and in the United States. Reagan determinedly opposed this movement, arguing that the United States should build up its forces and deploy Pershing missiles in Europe to offset the military power of the Soviet Union.

It seems likely, however, that Reagan's opposition to nuclear weapons crystallized during these early years in the White House. Once he became president, Reagan was gradually obliged to confront the reality of what nuclear war would mean, and to recognize the necessity of split-second judgments and the possibility of error. By several accounts, including Reagan's own, he was taken aback when he was briefed by the Pentagon about the details of America's nuclear war planning—how many Soviet cities would be attacked, how many people would be killed, and what would happen to the United States as result of a Soviet attack. The White House and Pentagon carried out detailed exercises for nuclear war, in which Reagan was sometimes obliged to participate. A 1982 briefing on the Pentagon's war plan, known as its SIOP, or Single Integrated Operational Plan, "made clear to Reagan that with but a nod of his head all the glories of imperial Russia, all the hopes and dreams of the peasants in Ukraine, and all the pioneering settlements in Kazakhstan would vanish," wrote one U.S. official present for the briefing.[4]

In the fall of 1983, at the height of the nuclear freeze movement, ABC television produced the movie *The Day After*, an account of what would happen to a single town, Lawrence, Kansas, in a nuclear war. In the film, Kansas City was hit by nuclear missiles, and nearby Lawrence suffered from the fallout of the attack. After viewing a tape before it was aired, Reagan wrote in his diary that it was "very effective and left me very depressed. . . . My own reaction: we have to do all we can to have a deterrent and to see there is never a nuclear war." Not long afterward, Reagan was again briefed on nuclear war planning in the White House Situation Room, and he wrote that it reminded him of the movie. "Yet there were still some people at the Pentagon who claimed a nuclear war was 'winnable,'" Reagan observed. "I thought they were crazy."[5]

That fall, two other episodes underlined for Reagan the possibility of a miscalculation that could lead to nuclear war. On September 1, 1983, a Korean Airlines plane was shot down after flying off course into Soviet territory; Soviet officials had wrongly believed it might be a military plane. Two months later, when NATO conducted an extensive military exercise called Able Archer, U.S. intelligence officials discovered that Soviet officials monitoring the allies' activities believed that the Soviet Union was about to be attacked. Reagan recorded in his diary one day in November that the Soviets "are so defense minded, so paranoid about being attacked that without being in any way soft on them we ought to tell them no one here has any intention of doing anything like that."[6]

By late 1983, it appears, Reagan had seen, heard, and witnessed enough as president to be in favor of trying to abolish nuclear weapons. In November of that year, on a trip to Asia, he began to talk vaguely of his beliefs. "I know I speak for people everywhere when I say, our dream is to see the day when nuclear weapons will be banished from the face of this earth," Reagan said in a speech to the Japanese Diet. At the time, those words were understandably greeted with skepticism. Within weeks, Reagan began asking his speechwriters to insert into a speech on Soviet relations another expression of his hopes for a world without nuclear weapons. At meeting after meeting, he raised the subject of abolition. "The bureaucracy would not hear of it," Secretary of State George Shultz reported.[7]

Reagan persisted. Following his 1984 reelection and throughout his second term, he made increasingly clear to the high-ranking officials around him that he would like to find a way to move toward a world without nuclear weapons. His aides argued with him, to no avail. "He periodically would say, 'Let's get rid of them [nuclear weapons],'" recalled Frank Carlucci, who served as national security adviser in 1986–87. "And I resurrected an old paper that [John] Poindexter [Carlucci's predecessor] had done, saying we can't get rid of them, and redid it and sent it back in." Reagan wasn't persuaded and didn't change. At one point in 1987, Carlucci brought in Richard Perle, the staunch proponent of American military power who had been Defense Secretary Caspar Weinberger's principal adviser for Soviet policy, to try to convince Reagan it would be wrong to abolish nuclear weapons. Perle found that Reagan "was fixed in his ways on a nuclear-free world."[8]

George Shultz told his State Department colleagues that the president had earned the right to his views. "When you win forty-eight out of fifty states, you, too, can talk about eliminating nuclear weapons," Shultz said.[9]

Reagan and Gorbachev met each other for the first time in Geneva in November 1985. The event attracted nearly three thousand correspondents from around the world to analyze every word and gesture—for good reason, since this was the first superpower summit between American and Soviet leaders in more than six years. When Reagan emerged outside coatless and hatless in the frosty weather for his first meeting with the Soviet leader, the correspondents took it as a sign of Reagan's vitality. Years later, Reagan's personal aide, executive assistant Jim Kuhn, admitted that Reagan had himself put on an overcoat and scarf, and that Kuhn had repeatedly urged him to take it off for appearance's sake. "Gorbachev is much younger, and I thought, 'Gorbachev's going to get out of that car, no coat on, no hat on, Reagan's going to be bundled up like [an] old feeble man,'" Kuhn recalled. After several pleas, Reagan, clearly annoyed, pulled off the overcoat and threw it at Kuhn. "All right, damn it, have it your way," Reagan said. He went out to greet Gorbachev, who was bundled up in a dark overcoat and scarf and was carrying a fedora.[10]

The two leaders reached no far-reaching accords at Geneva. They did agree to a joint statement saying that "a nuclear war cannot be won and must never be fought," a declaration that, while seemingly self-evident, turned out to be of some modest significance as a spur for future, more concrete negotiations. During the meetings, Gorbachev repeatedly voiced strong opposition to Reagan's Strategic Defense Initiative, but Reagan refused to give ground. It was a summit in which the two leaders became acquainted with each other, taking each other's measure for the first time. Each leader was dubious about the other, yet each came away thinking about the possibilities for some solid deals in the future. They agreed to two further meetings over the following years in Washington and Moscow.

Reagan recorded his initial impressions of Gorbachev and his wife, Raisa, in a private letter to his old friend George Murphy, another former actor, who had eventually become a conservative Republican senator from California. "He is a firm believer in their system (so is she), and he believes the propaganda they peddle about us," Reagan wrote. "At the same time, he is practical and knows his economy is a basket case. I think our job is to show him he and they will be better off if we make some practical agreements, without attempting to convert him to our way of thinking."[11] For his own part, Gorbachev told others he had found Reagan was "so loaded with stereotypes that it was difficult for him to accept reason." Yet Gorbachev concluded that Reagan wanted to improve relations with the Soviet Union and that there was a chance for progress on important issues.[12]

Within two months, on January 15, 1986, Gorbachev suddenly unveiled a sweeping proposal for a nuclear-free world by the year 2000. His highly publicized initiative appeared on TASS, the Soviet news service, within hours after it was sent to the White House, and Soviet ambassador Anatoly Dobrynin later admitted, "It would not be honest to deny that Gorbachev's proclamation carried elements of propaganda." According to Jack Matlock, the Soviet specialist on the National Security Council at the time, most U.S. officials and agencies favored simply rejecting the idea outright, but Reagan personally intervened to insist upon a positive response. The White House then issued a statement saying that the United States would give the idea careful study.[13]

Gorbachev's initiative reflected an intensified determination to change the direction of his country's foreign policy. According to Anatoly Chernyaev, Gorbachev's principal foreign-policy adviser, the Soviet leader's initial strategy after taking office had been to try to create divisions between Western Europe and the United States, creating indirect pressure on Washington to limit its military spending. But by early 1986, after nearly a year as general secretary, Gorbachev had decided instead to push for arms control through a direct dialogue with the Reagan administration.[14]

In August, while Gorbachev was on vacation in the Crimea, the Foreign Ministry sent him a draft letter to Reagan that reflected the Soviet government's standard positions. After reading the paper, Gorbachev termed it "simply crap." He wanted to speed things up and to drive harder for a breakthrough.[15] He ordered his aides to propose that Reagan meet him relatively soon in London or Reykjavik, Iceland. Reagan soon gave his assent; American officials explained that the talks would be for the limited purpose of preparing for the Washington summit the two leaders had previously discussed.

Reagan and Gorbachev sat down in Reykjavik on October 11 and 12, 1986, for what turned out to be one of the most tumultuous summits of the entire Cold War. Reagan flew into the meeting against a backdrop of the usual admonitions in the United States that Gorbachev represented nothing new for Soviet foreign policy. "He was a protégé of Yuri Andropov, then head of the KGB, and Mikhail Suslov, then chief party ideologue," wrote Henry Kissinger in *Newsweek*. "Neither of these men was likely to have been a closet dove."[16] In Reykjavik, however, Gorbachev quickly departed from the Soviet past by unveiling a startling package of Soviet proposals on arms control; these represented a series of concessions toward the American positions. Gorbachev suggested that the United States and Soviet Union cut by half their strategic weapons, including heavy intercontinental ballistic missiles. He also proposed that the two countries eliminate all their intermediate-range missiles in Europe.

Reagan, Shultz, and the rest of the American team grew increasingly excited by Gorbachev's initiatives. By the second day, the two sides were trying to iron out the details of possible agreements. Reagan and Gorbachev began talking about going even further toward eliminating all ballistic missiles or possibly all nuclear weapons. "It would be fine with me if we eliminated all nuclear weapons," Reagan said. "We can do that," replied Gorbachev.[17] Yet it finally became clear that all of Gorbachev's proposals, from beginning to end, came with a single condition: that the United States accept severe limits on the development of Reagan's Strategic Defense Initiative (SDI), confining all research to laboratories. It was a condition Reagan was unwilling to accept. At the end of the second day, after coming tantalizingly close to the most farreaching arms control agreements in the history of the Cold War, Reagan and Gorbachev walked out of the Reykjavik summit with no deal at all.

Reagan left the meeting both angry and upset. "I'd just never seen Ronald Reagan that way before, had never seen him with such a look," said Kuhn, who accompanied him after the meetings and in his flight back to Washington. "He wasn't certain that he had done the right thing by saying that we had to have SDI in return, instead of giving it up in return for eliminating all nuclear missiles."[18]

At the time, Reykjavik was widely perceived as a failure. In retrospect, it was a turning point in the Cold War standoff over nuclear weapons, despite the absence of an agreement. Each side had seen how far the other was willing to go. Both sides came to realize that they could try again. "As we all know, once you put positions on the table, you can say, 'I've withdrawn them,' but they're not withdrawn," said Shultz. "They're there. We've seen your bottom line, and so we know where it is, and they all came right back on the table before long."[19]

Declassified documents show that soon after Reykjavik, Reagan attempted to galvanize the U.S. government to begin thinking about what the abolition of ballistic missiles would mean and how it could be accomplished. A memo from Poindexter to Reagan dated November 1, 1986, laid out plans for a study on "how best to make the transition to a world without offensive ballistic missiles." The president was told that such a study would be a "follow-up to the proposals you made at Reykjavik." (Soon, military officials began sending back replies on how expensive such a change would be: the U.S. Army would need more divisions, the Navy more antisubmarine warfare, the Air Force more bombers.)[20]

Reykjavik also seemed to alter the relationship between Reagan and Gorbachev. In the immediate aftermath, Gorbachev claimed to be irked. He told the Politburo two days after the summit ended that Reagan had "exhibited extreme primitivism, a caveman outlook, and intellectual impotence." Yet such remarks seemed to be tailored for the consumption of Communist Party hard-liners. Whatever annoyance he felt soon passed, and Gorbachev began to see Reagan in a different light. According to Chernyaev, Gorbachev's foreign-policy adviser, it was at Reykjavik "that he became convinced it would 'work out' between him and Reagan. . . . After Reykjavik, he never again spoke about Reagan in his inner circle as he had before. . . . Never again did I hear statements such as, 'The U.S. administration is political scum that is liable to do anything.'"[21]

-7-

CONSERVATIVE UPROAR

On the Sunday evening on which the Reykjavik summit ended in disarray, Brent Scowcroft was having dinner with Vice President George H. W. Bush at the Naval Observatory in Washington, the vice president's residence. They were old friends who had worked together closely in the past: Bush had been CIA director while Scowcroft had been national security adviser in the final year of the Ford administration. The two men watched on television the scenes of Reagan leaving the summit with a grim face and Shultz, exhausted and depressed, telling a press conference of his deep disappointment.

"Geez, isn't that a shame?" asked Bush, displaying his loyalty to Reagan. No, replied Scowcroft, "That would have been the worst thing that could have happened to us." He was happy that the deal had fallen through. What bothered Scowcroft especially was the idea that the United States should do away with ballistic missiles, or remove them from Europe, leaving the continent under the threat of the conventional forces of the Soviet Union and its Warsaw Pact allies. "It would have been a disaster for us, an absolute disaster," Scowcroft believed.[1]

Scowcroft was reflecting the climate of opinion among those who had

been involved in American foreign and defense policy over the previous decades. Even though no agreement was reached at Reykjavik, the realization
that Reagan and Gorbachev had come close—that they had, in fact, talked
about abolishing or restricting ballistic missiles and nuclear weapons—produced an intense counterreaction in Washington and among America's allies.
The British prime minister, Margaret Thatcher; West German chancellor
Helmut Kohl; and the French prime minister, François Mitterrand, all voiced
concern about the implication of removing American missiles from Europe.
Shultz and the State Department supported what Reagan had been willing to
accept at Reykjavik, but the response in the Pentagon and the National Secu-
rity Council was frosty. American military officials, including notably the
Joint Chiefs of Staff, were thankful that the dispute over the Strategic Defense
Initiative had held up an agreement that they didn't want in the first place.

"The chiefs thought they had dodged a bullet when Gorbachev insisted
that the price had to be SDI," recalled Colin Powell, who arrived in the Reagan White House a couple of months after Reykjavik. Admiral William
Crowe, chairman of the Joint Chiefs, told Reagan he and the other chiefs
were upset by the idea of doing away with ballistic missiles. John Poindexter,
the national security adviser, argued to Reagan the importance of nuclear
weapons. "Reykjavik scared everyone. It was seen as a scary proof that Ronald
Reagan might do something terribly reckless," recalled Nelson Ledsky, a staff
aide at Reagan's National Security Council.[2]

The objections to limiting missiles and nuclear weapons were linked to a
broader, more generalized unease: the perception, commonplace in Washington at the time, that Gorbachev was a typical Soviet leader seeking in the
usual fashion to reassert Soviet military power, and that Reagan might allow
this to happen. "I was on the hawkish side, and very fearful that this kindly
old gentleman [Reagan] was going to get suckered," Fritz W. Ermarth, another National Security Council aide under Reagan, recalled many years later.
"Now, you know, I think back on that [period] with some embarrassment. . . .
Some of us worried that Gorbachev would actually succeed in revitalizing the
system in some way.[3]

In the vanguard of this outpouring of criticism of Reagan's performance at
Reykjavik were Richard Nixon and Henry Kissinger. Since Nixon's resigna-

tion in 1974, he and Kissinger had gone their separate ways. Their estrangement was based, above all, on the fact that after Watergate led to Nixon's resignation in 1974, the former president had lived in ignominy and isolation, while his former secretary of state stayed in the limelight. During these years, Kissinger often got the credit for Nixon administration foreign-policy initiatives, such as the opening to China and détente with the Soviet Union, and not infrequently, Nixon's own role was minimized.

At Reykjavik, Reagan and Gorbachev had begun to chip away at the underpinnings of the Cold War by holding out the prospect of a world without ballistic missiles or nuclear weapons. During the following months, Nixon and Kissinger put themselves forward in public as the champions of the existing Cold War order. For a time the two men acted independently of each other, as they had over the previous twelve years. Eventually, however, Nixon and Kissinger decided to join together in a coordinated public campaign aimed at throwing cold water on Reagan's diplomacy with Gorbachev.

In April 1987, the Los Angeles Times Syndicate distributed a commentary that carried the byline "By Richard Nixon and Henry Kissinger," an unprecedented joint op-ed by the two onetime architects of the policy of détente. It was published not only in the *Los Angeles Times* but in the *Washington Post* and, a few weeks later, in William F. Buckley's *National Review*, the conservative magazine that had long been Ronald Reagan's favorite publication. "Because we are deeply concerned about this danger, we, who have attended several Summits and engaged in many negotiations with Soviet leaders, are speaking out jointly for the first time since both of us left office," wrote Nixon and Kissinger.[4]

The article was brooding in tone. It warned of impending disaster if Reagan continued on the course of Reykjavik. Nixon and Kissinger were worried in particular about trying to eliminate missiles or nuclear weapons from Europe. They suggested that the Reagan administration might, however inadvertently, "create the most profound crisis of the NATO alliance in its forty-year history—an alliance sustained by seven administrations of both parties." Nixon and Kissinger proposed that the Reagan administration should go along with the elimination of missiles in Europe only if this could be linked to a separate deal reducing conventional forces. Such a linkage would have made it difficult, it not impossible, to reach any agreement at all.

Nixon and Kissinger made plain that their concerns were not simply about NATO or Europe: they were profoundly opposed to the idea of eliminating nuclear weapons. "Soviet strategy since the end of World War II has been to exploit the West's fear of nuclear weapons by calling repeatedly for their eventual abolition," asserted Nixon and Kissinger. "Any Western leader who indulges in the Soviets' disingenuous fantasies of a nuclear-free world courts unimaginable perils." Amplifying on this theme in a separate interview with *Time* magazine, Nixon asserted that "nuclear weapons have helped keep the peace for 40 years."[5]

Their other broad theme was that Gorbachev was a traditional Soviet leader seeking to reassert traditional Soviet foreign policy and military power. Gorbachev's foreign policy "can be said to be a subtler implementation of historic Soviet patterns," the two men wrote. At the beginning of 1987, Kissinger had met with Gorbachev when he visited Moscow for the first time in a decade. Upon returning home, he pronounced his verdict. "Gorbachev and his associates seem less constrained by the past and more assertive with respect to Soviet power," Kissinger wrote in a column in *Newsweek*. Even if Gorbachev's domestic reforms succeeded, Kissinger said, "it does not automatically guarantee a more benign foreign policy. On the contrary, it may provide additional resources for expansionism and ideological challenges."[6]

Above all, Nixon and Kissinger warned Reagan against trying to play the role of a peacemaker or worrying about his place in history. A president, they said, "must always remember that however he may be hailed in today's headlines the judgment of history would severely condemn a false peace."[7]

Among Reagan's longtime supporters on the political right, the reaction to Reykjavik was considerably worse. Nixon and Kissinger had couched their criticisms in the careful idiom of foreign policy specialists. Others were not similarly constrained, particularly not the leaders of conservative groups.

In early 1987, Reagan met in the Roosevelt Room of the White House with a group of conservatives, such as Paul Weyrich of the Committee for the Survival of a Free Congress, Phyllis Schlafly of the Eagle Forum, and Howard Phillips of the Conservative Caucus. The conservatives condemned Reagan's policy toward the Soviet Union and his negotiations with Gorbachev. When the session ended, the president left amid a frosty silence. Outside, Reagan turned to Jim Kuhn and observed how different it had been from such meetings in the past. "There was no applause," Reagan observed.[8]

Conservative newspaper columnists were becoming increasingly savage. George Will, who had held six dinner parties for the Reagans at his Washington home and helped edit Reagan's Westminster speech in 1982, had turned against the president. "The prudent person's answer to Gorbachev's question—'What are you afraid of?'—is 'You—and perhaps Ronald Reagan,'" wrote Will in April 1987. "Reagan seems to accept the core of the catechism of the antinuclear left, the notion that the threat to peace is technological, not political—the notion that the threat is the existence of nuclear weapons, not the nature of the Soviet regime."

In a column called "Gorbachev's Iron Smile: Why do democratic leaders fall for it?" Charles Krauthammer repeatedly conjured up the traditional metallurgical metaphors. "Mr. Gorbachev, your iron teeth are showing," he wrote.[9]

Reagan had always been able to deflect questions about his Soviet policy from the political right. A few days before the Reykjavik summit, his former aide Lyn Nofziger had gone to the White House to warn Reagan that conservatives were concerned Gorbachev might try to deceive or manipulate him. In a one-on-one meeting in the White House living quarters, Reagan had quickly soothed Nofziger's anxieties. "I don't want you ever to worry about me dealing with the communists," Reagan said. "I still have the scars on my back from fighting the communists in Hollywood." Nofziger left the session reassured.[10] But by the spring of 1987, Reagan found that he would have to work considerably harder to overcome the mistrust of the conservatives—and indeed, they remained deeply critical of Reagan for the remainder of his time in the White House.

-8-

THE CONVERSATION

By the time of Nixon's clandestine visit to the White House on April 28, 1987, Reagan and his top aides, including Shultz and his new chief of staff, Howard Baker, were incensed. Nixon and Kissinger, once the architects of détente with the Soviet Union, were now giving high-level credibility to the argument that Reagan was being seduced by Gorbachev.

Frank Carlucci, Reagan's national security adviser, had recommended that the president meet, separately, with both Nixon and Kissinger. Reagan quickly rejected Kissinger, his main adversary of the mid-1970s. Nixon, however, was different; Reagan would not say no to the former president whom he had once supported so determinedly. When Carlucci suggested the idea of smuggling Nixon into the White House for a quiet chat, Reagan's response was, "Great idea."[1]

Once settled into a soft chair alongside Reagan in the White House residence, with Baker and Carlucci looking on, Nixon seized the initiative. He said he realized the administration was unhappy with the public criticism, but he and Kissinger were sincere. Nixon took Reagan and his aides through the arguments he had already made in public. A deal to eliminate missiles and nuclear weapons in Europe was wrongheaded; the Soviet superiority in conventional arms was far more significant than nuclear weaponry, and any agreement the Reagan administration negotiated must address this problem.[2]

Nixon sought to create divisions within the administration by taking direct aim at the secretary of state, who was not present at the White House that day. Nixon viewed Shultz as the driving force behind Reagan's diplomacy with Gorbachev. During the Nixon administration, Shultz had served in three cabinet-level jobs, but all had been concerned with the domestic economy, not foreign policy, and after Reagan was elected president, Nixon had opposed the appointment of Shultz as secretary of state. Now, in the secret White House meeting, Nixon made it clear he thought Shultz was not up to the job of dealing with the Soviet Union.

"I did get in one shot at Shultz, which I thought was quite effective," recalled Nixon in the memo he wrote for his own files a few hours later. Nixon had done this by employing his favorite rhetorical device of insisting he was not doing what in fact he was about to do. "I introduced it by saying I didn't want anyone to get the idea that I had anything against him [Shultz]," Nixon said, recounting his own conversation. "I said he had been a great Secretary of the Treasury, a great Secretary of Labor and a great director of OMB [the Office of Management and Budget], and that he did an outstanding job of negotiating with [AFL-CIO chairman George] Meany for a period. But I said that negotiating with Meany was much different from negotiating with Gorbachev."[3]

Reagan asked Nixon for his opinion of Gorbachev, who had been saying he did not want an arms race in either nuclear or conventional weapons. Nixon responded with skepticism that Gorbachev represented anything new. He "could not have gotten his present position or have retained it unless he wanted to be in a position to neutralize Europe or dominate it by either conventional or nuclear blackmail," said Nixon.

Reagan defended his proposal to eliminate ballistic missiles. Those were the weapons that worried him, he told Nixon, because "just a finger on the button could set them off." He confirmed that he and Gorbachev had talked about the idea of getting rid of all nuclear weapons, and made plain he would be happy to do so. "It is clear that Reagan thinks the Reykjavik formula (seeking a drastic reduction in ballistic missiles and nuclear weapons) is still a good idea," Nixon wrote. Moving to counter the claims about Soviet superiority in conventional arms, Reagan told Nixon that the United States and Western Europe together had "enormous superiority over the Soviet Union, which would mean that any kind of arms race would be one they would lose."

Twice during the meeting, Reagan probed for a compromise with Nixon, suggesting that their two positions on how to deal with Gorbachev were not too far apart. Nixon didn't respond; he wasn't interested. At another juncture, Baker suggested Nixon and Kissinger should reassure their contacts in the Soviet Union that all Americans were united in wanting a deal with Gorbachev. Nixon demurred. "I could see of course what he was driving at, and pointed out that I didn't think it was a good idea," he wrote. Trying once more, Baker said it would strengthen the American negotiating position if Kissinger and Nixon made clear they supported the administration. Nixon rebuffed the overture. "I am afraid we just don't agree on that point," he said.

The meeting of president and ex-president was strikingly lacking in warmth. Reagan "was courteous throughout, but I think I sensed a certain coolness on his part," wrote Nixon. "I don't know whether Nancy was in the Residence at the time, but if she was, he did not suggest that she come in and say hello. My guess is that she is probably as teed off as Shultz is."

Nixon came out of the meeting believing that Reagan looked "far older, more tired, and less vigorous in person than in public." Moreover, Nixon thought, "Reagan, candidly, did not seem to be on top of the issues—certainly in no way as knowledgeable as Gorbachev, for example, which of course would not be surprising."

Nixon's conclusion about the president was damning: "There is no way he [Reagan] can ever be allowed to participate in a private meeting with Gorbachev."

-9-

REVERSAL OF ROLES

Reagan and Nixon had completed a remarkable reversal of roles. In the 1970s, Nixon had pursued a working accommodation with the Soviet Union; eventually, Reagan had emerged as the leading Republican critic of this policy of détente. Now, in the 1980s, Reagan sought agreements with the Soviet Union that would ease the nuclear dangers of the Cold War—and Nixon, joined by Henry Kissinger and other veterans of the Nixon administration, disparaged his efforts. Reagan the hawk had become a dove; Nixon the dove had returned as a hawk.

It is useful to summarize the powerful interests that were arrayed against Reagan in early 1987 as he and Gorbachev sought limits on missiles and nuclear weapons. First, Reagan's bedrock conservative supporters had abandoned him—if not in all respects, then certainly in his policies toward the Soviet Union. "For Western Europe, the lights may soon be going out again," mourned *National Review* in one Cassandra-like editorial; it deemed Reagan's attempts to negotiate a deal with Gorbachev to be "catastrophic."

Second, the U.S. intelligence community maintained that, stylistic changes aside, Gorbachev was trying to reassert Soviet power in the traditional fashion. Summarizing his views of Gorbachev through the end of 1987, Robert Gates, the CIA's deputy director and leading Soviet specialist, concluded: "He changed the tone and the face of Soviet foreign policy, but not the substance."[1]

Third, many in America's national-security elite—those who, like Nixon and Kissinger, had been directly involved in setting policy toward the Soviet Union for the previous four decades—were determinedly resisting Reagan's attempts to curb or eliminate nuclear weapons and ballistic missiles. Even Frank Carlucci, whom Reagan brought in as his national security adviser at the end of 1986, told the president he had problems with the far-reaching ideas that had been discussed at Reykjavik.[2]

Against all these forces, Reagan enjoyed a couple of advantages of his own. The first was his own personal popularity, underlined by his overwhelming victory in the 1984 election. The second was the latitude he enjoyed as a second-term president. While retaining the powers of the nation's chief executive, he would not be obliged to run for reelection again.

What accounted for the striking divergence between Reagan and his critics from the right wing and from Washington's foreign-policy establishment? Why was Reagan so much more willing to contemplate far-reaching changes in the Cold War, to view Gorbachev as at least potentially an agent of fundamental change in the Soviet Union? How did Reagan and Nixon come to such different conclusions?

Many attributed Reagan's behavior as a short-term response to the political problems he faced at the time. In late 1986, the Iran-Contra scandal broke; it was revealed that Reagan's National Security Council had been secretly selling weapons to Iran and using the profits to fund the Contra rebels fighting against the government of Nicaragua. In the months that followed, Reagan's presidency had hit its nadir. He had shuffled the top ranks of his administration; Carlucci had been brought in to replace John Poindexter as national security adviser, and Baker had taken the place of Donald Regan as White House chief of staff. On March 9, 1987, the cover of *Time* magazine carried a picture of Reagan with the question: "Can He Recover?" By this analysis, Reagan's eagerness for a deal with Gorbachev represented an attempt to revive his own flagging administration after Iran-Contra.

Yet this explanation does not fit the facts. Nixon and the other critics of

Reagan's Soviet policy had been upset above all by his willingness at Reykjavik to contemplate the elimination of ballistic missiles and nuclear weapons. But the Reykjavik summit took place well before the Iran-Contra scandal burst forth. Iran-Contra had not prompted Reagan's attempt to eliminate ballistic missiles; on the contrary, it had slowed down the effort that was already under way. The declassified archives show that soon after Reykjavik, the Reagan White House told the Pentagon to begin examining and making plans for Reagan's goal of eliminating ballistic missiles. The initiative flagged when Iran-Contra led to Poindexter's resignation, and Carlucci, his successor, made plain his dislike for what had taken place at Reykjavik. "Carlucci did not agree with the president's proposal to destroy ballistic missiles or with his aspiration to eliminate nuclear weapons," Jack Matlock, then the NSC's leading Soviet expert, concluded sadly.[3]

Reagan's determination to do business with Gorbachev thus demands other explanations beyond Iran-Contra. One is that Reagan and Secretary of State George Shultz had more firsthand contact with the new Soviet leadership than other Americans. They were dealing directly with Gorbachev and his foreign minister, Eduard Shevardnadze, and this put them in a better position to sense Gorbachev's eagerness, indeed growing desperation, for a deal with the United States that might limit Soviet military expenditures and free resources for the failing Soviet economy. Gates and others at the CIA were able to scrutinize all the objective signs of change, or lack of change, in the Soviet Union, yet from the distance of Washington, it was not easy for them to judge Gorbachev's intentions or state of mind.

Even those who were able to meet with Gorbachev a single time, like Nixon, tended to view him through the prism of the Cold War, with all its stale imagery of velvet gloves and steel fists. Reagan and Shultz, meeting Gorbachev more than once, were able to intuit, however imperfectly, that these clichés didn't fit. Fritz Ermarth, who succeeded Matlock as the Soviet specialist at the National Security Council, was deeply suspicious of Gorbachev's intentions at the time. Many years later, he reflected on why he had been wrong and Reagan and Shultz more accurate. "A lot of Gorbachev's revolutionary potential—not just his avowed purposes, but these areas of naiveté— were revealed in these one-on-one meetings," Ermarth said. General William Odom, the army intelligence official who served as director of the National

Security Agency from 1985 to 1988, said two decades later that he felt he, too, had underestimated Reagan during this period. "Reagan grasped what Gorbachev was trying to do, and he wanted him to do as much of it as possible," said Odom.[4]

Reagan's views and behavior cannot be explained entirely as an outgrowth of his direct contact with Gorbachev. He was also following through on ideas and policies he had begun to articulate in his first term, well before Gorbachev had become the Soviet leader. Those ideas included a desire to talk to the Soviet leadership even while seeking far-reaching change in the Soviet political and economic systems. Both of these goals had been enshrined in NSDD-75, the policy directive that set forth the Reagan administration's underlying approach toward the Soviet Union; the document had been approved a few weeks before Reagan's "evil empire" speech.

The hawks who championed tough policies toward the Soviets discovered that Reagan, while supportive, also broke into high-level discussions to emphasize the importance of compromise and diplomacy. Conservatives who were heartened by Reagan's rhetoric and his defense buildup either missed or intentionally overlooked this aspect of Reagan. For their own part, liberals tended to overlook or to dismiss Reagan's talk about abolishing nuclear weapons. This strand of Reagan's thinking, too, could be found in his speeches even before Gorbachev's rise to power. It was considerably more significant than anyone appreciated at the time.

Beyond these other factors, there was the most important difference of all between Reagan on the one hand and critics like Nixon on the other: a disagreement about the nature of the Cold War. Nixon's view of the Cold War as a geopolitical contest, with each side able to annihilate the other, implied that neither side could ever win. For Reagan, however, America's contest with the Soviet Union was about economic systems and ideals. When the Cold War was viewed in this fashion, it was conceivable to imagine that one side might fail and end up on "the ash heap of history."

Gorbachev's ascent to the job of Soviet leader brought these underlying differences to the surface. The early characterizations of Gorbachev in the West focused on his appearance and style: telegenic and charismatic, confident and poised. To Nixon, such traits were inherently suspect, and it was only a small logical step for him to begin portraying Gorbachev's ascent to preeminence as merely a superficial change covering up an underlying continuity. But to Reagan, the career actor, Gorbachev's public-relations skills were no defect.

As it became clear that the new Soviet leader was pressing for domestic reforms, skeptics such as Nixon and Kissinger at first worried, wrongly, that Gorbachev might be attempting to reassert Soviet military power and an aggressive foreign policy. By contrast, Reagan became ever more eager for a deal with Gorbachev, sensing that the United States could get good terms, and at the same time, give Gorbachev some of the help he needed to keep pushing for domestic reform inside the Soviet Union—a change in the Soviet system that had always interested Reagan more than Nixon.

Nixon and Reagan were contemporaries. They had been, since the 1940s, America's most prominent and most successful anti-Communist politicians. Yet by the 1980s, they had different perspectives and policy prescriptions. One of them, Nixon, instinctively viewed events in the Soviet Union as a continuation of the past. The other, Reagan, searched for fundamental changes.

PART II
INFORMAL ADVISER

-1-

A NEW FRIEND

In forming his perceptions of the Soviet Union, Ronald Reagan had a friend—a well-dressed, attractive, Russian-speaking, fifty-year-old woman whose ideas about what was happening in Moscow and Leningrad made a bigger impression upon the president of the United States than the reporting and analysis of the Central Intelligence Agency. Her name was Suzanne Massie. She was a writer and author, not an established Soviet scholar. She first met the president on January 17, 1984, when National Security Adviser Robert C. McFarlane brought her into the Oval Office to give Reagan a report on a recent visit to the Soviet Union. They hit it off immediately.[1]

The setting was hardly intimate. Reagan was flanked by several other senior officials, including McFarlane, Vice President George Bush, and Reagan's three top White House aides: Michael Deaver, James Baker, and Edwin Meese. Nevertheless, as Massie proceeded to describe the mood in Moscow, she focused directly on the president as though he were the only person in the room. Whatever she did worked. Reagan was by nature so remote and impersonal that even distinguished visitors sometimes left wondering if he knew their names—and yet on this occasion, Reagan forged some sort of bond with

Massie. He invited her to return to the White House after her next trip to Moscow, and she came back again and again and again. The records of the president's appointments show that Massie met Reagan at the White House roughly twenty times during the following years, more often than any Soviet expert or indeed anyone else outside his own immediate subordinates. Sometimes, Reagan was joined in these sessions by top-level officials, such as his national security adviser. Sometimes, the advisers weren't invited. Asked many years later whether he had taken part in Reagan's White House meetings with Massie, Donald Regan, the White House chief of staff from 1985 to 1987, replied, "No, that was always private, and usually upstairs in the family quarters."[2]

Massie and Reagan began to send each other letters that were mostly about the Soviet Union but occasionally veered toward the personal. "How do you do it, Superman?" Massie asked in a letter in the summer of 1985, after Reagan had returned to the White House from surgery for a polyp in his colon. She sent Reagan little notes on his birthday. Reagan reciprocated. When Massie became a grandmother, the president not only congratulated her but wrote out a separate note addressed to the grandson, Samuel Robert Massie, that began, "Welcome! Your arrival in this exciting and challenging world is a cause for joy far greater than you can know right now. . . ." Reagan's White House aides began to describe Massie in their memos to one another as a personal favorite of Reagan's. Asking that some time be set aside for Massie on Reagan's schedule, one aide wrote to another: "This is important to the President—he likes Suzanne very much."[3]

There is no evidence that this was some sort of romantic affair; Massie was no Monica Lewinsky. She was fascinated by the Soviet Union, interested in creating a role for herself, and also exceedingly skilled in making connections to powerful people. Before meeting Reagan, she had succeeded in courting and befriending a series of American military leaders and U.S. senators. She disdained formality and institutional structures, and in this respect above all she had something in common with Reagan himself. Massie's rival for attention within the Reagan White House—the individual whom she disliked, disparaged, and envied—was not Nancy Reagan. It was Jack Matlock, the National Security Council's leading Soviet specialist, who personified to Massie the U.S. government bureaucracy that she frequently sought to circumvent. (For his own part, Matlock, who went on to become a distinguished U.S. ambassador to Moscow, saw Massie as a marginal figure, despite her frequent meetings with the president.)

In a 1986 letter that epitomized Massie's style and approach, she told Reagan: "I have some thoughts about this [the situation in Leningrad] that I would like to share with you informally. Is there anyway [*sic*] that we could do this alone, or best of all, with Mrs. Reagan, whom I have always wanted to meet?"⁴ Shrewd in the ways of power, Massie no doubt recognized that Nancy Reagan could be a powerful ally and supporter. Mrs. Reagan did in fact join her husband a couple of times for conversations with Massie, but never developed the same warm relationship with her as the president did.

In an interview for this book, Nancy Reagan looked back with chilly detachment at Massie and the role she played. "She was pushy," Mrs. Reagan observed tersely. Nancy Reagan made sure, however, that Massie was invited to major ceremonial events, including the 1987 White House state dinner for Mikhail Gorbachev and, many years later, Ronald Reagan's funeral. Massie was grateful for these invitations. She recognized that everyone considered Nancy Reagan to be a tough operator, but Massie believed this was a role Mrs. Reagan was obliged to play in order to offset her husband's habitual congeniality and his dislike of confrontation. She compared the situation to a doctor's office. "You know how always when there's a wonderful gynecologist, he's got a nasty nurse?" Massie asked.⁵

Reagan obtained a series of benefits from his regular contacts with Massie. She was his source of Russian stories and proverbs. It was Massie who introduced to Reagan the Russian proverb he memorized and then repeated again and again, to Mikhail Gorbachev's considerable annoyance, throughout the summitry and arms-control negotiations of his second term: *Doveryai no proveryai* ("Trust, but verify").

Reagan also derived from Massie his impressions of the Russian people and their history, as an entity separate from the Soviet government or Communist Party. When Reagan went to Geneva for his first meeting with Gorbachev, he was carrying Massie's book *Land of the Firebird: The Beauty of Old Russia*. He was reading it so carefully that in one preparatory session devoted to the coming summit, Reagan interrupted Paul Nitze, his chief arms-control negotiator, to say: "I'm in the year 1830 [in Massie's book]. . . . What happened to all these small shopkeepers in St. Petersburg in the year 1830 and to all that entrepreneurial talent in Russia? How can it have just disappeared?" Reagan's reliance upon *Firebird* was startling, because when Massie's book had first been published in 1980, a scathing review in the *New York Times* had dismissed it as "a heavy breathing comic strip" and "a lollipop speaking baby-talk."[6]

Massie served other purposes as well. Reagan occasionally used her trips to the Soviet Union for back-channel diplomacy. The histories and memoirs of Soviet-American relations during the Reagan years, such as the books by Matlock and Secretary of State George Shultz, give short shrift to Massie. However, the declassified files of the Reagan administration show that at a couple of junctures, she played a more significant role than these histories described: she carried messages back and forth to Moscow concerning the timing, circumstances, and conditions of Reagan's summits with Gorbachev. Her interlocutors in Moscow included an official from the KGB. Eventually, Massie's direct access to Reagan became so threatening to others in the U.S. government that they campaigned against her, warning in secret memos that the KGB might somehow be using her to influence the president.

The Suzanne Massie saga offers a lens to examine Ronald Reagan's own ideas, instincts, and inclinations concerning the Soviet Union. In evaluating the Reagan administration and in particular its policies toward the Soviet Union, it is sometimes hard to distinguish which elements are distinctly Reagan's and which represent merely his approval of what others were doing. Some parts of Reagan's arms-control diplomacy, for example, were largely the work of foreign-policy advisers such as Shultz, who had been carefully nudging Reagan since 1983 to try to seek some agreements with Moscow. Reagan's political advisers and friends also influenced him on Soviet policy—above all, Nancy Reagan, who years later admitted, "Yes, I did push Ronnie a little" into negotiations with Gorbachev.[7] Yet Reagan's continuing use of Massie was his own doing. He chose to meet with her and listen to her, from among all the scholars and experts available to him; and so it is worth exploring where she came from, what she represented, and what ideas about the Soviet Union made her of interest to Reagan.

Reagan's contacts with Massie are also significant because they illuminate how the president's outlook on the Soviet Union changed during his later years in the White House. In 1984, when Massie was introduced to Reagan, a national security adviser (McFarlane) was attempting to use her to moderate the president's hawkish inclinations. In contrast, three years later another national security adviser (Carlucci) sought to restrict Massie's access to Reagan because of concerns that Reagan had become too *dovish* toward the Soviet Union. Throughout this period, Massie herself remained a constant; she continued to say the same things about Russia and its people. But the president's ideas about the Soviet Union changed considerably. Massie didn't cause this shift, but through her continuing trips to the White House, one can trace Reagan's gradual evolution.

-2-

BANNED FROM THE LAND OF THE FIREBIRD

If Ronald Reagan was immediately taken with Suzanne Massie, it was because her life story seemed like the stuff of the B movies to which he had devoted much of his Hollywood career. It contained elements of tragedy and hope, of adversity and overweening ambition. Massie's ideas about Russia—intensely romantic, spiritual, even mystical in nature—grew out of the extraordinary circumstances of her own life, especially the shattering experience of having a hemophiliac son.

Massie's mother, a Swiss woman named Suzanne Nobs, had lived in Russia as a teenager during the final years of Czar Nicholas. She was visiting a Russian family in 1914 when World War I broke out. Trapped inside the country, she stayed there for several years, through the upheavals of the Russian Revolution, before finally managing to flee. She later married a Swiss diplomat, Maurice Rohrbach, who was assigned to the United States. Massie, the eldest of three daughters, was born in New York City, but the family lived for most of her childhood in Philadelphia, where her father was serving as the Swiss consul general. Her mother taught Suzanne to love Russian ballet and introduced her to Russian friends.

After graduating from Vassar, Massie was one of five women from colleges across the nation chosen by Time Inc. as a trainee. She went on to work as a researcher at *Time* magazine (a job reserved exclusively for women) and as a cub reporter for *Life*. Following the custom of the 1950s, she shelved her budding career when she got married. Her husband, Robert Massie, a former Rhodes Scholar and U.S. Navy intelligence officer, became a magazine writer, first for *Collier's* and then for *Newsweek*. Struggling for money, the couple moved from a furnished room on the Lower West Side of Manhattan into a cramped apartment in Westchester County, where their first son, Robert, was born. Five months later, their suburban routines were upended: Suzanne noticed bruises on her son's body, and a toe prick from a lab test would not stop bleeding. The inevitable diagnosis: hemophilia. The Massies entered into a life of recurrent medical crises and unending fear of injury, of begging for blood donations and battling with doctors and hospitals.[1]

After several years, Suzanne Massie looked for something that would enable her to escape her son's illness for a few hours at a time. "To keep my mind intact, to keep from turning around in my cage like a panic-stricken animal, I had to do something hard, something mentally challenging," she later wrote. She decided to study Russian. Her mother had gotten to know the language in the midst of the Russian Revolution, in a milieu akin to that in *Doctor Zhivago*; by contrast, the setting for Suzanne Massie's study of Russian could not have been more mundane. She enrolled in the adult education program at White Plains High School, which was offering language courses for eight dollars a semester. On the first night of class, a woman named Svetlana told her, "Suzanne, you have a Russian soul." Massie took those words to heart.[2]

Meanwhile, Robert Massie had moved to another magazine, the *Saturday Evening Post*. For years he had been proposing to various magazines an article about hemophilia. Finally, the *Post* bought the idea. Along with a general article about hemophilia, Robert Massie also submitted a brief sidebar called "The Most Famous Hemophiliac," about the Russian czar Nicholas; his wife, Alexandra; their hemophiliac son, Alexis; and their faith healer, Gregory Rasputin. The *Post* killed this second piece for lack of space, but Suzanne Massie encouraged Robert to turn the story into a book that would narrate Russian history and at the same time tell the world about hemophilia, their son's disease. Robert Massie spent several years in the New York Public Library;

Suzanne served as his researcher and editor. The book, published in 1967, was *Nicholas and Alexandra*; it became a best seller and eventually, a Hollywood movie.[3]

After the book was published, the Massies traveled for the first time to the Soviet Union. The impact on Suzanne Massie was profound. She identified the travails of the Russian people with her own plight. She later wrote:

> *The contact I felt was deep and immediate. Hemophilia had been preparing me for ten years for these meetings. They knew the terror of the knock on the door, the telephone in the night, the anguished knowledge that in one awful moment a life might be shattered. The causes were different, but the psychological result was the same. We shared the reflexes of people who live with fear. I knew what it was to feel suffocated, to be unable to travel, unable to determine my career, to live in isolation from the rest of the world.*[4]

Over the next few years, Suzanne Massie returned to Russia again and again: eight trips in little more than four years. She interviewed Russian writers for a book called *The Living Mirror: Five Young Poets From Leningrad*; one of the subjects of the book was a dissident writer named Josef Brodsky, eventually the winner of the Nobel Prize for Literature.

Then, as Massie was preparing to make her ninth visit in 1972, Soviet authorities denied her request for a visa, without explanation. She had apparently become too close to the Russian dissident community. Massie was suddenly cut off from the country and culture that had become the focus of her life. The hunt for a visa brought Massie to Washington. She began to cultivate political friends and allies who might persuade or pressure Soviet authorities to change their minds. She spoke with Senator Henry Jackson, the leading opponent of the Nixon administration's détente with the Soviet Union. Jackson had just introduced what was known as the Jackson-Vanik amendment, a provision that denied trade benefits to the Soviet Union until authorities opened the way for Jewish emigration. Massie encouraged Jackson's efforts, hoping that while finding a way to get Jews out of the Soviet Union, the senator might also find a way to get her back in. During the following decade, while continuing to talk with Jackson, Massie also cultivated several other members of the Senate: Bill Cohen of Maine, John Heinz of Pennsylvania, Sam Nunn of Georgia, Al Gore Jr. of Tennessee, Ted Stevens of Alaska. Massie was so thoroughly obsessed with returning to the Soviet Union that, failing to obtain a visa, she twice signed up for tourist cruises on ships that stopped briefly in Leningrad.[5]

She spent the late 1970s writing *Land of the Firebird*, which would later attract the attention of Ronald Reagan. It was a history of Russian culture before the Soviet era, narrated in a romanticized way. "It is the darker side of Russia's history which has most often been emphasized, not only in the Soviet Union, but also in the West," she wrote in the introduction to the book, published in 1980. "As a result of this lopsided concentration, the picture of old Russia that has emerged is too often a stereotype, lacking in depth and accuracy. . . . These manifestations of beauty which old Russia produced so brilliantly, permeated by the spiritual qualities of the Russian people, are perhaps what we most need to rediscover now, to offset the coldness and impersonality of an increasingly heartless, technological and materialistic modern world." The relentlessly negative review in the *New York Times* went out of its way to recommend, as an alternative, James Billington's book *The Icon and the Ax*.[6]

During the 1970s and early 1980s, Massie also developed ties to the American military services. She was invited to lecture about Russian culture at the United States Military Academy at West Point and went on to appear at military institutions such as the Army War College in Carlisle Barracks, Pennsylvania. She found that she got along much more easily with American military officials than with scholars or diplomats. When she had approached the State Department for help in obtaining a Soviet visa, the Soviet desk officer, Jack Matlock, had seemed to brush her off, saying that her persistent requests were inappropriate. But the men in uniform had more time for her; they provided a receptive audience for her thoughts about Russian life and history. Her network of friends and contacts in the military included Andrew J. Goodpaster, the former NATO commander who became superintendent at West Point; William E. Odom, a West Point professor who eventually became head of the National Security Agency; and Tyrus W. Cobb, another West Point professor who later served on the National Security Council staff.

When Cobb was invited to the Soviet Union on a formal military exchange program, he asked Massie for seven signed copies of her book for Soviet officials, and Massie, still pursuing her quest for a visa, was happy to comply. One of the recipients sent back word that she should get in touch with a Soviet embassy official in Washington. Massie began courting him, much as she had pursued American officials. When Yuri Andropov, the long-time leader of the KGB, rose to become the Communist Party leader in 1982, Massie's Soviet contact in Washington asked her to inscribe a copy of *Land of the Firebirds* for Andropov. She did, cautiously signing the book "with hope for the future of the great Russian land"—words that deliberately avoided any mention of the Soviet Union or government.

Finally, these efforts paid off. In the spring of 1983, she was invited to the Soviet mission to the United Nations in New York for a meeting with Georgi Arbatov, the director of Moscow's Institute of the USA and Canada and a senior adviser to Andropov. He said he had heard she was still having trouble with a visa.

"Try again," Arbatov said. She did. Soon afterward she got a Soviet invitation for a visit to Moscow, the approval for which she had been waiting for more than a decade.[7]

-3-

WAR SCARE

Massie flew to Moscow in September 1983. By coincidence, her trip, which was planned well in advance, took place during a peak in tensions between the United States and the Soviet Union. A few days before she arrived, the Soviet military had shot down South Korean commercial flight KAL 007 over Sakhalin Island, killing 269 passengers, including 61 Americans. The International Federation of Air Line Pilots Associations responded by calling for a ban on commercial flights to Moscow, and for two weeks most Western airlines complied. Moscow had no flights to or from New York, London, Rome, Frankfurt, or Tokyo. Massie flew to Paris and caught a flight with Air France, the only major Western airline that, through the use of nonunion pilots, defied the boycott. The plane she took to Moscow had only one other passenger. When she arrived at Sheremetyevo Airport, it was virtually deserted.[1]

Those weeks brought frequent reminders of the rancor between the Soviet Union and the Reagan administration. Soviet leader Yuri Andropov called the KAL incident a "sophisticated provocation" by American intelligence agencies. In an extraordinary statement to the Soviet people, Andropov accused the Reagan administration of threatening world peace. "Even if someone had any illusions as to the possible evolution for the better in the policy of the present American administration, the latest developments have finally dispelled them," the Soviet leader said. Soviet foreign minister Andrei Gromyko canceled a visit to the United Nations after the governors of New York and New Jersey refused to let his civilian jet land at civilian airports in their states. The Soviet Union called home twenty Soviet scholars who had been studying at American universities; they had been the last Soviet researchers in the United States under a cultural agreement that had been allowed to lapse in 1979 after the Soviet invasion of Afghanistan.[2]

In Moscow, Massie phoned the Institute of the USA and Canada, her official hosts, to thank them for approving her visit after so many years of visa denials. She had expected to spend her time in Moscow looking at churches and museums. Instead, she was quickly invited to the institute for a chat. Once there, she was ushered into the office of Radomir Bogdanov, the deputy director.

The Institute of the USA and Canada was no independent think tank. It worked closely with and for several parts of the Soviet regime, including the Communist Party Central Committee, the Foreign Ministry, the armed forces, and the KGB. The institute, which housed about three hundred employees, had been set up in the 1960s by Georgi Arbatov, Moscow's leading specialist on the United States, the official who had opened the way for Massie's visit. Arbatov was particularly close to Soviet leader Yuri Andropov, the former KGB chief.[3]

During the early 1980s, Arbatov and his institute were at the height of their influence in Moscow, not only because of Andropov's ascent but also because of what was happening in Washington. After Reagan took office, the veteran Soviet ambassador Anatoly Dobrynin found that he no longer enjoyed the same access to top levels of the administration that he had held in the Nixon-Kissinger years. From Moscow's perspective, the Reagan administration wasn't talking much to the Soviet embassy in Washington, and Dobrynin wasn't offering much insight. As a result, the job of the USA Institute was to address from Moscow the large questions that were not being answered by the Soviet embassy in Washington: What did the new Reagan administration represent? What were the sources of Reagan's power? Why was he so popular in the United States? Was he planning to take the United States to war with the Soviet Union?

Radomir Bogdanov, the deputy director, was short, chunky, and balding; he bore a slight resemblance to Nikita Khrushchev. His colleagues at the institute regarded him as crude and vulgar. He had a biting sense of humor and several girlfriends.

He had not come to the institute from academia or the Foreign Ministry, the route taken by some of its specialists. Rather, Bogdanov was a leading intelligence official of the KGB. He had served as the KGB's resident, or station chief, in New Delhi in the 1960s, during the era when the Soviet Union solidified its ties with India. Within the KGB, he was considered one of the most experienced veterans in "active measures," that is, the spread of false rumors and other disinformation.[4]

Bogdanov was a familiar figure to American journalists, embassy officials, and arms-control specialists. He served regularly as an interlocutor for visitors from the United States, offering the official Soviet point of view in words that went beyond the formulations of the Foreign Ministry. From the institute in Moscow and at disarmament conferences overseas, Bogdanov volunteered opinions and themes that fit with Soviet policy objectives. "Throughout the late stagnation and early glasnost years, Bogdanov was one of the few people visiting foreigners could come to for an interview," observed David Remnick, a *Washington Post* correspondent in Moscow in the 1980s.[5]

Many of those who dealt with Bogdanov realized that he was from the KGB. So did Massie, by her subsequent account. She was familiar enough with Soviet institutions to know that the deputy director of an organization was frequently a KGB representative.[6] If anything, Bogdanov's intelligence connections enhanced his status. When Andropov became Communist Party general secretary after Brezhnev's death in November 1982, his ascent demonstrated that the KGB stood at the top of the institutional hierarchy in Moscow.

Throughout the early 1980s, Bogdanov issued a steady stream of warnings to visiting Americans that the policies of the Reagan administration were going to lead in some way or another to disaster. "In this Reagan administration, you have people who are ready to push the button," Bogdanov told Nicholas Daniloff of *U.S. News and World Report* in early 1982. "They are dangerous people, and they are sure there is only one way to deal with the

Soviet Union—to destroy it in a nuclear war." To Strobe Talbott of *Time*, he declared later that year, "These people in the White House are unpredictable ideologues. They think we are so weak that we can be crushed by economic pressure. They don't understand how this dangerous illusion might play into the hands of some people here."[7]

In the meeting with Massie in September 1983, Bogdanov conveyed his usual message of gloom about Soviet-American relations. This time, he went a step further. "You don't know how close war is," he told her. Massie had been observing the Soviet Union from the United States, not Moscow, and her focus had been on Russian culture, not high-level diplomacy. Now she was unexpectedly getting a warning about a potential outbreak of war from a well-connected official at a time when, after the KAL incident, the Soviet Union seemed increasingly isolated from the West.

She returned to the United States in dismay, determined to find some way to ease the hostility. She pursued this quest with her usual tenacity, working the high-level connections she had been relentlessly cultivating for the previous decade. At first, she tried to gain an appointment with Reagan's national security adviser, William Clark, by going through the famed Russian cellist Mstislav Rostropovich, an acquaintance who knew Clark well. That plan fell through because on October 17, before Massie could land a meeting, Reagan suddenly replaced Clark at the National Security Council, with Robert C. "Bud" McFarlane.

Undeterred, Massie turned to Bill Cohen, one of the senators she had befriended. Cohen and McFarlane were old friends. For a time in the late 1970s, McFarlane had served as a Republican staff aide to the Senate Armed Services Committee, of which Cohen was a Republican member. Massie told Cohen that what she had seen and heard in Moscow seemed to go beyond the usual Soviet truculence. The United States should do something to try to turn things around, she said. Cohen called the new national security adviser, who agreed to see Massie. She relayed to the White House Bogdanov's mutterings about the possibility of war. The two governments needed to find ways to start talking again, Massie argued. Even small steps, specific steps, would help. She offered to go back to Moscow to try to negotiate a new cultural agreement between the two countries to replace the one suspended when Soviet troops entered Afghanistan.

To McFarlane, Massie's report of the mood in Moscow was merely one more sign that the climate between Washington and Moscow was becoming dangerous. He had already seen other, more serious indications. That fall, Reagan and his administration were confronted with what became known as the war scare of 1983.

The CIA began receiving reports that the Soviet Union believed the Reagan administration might be preparing to launch a surprise nuclear attack on the Soviet Union. The principal source was Oleg Gordievsky, the KGB's resident, or station chief, in London, who nine years earlier had been recruited by MI6, the British intelligence service. Gordievsky told his British handlers that during the first year of the Reagan administration, Andropov, then the head of the KGB, had ordered Soviet intelligence officials throughout the world to monitor American activities for signs of preparations for war; he was afraid the new team would launch a nuclear first strike. In the fall of 1983, Gordievsky reported that Soviet officials had grown even more alarmed as they observed the United States and NATO countries begin preparing for the military exercise known as Able Archer 83. This was a test of the procedures for how the NATO chain of command would obtain approval from member countries for the release of a nuclear weapon. Under the original plans, Reagan himself was going to take part in the exercise.[8]

The reports that the Soviets were afraid they were about to be attacked began flowing into the White House in the early autumn of 1983. McFarlane at first dismissed the accounts; he believed they represented a Soviet attempt to create divisions between the United States and its allies before the deployment of American Pershing missiles in Europe later that fall. But other reports from the Warsaw Pact countries of Eastern Europe and from European diplomats seemed to corroborate what Gordievsky was saying: Soviet officials were openly expressing anxiety about a possible American attack. McFarlane took these accounts seriously enough to tell Reagan not to participate in Able Archer, and the exercise went forward without him.[9]

During Able Archer, NATO forces changed their message formats in a way that Soviet intelligence officials had not seen in previous NATO exercises. In the practice drill, NATO also moved imaginary forces up several stages of readiness to high alert. Gordievsky reported that the KGB, in monitoring

Able Archer, believed that genuine forces had gone on high alert and took seriously the idea that NATO might be on the verge of a preemptive attack. Gordievsky himself began to worry; he was growing increasingly upset with his British handlers and the CIA. "It was, 'Jesus, what's happening? I'm work- ing for you guys in the name of peace, not in the name of confrontation and war,'" recalled Fritz Ermarth, who later studied the Able Archer episode for the CIA. "He was disturbed by the trend of events and the atmospherics and was ready to place some of the blame for this on U.S. policy."[10]

In Washington, CIA director William Casey was carrying Gordievsky's reports about a Soviet war scare directly to Reagan and McFarlane. Some of the more hawkish Soviet experts in the U.S. intelligence community, includ- ing Ermarth, thought at the time that Casey should not have been passing along the alarmist messages. "I was concerned that they [Soviet officials] were doing influence operations here and in Europe, getting messages through, that they were trying to spook us," said Ermarth in an interview. "I was mad at Casey that he hadn't sufficiently snake-checked this thing. Not that Gordievsky wasn't being honest."

In early 1984, under Ermarth's direction, the CIA did a Special National Intelligence Estimate that dismissed the "war scare" as merely a Soviet propa- ganda campaign. "We believe strongly that Soviet actions are not inspired by, and Soviet leaders do not perceive, a genuine danger of imminent conflict or confrontation with the United States . . . ," it concluded. "Recent Soviet 'war scare' propaganda . . . is aimed primarily at discrediting U.S. policies and mobilizing 'peace' pressures among various audiences abroad." However, a study by British intelligence that same year determined that Soviet officials had taken seriously the possibility of a nuclear strike against them. Several years later, another review by the President's Foreign Intelligence Advisory Board similarly found that Soviet officials had not been merely posturing but had, in fact, been genuinely afraid of war.[11]

Although the intelligence community was divided on the significance of the "war scare," the episode had a clear and indisputable impact on Reagan him- self. One day in late November 1983, at the end of his morning intelligence briefing, the president asked McFarlane if the Soviets really thought the United States was planning a nuclear attack. "How could they believe this?"

he wondered. McFarlane reminded the president that the Soviets were edgy because the new Pershing missiles the United States was installing in Europe could hit Soviet targets within seven minutes, much more quickly than intercontinental missiles from the United States. Reagan himself later admitted to growing concern during this period with how Soviet officials viewed the United States. In his 1990 autobiography, he said that by the end of 1983, he had begun to realize "that many Soviet officials feared us not only as adversaries but as potential aggressors who might hurl nuclear weapons at them in a first strike."[12]

When the Reagan administration and its allies began deploying the new Pershing missiles in Europe in late 1983, the Soviet Union, in response, suspended participation in all arms-control talks with the United States. According to McFarlane, in December, just before leaving Washington to spend Christmas in California, Reagan said he would like to find some way to start new high-level talks with Moscow. As secretary of state, Shultz had been gently encouraging the president for more than a year to establish more regular and direct contact with Soviet leaders. At the end of the year, over a round of golf in Palm Springs, Reagan and Shultz talked at length about the importance of opening new channels to the Soviet leadership.[13]

There was a political dimension to Reagan's growing eagerness for dialogue. He was preparing to run for reelection in 1984, and his Democratic opponents were already beginning to seize upon the heightened tensions with the Soviet Union as a possible campaign issue. On January 3, 1984, in a speech to the National Press Club, former vice president Walter F. Mondale, the leading candidate for the Democratic nomination, warned that under the Reagan administration, the "risk of nuclear war" had increased. "It's three minutes to midnight, and we are scarcely talking to the Soviets at all," Mondale asserted. He promised that if he were elected president, he would have "regular contacts" with Moscow. "Mr. Reagan may become the first president since Hoover never to have met with his Soviet counterpart," Mondale declared.[14]

Reagan countered two weeks later, on January 16, 1984, with a speech about the Soviet Union that was strikingly conciliatory in tone. It marked a distinct change in emphasis from his public statements of the previous three years. In his Westminster speech in 1982, Reagan had relegated the communist system to the "ash heap of history," and the following year, he had denounced the Soviet regime as "the evil empire." This time, however, the president emphasized the importance of reducing the possibility of confrontation between the two countries. "Neither we nor the Soviet Union can wish away the differences between our two societies and our philosophies," Reagan declared, "but we should always remember that we do have common interests and the foremost among them is to avoid war and reduce the level of arms."[15]

Reagan had instructed his aides several weeks earlier to prepare a speech that could launch a concerted attempt at new discussions with Moscow in 1984. The speech had been ready before the end of December but had been delayed until January at the request of Nancy Reagan, in consultation with her astrologer, Joan Quigley. Most of the speech had been drafted by Jack Matlock, then the National Security Council aide for Soviet affairs, and by State Department officials. However, Reagan himself wrote the final section of the speech, which cast the abstract idea of common interests between the United States and the Soviet Union in his own distinctive style, a sentimental appeal to ordinary, unsophisticated Americans:

> *Just suppose with me for a moment that an Ivan and an Anya could find themselves, oh, say, in a waiting room, or sharing a shelter from the rain or a storm, with a Jim and Sally, and there was no language barrier to keep them from getting acquainted. Would they then debate the differences between their respective governments? Or would they find themselves comparing notes about their children and what each other did for a living? Before they parted company, they would probably have touched on ambitions and hobbies and what they wanted for their children and problems of making ends meet. And as they went their separate ways, maybe Anya would be saying to Ivan: 'Wasn't she nice? She also teaches music.'. . . They might even have decided they were all going to get together for dinner some evening soon. Above all, they would have proven that people don't make wars.*[16]

The passage was implausible, old-fashioned, and saccharine. According to Matlock, what Reagan had first written had to be revised, because it was also sexist: in Reagan's draft, Ivan and Jim talked about their work while Anya and Sally swapped notes about children and cooking.[17] Nevertheless, giving the speech signified that Reagan was for the first time seeking public support in America for the idea of easing hostilities with the Soviet Union. At the time, Soviet officials dismissed the overture as a political stunt. "At any other time, such a speech by an American president would have been regarded as a tangible step toward improving relations with the Soviet Union," reflected Dobrynin many years later. "But with all the other negative factors, to say nothing of the imminent presidential election, it was hard to believe in Reagan's sincerity."[18]

-4-

IMPROBABLE EMISSARY

The National Security Council decided to take Massie up on her suggestion that she return to Moscow as an informal intermediary. The hope was that she might be able to help in obtaining a resumption of cultural exchanges between the United States and the Soviet Union, a first step toward an easing of the broader tensions. A plausible case could be made for sending Massie, who had written a book on Russian culture.

From the Reagan administration's standpoint, there were several advantages to using Massie in this fashion. She was not an official representative of the U.S. government and thus could not be besieged by the Soviets with demands to justify all of the Reagan administration's actions and utterances of the previous three years. If the Reagan White House had itself proposed a resumption of cultural exchanges, the Soviets would probably have dismissed the idea as a ruse to divert attention from the recent deployment of Pershing missiles in Europe. Moreover, through Massie and her unofficial contacts in Moscow, the Reagan administration was hoping to circumvent the two senior Soviet officials who had regularly dominated all decisions about the United States: Anatoly Dobrynin, the ambassador to Washington, and his boss, Andrei Gromyko, the foreign minister. "We didn't want everything to go through Dobrynin," said Jack Matlock, the NSC's Soviet expert, who felt both Gromyko and Dobrynin would be cold to the idea of resuming contacts.[1]

Sending a private citizen like Massie was irregular, but Robert McFarlane, Reagan's national security adviser, had a penchant for doing business with other governments outside regular channels. He had learned about the conduct of American foreign policy as a military aide to Henry Kissinger, at a time when Kissinger, as national security adviser, was keeping the State Department, even the secretary of state, in the dark about the Nixon administration's diplomacy with the Soviet Union, China, and North Vietnam. McFarlane's own clumsy attempts at Kissingerian secret diplomacy would eventually culminate in the Reagan administration's biggest disaster, the Iran-Contra scandal, when McFarlane tried to go outside the U.S. government bureaucracy to deal with the leadership in Tehran.

Massie was not Reagan's only conduit for back-channel discussions with Moscow. During this same period, the administration also received an offer of help from an unlikely source: Senator Edward Kennedy, Democrat from Massachusetts, one of the administration's most prominent critics. One of Kennedy's aides, Dr. Lawrence Horowitz, had been meeting in Moscow with Vadim Zagladin, deputy chief of the Communist Party Central Committee's International Department. For several years, Horowitz served as a secret message carrier between Reagan's NSC and Zagladin. Kennedy was aware of these secret exchanges; for a long time Secretary of State George Shultz was not.[2]

At one juncture, McFarlane also sought to have Reagan designate Brent Scowcroft, the former national security adviser and onetime aide to Kissinger, as an emissary for private conversations with top Soviet leaders. But soon after McFarlane broached the idea with Reagan and invited Scowcroft to come to the White House to discuss the mission, Shultz passionately objected, arguing that all Soviet diplomacy should go through him and the State Department. Reagan knew how to handle turf battles like this one in a genial, nonconfrontational way. When Scowcroft arrived at the White House a few days later to talk in further detail about what he should say on Reagan's behalf on an upcoming visit to Moscow, Reagan told him stories about the movie *Patton* for twenty minutes: how the movie was made, why Patton's speech was in the beginning of the film. The president then stood up and said, "Well,

good luck!"—thus leaving Scowcroft bewildered, Shultz mollified, and Mc-
Farlane not really humiliated.[3]

Massie, who had never served in government, was a different sort of intermediary from Scowcroft. She was not being sent to meet with top Soviet
leaders; she was being asked to explore merely routine cultural exchanges, not
major diplomatic issues such as arms control. Still, Massie moved quickly and
shrewdly to enhance her status. Before leaving for Moscow on the cultural
mission for the NSC, Massie said she had a single request. She wanted to
meet, face-to-face, with Reagan. She argued that it would be important to be
able to tell Soviet officials that she had met with the president and that what
she was saying had his personal imprimatur.[4]

McFarlane gave his assent. He liked the idea of introducing Massie to the
president. He felt that she could help Reagan to develop a better feel for
people and ordinary life inside the Soviet Union. He had discovered that the
president was uncomfortable dealing with conceptual matters such as arms
control and balance-of-power diplomacy, and that Reagan always found issues more appealing if they were cast in human terms. Massie was the perfect
vehicle for McFarlane's goal of bringing the Soviet Union alive to Reagan, so
that he would begin to see America's Cold War adversary as more than an
abstraction.

The meeting was set for January 17, 1984, the morning after Reagan's
"Ivan and Anya" speech. The president had talked in that same address about
the need to search for "concrete actions that we both can take to reduce the
risk of U.S.-Soviet confrontation." Seated in the Oval Office with Reagan
and his advisers, Massie asked what she should say while she was in Moscow.
Could she tell Soviet officials that she had met with the president and that his
newly announced effort to improve relations with the Soviet Union was more
than just an election-year ploy? Could she say that if Reagan won reelection
in November, his approach of seeking to avoid confrontation would continue
to guide Soviet policy during his second term? Reagan said she could.

As McFarlane had hoped, Massie also began describing the situation inside the Soviet Union. She was lively: she told Russian jokes; she recounted in
an animated way her arguments with Soviet officials about American policy;
she spoke of the hardship of the Russian people, their economic desperation
and their capacity for suffering. She also talked about subjects Reagan's

foreign-policy advisers rarely mentioned, such as the quest for spiritual values inside the Soviet Union. Reagan paid close attention. The session, held just after Reagan's regular morning national-security briefing, lasted not more than half an hour. But Reagan was intrigued. He invited her to come back.

Reagan was seventy-two years old. It is worth recalling that at this point, three years into his presidency, he had had remarkably little contact with the Soviet Union, its leaders, or its people. He was by now interested in trying to ease tensions with Moscow and to reduce or eliminate the dangers of nuclear weapons, but he had little in the way of personal experience to guide him. He had never traveled to the Soviet Union. He had met a Soviet leader only once in his life, while he was governor, at the party President Richard Nixon gave in California during Leonid Brezhnev's visit to the United States. In early 1983, after taking over from Alexander Haig as secretary of state, Shultz recalled, "It finally dawned on me that President Reagan had never had a real conversation with a top Communist leader, and that he wanted to have one." Shultz had arranged a White House meeting in which Reagan talked for the first time with Anatoly Dobrynin, the Soviet ambassador, and the session had gone well. Nevertheless, Reagan's ideas about the Soviet Union and its leaders had been formed four decades earlier, during the anti-Communist battles in Hollywood in the 1940s, and his early impressions lingered. A couple of years later, when Dobrynin was leaving his job as ambassador to return to Moscow, Reagan expressed astonishment that such a polished, urbane diplomat could represent the evil empire. "Is he *really* a communist?" Reagan asked.[5]

Suzanne Massie began to serve as Reagan's window on the Soviet Union. She described the country and the Russian people to the president in terms that he understood and found useful. Reagan was perennially on the lookout for stories, anecdotes, and proverbs about subjects he would have to address in public. With respect to the Soviet Union, he didn't want to have to keep making up fictitious Ivans and Anyas; he preferred to talk about people and details taken (selectively) from real life. Reagan needed this material not just for his speeches and press conferences but for his private meetings too. As Scowcroft and countless other visitors had discovered, Reagan's almost compulsive habit of telling stories served the purposes of avoiding confrontation, overcoming bureaucratic disputes, and steering clear of the finer points of policy, in which Reagan often was not well versed. His aides talked to Reagan about throw weights, SLCMS (submarine-launched cruise missiles), and CFE (conventional forces in Europe). For Reagan, such briefings were necessary, but not sufficient. He was a political leader who needed to be able to justify his policies in public, and he was looking for new ways to think about and talk about the Soviet Union on his own terms. For this purpose he reached out, past his advisers, to Massie.

In early 1984, Massie was anything but an imposing figure. She had separated from her husband and was living in a friend's apartment in New York City. She was also virtually penniless. She could barely afford the cost of a train ticket from New York to Washington. McFarlane's National Security Council had agreed to pay the costs for her trip to Moscow, but she was required to put the expenses on her credit card and then struggled with the paperwork to obtain repayment. She was as improbable an emissary as could be imagined for conversations between the world's two superpowers.

-5-

HUNGER FOR RELIGION

Less than a month after their first meeting, Reagan sent a note to Massie that provides an indication of how the president was viewing events in the Soviet Union and why Massie had attracted his interest. During the intervening time, on February 9, 1984, the Soviet leader Yuri Andropov had died. Reagan's letter to Massie—drafted in his own handwriting, retyped by his staff, and sent on February 15—opened by alluding to the "great change" in Moscow. "I dare to hope there might be a better chance for communication with the new leadership," Reagan said. Then the president got to his larger point: "Watching scenes of the (Andropov) funeral on TV, I wondered what thoughts people must have at such a time when their belief in no God or immortality is faced with death. Like you, I continue to believe that the hunger for religion may yet be a major factor in bringing about a change in the present situation."[1]

Reagan had been talking and writing about religion in Eastern Europe, and its potential for bringing about political change, since the early days of his presidency. He had paid careful attention to the extraordinary impact of Pope John Paul II's trip to Poland in 1979. "I have had a feeling, particularly in view of the Pope's visit to Poland, that religion might very well turn out to be the Soviets' Achilles' heel," wrote Reagan in one letter a few months after he came to the White House.[2]

Throughout his career, Reagan was always more attuned to religious themes than his political aides or foreign-policy advisers. "He believed in Armageddon, a very nervous subject with me," recalled his longtime political adviser Stuart Spencer. "I argued with him about it, not that I'm an expert on Biblical stuff, but I'd just say, 'That's kind of scary to be talking about.' He'd say, 'Yeah, but it's going to happen.'" In dealing with the Soviet Union, Reagan continued throughout his presidency to raise questions about religion and churches. Colin Powell, who served as the last of Reagan's national security advisers, said he and other officials had to warn Reagan from time to time about overemphasizing religion in his dealing with the Soviets.[3]

Suzanne Massie was in a position both to encourage Reagan's own instincts on the subject and to supply the anecdotes he craved. Religion had been an essential component of Massie's own interest in the Soviet Union. "In Russia, I saw religion alive; beleaguered, tormented, but alive," Massie had written after her first visit in 1967. "In a state where great cathedrals have been turned into obscene 'anti-religious' museums, where God has officially been declared dead, this was a sublime example of His enduring strength in the hearts of men." She had studied the history of the Russian Orthodox Church for her book *Land of the Firebird.* "The church has always represented the aspirations of the Russian people and provided them with inspiration and strength in the darkest hours of their history," Massie asserted in a speech at an Orthodox seminary in 1981. "There have been no darker days than those of the past 60 years."[4]

In establishing her relationship with Reagan, Massie seems from the start to have relied heavily on their joint interest in religion. Her initial letter to Reagan, a thank-you note she wrote after their meeting in January 1984, said of the Soviet Union: "The most inspiring and hopeful aspect is the great renaissance of spirituality, particularly among the young." A few weeks later, Massie sent the president and his wife copies of *Land of the Firebird* and her two other books, with a cover note that said: "It is said that God writes straight with crooked lines."[5]

Along with her interest in religion, Massie regularly advanced one other

related theme: the idea that Reagan should draw a clear distinction between the Soviet Union and the Russian people. Massie was both an anti-
Communist and a Russophile: she was antipathetic toward the Soviet regime
and also deeply sentimental, if not mystical, about the Russian "soul." The
snippets of ordinary life inside the Soviet Union that she offered to Reagan
during their meetings conveyed a sense of the distance between the Russian
people and their Communist Party leaders. She reported to Reagan that people in Leningrad and Moscow talked of Russians as *we* or *us*, but referred to
the Soviets as *they* or *them*. "Quietly, but unmistakably, every day in every
way, the Russians are beginning to look and act more like Russians," she said
in one speech.[6]

Massie's way of looking at the Soviet Union had obvious appeal to Reagan, because it seemed to fit with the distinction he often made when talking
about the United States: ordinary people (whom Reagan portrayed as humble
but wise) versus the government (which was inherently remote and malign).
Nevertheless, in some respects Massie's portrayal also seemed to contradict
some of the images of the Soviet Union that had been advanced throughout
the years by American conservatives, including Reagan himself. She argued
that the Soviet Union was not a monolith and that day-to-day life went on
there outside the control of the authorities.

What Massie offered was a brand of Russian nationalism, but one that
was different from the version put forward by Soviet authorities. She belittled
what she called the "cult of World War II," asserting that the Soviet regime
stoked memories of what was called the Great Patriotic War in order to portray itself as the protector of Russian territory against invaders. This was a
"manipulated" nationalism, Massie argued, in contrast to the more genuine
version, which emphasized Russian religion, history, and culture.[7]

Like everyone else who met Reagan, Massie found him to be opaque.
(Even Nancy Reagan once said of her husband, "There's a wall around him.
He lets me come closer than anyone else, but there are times when even I feel
that barrier.") Massie, who had piqued Reagan's interest enough to be invited
back to talk with him over and over again, said in an interview two decades
later, "Frankly, Reagan was the most closed, the most reserved person one
could ever meet, and I found that interesting." During their meetings, she
said Reagan spent most of the time asking questions and listening to her talk

about Russian life, without saying much. She gradually got a sense of what Reagan was seeking: "He was trying to understand the Russian character, he was trying to understand something about the people." Most of the Soviet experts in the U.S. government didn't talk or think like Reagan and weren't attuned to his interests. Most of the CIA's experts didn't tell stories well; Massie did.[8]

In the fall of 1985, as Reagan was preparing for his first summit with Mikhail Gorbachev in Geneva, the CIA launched an extensive campaign to get him ready. There were memos, briefing papers, and stacks of other material. CIA director William Casey arranged an hour-long briefing for the president with the CIA's Soviet experts, led by Robert Gates, then the agency's deputy director for intelligence. Gates and other CIA experts talked at some length about strategy and geopolitics, about Gorbachev and the Politburo, about Soviet defense spending and its role in the third world. They found that the president was not particularly interested. Reagan began to pay much closer attention when a CIA analyst named Kay Oliver began talking about daily life in the Soviet Union and about problems such as alcoholism, corruption, economic stagnation, and the revival of religion. "He was riveted by Oliver's briefing, I think, because she described the Soviet Union in terms of human beings, everyday life, and the conditions under which they lived," Gates later wrote.[9]

During the weeks before this initial summit in Geneva, Reagan was determined to make sure that it would bear his own imprint. One of the common stereotypes about Reagan is that he was so passive he merely went along with what his subordinates told him. This was often true on routine matters, but on those few major events in which he took a special interest, Reagan could prove to be more actively engaged and more involved in minute details than even such notorious presidential micromanagers as Richard Nixon and Jimmy Carter. When State Department officials, in explaining the plans for the Geneva summit, made the mistake of referring to his private meeting with Gorbachev as a *"tête-à-tête,"* Reagan cut them short and banned the French phrase. "If we're not careful, we're going to go from *tête-à-tête* back to *détente,*" he told them. "Let's call it a 'one-on-one.'"[10]

This was mere semantics, but Reagan's insistence on personal control went to the heart of the Soviet-American diplomacy as well. Throughout the fall of 1985, State Department officials and their Soviet counterparts tried to work out a joint communiqué that Reagan and Gorbachev could sign at the end of their talks in Geneva. These officials were merely following past practice; it was commonplace for American presidents and foreign leaders to arrive for a summit with the formal written results already settled before the start of the talks. Before the Geneva summit, to the dismay of officials at the State Department and National Security Council, Reagan adamantly refused to go along with this standard procedure. No precooked communiqué, the president ordered. "He wanted the meeting in Geneva to be *his* meeting; he believed any statement should be composed after he met Gorbachev, and should reflect what happened," recalled Jack Matlock, then the Soviet specialist on Reagan's National Security Council. Matlock admitted that, at the time, he thought the president was being unreasonable. But in hindsight, Matlock said, he realized Reagan had accurately perceived that a prearranged communiqué would be too constraining. "If we were to move away from the confrontational psychology that had marked relations up to then, it was better not to tie the hands of our leaders, even loosely, before they met," said Matlock.[11]

Soviet diplomats were particularly distressed when they learned about Reagan's preparations for his first meeting with Gorbachev. Their principal source was Arthur Hartman, the American ambassador in Moscow, who came back to Washington to help with the summit and spoke during his stay with Soviet ambassador Anatoly Dobrynin. "In order to keep abreast of the times, Reagan was examining history to obtain a better idea of the Russian 'soul,' the Soviet Union and the motives behind its policy," Dobrynin reported to Moscow after talking to Hartman. "He preferred oral reports and stories from people who had lived in the Soviet Union, especially those who had met Soviet leaders."[12]

Dobrynin's sarcastic reference to Reagan's study of the Russian "soul" hinted at how Reagan was borrowing from Massie and her ideas. During this period she was traveling back and forth to the Soviet Union for a book about Leningrad. White House records show that Reagan talked on the phone with Massie at her summer home in Maine in August and then met with her in the Oval Office on September 3, 1985, with Vice President Bush, McFarlane, and Matlock sitting in. Reagan had asked his schedulers to arrange for her to come to the White House before Massie departed for another trip to Leningrad in late September.[13] The president was reading Massie's *Land of the Firebird* during this period and asking senior American officials about the early Russian history he was gleaning from the book.

From Leningrad, Massie sent the president a letter wishing him well at the summit and providing a description of the mood of the Russians. "There is a great deal of hope that somehow our relations will get better," she wrote. "Life is really so hard, there are so many things that need improving, and that is what seems to be uppermost in everyone's mind." She enclosed a picture of Leningrad's Theater Street, including the theater where Nikolai Gogol's play *The Inspector General* had opened in 1836. She had guessed that Reagan, as a former actor, might be interested, and he was. He responded with a letter sent through the diplomatic pouch and delivered to Massie by the U.S. consulate in Leningrad. Once again, the letter was drafted in Reagan's own handwriting:

> *Dear Suzanne:*
>
> *Thank you very much for your letter and the picture of 'Theater Street.'*
>
> *Believe it or not, I had just read about architect [Carlo] Rossi designing the theater and other buildings. Of course I had read about it in your magnificent book which I'll have with me in Geneva because I'm only half way through it. Thank you so much for sending it to me. I'm really enjoying it, and it has also helped for the forthcoming meeting.*
>
> *I hope we can open a few doors and really get on with the business of a world at peace. I'm grateful for your good wishes and your prayers. Again, my heartfelt thanks.*
>
> *Sincerely yours,*
> *Ronald Reagan*[14]

In Geneva, during the second day of meetings with Gorbachev, Reagan gave Secretary of State George Shultz his approval to move ahead with something in writing that the two governments could issue at the end of the summit. (Shultz, carefully deferring to Reagan's dislike of French words and phrases, decided to stay clear of the word *communiqué* and termed it an *agreed statement* instead.) The two leaders settled on their vague, generalized assertion that a nuclear war could not be won and should never be fought—words that echoed some of Reagan's speeches of the previous two years.

At Geneva and in its aftermath, Reagan seemed to be wondering whether Gorbachev might secretly be a religious believer—a question that was closely linked to his discussions with Massie about the spiritual nature of the Russian people. "Strangely enough in those meetings he twice invoked God's name," Reagan wrote in a letter to Elsa Sandstrom, a California Republican activist who had worked on his political campaigns and had sent the president her prayers before the Geneva summit. Responding to another letter writer, Reagan wrote, "He [Gorbachev] has aroused my curiosity—twice in our meetings, he invoked the Lord's name and once cited a Bible verse."[15]

In reality, Gorbachev was not religious. The Soviet leader's fleeting allusions to God and the Bible probably represented an effort to tailor his message and arguments in ways that might appeal to Reagan. Whatever the intent of Gorbachev's words, the Geneva summit represented the beginning of a new trend: throughout the later years of his presidency, Reagan continued to harbor the dream that Gorbachev might be a religious believer. When Gorbachev briefly used the phrase "God bless" at a subsequent summit meeting, Reagan took notice and pointed it out to Colin Powell, then his national security adviser. "I had to tell the president, 'Don't see this as an expression of religious faith,'" recalled Powell. 'It's almost idiomatic. He's not ready to get down on his knees for you.'"[16]

-6-

AN ARREST AND ITS CONSEQUENCES

In 1986, while Reagan was trying to calculate his next steps with Gorbachev, Massie was a frequent presence in the White House, meeting with the president before or after her trips to the Soviet Union. White House records show, for example, that Reagan talked to Massie in the Oval Office for about forty-five minutes on May 20, 1986, with White House chief of staff Donald Regan, National Security Adviser John Poindexter, and Nancy Reagan in attendance. She came back less than three weeks later, on June 6, to lunch alone with the president and first lady on the patio outside the Oval Office. On September 23, she returned for a lunch that lasted an hour and forty minutes in the Oval Office—and once again, the Reagans elected to talk with Massie on their own, without Regan, Poindexter, or any of the Soviet specialists from the National Security Council or State Department. (After the September lunch, Massie had a separate afternoon session with Poindexter.)[1]

The president and his wife were at this point weighing the possibilities for further summits with Gorbachev before the end of Reagan's second term. The Geneva summit had been held on neutral ground. Before leaving, Gorbachev had agreed in principle to the concept of two more summits, first in

Washington and then in Moscow. However, the details had not been set. Gorbachev was balking at fixing a date for the next summit, because he wanted assurances in advance that it would produce concrete results, particularly something on arms control.

During these visits to the White House in 1986, Massie offered the president new descriptions of daily life inside the Soviet Union: the shortages of goods, the long lines, and other signs of economic decline and social distress. She also passed along impressions of what ordinary people in the Soviet Union were saying.

By far the most significant event that year was the nuclear accident at Chernobyl on April 25–26. Massie told Reagan and Secretary of State George Shultz that ordinary Russians viewed the disaster as confirmation of a biblical prophecy. The Book of Revelations refers to a star called Wormwood, which falls to the earth, poisoning the waters and killing many people. Wormwood is the name for a common herb, and the Ukrainian word for it is *chernobyl.* This apocalyptic interpretation of the Chernobyl disaster was bound to attract the attention of Reagan, given his occasional references to Armageddon. According to Shultz, Massie also had a more political interpretation: "Chernobyl was of great symbolic importance, she felt: it showed that Soviet science and technology were flawed, that the leadership was lying and out of touch, that the party could not conceal its failures any longer." Massie was merely passing along what ordinary Russians were saying (and what foreign correspondents were reporting); she was, however, calling attention to these views through her face-to-face meetings with the president and secretary of state.[2]

Reagan was using Massie not only for her accounts of Russian street life and conversations, but also for the occasional messages she carried back and forth between Moscow and Washington. The specific mission for which Reagan had first agreed to see Massie in early 1984—to send word to Moscow that he would like to resume talks about a new cultural agreement—had been soon passed back to the professional diplomats. (Eventually, in Geneva, Reagan and Gorbachev reached final agreement on a series of cultural, educational, and scientific exchanges.)

Nevertheless, Massie kept on seeing her Soviet contact Bogdanov during her visits to Moscow. His KGB affiliation did not deter her. She had noticed that many of the people in the Soviet leadership who read books or traveled widely had some connection to the KGB. She believed, furthermore, that the core of Gorbachev's support in those earlier years was an enlightened group or faction within the KGB.[3]

In Moscow, Massie did nothing to dispel the impression that she had personal ties to Reagan and could convey the messages of Soviet officials directly to the Oval Office. For his own part, Bogdanov, her main interlocutor, seems to have suggested to Massie that what he said represented the views of the top Soviet leadership, including Gorbachev himself.

These messages from Moscow outside of official channels drove Shultz crazy. They were also sometimes confusing even to Reagan himself. In the fall of 1985, during a meeting with Soviet foreign minister Eduard Shevardnadze, he sent a message to Gorbachev that the two leaders might want to set up a single confidential channel for informal exchanges. Reagan explained to Gorbachev that he was eager "to resolve certain ambiguities in how we communicate."

> *From time to time in recent months Soviet officials have approached American officials or private citizens who are in touch with senior officials in our government and offered comments which, they suggest, represent your views. . . . However, the comments received in this manner have not always been consistent and thus I have difficulty determining to what degree they in fact represent your views.*[4]

Gorbachev said he liked the idea of a confidential channel for unofficial messages and then named his ambassador to Washington, Anatoly Dobrynin, as his representative. Reagan responded that Dobrynin could carry Gorbachev's confidential messages to Shultz and said he hoped Gorbachev would grant similar access to Arthur Hartman in Moscow. In theory, the backchannel emissaries, such as Massie and Bogdanov, were cut out. Yet this episode in 1985 didn't end the informal message carrying (and, in fact, may have merely represented an effort by Reagan to mollify Shultz, who wanted all communications to go through him). Afterward, Massie still carried to the White House messages from Bogdanov that were taken by the president as coming directly from Gorbachev. Reagan on occasion still gave Massie private messages to take back to Moscow.

In the early fall of 1986, Reagan was confronted with a new crisis when Nicholas Daniloff, the Moscow correspondent for *U.S. News and World Report*, was suddenly detained and charged with espionage. The Soviet action came precisely one week after the FBI had arrested Gennadi Zakharov, a Soviet scientist on the staff of the United Nations Secretariat in New York, and charged him with spying during a three-year period in which he sought to recruit and pay an employee of an American defense contractor. Zakharov was subject to prosecution in the United States; he did not enjoy diplomatic immunity because he was not part of the Soviet mission to the United Nations. In moving against Daniloff, the Soviets clearly seemed to be aiming for a trade: Daniloff for Zakharov.

Reagan was incensed. The CIA assured him that Daniloff was not a spy. Moreover, Daniloff's arrest was merely the latest in a series of similar episodes. "This whole thing follows the pattern," he wrote in his diary. "We catch a spy, as we have this time, and the Soviets grab an American—*any* American and frame him so they can demand a trade of prisoners."[5]

The case touched off nearly a month of frenetic diplomacy between the United States and the Soviet Union. It also produced intense internal frictions within the Reagan administration. At the NSC, Poindexter and his aides wanted to draw the line, strictly barring any sort of trade; but Shultz and the State Department were urging caution and quiet diplomacy. Shultz was furious at the CIA, believing that its operatives had compromised Daniloff by using the correspondent's name in trying to contact a source in Moscow and by mentioning his name in a written communication. The secretary of state told Reagan that because of the CIA's bungling conduct (of which Daniloff was unaware), Soviet officials had sufficient legal grounds to attempt to bring Daniloff to trial.[6]

Massie's private lunch with the Reagans on September 23, 1986, took place at the very peak of these tensions. There is no record of their conversation, but Reagan afterward sent her to meet with Shultz. The secretary of state recorded what she told him in his own memoir.

> *Her message was that Gorbachev almost certainly had not or-*
> *dered Daniloff picked up—it was the 'theys' of the regime. Gor-*
> *bachev, she said, now was referring to 'they,' as in 'they' got*
> *Khrushchev. He was under pressure from hard-liners, and his*
> *room for maneuvering was narrow. She had urged the president*
> *not to push Gorbachev too far on the Daniloff matter, for she*
> *felt such pressure would serve those in the USSR 'who want to*
> *stop this process of improvement.'[7]*

The impasse over Daniloff had been holding up all other business between Reagan and Gorbachev. The president was trying to arrange a summit
in Washington, which would in turn clear the way for him to visit Moscow
before he left the White House. Gorbachev was even more eager for another
meeting with Reagan, at which he hoped for new agreements on arms control
that would enable him to cut back on defense spending. In mid-September,
in the midst of the Daniloff affair, Shevardnadze suddenly brought Reagan a
proposal from Gorbachev for a quick meeting soon in Reykjavik, one that
could prepare the way for a fuller summit in Washington.

On September 28, five days after Massie's private lunch with the Reagans, a deal was worked out for Daniloff's release. Shultz and Shevardnadze
worked out the plan at a meeting in New York City. It involved a sequence of
orchestrated steps. First, Daniloff was set free and flown out of the Soviet
Union. Next, Zakharov pleaded no contest to espionage charges and was immediately expelled from the United States. Then the Soviet authorities agreed
to allow a leading dissident, Yuri Orlov, and his wife to leave the country. The
release of Orlov enabled the Reagan administration to assert that it was not
simply making a trade of Zakharov for Daniloff, a spy for a newspaper correspondent. Finally, on September 30, the White House announced that Reagan and Gorbachev would meet in Reykjavik only ten days later.

The outcome—the resolution of the Daniloff case and the agreement to meet
in Reykjavik—represented a fundamental turning point for Reagan, for his
Soviet policy, and for his relationship with his own conservative supporters.
This was the point when the right wing turned irreversibly against Rea-

gan's policies toward the Soviet Union, and when the president decided to move ahead with Gorbachev anyway, in the absence of his usual support from the hawks. Reagan's conciliatory "Ivan and Anya" speech of January 1984 could be explained away as election-year politics. The harmonious Geneva summit of 1985 could be seen as merely a meeting without concrete results. But Reagan's actions in the fall of 1986 could not be written off in similar fashion.

In Congress, conservatives such as Representative Jack Kemp rose up in fury over the handling of the Daniloff case. On the newspaper op-ed pages, commentators including William Safire and Charles Krauthammer ridiculed the administration. Reagan's favorite columnist, George Will, was particularly scathing. "When an administration collapses, quickly and completely, as the Reagan administration has done in the Daniloff debacle, a reasonable surmise is that the administration, like a balloon, had nothing in it but air," Will wrote in a column published September 18, 1986. In another column two weeks later, Will condemned the administration for failing to recognize the enduring ideological differences between America and the Soviet Union. "The administration believes that Gorbachev wants to end the arms race so he can raise his people's standard of living," Will wrote. "The administration partakes of the national vanity of believing that if Soviet leaders just see our supermarkets and swimming pools, they will see the folly of trying to win an arms race with a nation this rich."[8]

Vanity or not, this was precisely what Reagan believed. Will was paraphrasing one of the president's favorite lines; Reagan often said he wished he could give Soviet leaders a tour of the United States so that they could see its prosperity. Frank Carlucci, who served as Reagan's national security adviser and defense secretary, recalled the time he was riding with Reagan in a helicopter: "He looked down and said, 'See all those nice homes? If I could just have Gorbachev come in and look at some of those homes, I'm sure he'd change his ways.' "[9]

In fact, Reagan's perceptions of the Soviet Union and of Gorbachev were much closer to the truth than were those of his conservative critics. The memoirs and histories of the Gorbachev era demonstrate that in the late summer of 1986, the Soviet leader decided he urgently needed a new agreement with the United States to limit Soviet military spending. "If we don't back down on some specific, maybe even important issues, if we won't budge from the positions we've held for a long time, we will lose in the end," Gorbachev told his colleagues in the Politburo. "We will be drawn into an arms race that we cannot manage. We will lose, because right now we are at the end of our tether."[10]

Soon after Will's columns about the Daniloff case were published, he received a call from the president. "George, I'm not enjoying reading you as much as I used to," Reagan said. Will replied that "I'm not enjoying watching you as much as I used to." Reagan invited him to the White House for a talk, at which he urged the columnist to consider what was happening on the ground in the Soviet Union. Things are really changing over there, Reagan told him; life is opening up. For example, Reagan said, some of these people going into churches in Russia aren't old babushkas, but young people. In saying this, Reagan was passing along the views of Soviet life he had obtained from Massie.

Indeed, in the fall of 1986, one press account briefly identified Massie as having contributed to Reagan's changing views of the Soviet Union: In early October, perhaps spurred on by Will's columns and other criticisms of the way he had handled the Daniloff case, *Time* magazine did a story titled, "Has Reagan Gone Soft?" It said that Reagan "has come to view the Russians no longer as cardboard-cutout Communists, but as human beings in a multi-dimensional society, with a history that goes back beyond the 1917 Revolution." The article went on to report that Suzanne Massie was a writer "with whom Reagan developed a particular rapport."[11]

Reagan's advisers sometimes joked to one another that he had an actor's memory: Once Reagan got something into his head, they said, it was hard to get it out. When the president sat down with Gorbachev in Reykjavik in mid-October, he had memorized a new line. It was the Russian proverb that Suzanne Massie had taught him: *Doveryai no proveryai* ("Trust but verify"). He used this phrase on the opening morning of the Reykjavik summit and then repeated it so often over the following two years, both in public speeches and in private meetings, that at one summit, Gorbachev grumbled, "You say that every time." In practical terms, the line didn't mean much. But it did convey an attitudinal shift at the Reagan White House, a willingness to try to do business with Gorbachev and to explore, however warily, the possibility of agreements with him.[12]

It is easy to imagine this series of events in the fall of 1986 coming out differently. At this point, Reagan could well have gone along with those who favored taking a tough stance with Gorbachev. Not only conservative columnists but some advisers within his own administration were urging him to do just that. As a matter of principle, the president would have been on reasonable ground. The detention of Daniloff represented an obvious attempt by Soviet authorities to respond to Zakharov's arrest by taking a hostage who could be used for a trade. Reagan might have rejected any deal concerning Daniloff and instead taken the position that the American correspondent should be released and sent home without any negotiations. Moreover, Reagan could have spurned Gorbachev's request in the midst of this crisis for a sudden, quick meeting in Reykjavik.

What would the result have been? Of course one can never know for sure. But it is worth keeping in mind the political dynamics in Moscow in 1986. Gorbachev's own power as Soviet leader rested upon the same institutions as that of his predecessors: the Communist Party, the KGB, and the Soviet military. At the same time, Gorbachev was also beginning to try to reform the Soviet political system. Over the long run, those two aspects of Gorbachev's leadership turned out to be fundamentally incompatible with each other. Gorbachev didn't know that, however, and in 1986, after just a year in office, he was only starting the process of political change.

By deciding to deal with Gorbachev at this critical juncture, Reagan was giving the Soviet leader the time and leeway he needed to move forward with his domestic reforms. Gorbachev was able to show the "power ministries" in Moscow—above all, the KGB and the military—that as Soviet leader, he could handle the Americans and could win compromises from Reagan. This, in turn, strengthened Gorbachev in Moscow as he launched his domestic reforms. Those changes turned out to be irreversible; five years later, when the KGB organized a hard-liners' coup against Gorbachev, they failed, because it was too late to return to the pre-Gorbachev era. But in 1986, the changes were not entrenched; indeed, they had barely begun. He told his closest aides in one meeting early that year that "here at the top, we're better informed. We see more clearly than anyone that drastic change is necessary." Yet Gorbachev was at that point too inhibited by traditional Soviet ideology and by commitments to his old friends and allies to bring about any such drastic change.[13]

If Reagan had spurned Gorbachev in the fall of 1986, it would have weakened Gorbachev's hand, particularly in dealing with the KGB and Soviet military. They would have had greater power to resist his reforms, both at home and abroad; the traditionalists in Moscow could have argued that the Soviet Union still confronted an unyielding, unchanging threat from its American adversary. It is hard to imagine Gorbachev's persuading the Soviet military to stand by and permit peaceful democratic revolutions in Eastern Europe in 1989 if Soviet-American relations had remained tense and adversarial for the previous three years.

Was Reagan, in the summer and fall of 1986, following an explicit, conscious strategy of giving Gorbachev time to dismantle the Soviet system? Of course not. Gorbachev himself didn't know at this stage where his domestic reforms were headed. But Reagan had gotten a sense of Gorbachev's style and his personality during their first meeting in Geneva, and he was also getting reports of the changes unfolding in Soviet society from Massie and others.

It is worth noting how the views of Reagan and Shultz contrasted with what the CIA's Soviet specialists were saying about Gorbachev at the time. In a memo in early 1986, Robert Gates, the CIA's leading Soviet analyst and soon to become its deputy director, argued that "all we have seen since Gorbachev took over leads us to believe that on fundamental objectives and policies he so far remains generally as inflexible as his predecessors."[14]

The interpretation of Gorbachev that underlay Reagan's policies during this period was essentially the one that Massie had conveyed: that Gorbachev was seeking to move the Soviet Union in new directions and should not be pushed too hard, because he was under pressure from hard-liners who wanted to stymie his reforms. This view may have been slightly too simplistic, because Gorbachev wasn't completely separate from those hard-liners in the Communist Party, KGB, and military; he had been brought into office by them and maintained extensive ties to them. Yet the Reagan outlook, shared by Shultz, proved to be more accurate than that of the CIA or of American conservatives who were portraying Gorbachev as just another Soviet leader, merely a creature of the usual forces in the Soviet apparatus. Reagan was acting on instinct, and at this important moment, his instincts turned out to be right.

-7-

KEEP HER AWAY

Her frequent visits to the White House eventually caught up with Suzanne Massie. She made the mistake, as did so many others in dealing with Ronald Reagan, of overplaying her hand and overestimating the depth of his friendship. At the beginning of 1987, Massie suffered two serious setbacks. First, she tried and failed to turn her informal role as adviser and message carrier into an official, high-level government job. Second, the officials on a reconstituted National Security Council mounted a campaign against her, insinuating that she might be a conduit or dupe for attempts by the KGB to influence Reagan.

Massie had been operating with remarkably little in the way of institutional backing. She held no formal academic position; she could claim only a loose affiliation, as fellow and visiting scholar, with Harvard's Russian Research Center (now the Davis Center for Russian and Eurasian Studies). She was short of money. By her own logic, since she was already serving as presidential consultant and emissary, why not turn those activities into a salaried job? In mid-1986, Senator Bill Cohen and Senator John Heinz, two of her friends, suggested to Reagan that he hire her. "Her presence in the U.S.S.R.

in an official capacity for your administration could provide a two-way conduit for promoting understanding and improved relations," argued the two Republican senators in a letter to the president.[1]

Their letter did not specify what job Massie should be given, but within months, Massie herself did. Her ambition was breathtaking. The administration had announced that Arthur Hartman, who had served as the U.S. ambassador in Moscow since 1981, would be coming home. Massie sought the nomination to replace him. "I want this job because I know that in this critical and exciting time of change in the Soviet Union, I can do this job for you better than anyone else," Massie wrote in a note she sent directly to Reagan. She had badly miscalculated. While the appointment had not yet been announced, Reagan had already settled on his nominee by the time Massie's note arrived, and it was an obvious choice: Jack Matlock, the NSC's Soviet expert since 1983.[2]

Reagan hurriedly sent Massie back a note, claiming that he had been "surprised" to get her request. "I had no idea that you would be interested in being 'Our Man' in Moscow," the president wrote. Underneath the typed letter Reagan scrawled a postscript. "You really are a 'trusted adviser . . .' and I hope you'll continue to be," he said.[3]

But soon Massie's advisory role was called into question, caught up in the travails of the Reagan administration and the conflicts over Reagan's diplomacy with Gorbachev. The Iran-Contra scandal burst forth in November 1986, exposing the National Security Council's furtive operations to establish contacts with Iran and to obtain funds for rebel forces fighting Nicaragua's leftist Sandinista government. Amid the unfolding investigations in Congress and at the Justice Department, Reagan brought in a new national security adviser, Frank Carlucci, and a new deputy, Colin Powell. They carried out a thorough housecleaning at the NSC, changing most of its personnel and imposing new orders that everything was to be done aboveboard and by the book. No secret operations and no "freelancing," Powell warned the new NSC team.[4]

Massie had no connection with Iran-Contra. Nevertheless, her ties to the Reagan White House had been established under the same two national security advisers, Robert McFarlane and John Poindexter, who had been responsible for the secret contacts with Iran. When Carlucci took over, he wasn't worrying about Massie; he had far more serious concerns, above all trying to prevent what seemed like a possible collapse of the Reagan presidency. Nevertheless, Massie soon caught his attention.

On February 3, 1987, Massie arrived at the White House and had another one-on-one session with Reagan. At the time, he was reported to be in seclusion, with his administration in disarray. Over the previous week, a Senate select committee had issued its first public report on Iran-Contra, and the ailing CIA Director William Casey had resigned. That day, Massie spoke with Reagan for only five minutes, but she handed him a handwritten message she had obtained in Moscow, one that was said to have come from Mikhail Gorbachev. Reagan dispatched Massie and her note over to Secretary of State George Shultz at the State Department. "I know that you are seeing Suzanne Massie this evening," Reagan wrote. "She delivered this handwritten note from Gorbachev. He asked her to deliver this to me personally."[5]

Massie had been talking frequently to Bogdanov in Moscow. "Occasionally, I was given little missives for Reagan, always worded carefully and from the top," she said. The note Massie was carrying on this occasion suggested some form of Soviet-American agreement for "national reconciliation" in Afghanistan, one that would open the way for an end to the war Soviet troops were fighting there. Reagan told Shultz he felt the United States shouldn't go along with that Soviet proposal, and the secretary of state agreed with the president. Shultz was, however, irritated by Reagan's willingness to go along with Massie's back-channel diplomacy. "I was skeptical that this message actually came from Gorbachev," Shultz later wrote. "It had been given to Suzanne Massie by Radomir Bogdanov, deputy director of the Soviets' Institute of the USA and Canada and a KGB officer. . . . This was yet another instance of the confusion that multiple, unofficial channels create."[6]

Massie returned for another session with Reagan at the White House less than three weeks later, on February 25, having visited Moscow in the meantime. This time, however, there was no one-on-one meeting. Carlucci had put out the word: whenever Massie met with the president, he wanted to be there. "She [Massie] didn't seem to have any agenda—but that's why I wanted to get in on the meeting. I wanted to make sure," Carlucci explained in an interview two decades later. "They had a wonderful relationship, and at the end of the meetings, she would give him a kiss on the cheek. She was perfectly harmless."[7]

Others within the U.S. government were not so sure, and they sought to cut off Reagan's contacts with Massie entirely. Carlucci's fleeting reference to the question of whether Massie had an "agenda" hints at the larger underlying issue: it was not Iran-Contra, but the Reykjavik summit and the suspicion that, as *Time* magazine phrased it, Reagan had "gone soft" on the Soviet Union. The Reykjavik summit with Gorbachev the previous October had produced Reagan's stunning assertion that he would be willing to move toward the elimination of nuclear weapons. Even though those negotiations had broken down when Reagan refused to restrict his Strategic Defense Initiative, the reverberations continued to be felt for a long time, particularly within Washington's national-security establishment. Hawkish officials in the Pentagon, the CIA, and other agencies—the legacy of four decades of Cold War—feared what Reagan might do in his future dealings with Gorbachev. "After Reykjavik, Reagan was watched by someone all during the rest of his term in office," recalled Nelson Ledsky, who served on Reagan's National Security Council in 1987–88. "He was surrounded by people like Carlucci, Powell, [White House chief of staff Howard] Baker, Shultz."[8]

Inevitably, the national-security bureaucracy's growing mistrust of Reagan spilled over all the more to Massie, who had been identified in public just before Reykjavik as one of the leading influences on the president's thinking about the Soviets. In early 1987, uneasiness about Massie crystallized into a high-level whispering campaign—although, true to form in Washington, it was one that was waged in secret with the use of classified documents.

Beginning in early March 1987, the White House memos on Suzanne Massie—that is, the routine paperwork discussing the times or talking points for her meetings with the president—began to be accompanied by another secret file. It was labeled "NSC Intelligence Document." While the cover page for this intelligence document now sits in the files of the Reagan Presidential Library, its contents have not been declassified. However, interviews with one of the senior officials on Reagan's National Security Council during this period establish the gist of the intelligence document: it apparently suggested that Massie was being used by the Soviet KGB in an attempt to influence Reagan. The specific allegation was especially nasty: it smeared Massie by attempting to link her, in a tangential way, to a tawdry, sensationalized Moscow spy case that had filled the newspapers during that period.

In January 1987, Clayton Lonetree, a former marine security guard at the U.S. embassy in Moscow, had been charged with espionage after he confessed to passing classified information to the Soviet Union. The marine had started to have an affair with a woman who was a Russian interpreter at the embassy, and she in turn then introduced Lonetree to her "Uncle Sasha." He turned out to be a KGB officer, who began obtaining classified documents from Lonetree. When the case became public in the early weeks of 1987, newspapers carried front-page stories claiming that Lonetree had allowed KGB agents to wander through the American embassy at night.[9]

None of this had anything to do with Massie. But the secret Washington campaign against Massie alleged that "Uncle Sasha," the KGB agent running the Lonetree case, was the very same KGB official who was, separately, talking to Massie. "'Uncle Sasha' was also Suzanne Massie's handler," one official who worked on Reagan's National Security Council asserted in an interview for this book.[10] The allegation was not that Massie was knowingly working for the KGB, but that she was a dupe, unwittingly being used by the KGB as what U.S. intelligence officials in that Cold War era usually called an "agent of influence."

It seems extremely likely that even this flimsy allegation was false. Massie's contact in the KGB was Bogdanov—a fact that she had made known at the Reagan White House from the very start of her 1983 conversations with McFarlane at the National Security Council. During the prosecution and trial of Clayton Lonetree, "Uncle Sasha" was subsequently identified as a KGB official named Alexei Yefimov, not Bogdanov.[11] It made sense that they would have been different people. Would the KGB really have assigned the covert work of entrapping lowly marine security guards to the very same person who spent his days disseminating the Soviet point of view about arms control and world affairs to prominent American scholars, journalists, and diplomats? If so, the supposed "Uncle Sasha" must have been both the KGB's busiest and its most versatile agent.

As it turned out, the allegations against Lonetree turned out to be considerably less damaging than originally reported. A detailed review later concluded that Lonetree had never allowed KGB agents into the embassy. Nonetheless, in the early months of 1987, after the Lonetree story broke, the Moscow embassy affair was used in Washington to discourage Shultz from trying to do business in Moscow.[12] And at the same time, the allegation linking Massie to "Uncle Sasha" was employed in an attempt to discourage Reagan from talking to Massie.

Officials on the National Security Council resorted to other gambits as well to seek to curtail Massie. When she returned from another trip to the Soviet Union in April 1987 and asked, as usual, to meet with Reagan, Fritz Ermarth, the leading Soviet specialist at the NSC, drafted a note to Massie for the president to sign. Ermarth sent the proposed letter to Carlucci on April 23, 1987, with an accompanying memo that said that what he had written was "designed to discourage future visits." It said:

Dear Suzanne:

Thank you very much for your letter of April 13.

I am delighted that your trip to the Soviet Union went well. As you can imagine, the pace around here has become pretty tempestuous. It is for that reason that I was unable to take your call, and won't be able to visit with you around May 1. I would very much appreciate it, however, if you would brief Frank Carlucci or key members of his staff on your impressions of the current Soviet scene or, perhaps, send him a more detailed report of your impressions.

Nancy and I send our best regards.

Sincerely,
[Ronald Reagan]

Ermarth explained the letter to Carlucci in a cover memo: "The President may find it too unfriendly. But, if he responds with his natural style, he will certainly encourage future requests for access. This is getting to be a case where we need his advice."[13]

As Ermarth surmised, Reagan did indeed apparently find the letter too unfriendly. It was never sent. Instead, Massie was granted the meeting she had requested with Reagan. Yet the effort to separate Reagan from Massie continued. On April 30, Carlucci sent Reagan a memo, with copies to Vice President George Bush and White House chief of staff Howard Baker, which called into question Massie's views about the Soviet Union, and particularly her positive embrace of Russian nationalism. Carlucci wrote:

> *Apart from her artistic projects, Ms. Massie is an enthusiastic student of what she calls the "revival of the Russian spirit," a rebirth of interest among Russians in their history, culture, folkways, and religion. This revival has, from our point of view, many positive aspects, e.g., the search for a moral compass that Communist ideology has failed to provide. It also displays negative features, however, such as extreme chauvinism towards non-Russians (nearly 50% of the Soviet population), anti-Semitism, and hostility to all Western influences, including democracy and freedom of thought.*[14]

-8-

CARLUCCI'S NOTES

The mystery remains: What sort of business was being transacted in Massie's shuttling back and forth between Moscow and the Oval Office? Any evaluation of Massie's role as a message carrier depends upon the nature of the messages. What were Reagan and Gorbachev (or Bogdanov, purporting to represent him) trying to tell one another?

The answer can be found in the handwritten notes taken during Massie's meeting with Reagan on February 25, 1987—the meeting that Carlucci had insisted on attending. These notes are in Carlucci's handwriting, as he verified in an interview for this book. They demonstrate that the discussions being conducted indirectly, through Massie, went directly to the heart of Reagan's summit diplomacy with Gorbachev.

The tumultuous meeting at Reykjavik had ended without resolving the question of when or even whether the two leaders would see each other again. In theory, Gorbachev was supposed to go to Washington for the next summit and then Reagan to Moscow. But no dates had been set—and in fact, Gorbachev was making clear that he did not want to proceed to another meeting with the president unless he could be sure there would be tangible results.

At the beginning of the February 25 meeting, Carlucci's notes show, Massie offered an overview of the situation inside the Soviet Union and of Gorbachev's role as Soviet leader. He was "lurching forward," she said. He and his team were working toward decentralization and greater cultural openness. She spoke of an effort to revive life in the villages, and a "modest attempt towards pluralism."

Next, the notes show, Massie couldn't resist a belittling reference to Matlock, the new U.S. ambassador to Moscow. "Jack bureaucrat, Wrong message," Carlucci wrote to summarize what Massie was telling the president. *Matlock was a bureaucrat, and his appointment sent the wrong message to the Soviets.*

Soon the discussion turned to Soviet-American diplomacy. Massie argued that the president should make a crucial concession to Gorbachev: Reagan should go to Moscow first, some time in 1987, before any summit in Washington. She contended that switching the order of the summits would appease Soviet pride. She also said she had been told by a Soviet official (that is, Bogdanov) that Gorbachev was worried about his personal safety; there was a threat that he might be assassinated if he came to the United States.

Reagan wasn't buying any of these Soviet arguments, Carlucci's notes show. He told Massie:

> *I waiting their reply. Want to be here. Then I go there. If they wait much longer, I won't be able to go there.*[1]

Reagan was insisting on a Washington summit first. He was warning that if the Soviets didn't accept the Washington invitation soon, there would be no time for him to visit Moscow for a second summit later on.

Carlucci's notes then show a direct dialogue between the president (P.) and Massie (S.M.)

S.M.   *If you have something for me to say to him, I could get to him + hear what has to say.*

P.   *Say, I realize how busy he is, but we most eager to receive him here. Are things going on at Geneva* [the site of U.S.-Soviet arms control negotiations] *to talk about. R* [Reykjavik] *was to set path for solution. We not cooled off. Very eager to have him here.*

S.M. *He has nothing to show. Needs something to show. To come here looks like he running after you.*

P. *We would hear his reaction.*

S.M. *I could read his answer.*

P. *We still eager to go there.*[2]

It is hard to escape the conclusion that the KGB's Bogdanov and the president of the United States were employing Massie's trips for their own purposes. Bogdanov, and perhaps others in Moscow, were using Massie to persuade the president to make greater concessions out of sympathy for Gorbachev. Bogdanov could float ideas, offer proposals or arguments, and plead for understanding in Washington in a way that Gorbachev could not have done on his own. The president, for his own part, was using Massie to carry messages to Gorbachev that did not have to go through the State Department or other official government channels.

On March 2, 1987, five days after Massie's session with Reagan and Carlucci, officials at the White House prepared a written statement for Massie to deliver in Moscow. A copy of it now lies buried in the archives of Reagan's presidential library. The single-spaced, five-line message says:

> *The First Lady and I are still very much looking forward to the opportunity to welcome you and Mrs. Gorbachev in the United States in 1987, with my coming to the USSR in the following year. There is much to discuss in our continuing face-to-face dialogue and I would hope to hear from you at an early date.*[3]

The files show that White House staff aides planned to deliver this message by Federal Express to Massie's apartment in New York. In an interview two decades later, Massie said she never received such a FedEx, because she had by that time moved from New York City to Cambridge. But Massie confirmed that she had received this same message from the Reagan White House, either in person or over the phone, and had delivered it to Moscow.[4]

With or without Federal Express, this was Reagan's back-channel diplomacy in its quintessence. The president of the United States was communicating with the general secretary of the Communist Party of the Soviet Union not by diplomatic pouch, not through his secretary of state, not through the hotline installed in the White House and Kremlin, but through a lone, idiosyncratic message carrier—a nervy, enterprising American author with no formal credentials, but with a boundless belief in the "soul" of Russia.

PART III
BERLIN

-1-

THE SPEECH

During the spring of 1987, as conservatives railed at Ronald Reagan's conciliatory approach to Mikhail Gorbachev, his aides were bickering over a speech the president was supposed to give on a trip to Europe. The president was scheduled to go to Venice in June for the annual economic summit meeting of the leaders of the seven largest industrialized nations. From there, plans called for him to stop over for a day in Berlin. The question was what he should say there.

The speech Reagan eventually delivered now stands as one of the best-remembered moments of his presidency. The video images of that speech are played in virtually every documentary about the Reagan administration or the end of the Cold War. On June 12, 1987, Reagan, standing in front of the Brandenburg Gate and the Berlin Wall, issued his famous exhortation to Gorbachev: "Mr. Gorbachev, tear down this wall."

The Berlin Wall speech lies at ground zero in the historical disputes over Ronald Reagan and his presidency. In the ensuing years, two radically different perspectives have emerged. In one, the speech was the single triumphal moment leading toward the end of the Cold War. In the other, the speech was mere showmanship, without substance. Both perspectives are wrong. Neither deals adequately with the complexities or the underlying significance of the Berlin Wall speech.

For American conservatives, the Berlin Wall speech has taken on iconic status. This was Reagan's ultimate challenge to the Soviet Union—and, so they believe, Mikhail Gorbachev effectively capitulated when, in November of 1989, he failed to intervene as Germans suddenly began tearing down the wall. At the museum of Ronald Reagan's presidential library in Simi Valley, California, a section of the Berlin Wall stands outside the main doors, overlooking the view to the Pacific Ocean, the monument chosen as the enduring symbol of the Reagan presidency.

Among Reagan's most devoted followers, an entire mythology has developed about the Berlin Wall speech. Theirs is what might be called the triumphal school—the president spoke, the Soviets quaked, the wall came down. Representative Dana Rohrabacher, a California congressman and former Reagan speechwriter, maintained in an interview for this book that one day after Reagan's speech, Mikhail Gorbachev gathered his aides together and said, "You know, this Reagan, once he grabs on to you, he never lets go . . . and if he's talking about this wall, he's never going to let go unless we do something. So what we have to do is find a way to bring down the wall and save face at the same time."[1]

This is fiction: over the two decades since Reagan's speech, no evidence has turned up to corroborate Rohrabacher's account. The triumphal school fails to explain the connection between Reagan's speech and the events of 1989. Even more problematically, the triumphal school ignores Reagan's actual policies toward the Soviet Union at the time of the Berlin Wall speech. From the autumn of 1986 through the end of his presidency in January 1989, Reagan was in fact moving steadily toward a working accommodation with Gorbachev, conducting a series of summits and signing arms-control agreements with the Soviet leader. At the time, many American conservatives who now belong to the triumphal school were furious at Reagan.

The opposing perspective on Reagan's Berlin Wall speech holds that it was nothing but a stunt. The adherents of what might be called the theater school are not merely liberals or Democrats with a generalized animus toward Reagan. The theater school also includes, prominently, the veterans of the

George H. W. Bush administration of 1989–93: the so-called realists who tended to view the Reagan administration as overly moralistic in its foreign policies and insufficiently attuned to concerns such as stability and the balance of power. Adherents of the theater school point out that, when viewed strictly as a statement of foreign policy, the Berlin Wall speech didn't even say anything particularly new. It was a long-standing tenet of American policy that the wall should come down.

In their 1995 book on the end of the Cold War, *Germany Unified and Europe Transformed*, Philip Zelikow and Condoleezza Rice, who had both served in the George H. W. Bush administration, belittled the significance of the Berlin Wall speech. They argued that the Reagan administration did not seriously follow up the speech with actions. "American diplomats did not consider the matter part of the real policy agenda," they wrote.[2]

In an interview for this book, Brent Scowcroft, who served as national security adviser to George H. W. Bush, called Reagan's tear-down-this-wall line "corny in the extreme. That [speech] is what everyone remembers now. It was irrelevant, that statement at that time." Despite Scowcroft's view, President George H. W. Bush felt compelled to repeat Reagan's language on his own first presidential visit to Europe in the spring of 1989. "I tried to get him [Bush] not to," recalled Scowcroft. "He felt a lot of loyalty to Reagan. He was not going to depart from the Reagan agenda."[3]

Inside the Reagan administration itself, even some of the foreign-policy officials who were central to and especially admiring of the president's overall diplomacy with the Soviet Union seem to have subscribed, at least implicitly, to the theater school's interpretation. In his memoir of 1,138 pages, the most detailed account that exists of Reagan's foreign policies, Secretary of State George Shultz did not mention the speech at all. Jack Matlock, who served first as Reagan's Soviet adviser on the National Security Council and then as U.S. ambassador to Moscow, also took no note of the speech in his own book on Reagan and Gorbachev.

Yet the theater interpretation doesn't hold up either. It fails to take account of Reagan's role as political leader. As president, Reagan was responsible not merely for determining American foreign policy but for winning and maintaining public support for it. That task is what makes any president fundamentally different from his foreign-policy advisers; it is why Richard

Nixon's role in the American rapprochement with China was of greater weight than that of Henry Kissinger.

At the time of the Berlin Wall speech, Ronald Reagan was already under attack in the United States for having supposedly been taken in by Gorbachev. Conservatives were especially outraged. In September 1986, when the KGB had seized the American magazine correspondent Nicholas Daniloff in retaliation for the arrest of a Soviet agent in the United States, Reagan had negotiated an exchange rather than drawing a firm line. Separately, hawks in the national-security establishment were upset that at the Reykjavik summit in October 1986, Reagan had spoken of abolishing nuclear weapons.

And yet for Reagan, these events were merely prologue: there was considerably more business he wanted to conduct with Gorbachev. By the spring of 1987, he was well into negotiations for two more summits in Washington and Moscow. Even more important, his administration was moving toward a groundbreaking arms-control agreement with the Soviet Union: the Intermediate Nuclear Forces Treaty, which would eventually have to be ratified by the Senate. The idea of such a treaty was beginning to attract considerable opposition in Washington.

The Berlin Wall speech cut in precisely the reverse direction from the way it appeared. It was an anti-Communist speech that helped preserve support for a president seeking to upgrade American relations with the Soviet Union. It demonstrated to the American public that, even as he proceeded to do business with Gorbachev, Reagan had not been beguiled by the charismatic Soviet leader and had not altered his beliefs about the nature of the Soviet system. The Berlin Wall speech was, in a real sense, the political prerequisite for the president's subsequent efforts to work with Gorbachev in easing the tensions of the Cold War.

This is not to suggest that Reagan's speech was merely politics or a grand deception. It carried considerable substantive meaning as well. By demanding that Gorbachev "tear down this wall," Reagan was setting forth what amounted to American terms, or at least ideas, for the end of the Cold War. At the time of the speech, it appeared that the Cold War atmosphere of the prior four decades was already giving way to something new. Gorbachev was searching for a new relationship with the United States. West and East Germany were moving toward each other.

The open question was where all of this would lead. The Berlin Wall speech served notice that the United States was willing to reach accommodations with Gorbachev, but not at the expense of accepting the permanent division of Berlin (or by extension, the permanent division of Germany or Europe). In this sense, the speech was directed to Europeans as well as Americans.

On the surface, the Berlin Wall speech seemed like the obvious successor to a series of earlier anti-Communist speeches by Reagan: the 1982 speech where he consigned Marxism-Leninism to "the ash heap of history" and the still more famous address of 1983 in which Reagan branded the Soviet Union "the evil empire." The Berlin Wall speech was different, however, because it had to reckon with a new factor: the ascent of Gorbachev. While many in the United States were dismissing Gorbachev as merely a new face for the same old Soviet policies, Reagan and Shultz did not. It was for precisely this reason that Reagan's Soviet policies were under attack.

Thus, while the Berlin Wall speech reaffirmed the anticommunism on which Reagan had based his entire political career, it also gave recognition to the idea that the Soviet system might be changing. "We hear much from Moscow about a new policy of reform and openness," Reagan said in Berlin. "Some political prisoners have been released. Certain foreign news broadcasts are no longer being jammed. . . . Are these the beginnings of profound changes in the Soviet state?"

The speech did not attempt to answer that question. But it went on to establish a new test for evaluating Gorbachev and the new Soviet leadership:

> *There is one sign the Soviets can make that would be unmistakable, that would advance dramatically the cause of freedom and peace. General Secretary Gorbachev, if you seek peace, if you seek prosperity for the Soviet Union and Eastern Europe, if you seek liberalization: Come here to this gate! . . . Mr. Gorbachev, tear down this wall!*

Reagan's speech also offered Gorbachev the same thematic message that other Reagan administration officials, notably Shultz, had been conveying repeatedly in private meetings: it suggested that the way to make the Soviet Union more prosperous was to join the international system and to break down the barriers that divided the Soviet Union and its Eastern European allies from the rest of the world. The Soviet leader needed to tear down walls if he wanted to revive his country's economy.

The Berlin Wall speech was the product of a torturous process within the Reagan administration. The drafting of the speech, and Reagan's decision to deliver it, reflected the swirling dynamics of the final years of the Cold War, both overseas and in Washington. It was, indeed, a remarkable story.

-2-

TWENTY-FIFTH ANNIVERSARY

On August 13, 1986, West and East Berlin commemorated separately and in different ways the twenty-fifth anniversary of the epochal day when East German security officials had suddenly put up barbed wire, dividing the city. The initial barriers, constructed overnight on August 12–13, 1961, had quickly been replaced by the concrete structure with accompanying watchtower and floodlights known as the Berlin Wall. A quarter century later, the wall remained the enduring symbol of the Cold War, a barrier nearly thirty miles long that split up neighborhoods, separated families, and prevented the residents of East Berlin from fleeing to the West, as they had been seeking to do in ever-increasing numbers.

In East Berlin, the twenty-fifth anniversary was marked by a military parade. Large formations of troops and armored cars moved slowly up the wide, spacious boulevard called the Karl-Marx-Allee. East Germany's Communist Party general secretary Erich Honecker (who in 1961, as the top security aide to the preceding East Germany leader, Walter Ulbricht, had personally overseen construction of the wall) stood on a grandstand alongside other Communist Party and military officials. A giant banner on the grandstand proclaimed "25 Years of an Anti-Fascist Defense Wall." Posters on nearby streets displayed a picture of a uniformed, helmeted East German solider with the words, "Aug. 13, 1961–86: An example for the workplace and the armed forces."

In West Berlin, German chancellor Helmut Kohl, in ceremonies at the German Reichstag (parliament building), proclaimed that "we will never and can never get used to this monument of inhumanity." The Berlin Wall, Kohl continued, "is perhaps the most visible expression of the moral gulf between free democracy and totalitarian dictatorship."[1] There were a handful of small popular protests by West Germans at the wall. In one, at Checkpoint Charlie, a crossing point between East and West Berlin, about three hundred people gathered at night, in some instances lunging across the border for a few brief moments before they were thrown back by East German security officials or prudently leaped back on their own. A couple of protesters threw stones at the East German guards. The Soviet ambassador to East Germany, Yuli Kvitsinsky, subsequently filed a formal protest to Allied authorities in West Berlin, calling the demonstrations "a wide-ranging provocative campaign."

On the whole, however, the West Berlin observances of the anniversary were subdued. West Germans had become increasingly nervous about the possibility of a nuclear confrontation between the United States and the Soviet Union. They were beginning to learn to live with the wall and to move toward an acceptance of and reconciliation with East Germany. Kohl himself, after denouncing the immorality of the wall, carefully added a few notes of hope for better relations with Honecker's government. "We remain prepared for a policy of small steps in the interest of the German people," he said. Other West German officials went further. Eberhard Diepgen, the mayor of West Berlin, was supervising plans for a reconstruction of the area around the Reichstag alongside the border between the two parts of the city; the plan was based on the notion that it was time for West Berliners to be realistic and stop dreaming that the wall would come down.[2]

The American perspective was different. Two days before the twenty-fifth anniversary of the construction of the wall, the White House released the transcript of a so-called interview that President Ronald Reagan had given to *Das Bild*, the newspaper with the largest circulation in West Germany. Reagan's words were, in fact, merely a set of written answers to written questions submitted by the paper—the sort of responses that were routinely drafted in the president's name by lower-level Reagan administration officials. Still, Reagan's remarks were front-page news in Germany. "I would like to see the wall come down today, and I call upon those responsible to dismantle it," he asserted. "No regime can attain genuine legitimacy in the eyes of its own people if those people are treated as prisoners by their own government."[3]

The president may never have seen these words before they were released. But the following day, Reagan was asked once again about the Berlin Wall at a press conference in Chicago. The president rambled a bit, then offered a reply similar to what had been said in writing the previous day. "Isn't it strange that all of these situations where other people build walls to keep an enemy out, and there's only one part of the world and one philosophy where they have to build walls to keep their people in?" he asked. "Maybe they're going to recognize that there's something wrong with that soon."[4]

By the 1980s, Berlin had been for many years a subject that American leaders avoided. "Berlin was a third rail for everyone," observed Barry Lowenkron, a European specialist in the State Department. "The subject was just off the table."[5] The reason lay in Berlin's stormy history at the center of the early disputes of the Cold War, and the uneasy equilibrium that had resulted from the construction of the Berlin Wall at the beginning of the Kennedy administration.

Germany had been divided ever since American, British, and French troops and the Soviet Red Army occupied the country after World War II. In the following years, the zones of the three Western allies were consolidated into West Germany, while the area under Soviet control became East Germany. The city of Berlin, located inside East Germany more than a hundred miles from the West, was itself split up by the occupying powers, and these divisions eventually became West and East Berlin. Under Josef Stalin, the Soviet Union imposed a land blockade to attempt to force the Western powers out of Berlin, but the Allies responded with the Berlin Airlift of 1948–49, and the Soviets finally backed down.

For the first sixteen years after the end of the war, there had been freedom of movement within the separate sections of Berlin. That meant, effectively, that residents of East Berlin could respond to the economic deprivation and political repression under East Germany's Communist government by moving to West Berlin and often from there onward to other locations in West Germany. Many East Berliners and other East Germans took this route—all the more so after the East German regime headed by Walter Ulbricht crushed a rebellion that erupted in East Berlin in 1953. Ulbricht repeatedly urged Moscow to do something to stem the outflow, or to let him act on his own.

In 1958, Nikita Khrushchev set off a new Berlin crisis by declaring that within six months he would either end the formal four-power arrangements for occupation of the city or turn over the control of access to Berlin to Ulbricht's East Germany. He was, at the time, reflecting the heady confidence in Moscow following the Soviet launch of its *Sputnik* satellite. "Berlin is the testicles of the West," Khrushchev once said. "Every time I want to make the West scream, I squeeze on Berlin." However, the Eisenhower administration held its ground, and Khrushchev let the deadline pass, choosing instead to pay a visit to the United States.[6]

In East Germany, Ulbricht sought in 1959 to collectivize remaining private farmland, touching off a new exodus to the West that soon reached a rate of 10,000 people a month and then kept on climbing. More than 120,000 East Germans left the country in 1959, and more than 180,000 in 1960. East Germany's overall population was in decline.[7] Not only did the flood of refugees deprive the East German economy of professionals and other needed personnel, it also undermined the Communist regime's control over the country. Ulbricht and his aides had to be careful in cracking down on dissent, or in imposing labor discipline or carrying out military conscription, because they had to worry that those who were unhappy would leave for the West.

Ulbricht pressured Khrushchev to give him more support and to help stop the outflow. In 1961, soon after John F. Kennedy succeeded Eisenhower as president, Khrushchev deliberately renewed the tensions over Berlin, suggesting once again that he might force out the Western powers or limit their access to the city. Kennedy's response seemed to be a tough one: At a summit meeting in Vienna in early June, he made clear that the United States would be willing to use force to protect the Western presence in Berlin and the right of the Allied powers to travel into and out of the city. In an address to the American people a few weeks later, Kennedy said, "We cannot and will not permit the Communists to drive us out of Berlin, either gradually or by force." He also raised the defense budget, moved to increase the size of the army, and sought authority to call up reserves.[8]

Yet Kennedy's response also left an opening, an opportunity that first Ulbricht and subsequently Khrushchev decided to seize. To be sure, the American president had been specific about defending the Western presence in Berlin; essentially, Kennedy was holding to the policies of the Truman administration during the Berlin Airlift. At the same time, however, Kennedy had made no commitments to the residents of East Berlin. This suggested to Ulbricht and Khrushchev a possible solution: Why not go along with Kennedy and leave the Western powers undisturbed in West Berlin, but also shut off East Berlin from the West?

Two weeks after the Vienna summit, Ulbricht held a press conference at which, when discussing the different sections of Berlin, he at one point issued a strange denial: "No one has the intention of building a wall." Those remarks touched off what the Germans called *Torschlusspanik*—fear that the open door from East to West was about to be closed. The number of refugees shot up still higher.[9]

During the following weeks, throughout July and early August 1961, Ulbricht won support from Moscow and his Warsaw Pact allies to build a barricade between East and West Berlin. Finally, in the overnight hours of August 12–13, Ulbricht's aides and the Ministry of Security, or Stasi, carried out Operation Rose, the code name they had used in their preparations. They put up the barbed wire they had been secretly stockpiling for weeks; severed phone lines between East and West Berlin; and restricted car, subway, and train movements between the two parts of the city. They carefully did nothing to restrict transportation between West Berlin and West Germany, thus avoiding any repetition of the failed embargo of 1948–49.

Kennedy had told his advisers he expected the construction of a wall, or something like it. This would be, Kennedy calculated, a way to end the Soviet-American tensions over Berlin without a war. It was a solution that would stabilize the city and beyond that, preserve the status quo in Europe. "President Kennedy at the time—and this was about ten days before the Wall went up—judged that they would have to put something up, because East Germany was bleeding to death in terms of the outflow of people, extremely valuable people, and this would disrupt the whole Eastern bloc, which the Soviets regarded as fundamental to their security," recalled Walt W. Rostow, Kennedy's deputy national security adviser, in an interview a quarter century later. "President Kennedy went on to say that when they put up the wall, or whatever it was that would block exit, we would not be able to do anything about it, because he could barely hold together the Western alliance in defense of West Berlin. . . . If we had knocked down the barbed wire, they could have done other things to stop the outflow, put the wall further back," Rostow said. "It would have been useless to knock it down. The Soviets were not about to witness the dissolution of the Eastern alliance. And the West was not about to force the dissolution of the Eastern alliance."[10]

Two years later, when the wall had become a permanent fixture in Berlin, Kennedy paid a visit to the city, choosing to deliver there one of his best-remembered speeches, an address that contained fervently anti-Communist themes:

> *There are many people in the world who really don't understand, or say they don't, what is the great issue between the free world and the communist world. Let them come to Berlin!*
> *There are some who say that communism is the wave of the future. Let them come to Berlin!*
> *And there are some who say in Europe and elsewhere we can work with the communists. Let them come to Berlin! . . .*
> *All free men, wherever they may live, are citizens of Berlin, and therefore, as a free man, I take pride in the words, 'Ich bin ein Berliner.'*

Arthur M. Schlesinger, Jr., Kennedy's aide and later his biographer, reported that Kennedy's visit was received "as if it were the second coming." When the president spoke outside the Rathaus Schöeneberg, West Berlin's city hall, "The hysteria spread almost visibly through the square. Kennedy was first exhilarated, then disturbed; he felt, as he remarked on his return, that if he had said, 'March to the wall—tear it down,' his listeners would have marched."[11]

In fact, however, the reaction of West Germans to Kennedy was considerably more complicated than Schlesinger's triumphal account recognized. In allowing the construction of the Berlin Wall to go unchallenged, Kennedy had settled upon a solution that avoided a war between the superpowers. However, he had also demonstrated to West Germans that he was willing to accept the division of Berlin.

Some residents of West Berlin, including a few of the city's most prominent residents, had been dismayed by the American passivity. Among them was the mayor of West Berlin, Willy Brandt (who had, in fact, stood on the podium alongside Kennedy during his "Berliner" speech). In an interview more than four decades later, Egon Bahr, Brandt's longtime associate and foreign-policy adviser, recalled that when the East Germans built the wall, "that was a bitter situation for us," one that prompted Brandt to send an angry protest to Kennedy. "Nobody helped us," Bahr said. "This damn wall was the beginning of our thinking that we have to take care of German interests on our own."[12]

"I'm not a great fan of Kennedy," said Eberhard Diepgen, who was twenty years old when the wall was built and later served as mayor of West Berlin in the 1980s and mayor of a reunified Berlin in the 1990s. "Through his policies, he basically created the problem of the Wall. When he reduced the American guarantees from all of Berlin to the western part of the city, he made the building of the wall politically possible."[13]

For these Germans, Kennedy's acceptance of the Berlin Wall taught a lesson: those who sought to overcome the division of Berlin or of Germany couldn't rely solely on the Americans. They needed to look to the other side: to Moscow or East Germany or East Berlin.

There was a rough correlation between those West Berliners who were upset about the American decision to permit construction of the wall and those who played an active role years later in seeking to improve relations with the Soviet Union or to distance themselves from American foreign policy. Within a decade after the wall went up, Brandt, as German chancellor, launched his policy of *Ostpolitik*, working out groundbreaking agreements with the Soviet Union, Poland, and then East Germany.

For his own part, Diepgen years later often sought to obstruct whatever the Americans wanted to do in Berlin. When U.S. officials began talking in early 1987 about the possibility that Reagan would deliver a speech in front of the Berlin Wall and the Brandenburg Gate, the leading opponent of this idea was West Berlin's mayor, Eberhard Diepgen.

After Kennedy's famous speech, the subject of Berlin virtually vanished from American political discourse. It was a subject best left alone, too risky to discuss.

-3-

DAY VISIT OF A PRESIDENTIAL CANDIDATE

Over the years, Ronald Reagan had repeatedly made the same complaint about the Berlin Wall as had Willy Brandt: that John F. Kennedy should have done something to stop its construction. In one letter written shortly before his 1980 presidential campaign, he told one of his followers: "I agree with you about the lost opportunity in Berlin, when we could have knocked down and prevented the completion of the wall with no hostilities following."[1]

Reagan had visited Berlin only once for less than a day before his arrival in the White House. It was during a tour Reagan had made of several European capitals at the end of 1978, just as he was preparing his second campaign for the Republican presidential nomination. Reagan's foreign-policy advisers, led by Richard Allen, a former aide to Richard Nixon, were eager to help Reagan overcome perceptions that he would be too dangerous in foreign policy—precisely the unease that had sunk the candidacy of Reagan's conservative Republican predecessor Barry Goldwater in 1964.

In a memo addressed directly to Reagan in the summer of 1978 from his office at the Hoover Institution at Stanford University, Allen said:

For many, you come across as a "saber rattler," a "button pusher,"
or as "too willing to send in the Marines." This false image is
happily amplified by the media . . .

Allen suggested that without changing his strong views, Reagan might
want

to soften the delivery of your message. . . . You are, after all, try-
ing to put your best foot forward; in so doing, you will have to
sound more "Presidential" than a quiz show respondent.[2]

With Reagan on his trip to Europe in late 1978 were Allen; his wife,
Nancy; and Reagan's longtime adviser Peter Hannaford. At their first stopover
in London, Reagan visited Parliament for talks with the Conservative Party
opposition leader, Margaret Thatcher (who within five months would become prime minister). They had met once before, when Reagan had visited
London three years earlier. On that occasion, Reagan and Thatcher had talked
in general about economic issues and the importance of free markets. This
time, the principal subject of discussion was the new, mobile Soviet SS-20
ballistic missile, a medium-range weapon that could reach targets in Western
Europe from inside the Soviet Union.[3]

In Bonn, Reagan met with German chancellor Helmut Schmidt and also
with Helmut Kohl, then the leader of the conservative Christian Democratic
Union. Schmidt was disdainful, and even Kohl was struck at the time by
Reagan's lack of experience. "He had no idea about Europe, or about Germany," reflected Kohl in an interview three decades later. "He had, let us say,
a minimum knowledge about the world. But he was very open, and in his
dealings with me, Reagan was incredibly friendly, right from the start."
Within a few years, Reagan's friendship with Kohl would turn out to be of
profound importance for the strong relationship between the United States
and Western Europe.[4]

Reagan and his party flew on to Berlin, where they stayed at the Kempinski
Hotel. The next morning, Berlin officials gave Reagan and his party a tour of
the city. The Reagans saw the Berlin Wall and had their picture taken at Checkpoint Charlie, one of the crossing points between East and West Berlin.

Later, after an American military briefing, Reagan said he would like to cross into East Berlin. U.S. consular officials accompanied him and his party on a very brief tour through Checkpoint Charlie to East Berlin's Alexanderplatz, less than half a mile away. This afternoon excursion was the only time Reagan set foot in a Communist country on the other side of Europe's Iron Curtain until near the end of his presidency; he did not visit the Soviet Union until his trip to Moscow in 1988.

Reagan and everyone else in his party were instructed to keep their American passports out and pressed against the glass of the car. At Alexanderplatz, in the heart of East Berlin, Nancy Reagan and Hannaford's wife went off to have a look at a state-run department store, while Reagan, Allen, and Hannaford waited outside. Suddenly, the three men witnessed East German Vopos (short for *Volkspolizisten,* the "people's police") stopping a lone young man carrying shopping bags. "They required him to produce identification documents and their treatment appeared to be pure harassment," Hannaford later wrote.

None of them heard the conversation between the man and the police or saw anything else transpire. Yet Hannaford later claimed, "Looking on at this scene, Ronald Reagan, as strong a champion of liberty as could be found, saw it as an example of authoritarian oppression in action. It is an event he would mention many times upon his return to the United States."[5] If so, it was the thinnest possible reed on which to base foreign policy judgments; it raised the question of whether Reagan knew what sometimes takes place at traffic stops of racial minorities in the United States.

Decades later, the aides who accompanied Reagan made much of the broader meaning of this 1978 trip. Allen asserted in an interview that Reagan, standing at the Berlin Wall, had told him, "Dick, we've got to find a way to tear this thing down." Hannaford said the glimpse of East Berlin "had a very powerful effect on the Reagans." Upon being shown the point where a young East German had earlier been shot trying to escape, Hannaford said, "You could see the muscles in [Reagan's] jaw tightening, and the sense of resolve was very, very powerful."[6]

Yet Reagan's aides offered these recollections only many years later, with hindsight after the fall of the Berlin Wall. It is not clear how much the Berlin stopover meant to Reagan at the time. A news story about Reagan the following day in *Die Welt*, West Germany's conservative daily newspaper, focused on his criticisms of the Carter administration and, in particular, the unease in Europe over the Soviet SS-20 missiles. The newspaper's picture of the Reagans at Checkpoint Charlie shows the couple standing stiffly and forlornly in the rain, with Nancy Reagan protecting herself under an umbrella.[7] Berlin seemed to be little more than another desultory precampaign stop for an aspiring presidential candidate.

When Reagan next returned to Berlin in mid-1982, the city was in tumult. By then he had already been president for nearly a year and a half, and his administration was in the midst of a drive to install new American intermediate-range Pershing and cruise missiles in Europe to help offset the Soviet SS-20s. Although those efforts had been strongly endorsed by the West German government of Chancellor Helmut Schmidt, they had also galvanized a strong opposition movement.

At a NATO summit meeting of Western leaders in Bonn, Reagan was greeted by three hundred thousand antiwar protesters, the largest single gathering of Germans since World War II. There were similar gatherings that week in London, Paris, Rome, and New York City. Reagan sought to deflect the antinuclear movement by declaring in a speech to the West German parliament, "To those who march for peace, my heart is with you. I would be at the head of your parade if I believed marching alone could bring about a more secure world."[8]

When Reagan flew on to West Berlin for a three-hour visit on June 11, 1982, tens of thousands of demonstrators assembled to denounce him, carrying signs that said "Back to Hollywood" and "Get Out, Cowboy." Church bells chimed during the march, underlining the support of West German churches for the antinuclear movement. Eventually, the West Berlin rally descended into violence, as thousands of young protesters, wearing helmets for protection, shattered store windows, overturned cars, threw rocks and paving material, and set fires. In an attempt to contain the upheaval, the West Berlin police rolled out barbed wire; used tear gas, water cannons, and clubs; and waged pitched battles with the demonstrators along the Kurfürstendamm, the wide boulevard at the heart of West Berlin.[9]

Reagan chose the occasion to unveil what he called a "new Berlin initiative." It was a collection of proposals, none of them far-reaching, to reduce the risks of nuclear war through exchanges of information and notification of military exercises. He offered to keep American missiles out of Europe if the Soviets would eliminate their SS-20s and other intermediate-range missiles. "If Chairman Brezhnev agrees to this, we stand ready to forgo all of our ground-launched cruise missiles and Pershing II missiles," Reagan said. Soviet president Leonid Brezhnev was by then in the final six months of his life, and Reagan's proposals went nowhere.[10]

Reagan did not ignore the subject of the wall. Indeed, during his 1982 trip, he offered a preview of the themes he would advance more fully five years later. Immediately upon his arrival in West Berlin, he told one audience:

> *You know, if I had a chance, I'd like to ask the Soviet leaders one question—in fact, I may stuff the question in a bottle and throw it over the wall when I go there today. I really want to hear their explanation. Why is that wall there? Why are they so afraid of freedom on this side of the wall? Well, the truth is they're scared to death of it because they know that freedom is catching, and they don't dare leave their people have a taste of it.*[11]

Reagan paid another quick visit to Checkpoint Charlie. He was asked what he thought of the wall. "It's as ugly as the idea behind it," he said.[12]

During the 1980s, West Germans in general and West Berliners in particular became increasingly unreceptive to such rhetoric from American leaders. At one point during his 1982 visit, Reagan sought to call attention to the bonds between Americans and the people of Berlin by recalling memories of John F. Kennedy's declaration *"Ich bin ein Berliner."* While Reagan complained from time to time about Kennedy's inaction in allowing the wall to be built, he seemed happy to link himself to the Kennedy speech that Americans knew so well. "We all remember John Kennedy's stirring words when he visited Berlin," said Reagan. "I can only add that we in America and in the West are still Berliners, too, and always will be."[13]

Nevertheless, these invocations of Kennedy's rhetoric served only to obscure the differences that had emerged between the United States and West

Germany. Indeed, in 1983, when American officials suggested the idea of a large-scale celebration to commemorate the twentieth anniversary of Kennedy's "Berliner" speech, they discovered to their dismay that the Germans weren't particularly interested.[14] In the United States, the speech was a source of pride; in West Berlin, it was remembered with a tinge of melancholy. As a result, the anniversary was allowed to pass by in obscurity.

The prolonged test of wills between the United States and the Soviet Union over intermediate-range missiles in Europe had increasingly unsettled the Germans. The West German governments of both Schmidt and Kohl, who succeeded him in October 1982, had supported the deployment of the Pershing II and cruise missiles. The rationale was clear: without those American missiles, the Soviet SS-20s might enable Moscow to subject Western Europe to nuclear blackmail. Yet once the Reagan administration and its Western allies decided that NATO should deploy its own intermediate-range missiles in response to the Soviets, then many in West Germany began to voice a new set of fears: that the Cold War could erupt into a nuclear conflict, one that might begin on German soil. Perhaps with the new deployments of missiles that could not cross the Atlantic Ocean, the Reagan administration and the Soviet Union—whose relations, in 1983, were more acrimonious than at any time since the Cuban missile crisis—might be less hesitant about waging a limited nuclear war that would affect only Europe. "The Europeans were afraid that America would not be sufficiently interested in the dangers of these new weapons, because they couldn't reach America anyhow," explained Richard von Weizsäcker, who served as mayor of West Berlin in the early Reagan years and became the West German president in 1984.[15]

The groundswell of antinuclear sentiment contributed to an unusual new form of German nationalism, one that sometimes spanned the long-standing divisions between West and East Germany. At one point, former West German chancellor Willy Brandt called the new missiles being stationed on German soil "the work of the devil." East German president Erich Honecker picked up Brandt's phrase and began to use it himself. Honecker also began to speak of a "coalition of reason" between Bonn and Berlin, suggesting that he would like to see both the American and the Soviet missiles removed from German soil.

According to Egon Krenz, Honecker's top aide and heir apparent, Soviet officials were angered by what Honecker was saying. In July 1984, two articles in *Pravda,* the Soviet Communist Party organ, suddenly warned of the dangers of German reunification. A few weeks later, Honecker was summoned to a secret meeting in Moscow. There, the senior-most leaders of the Soviet Union—among them Communist Party general secretary Konstantin Chernenko, Defense Minister Dmitri Ustinov, and the rising young Communist Party official Mikhail Gorbachev—served notice to Honecker that he should keep his foreign policy in line with that of Moscow and should not get too friendly with the West Germans.

Chernenko warned that "the issue concerning development of the relationship between the GDR [East Germany] and the FRG [West Germany] is a question of our common global policy. This question directly affects the Soviet Union and the entire socialist community." He said he could not see how warming up to West Germany would do anything to offset the harm caused by the American missiles.[16]

Gorbachev, as an aide to Chernenko, was particularly outspoken in warning the East Germans not to go astray. "In these negotiations, Gorbachev played the hard-liner, so to speak," recalled Krenz. "He criticized Honecker very sharply."[17]

Other factors besides the missile deployments were also driving West and East Germany toward each other. During the mid-1980s, powerful economic forces had prompted Honecker to turn toward the West. The East Germans were desperate for hard currency. In 1983, Franz Josef Strauss, the Bavarian prime minister who was West Germany's most prominent conservative politician, helped arrange a government-backed loan of one billion marks (then about four hundred million dollars) to East Germany, a landmark deal.

In the years that followed, Honecker sought and was given ever-increasing amounts of financial help from West Germany. In return, Honecker was willing to permit increasing numbers of East Germans to emigrate to the West and to make it easier for West Germans to visit their families in the East. By mid-1984, Honecker was talking eagerly, and in public, about making what would be the first visit to West Germany by an East German leader. Resistance from Moscow forced him to postpone the idea. In the same *Pravda* commentary that argued against German reunification, the Soviets also warned that West Germany was using "economic levers and political contacts" to undermine East Germany's Communist system.[18]

In short, by the mid-1980s, West Germany was beginning to pursue a conscious strategy of easing Cold War tensions through accommodation with East Germany. In a sense, this effort was the natural follow-up to the 1970s policy of *Ostpolitik,* Brandt's drive to improve relations with the Soviet Union and Eastern Europe. "We were ultimately convinced—I can say this also on behalf of Willy Brandt—we were trying to overcome the division of Germany," said Egon Bahr, Brandt's longtime aide and adviser.[19]

The West Germans were increasingly tired of Cold War confrontation and skeptical about American policy. The shift in mood could be detected not merely in public opinion or within the opposition Social Democratic Party, but also among West German's more conservative leaders. In West Berlin, Mayor Eberhard Diepgen, a member of the conservative Christian Democratic Union, began seeking new cooperation with the East Germans on such local issues as traffic and gas supplies. "In those times, West Germans were on the way to accepting, more and more, the division of Germany," reflected Diepgen in an interview many years later.[20]

Kohl, as West German chancellor, generally resisted these trends. He emerged as a particularly strong supporter of Reagan and, more generally, of American policy in Europe. Kohl warned of the dangers of "Finlandization," a reference to Finland's policy during the Cold War of maintaining neutrality and declining to challenge the authority of the Soviet Union in international affairs. West Germany's peace movement had revived a proposal first put forward by former Polish foreign minister Adam Rapacki for a nuclear-free zone that would cover East and West Germany, Poland, Czechoslovakia, and perhaps eventually other countries as well. Kohl summarily rejected the idea, arguing that it would mean that the Americans would be effectively pushed back to the English Channel, leaving the Soviet Union to dominate Europe.[21]

However, Kohl and the West German government were also moving toward doing business with East Germany in ways that made the Reagan administration uneasy. American officials complained that the West Germans were conferring too much legitimacy upon Honecker's government. To be sure, the Soviet Union didn't like the idea of Honecker's visiting West Germany, but the same prospect put the Reagan administration on edge too. In mid-1986, for example, American officials became alarmed by reports that Kohl's government was thinking about an agreement with Honecker that would formally accept as permanent the post–World War II division of the city of Berlin; the West Germans would formally recognize East Berlin as part of East Germany, and the East Germans would accept the incorporation of West Berlin into West Germany.[22]

Even ceremonial events were becoming problematic. The city of Berlin was officially observing its 750th anniversary in 1987, and West and East German officials began preparing separate events to commemorate the event. By the fall of 1986, the three allied powers in Berlin had let it be known that their three heads of state—Queen Elizabeth, French president François Mitterrand, and President Reagan—would visit West Berlin at some point during the anniversary year. But then Honecker extended an invitation to the young mayor of West Berlin, Eberhard Diepgen, to come to East Berlin for its celebration. Allied officials feared such a visit would undermine their legal position that Berlin should still be considered a united city governed by the World War II Allies; Diepgen's visit might instead buttress Honecker's claim that East Berlin was the capital of East Germany.

American officials were increasingly dismayed. "The West Germans were spending a lot of time cuddling up to the East Germans, to Honecker," said Nelson Ledsky, who served as the U.S. minister in West Berlin until 1985 and later worked as a European specialist on Reagan's National Security Council. John C. Kornblum, who succeeded Ledsky in West Berlin, maintained in an interview years later, "At this point in German history, the West Germans had basically given up on reunification. And they were trying to arrange themselves with the East."[23]

Gradually, by late 1986, the top American officials dealing with West Germany decided the United States needed to do something dramatic to arrest the drift toward accommodation and mutual acceptance between the two Germanys. "There was a German attitude that we have to live with the Wall," asserted Richard Burt, who served as Reagan's ambassador to West Germany. "They thought, 'We have to find little ways to come together.' And their idea of 'little ways' was mostly ways to pump deutschmarks into the East to buy off the East Germans." By late 1986 and early 1987, Burt said, American officials came to the conclusion that "it was incumbent upon us to remind the West Germans that this was still a divided country."[24]

-4-

"HE BLEW IT"

Ronald Reagan was not paying attention to Germany during the first months of 1987. Neither were his domestic advisers or his White House staff. All of them were trying to save his presidency from collapse.

The Iran-Contra scandal had burst open in November 1986. The revelations that the administration had secretly supplied arms to Iran and then used the profits for rebel forces in Nicaragua prompted a series of investigations without parallel since Watergate. Attorney General Edwin Meese conducted a limited inquiry, then a special commission headed by Senator John Tower carried out a three-month policy review, and eventually a special prosecutor, Lawrence Walsh, conducted an extensive criminal investigation. Congress, meanwhile, set up its own joint committee to examine the affair. For months the press was full of suggestions that Reagan might be impeached or forced to resign, as Richard Nixon had twelve years earlier.

The Reagan administration was in turmoil. Several of its top officials either were fired or resigned. National Security Adviser John Poindexter was quickly ousted along with Oliver North, the central operative in the Iran-Contra affair; Frank Carlucci replaced Poindexter. Within three months, Reagan fired his White House chief of staff, Donald Regan, and appointed former senator Howard Baker to replace him. Adding to the sense of upheaval, CIA director William Casey suffered a stroke, underwent brain surgery, and resigned; he died within months. Robert McFarlane, the former Reagan national security adviser who had approved the Iran initiative, attempted suicide.

The drama unfolded against a backdrop of intrigue that was unusual even for the Reagan White House. The firing of the White House chief of staff had followed several weeks of maneuvering in which Nancy Reagan had played the central orchestrating role. She had clashed repeatedly with Regan, who at one point had hung up the phone on her; she believed her husband failed to see that Regan was to blame for many of the administration's difficulties. "Ronnie never saw the Don that everybody else saw, because Don didn't let him," she recalled years later. "So Ronnie never knew all these things that were going on in the office, and all the people who were coming to me saying, 'You've got to do something to get that man out of there.'"[1] Eventually, Mrs. Reagan put together a much larger team, including Reagan adviser Michael Deaver, political strategist Stuart Spencer, and eventually Vice President George Bush, to force Regan's resignation.

The scandal had an impact not merely on the White House staff or the rest of the administration, but upon Reagan himself. In a series of press conferences, speeches, and testimony to the Tower Commission, he sought repeatedly to justify what had happened, but his explanations failed to win public support. "Always before, he had the view that 'I'll do what's right, and if it's right I can take it to the American people and then sell it to them,'" reflected his secretary of state, George Shultz, many years later. "And you had to say, 'This time, Mr. President, what you did was wrong, that's why you couldn't sell it, because everyone could see it was wrong.'"[2] On February 26, 1987, the Tower Commission reported its finding that, contrary to Reagan's own earlier claims, his administration had, in fact, been trading arms to Iran in exchange for the release of American hostages in Lebanon. Reagan was upset by the report. Reagan's executive assistant, Jim Kuhn, noted that the day of the Tower report "was one of only three days during Ronald Reagan's presidency when he seemed off stride. (The other two instances, he said, were the last day of the Reykjavik talks with Gorbachev and the day of Nancy Reagan's breast surgery.)[3]

By the end of February, the Reagan administration was in such disarray that the *New York Times* was running daily packages of news stories under the umbrella headline WHITE HOUSE IN CRISIS. Reagan was widely portrayed as a lame-duck president whose administration would be too crippled to accomplish anything during its final twenty-two months in office. The cover of *Time* for March 9, 1987, showed a picture of a clearly aging Reagan, his face lined and puffy. The cover line asked, "Can Reagan Recover?" The magazine quoted one rising young Republican who felt the answer was no: "Says Newt Gingrich, a conservative Republican Congressman from Georgia: 'He will never again be the Reagan that he was before he blew it. He is not going to regain our trust and our faith easily.' "[4]

At the beginning of March 1987, Howard Baker took over as Reagan's White House chief of staff, bringing in a new team of aides with him. The new team took as its principal mission a desire to revive Reagan's presidency and to restore his popularity. "Reagan was at 37 per cent in the polls. He wasn't a lame duck, he was a dead duck," recalled Ken Duberstein, who had worked for Reagan during his first term and returned, under Baker, as deputy White House chief of staff.[5]

"We had to do things that showed that he could still govern," said Thomas Griscom, another new White House staffer. Griscom, a former Senate aide to Baker, had been brought in as the White House director of communications, replacing the archconservative Patrick Buchanan. More than any other, that personnel shuffle seemed to symbolize the larger change in mood within the administration: from combative to conciliatory, from challenging the existing order and institutions to working inside them.

But how should the new team demonstrate that Reagan could still govern? One of the first decisions was that the president should travel as much as possible, particularly throughout the United States but also overseas. The Baker team compared Reagan's situation to Nixon's during Watergate. "We were not going to let him get trapped in the White House," said Griscom. "I remembered those images of Richard Nixon sitting there in the White House, watching the TV set. We weren't going to let that happen."[6]

Griscom worked closely with Reagan's chief pollster, Richard Wirthlin. They discovered that although Americans weren't rushing to accept Reagan's explanation for Iran-Contra, the public also wasn't following closely the day-to-day developments. Washington was consumed by Iran-Contra, but the public didn't understand it well. Thus there was an opportunity for Reagan to deflect attention from Iran-Contra by showing that he was actively engaged on other issues and in other places.

Reagan hadn't left the United States for five months, not since his summit meeting with Mikhail Gorbachev in Reykjavik in October 1986. Even in the early spring, the president ventured outside the country only once, and then not far: he made a two-day trip to Ottawa to see Canadian prime minister Brian Mulroney. However, later that spring Reagan's schedule called for him to attend, as usual, the annual meeting of the leaders of the world's leading industrialized nations. The session was to be held in Venice. Once he was already in Europe for the economic summit, he would have a chance to go elsewhere. For example, the United States had already promised that Reagan would go to West Berlin sometime during 1987 to the 750th anniversary celebrations of Berlin's founding. Reagan's advisers began looking at the Berlin stopover as a chance to show the American public and the world that Iran-Contra hadn't ended the Reagan presidency.

-5-

ANTI-SOVIET JOKES

Ronald Reagan's repertoire included a seemingly endless supply of anti-Communist jokes. When he met with visitors from the Soviet Union or other places on the front lines of the Cold War, he invariably offered something from this storehouse of material. Telling these jokes came naturally to Reagan, but they also served other purposes. They kept the tone and mood of a meeting light, deflecting discussion away from weighty details of policy on which Reagan was not well versed. Not accidentally, they also conveyed Reagan's own underlying beliefs and values.

"Question: What are the four things wrong with Soviet agriculture?" he would ask a dumbfounded visitor. "Answer: Spring, summer, fall and winter." Reagan would recount with relish the story of the Moscow resident who purchased a car and was told by the salesman that it would be ready on a specific date a quarter century later. "Morning or afternoon?" the customer asked. "Why does it matter for a date so far away?" the salesman wondered. "Because the plumber is coming in the morning." In a meeting with West German chancellor Helmut Schmidt, which Schmidt had hoped would be about the need to revive détente with the Soviet Union, Reagan suddenly asked whether the German leader had heard what happened when Soviet president Leonid Brezhnev showed off his personal supply of expensive foreign cars to his mother. "Very fine," his mother replied. "But what happens if the Commies come and take them away?"[1]

Most of this humor was about life inside the Soviet Union. But Reagan even kept a few extra stories handy about life in other Communist countries. When West Berlin mayor Eberhard Diepgen paid a brief visit to the White House on March 4, 1987, the president was ready for him. He first welcomed Diepgen with a few words of German, some of the only German he knew. *"Haben Sie einen Streichholz?"* he asked the mayor—the German for "Do you have a match?" It was a phrase the president had learned from a German actress during his days in Hollywood.

Then Reagan quickly reached into his bag of jokes. "Why was [Communist Party leader] Erich Honecker the last person to leave East Germany?" Reagan asked. Diepgen couldn't guess. "Because someone had to turn out the light," Reagan told him.[2] Under the circumstances, the joke was a rather pointed one. At the time, Diepgen was considering Honecker's invitation to visit East Berlin. He was eager to go, but the allies objected, holding to their long-standing position that East Berlin was temporarily under Soviet control and not under Honecker's domain. Reagan, as usual, avoided becoming entangled in the complexities of these issues. His session with Diepgen took place days after the Tower Commission had reported on Iran-Contra and Donald Regan had been fired as White House chief of staff. Reagan was preparing for a televised address to the nation that night, in which he would concede for the first time in carefully worded sentences that "it was a mistake" for his administration to have sent arms to Iran. The twenty-minute meeting with Diepgen was confined to generalities.

The task of admonishing Diepgen fell instead to John Whitehead, the deputy to Secretary of State George Shultz. Whitehead, a former investment banker with Goldman Sachs, had precisely the right credentials to keep the mayor in line. He was a World War II veteran, had taken part in the D-Day invasion at Omaha Beach, and later, as a visiting American businessman, had seen Berlin at the time the Berlin Wall was constructed. Whitehead had just returned from a trip to Eastern Europe, where, on Shultz's instructions, he had been exploring the prospects for change there; in Warsaw, he had met

both with General Wojciech Jaruzelski and with Lech Walesa, thus conveying
U.S. support for Walesa's Solidarity movement.[3]

Whitehead made it clear that the United States, not Diepgen, would play
the lead role in deciding the timing and conditions of any meetings with a
Communist leader such as Honecker. He reminded the mayor that the allies
were still sovereign in West Berlin, and that the city owed its continuing freedom to the Berlin Airlift of 1948–49. Americans had long-standing emotional ties to the city, Whitehead went on; he had seen firsthand how residents
of the city even dug tunnels to flee to the West. Diepgen argued that it was
time to make the Berlin Wall more permeable; greater contact between the
two German governments might cause the residents of East Germany to
question the regime. The deputy secretary of state rejected his pleas. When it
comes to the Berlin Wall, you shouldn't shy away from confrontation, he told
Diepgen. The West Germans couldn't deal on their own with East Germany
because they would just be too soft.[4]

The West German mayor failed to win the Reagan administration's approval for his proposed visit to East Berlin. Instead, he was offered a consolation prize, one that might help buttress Diepgen's standing back home.
During his visit to Washington, the White House announced that Reagan
had formally accepted Diepgen's invitation to visit West Berlin in June.

The United States would take part in the Berlin anniversary celebrations,
but on its own terms—terms that emphasized the continuing Soviet presence
in Eastern Europe.

That same week, on March 6, 1987, American officials in West Germany sent
to Washington the first draft of the speech they wanted Reagan to deliver in
West Berlin. A copy of that original twenty-three-page text, stamped "Secret," was obtained for this book under the Freedom of Information Act. It
was written by John Kornblum, a round-faced, bespectacled Foreign Service
officer who was serving at the time as U.S. minister and deputy commandant
in West Berlin, the official in charge of the American presence there.

Kornblum had spent most of his career working on German and central
European issues in Washington, Bonn, and Berlin. What he wrote reflected
the anxieties within the U.S. government about the drift of events in West
Germany—in particular, the concerns that either Kohl's government in Bonn

or Diepgen's in West Berlin would accept the permanent division of Berlin or recognize East Berlin as part of East Germany. The key section of Kornblum's draft came near the end of the speech, where he wanted Reagan to say: "We have no need to sacrifice our principles, such as the status of Berlin, in search of weak compromises from the East."[5]

Kornblum did not avoid the subject of the Berlin Wall. On the contrary, his draft repeatedly pointed to the wall. That fact was not surprising. Reagan himself had already attacked the wall, both during his 1982 trip to Berlin and in his remarks in 1986 on the twenty-fifth anniversary of its construction. Calling attention to the evils of the Berlin Wall was not something original or unique to Reagan; it was a regular refrain in speeches by U.S. officials. Kornblum's draft of the speech included some of the usual themes:

> *Berliners on the East side of that wall have little to celebrate.*
> *They are being forced to endure a glorification of communist*
> *dictatorship . . . Your courage and your unity will ensure that—*
> *one day—this ugly wall will disappear. . . .*
>
> *Europe must be reunited. Barriers to contact must be torn*
> *down. We should begin with the ugly wall which divides this*
> *great city. We should continue by helping people in East Ger-*
> *many and Eastern Europe to enjoy full self-determination and*
> *democratic rights.*[6]

Although the Kornblum draft reviled the wall and urged its destruction, it did not include what would later become the most bitterly debated and eventually the most celebrated element in Reagan's speech. His text did not call upon Soviet leader Mikhail Gorbachev to tear down the wall.

The Soviet leader, in his first two years on the job, had engaged in a flurry of diplomacy that had attracted considerable excitement, particularly in Western Europe. He had proposed the elimination of nuclear weapons by the year 2000; he had also started to establish good working relationships with Margaret Thatcher and François Mitterrand. The perception had taken hold that Gorbachev was innovative, while the United States was clinging to the status quo. The idea behind this early draft of the speech was that Reagan needed to respond to Gorbachev, not to challenge him. A cover letter explained that the speech "will help counter the impression that Gorbachev has seized the initiative." In particular, Kornblum proposed that Reagan make a series of specific policy suggestions. The United States, he said, should propose an improvement in air links to Berlin. It should call for international conferences to be held concurrently in West and East Berlin. Perhaps the 1992 Olympics could be held in both parts of the city.

These ideas were designed to convey the idea that American policy toward Europe was open to change—even as the United States was quietly rebuffing the idea of upgraded ties between the two Germanys. The cover letter that accompanied Kornblum's draft said Reagan should emphasize that "we are not sitting on a static line in Europe—we are going somewhere." Reagan's address in West Berlin should also demonstrate to Soviet officials that while the United States was ready to deal with Gorbachev, "we will not abandon positions of principle to do so."[7]

Many years later, after the end of the Cold War, Kornblum would become embroiled in an acrimonious dispute with Reagan's speechwriters over his role in the Berlin Wall speech. Kornblum sometimes claimed credit for having been the inspiration for the key line in the speech. Two decades later, he wrote that Reagan "needed, in our view, to issue a direct call to Gorbachev to open the Berlin Wall."[8] However, the idea of an exhortation addressed specifically to Gorbachev is not contained in the speech Kornblum sent to Washington, nor does it appear in other records. Kornblum's speech would have had the president inveigh against the wall, but in a more impersonal way; there would have been no appeal to the leader of the Soviet Union to remove it.

Reagan's former speechwriters, on the other hand, claimed that Kornblum wanted Reagan to avoid the subject of the Berlin Wall entirely. One of them, Peter Robinson, attributed to Kornblum the view that the president's speech should contain "no chest-thumping. No Soviet-bashing. And no inflammatory statements about the Berlin Wall."[9] The record demonstrates, however, that this accusation is incorrect. The speech Kornblum sent to the White House in early March repeatedly denounced the Berlin Wall and urged that it be torn down.

Kornblum's draft was merely the first step in deciding what Reagan should say and do while in West Berlin. State Department officials and U.S. diplomats overseas could make suggestions for what Reagan could say. They could even put their ideas into the form of a draft speech. No matter what they did, the work of crafting prose for Ronald Reagan would always go to the White House speechwriters.

-6-

THE ORATOR AND HIS WRITERS

Reagan's political career was based in no small part on his ability to give a speech. He had first attracted national prominence in 1964 with his televised address on behalf of Barry Goldwater's losing presidential campaign—a speech that reflected the ideas he had been refining in front of audiences for more than a decade.[1] Twelve years later, with his concession speech to Gerald Ford at the Republican National Convention in 1976, he had put himself in position to take over the Republican Party.

When Reagan handled policy issues or the daily workings of government, he was frequently passive and aloof. But when it came to speeches, he was attentive to detail. He sometimes delivered a speech with a contact lens designed for reading in one eye but not the other, so that he could glance down and read the speech text if he needed to do so. Secretary of State George Shultz once heard Reagan advise Margaret Thatcher about how to use a Tele-PrompTer. Be sure the pages of the speech are numbered on the TelePrompTer and keep turning the pages of your written text, Reagan said, so that if the machine suddenly breaks down, you know where you are in the printed copy. Be sure to have a few quotes in the speech; it's appropriate to pull up the printed page and read those words—so that, by contrast, it will not seem to the audience as if you are reading the other parts of the speech.[2]

Reagan worked up the final text of a speech with markings every few lines, at each point he wanted to pause and take a breath, so that his delivery would flow evenly.[3] It was Reagan (no doubt thinking of Franklin D. Roosevelt's fireside chats) who came up with the idea of a five-minute live presidential radio speech each Saturday. When he rehearsed these radio broadcasts, he did it with a watch, noting down where he should be in the text after one, two, three, and four minutes. Once Reagan was on the air, an aide would gesture to him when each minute had passed. Reagan would either slightly speed up or slow down his delivery as necessary so that the speech would end in exactly five minutes—just what the broadcasters needed.[4]

Alone with his aides, Reagan sometimes indulged in the sort of bathroom humor or profanity that the public never saw. During his prepresidential trip to West Germany, he had laughed when he discovered that the German words for entrance and exit are *Einfahrt* and *Ausfahrt;* from then on, he and Richard Allen, the foreign-policy adviser who had accompanied him on the trip, used to swap *fahrt* jokes.[5] When Soviet leader Yuri Andropov died in 1984 and aides suggested that the president go to Moscow to attend the funeral, Reagan countered, "I don't want to honor that prick."[6]

In public, however, and particularly in his speeches, Reagan succeeded in conveying a world of innocence and goodness, a throwback to the era of Thornton Wilder's play *Our Town.* No one could better elicit emotions of nostalgia, childhood, and a romance for the America of small towns—the parts of the nation whose past was more glorious than their future. Richard Nixon used to try to appeal to the same small-town nostalgia by recalling how, as a boy, he used to hear the train whistle as it passed in the night. Yet Nixon managed to convey, instead, only the resentment of hard life in small towns. It was Reagan who could make the train whistle.

Reagan's speeches often told stories of ordinary people, of heroes who had not received the recognition they deserved. He spoke of Roy Benavidez, a Medal of Honor winner in Vietnam, or Lenny Skutnik, a federal worker who jumped into the icy waters of the Potomac River to rescue a woman after a plane crash. It was Reagan who introduced the custom of inviting one or more such heroes to attend his annual State of the Union address to Congress, so that he could point them out to a surefire burst of applause.

His worship of heroes was not confined to speeches. Frederick Ryan, who handled the president's appointments and scheduling, recalled that every week or two, Reagan would hand his aides some news story with a name circled—someone who had done something Reagan considered heroic, perhaps a fireman who had pulled someone out of a burning building. "I'd like to meet this person," Reagan would say, and the aides would scramble to bring the person to the White House.[7] In the speeches, however, the heroes and other ordinary Americans usually served a purpose. They were cited on behalf of the ideas Reagan wanted to convey: his hostility to big government, taxes, and communism, and his belief in a continually rising America. "Don't let anyone tell you that America's best days are behind her, that the American spirit has been vanquished," he said as he pointed to Skutnik during his first State of the Union address in 1982. "We've seen it triumph too often in our lives to stop believing in it now."[8]

Early in his career, Reagan wrote many of his own speeches. His work can be seen in the texts he crafted in his own handwriting, such as the radio commentaries he prepared on his own during the 1970s, between being governor and being president.[9] At the White House, Reagan, like other presidents, had a team of speechwriters to draft his remarks at his public appearances. On important speeches, Reagan would take part in an early meeting with top aides and the speechwriters to talk about what he should say. Later on, after a speechwriter had come up with a text, Reagan would edit the draft, crossing out paragraphs, adding additional thoughts. He liked particularly to do this on Wednesday afternoons, which he often took off from the Oval Office, or at Camp David on weekends.[10]

The speechwriting team served a number of functions. They helped come up with some of Reagan's one-liners for events such as the annual dinners of the Gridiron Club and the White House Correspondents' Association, two groups of Washington reporters. They were also responsible for making sure what the president *didn't* say, by screening and checking out the anecdotes that were passed on to him—because it was assumed that once Reagan got hold of a story he liked, he would tell it over and over again.

Dana Rohrabacher, who worked as a Reagan speechwriter, was once told a secondhand, unconfirmed story about an ailing veteran who had been on disability and then, against all expectations, had recovered. The man had called the Veterans Administration to say he didn't need his disability payments anymore, only to discover that it took many days because—so the story went—nobody knew how to stop a government payment. Rohrabacher mentioned this story to the president, not in a speech draft but in casual conversation. Reagan, who loved the tale, immediately began to use it. Rohrabacher was reprimanded. "Dana, just be aware—any time during this presidency that you say something [to Reagan], you'd better make sure that it's been checked out," a White House aide told him. "Because he assumes that you're telling the truth."[11]

The speechwriters didn't need to be experts on specific areas of policy. Some of them weren't even good at spelling. Rohrabacher was famous among the speechwriters for having once rendered "Hollywood Bowl" as "Hollywood Bowel" and for having turned the phrase "fait accompli" into a kind of Greek cheese: "feta compli."[12] What counted for a speechwriter was an ability to render ideas in simple ways and in Reagan's own idiom. Several of the speechwriters came out of the conservative movement, recommended to the Reagan administration by figures such as William F. Buckley, Jr., the editor of *National Review*. They had worked on conservative political campaigns, read magazines such as *Human Events*, and were steeped in books such as Whittaker Chambers's *Witness*, his memoir about the nature of communism after working for years as a Soviet agent.

The driving force in the speechwriting office was a figure named Anthony R. (Tony) Dolan. He had been a passionate conservative since the early 1960s, when, as a parochial school student in his early teens, he had joined the Citizens Anti-Communist Committee of Connecticut. He had been a journalist, first for the *Yale Daily News* and then at the Stamford *Advocate*, where, in 1978, he won a Pulitzer Price for an investigation of organized crime in Connecticut. He had written for *National Review* and gotten to know Buckley, who served as a mentor.[13]

Dolan had watched and admired Reagan ever since the early 1960s, when he read one of Reagan's speeches for General Electric. When Reagan announced he was running for president in 1980, Dolan sought a job in the campaign. At first nothing opened up, but eventually Buckley wrote to William Casey, who was at the time managing Reagan's campaign. After Reagan won the election, Casey recommended Dolan to the White House as a speechwriter. The result was an interesting and continuing connection: Casey, the head of the CIA who fought secret wars with the Soviets around the world, and Dolan, the speechwriter who drafted some of Reagan's most important speeches about the Soviet Union.

The combative Dolan saw the Soviet leadership as akin to the mob he had investigated in small-town Connecticut: a gang of leaders ruling primarily through fear, who might topple from power if someone called their bluff and if ordinary citizens were no longer afraid. To Dolan, dealing with the Soviet Union thus amounted to a remake of the 1950s movie *On the Waterfront*. That was simplistic, but it also reflected a view that others in the Reagan administration more restrained by their jobs than Dolan, up to and including Secretary of State George Shultz, had harbored at one time or another. "Shultz's interpretation of the Soviet Union was that it was the Mafia," observed Thomas Simons, a Soviet specialist who served as deputy assistant secretary of state for Soviet affairs in the Reagan administration. "It was very personalized. He thought they were kind of thugs."[14]

It was Dolan who had drafted Reagan's Westminster speech of 1982, saying that Marxism-Leninism would someday be left on "the ash heap of history." Dolan, again, was the principal speechwriter for Reagan's 1983 speech branding the Soviet Union the "evil empire." The process of drafting these speeches and others brought Dolan and the speechwriting team into frequent conflict with centrist, nonconservative officials in the Reagan White House—notably David Gergen, who served as Reagan's communications adviser, and Richard Darman, the top aide to White House chief of staff James Baker. The battles had been particularly intense before the Westminster speech about the Soviet Union; Gergen himself had written several drafts, Dolan had submitted competing versions, and Reagan had even quietly sent drafts to conservative columnist George Will for his suggestions. The battles continued from Washington to London until the hours before the speech was delivered; in the end, Reagan gave the speech Dolan had drafted, but with substantial deletions. Dolan, undeterred, reinserted some of the deleted passages into Reagan's "evil empire" speech nine months later.

The battles were more complicated when Reagan was speaking overseas. In those cases, the drafts would have to be sent to the State Department and National Security Council for comments on the foreign-policy implications. When Reagan was appearing at an event inside the United States, these foreign-policy agencies played a lesser role, and sometimes the speechwriters could slip in lines that would have been vetoed if Reagan had been speaking abroad.

Reagan's speech calling the Soviet Union an "evil empire" was delivered inside the United States, to the National Association of Evangelicals in Florida, an audience before whom Reagan could be expected to deliver a talk with conservative themes. From the start, that address was viewed more as domestic politics than as foreign policy, and thus the line about the "evil empire" was given considerably less scrutiny than if Reagan had been appearing in London or Moscow. By contrast, officials at the State Department and the National Security Council would review the drafts of Reagan's 1987 "tear down this wall" speech over and over, phrase by phrase, word by word.

Reagan himself stayed aloof from these battles. Dolan and other speechwriters sought to put forward what they saw as Reagan's conservative values, using slogans such as "Let Reagan be Reagan." The president often supported them, but he did so from a distance. "He had worked under the Hollywood system, where there are directors and writers," reflected Dolan many years later. "In Hollywood, you can't befriend the writers too much, or else they'll get too full of their own importance."

-7-

ONE NIGHT FREE IN WEST BERLIN

On Ronald Reagan's previous presidential trip to West Berlin in 1982, he had delivered his speech in front of the Charlottenburg Palace in a pleasant, mostly residential area a couple of miles from the heart of the city and the dividing line with East Berlin. Security had been one important factor. The planners had to worry about the huge antinuclear demonstrations against Reagan, which indeed turned out to be raucous and occasionally violent.

As soon as Reagan agreed to go to West Berlin again in 1987, U.S. officials there began trying to decide where he should speak. They were looking for a location that would attract attention. John Kornblum, the U.S. minister in West Berlin, began thinking about a site that would make a bold statement, one with deep resonance in German history. The president could appear directly in front of the Brandenburg Gate.[1] The gate is Berlin's most famous landmark, the very symbol of the city itself. It was constructed in 1791 as a symbol of peace, then played a symbolic role in Germany's turbulent history, from Napoléon's conquest through the rise of Hitler.

The Brandenburg Gate was located in East Berlin in the Soviet sector about fifty yards behind the Berlin Wall. The gate had been closed to the West ever since the wall was built. For Kornblum and other American officials, that was precisely the point. An American leader couldn't go directly up to the Brandenburg Gate (at least not without fear of being shot by East German border guards). But if the speaking podium was placed correctly, Reagan could appear on television with the mammoth gate framed directly behind him, and with the wall between himself and the gate. No image could better dramatize the continuing division of Berlin, of Germany, and of Europe.

Kornblum broached with West Berlin officials the idea of Reagan's speaking before the Brandenburg Gate. They told him it was impossible; the security problems would be too great. Kornblum, who was never reluctant to assert U.S. or Allied power and sovereignty in West Berlin, reminded officials there that the Americans, British, and French were still in charge of security in the city. Despite the West German anxieties, he recommended to Washington that Reagan give his speech with the Brandenburg Gate and the Berlin Wall as the backdrop.

Early on, Ronald Reagan's White House aides had little idea of what he might say in Berlin. The new White House communications adviser, Thomas Griscom, had started his job in early March along with his own boss, White House chief of staff Howard Baker. Griscom oversaw the speechwriters. Their principal goals were to help Reagan recover from the Iran-Contra scandal and to demonstrate that he was not a lame-duck president.

Griscom knew what he did not want: this should not be simply a speech about Germany or American policy toward Germany, he believed. Griscom's initial instructions for the speech were that Reagan should not try to imitate John Kennedy's famous *"Ich bin ein Berliner"* speech of 1963. He did not want "to have Ronald Reagan up there speaking German and trying to bond with the German people," Griscom subsequently explained. "That wasn't the president's style, and it had already been done very well by Kennedy." Reagan's speech should, instead, be cast in the larger context of America's changing relations with the Soviet Union.[2]

In early April, Reagan's chief speechwriter, Tony Dolan, assigned to a thirty-year-old assistant, Peter Robinson, the job of drafting Reagan's speech. Robinson, like Dolan, owed his job to William F. Buckley. Robinson was a political conservative; his favorite college professor, Jeff Hart, had worked

with Buckley at *National Review*. After graduating from Dartmouth, Robinson had studied at Oxford and tried unsuccessfully to write a novel. In
1982, three years out of college and jobless, he wrote to Buckley for advice
or help. It turned out that Buckley's own son, Christopher, was just leaving
a speechwriting job with Vice President George Bush. Robinson went to
work for the vice president and became a Reagan speechwriter a couple of
years later.[3]

In late April 1987, as preparation for writing Reagan's speech, Robinson
went to Europe as part of a White House and Secret Service advance team
arranging the presidential trip. In West Berlin, his first stop was a discussion
with Kornblum to discuss what Reagan should say.[4]

It was a frosty conversation. Kornblum was a professional diplomat who
spent his days dealing with West German officials and the State Department
back home. He was engaged above all in a fight to maintain American and
Allied sovereignty over West Berlin and to prevent the growing rapprochement between West and East Germany from going too far. The declassified
State Department cables from this period show that Kornblum was endeavoring to make sure that Eberhard Diepgen, the mayor of West Berlin, did not
attempt to go to ceremonies in East Berlin and did not invite East Germany's
Erich Honecker to ceremonies in West Berlin.[5]

Kornblum was not a humble man. He tended to be respectful toward
those with whom he did business from day to day, but also aloof and dismis-
sive to those he considered less knowledgeable. He was not inclined toward
patience with a young conservative speechwriter from Washington, even one
who worked at the White House. In fact, Kornblum believed he had already
drafted Reagan's speech anyway, making the speechwriter's trip superfluous.
For his own part, Robinson wasn't disposed to pay homage to a State Department bureaucrat. He had been assigned by the White House the task of drafting the president's speech, and he expected it to embody Reagan's traditional
anti-Communist values, which of course meant concentrating on the Soviet
Union. He didn't want to get bogged down in the details of intra-German
diplomacy.

The entire meeting lasted only about fifteen minutes. By Robinson's subsequent account, Kornblum told him the president should stay away from the
subject of the Berlin Wall. It would be unwise for Reagan to stir up public

feelings about the divided city. Robinson said Kornblum informed him that the residents of West Berlin "had long ago gotten used to the structure that encircled them."[6]

Robinson's description is puzzling, because in fact Kornblum's own draft speech for Reagan, sent to Washington the previous month, had attacked the wall and called for it to be destroyed. ("Barriers to contact must be torn down. We should begin with the ugly wall which divides this great city.")[7] It had, moreover, contained a denunciation of "communist dictatorship." However, Kornblum had also included a series of modest policy proposals (such as holding conferences jointly in West and East Berlin) intended to make Reagan's speech sound positive and future oriented. The goal was to convey a sense of change and thus to defuse public sentiment in West Berlin for a new, more harmonious relationship with the East.

It seems likely that in his meeting with the visiting White House speechwriter, Kornblum emphasized the specific policy measures he had suggested. He may well have cautioned Robinson against focusing too much on the Berlin Wall and argued that many West Berliners had become accustomed to the reality of a divided city. It seems plausible that Robinson may have taken what Kornblum said as a warning that Reagan should not criticize the presence of the Berlin Wall. At this juncture, Robinson had no idea Kornblum had himself written a speech that called for the wall to be dismantled. He had not seen Kornblum's earlier draft and realized, correctly, that Reagan was not going to deliver a speech drafted by the State Department. Robinson left the meeting angry, deciding that in gathering ideas for Reagan's speech, a diplomat like Kornblum was going to be of no help.

Robinson had a single night free in West Berlin. He had arranged to have dinner with a few West Germans. A friend had given him the name of Dieter Elz, a former World Bank employee who had lived in Washington for many years and then retired at age sixty to West Berlin. Elz and his wife, Ingeborg, had only recently moved back from the United States and didn't know many people in the city. When Robinson asked the Elzes to invite a few West Berliners over to their home, Dieter Elz had trouble finding anyone. He finally enlisted a couple of members of the local Rotary Club and their wives.[8]

Over dinner, Robinson asked the Germans around the table about their lives in West Berlin. What did they think an American president should say during a speech in the city? Midway through the dinner, Ingeborg Elz began to talk about the Berlin Wall. Every time the Elzes sought merely to visit family in East Germany or to drive through East Germany to summer vacations in Austria, they were required to deal with the wall and its many manifestations: frightening border checkpoints, threatening East German police, car searches, transit visas that required months of advance paperwork. To be sure, in Moscow, Mikhail Gorbachev was talking about change, using words like *glasnost* and *perestroika,* but in West Berlin those slogans didn't carry much practical significance.

As Ingeborg Elz spoke, Robinson was taking notes. At one point, the White House speechwriter scrawled down these words into his notebook: "If the Russians are willing to open up, then the wall must go. Open the Brandenburg Gate."[9]

Those two sentences made the crucial connection, the one that became the core element of Reagan's speech several weeks later: the linkage between Gorbachev's reforms and the Berlin Wall. To be sure, in the past, Reagan and other American officials had called for the destruction of the wall, but this idea went one step further: it turned the wall into the litmus test for whether the Soviet Union was really changing or not.

Gorbachev's continuing talk of far-reaching change had made the concept of tearing down the wall no longer unimaginable. What Ingeborg Elz told Robinson was an idea that was already in the air. Indeed, only a few weeks earlier, the *Washington Post* had published a commentary by Dimitri K. Simes, a specialist on Soviet affairs, which carried the headline: Tearing Down the Berlin Wall: Gorbachev Has a Chance to Hit a Public Relations Home Run. If Gorbachev were to do this, Simes wrote, then "the image of the evil empire so damaging to Soviet international effectiveness would disappear overnight."[10]

It was ironic that this dinner conversation at the Elzes' home had such a lasting impact. Robinson was talking not to a cross section of the citizenry of West Berlin, but merely to six English-speaking dinner guests hastily and randomly put together by a couple who had just moved home from the United States. The Elzes had few connections to West Berlin's political or intellectual elites; they were middle-class people, conservative but not involved, prosperous but not powerful. Still, what they told Robinson reflected the attitude of many other West Berliners: that the wall was not merely a diplomatic issue, but a continuing outrage and hardship to daily life of the city.

In attending this casual dinner, Robinson was behaving less like a speechwriter than a journalist or novelist; he was gathering material. In retrospect, the results were startling. His handwritten notes of the conversation that night show that in addition to the idea of opening up the Brandenburg Gate, the dinner guests offered several other details that would eventually emerge in Reagan's speech. One of the guests suggested that the president might quote the title of a Marlene Dietrich song: *"Ich hab' noch einen Koffer in Berlin"* ("I still have a suitcase in Berlin"). Another offered him the phrase *"Berliner Schnauze,"* a slang phrase for the blunt, cheeky personality that other Germans associated with Berlin. Robinson wrote down these phrases and put them into the president's speech.

The following day, U.S. and West Berlin officials gave the White House speechwriter a tour of the city, including the Brandenburg Gate and the Reichstag building. When the group stopped at the Berlin Wall, they noticed some graffiti, including a slogan that a West German official translated for Robinson. "This wall will fall," it said. "Beliefs become reality."[11] Robinson dutifully wrote the words in his notebook. They, too, became Reagan's.

Robinson did not talk to Kornblum again. The senior U.S. diplomat in West Berlin was paying far greater attention to the head of the White House delegation: Bill Henkel, who was in charge of advance preparations for Reagan's trip. West Berlin officials, up to and including Mayor Eberhard Diepgen, were still objecting to the idea of having an American president give a speech at the Brandenburg Gate.

"We discussed what would be the best place, and that was not very simple," explained Diepgen many years later. "In that time, we had in Berlin a very special situation. On the one hand, most of the people were thankful to the Americans, friends to Americans. And on the other hand, Berlin was a concentration point for the very fundamentalistic position of people from West Germany, because all of those who didn't want to go into the army, they came to [West] Berlin." Diepgen was alluding to the West German policy of encouraging young Germans to move to West Berlin by exempting them from military service. As a result, West Berlin became the center of the political left, and its political demonstrations were particularly prone to violence, as Reagan had discovered on his previous visit to Berlin five years earlier. "It was a question of security," said Diepgen of his opposition to a speech at the Brandenburg Gate.[12]

Kornblum realized that the West Berlin mayor would not agree to the Brandenburg Gate site, but he didn't care. "We can listen to the mayor, but we're in charge here," he told Henkel. They attended a meeting with West Berlin officials, who suggested four other venues, including a convention hall and a factory. Kornblum thought they were boring. He took Henkel to visit the other sites, and then to the one in front of the Brandenburg Gate. "Look, here's how it's going to look on TV," Kornblum said.[13] Henkel was convinced. Before leaving for Washington, he chose the Brandenburg Gate site.

-8-

COMPETING DRAFTS

Back in Washington to write Reagan's Berlin speech, Peter Robinson was determined to concentrate on the Berlin Wall and the differences between totalitarianism and freedom. He tried to set down on paper what he had heard over dinner in Berlin: that the standard for judging Mikhail Gorbachev's policy of *glasnost* (political openness) in the Soviet Union was whether he would open the Berlin Wall. In an early draft of the speech, Robinson wrote: "If you truly believe in *glasnost,* Herr Gorbachev, bring down this wall." Tony Dolan, who as Reagan's chief speechwriter was Robinson's boss, liked that idea but found the speech in general to be too prosaic. He sent it back to Robinson for a rewrite, saying he could do better.[1] In the second draft, Robinson included the words "If you are sincere about *glasnost,* Herr Gorbachev, take down this wall."

On May 20, 1987, Robinson completed a draft that Dolan approved. "Behind me stands a wall that divides the entire continent of Europe," the speech said. The armed guards and the checkpoints along Europe's divide served as "an instrument to impose upon ordinary men and women the will of a totalitarian state." Robinson's new draft continued:

We hear much from Moscow about a new policy of openness and liberalization—to use the Russian term, "glasnost." Some political prisoners have been released. BBC broadcasts are no longer jammed. . . .

Are these the beginnings of profound changes in the Soviet state? Or are they token gestures, intended only to raise false hopes in the West? It is impossible to tell.

But there is one sign the Soviets can make that would be unmistakable.

General Secretary Gorbachev, if you seek peace, come to Berlin. If you seek prosperity for the Soviet Union and Eastern Europe, come to Berlin.

Come here to this wall.

Herr Gorbachev, machen Sie dieses Tor auf.[2]

The final words were the German for "open up this gate." Robinson, following the example of John Kennedy's words *"Ich bin ein Berliner,"* had tentatively decided to put the key phrase in German. Dolan scrawled the phrase "tear down this wall" back into the draft.

This passage would survive and, with minor revisions, become the core of Reagan's speech in Berlin. Yet the May 20 draft was merely the opening scene in a protracted drama. After Dolan had given his assent, the speech began to circulate through the bureaucracy in Washington. What followed over the next three weeks was an epic struggle within the Reagan administration, pitting Reagan's domestic advisers and speechwriters against his foreign-policy team.

Officials at the State Department hated what Robinson had written. It seemed to be full of old Cold War rhetoric, a return to the past, at just the time when the situation seemed to be changing in the Soviet Union. "I just thought it was in bad taste," recalled Thomas Simons, a veteran Foreign Service officer who was serving as the deputy assistant secretary of state for European affairs. Rozanne Ridgway, Simons's boss, was particularly worried about the impact of the speech, because she believed that Gorbachev's own position at the top of the Soviet leadership was fragile. Ridgway feared that hard-liners in

Moscow might seize on a tough Reagan speech as ammunition against him, arguing that it was useless for Gorbachev to try to do business with the United States. "Those of us who were aware of the fact that there was a major struggle going on inside the Soviet Union were not really persuaded that you had to keep throwing stuff at this guy in public," Ridgway said.[3]

At the time, State Department officials were trying to move toward new arms-control agreements with the Soviet Union, and they felt that a speech like the one Robinson had drafted would make things more difficult. They were instinctively suspicious of Reagan's White House speechwriters, particularly when it came to anything involving the Soviet Union. "It just struck us that every time we were going somewhere, or were going to meet with the Soviets, the speechwriters came out," Ridgway said. State Department officials were also in the midst of a diplomatic campaign in Eastern Europe, designed to see if the United States could open up some distance between their Communist governments and the Soviet Union. The speech Robinson had written depicted Eastern Europe as under Moscow's control, and in this sense, too, it threatened State Department initiatives.

State Department officials and those at Reagan's National Security Council had their own agenda for Reagan's speech, and they had been holding meetings and sending out cables in pursuit of it. They viewed Reagan's stopover in Berlin as an opportunity for a new series of steps on policy—the ones that had already been laid out in the draft speech sent by John Kornblum, the U.S. minister in West Berlin. These included changing the rules for international aviation into and out of the city, holding international conferences jointly in West and East Berlin, and staging the Olympics or some other high-level sports competition in both parts of the city. However, State Department officials had expected that the Berlin Wall would serve as merely the backdrop, rhetorically and visually, for what they formally called a Presidential Initiative on Berlin. The emphasis was to be on diplomacy, not rhetoric.

Thus, while Reagan's White House speechwriters were refining the language of an exhortation to tear down the wall, his foreign-policy team was moving in entirely different directions. National Security Council and State Department officials were consulting the British and French (the other two sovereign powers in West Berlin) about the possibilities and details of future international conferences in Berlin and future exchanges between East and

West Berlin. One State Department cable, for example, said that the United States would "like to encourage more youth exchanges at the district level between the eastern and the western parts of the city." The National Security Council composed letters for Reagan to send to British prime minister Margaret Thatcher and French president François Mitterrand, which the president signed and sent out on May 16, 1987, seeking their support.[4] Years later, it is difficult to fathom how so much effort could have been spent on such small steps.

The Berlin "initiative" led to an arcane bureaucratic struggle involving the Pentagon and the U.S. intelligence community. The aviation rules for Berlin had not changed since the late 1940s: American planes were required to fly into the city at altitudes of ten thousand feet or less, while Soviet planes were required to fly at above ten thousand feet. The rules were designed to prevent collisions, and they had worked. However, with the arrival of jet airplanes, the American companies flying into West Berlin, such as Pan American, complained that the low-altitude rules wore down their engines and required them to spend many thousands of dollars on paint for their planes. On behalf of the commercial airliners, U.S. diplomats in West Berlin had recommended an easing of the altitude limitation. However, U.S. intelligence officials and the air force balked. They argued that the low-altitude flights made it easier for them to see and photograph Soviet and East German military equipment on the ground.

The declassified archives of the Reagan administration show that on May 6, 1987, the National Security Council held a special meeting of its Policy Review Group specifically to discuss Berlin. The participants included representatives of Vice President George Bush's office, the Central Intelligence Agency, the Joint Chiefs of Staff, the Defense Department, and the State Department. The subject of that meeting was apparently to reconcile the internal disagreements within the U.S. government over the idea of changing the aviation rules for Berlin.[5]

"The fact is that when I was sitting there in Berlin, I was more worried about the air initiative than I was about this sentence" to tear down the wall, acknowledged Kornblum in an interview two decades later. "The air initiative was the key part [of Reagan's speech], from an operational point of view."[6]

Reagan's conservative speechwriters had often been at odds with his more moderate domestic and political advisers. But in 1987, Reagan's new White House team, headed by Chief of Staff Howard Baker, was nervous about a dramatic erosion of support from the right. (One conservative leader, Richard Viguerie, had written that "the symbolic end of the Reagan revolution came with the installment of Howard Baker as White House chief of staff."[7]) The result was that for a change, the White House staff was inclined to support the speechwriters.

Reagan's new White House team was also especially eager to show that he was still an active and engaged president, despite Iran-Contra. Thomas Griscom, the longtime Baker aide installed as the White House communications director, liked Robinson's speech from the moment he saw it. "There were real questions at that point about whether this presidency was over," Griscom later reflected. The passage about the Berlin Wall would attract attention, he felt. It would be a line people would remember.[8]

Griscom was inclined to endorse the fiery rhetoric of the speechwriting team in a way that such predecessors as Richard Darman and David Gergen had not been. Inside the White House, Griscom became a leading advocate of Robinson's speech, along with Dolan, the chief speechwriter. Griscom decided to make sure, early on, that the president liked the idea. He wanted to know that Reagan saw the speech, understood its implications, and was comfortable with it.[9]

The White House speechwriters conspired to get Robinson's Berlin Wall speech into Reagan's hands early, before the State Department or National Security Council had time to marshal their opposition.[10] Other speechwriters, assigned to compose what Reagan might say during other appearances on his European trip, hurried to finish their own drafts so that the entire package could be sent to Reagan quickly.

On the morning of Monday, May 18, 1987, Griscom and the White House speechwriters went to the Oval Office for a session with Reagan to plan his visit to Europe. The aides outlined the main points in their speeches. One, Josh Gilder, gave an overview of what he was writing for the president's meeting with Pope John Paul II. Eventually, it was time for the Berlin Wall speech. Robinson asked Reagan what he thought of the draft. Reagan simply said he liked it. Disappointed, the thirty-year-old speechwriter asked whether the president had any further ideas. It was possible, Robinson pointed out, that this speech might be heard over the radio throughout East Germany, or even all the way to Moscow. Was there anything in particular the president wanted to say to people in Eastern Europe? "Well, there's that passage about tearing down the wall," Reagan replied. "That wall has to come down."[11]

Reagan's seemingly casual approval was hardly surprising, at least not when phrased in that way. As recently as the previous summer, on the twenty-fifth anniversary of its construction, he had himself called for the wall to come down. He had, however, never before called upon Gorbachev to tear it down; the new wording differed from what Reagan had said before. If the president noticed this distinction, he didn't discuss it during his session with the speechwriters. But the meeting had served its purpose. Griscom left the Oval Office satisfied that Reagan not only knew about the passage on tearing down the wall, but liked it.

During the following week, State Department officials, led by Ridgway, mounted an intensive campaign against the "tear down this wall" speech. They wanted Robinson's draft to be abandoned. Instead, they argued, Reagan should deliver some version of the draft that Kornblum had sent to the State Department from Berlin.

Ridgway took her complaints to the National Security Council. It was up to officials there to try to represent the interests of American foreign policy within the Reagan administration. The NSC was responsible for reconciling intramural disputes like this one.

Reagan's new national security adviser, Frank Carlucci, who had been brought to the White House after the Iran-Contra scandal broke, quickly discovered that he hated dealing with the White House speechwriters. He turned over the task of clearing Reagan's foreign-policy speeches to his deputy, Colin Powell.[12] In the spring of 1987, Powell was also new to his job. He had previously worked as the military aide to Defense Secretary Caspar Weinberger, and he wanted to return to his career in the army. He had been commanding an army corps in West Germany when Carlucci persuaded him to come to the NSC. In Powell's very first day there, he had clashed with the speechwriters. He had questioned whether a draft speech for Reagan to deliver about the defense budget was too shrill. Tony Dolan, the chief White

House speechwriter, had launched into a "tirade," Powell later recalled in his memoir. "This was going to be an even tougher neighborhood than the Pentagon front office," Powell concluded.[13]

When the dispute erupted over plans for the Berlin Wall speech, Powell represented the interests of the State Department, passing along its objections to Griscom. In one memo, Powell's team offered instructions for how to completely rewrite the speech. The call for Gorbachev to tear down the wall was replaced with a more anodyne "It's time for the Wall to come down."[14] On May 26, Powell and the National Security Council lost the first skirmish. The issue was whether to proceed with Robinson's draft, calling upon Gorbachev to tear down the Berlin Wall, or to throw it out. Somebody—probably Griscom or his boss, Howard Baker—decided that Robinson's draft would survive.

That day, Powell sent a note to Ridgway at the State Department. Written in Powell's script on White House stationery, it said:

Roz—

Here's the working draft from the speechwriters. We are working to reinsert elements of the Kornblum version as well as our own comments.

At this point, we need to work from this draft, as opposed to a brand-new draft.

Colin[15]

Powell's final sentence was crucial. Officials at the State Department and National Security Council would not be able to kill Robinson's draft, emphasizing the Berlin Wall as a symbol of the enduring differences between Western and Eastern Europe, between freedom and communism. They could seek to revise or edit what the speechwriters had written, but it would serve as the foundation for what Reagan was going to say.

-9-

WARSAW PACT

While White House aides were still debating exactly what Ronald Reagan would say to Mikhail Gorbachev about the Berlin Wall, Gorbachev himself was by coincidence visiting Berlin. On May 27, 1987, the Soviet leader, joined by his wife, Raisa, flew to East Berlin to meet with the general secretaries of the other Communist regimes of Eastern Europe. The occasion was a regular meeting of the Warsaw Pact, the military alliance organized under Soviet leadership as a counterpart to NATO.

Gorbachev was joined in Berlin by a group of aging leaders, each of them holding absolute power within his own domain. The group photos taken by an East German newspaper show their stiffness, formality, and utter lack of humor or flexibility—men lost in a time that was passing them by more quickly than they knew or could even fear.[1] Erich Honecker from East Germany served as the host. Besides Gorbachev, the visitors included General Wojciech Jaruzelski of Poland, Todor Zhivkov of Bulgaria, János Kádár of Hungary, Gustáv Husák of Czechoslovakia, and Nicolae Ceaușescu of Romania. By day, they talked in a conference hall. One night, they attended a concert in the ornate Schauspielhaus in honor of the 750th anniversary of the city of Berlin.

In such gatherings, Gorbachev sometimes gave voice to scathing attacks on Ronald Reagan, portraying him as unsophisticated and belligerent. Subsequently, and in other settings, Gorbachev was full of praise for Reagan, but that was not what he told his Eastern European colleagues, at least not during his early years. "His assessments of Reagan at the time were totally different from the things that he said later," recalled Egon Krenz, the East German Politburo member who attended the 1987 Warsaw Pact meeting in East Berlin as a top aide to Honecker and two years later became, briefly, Honecker's successor. Krenz said Gorbachev "used to tell us that Reagan was an old man who had a simplified view of the world, who intellectually couldn't follow him."[2]

The pretense of Communist solidarity prevailed. Yet under the surface there were tensions. By mid-1987, Gorbachev was moving in new directions. After two years in office, he had come to the conclusion that he couldn't achieve his aims—reviving the Soviet economy, easing the arms race with the United States, forging a new relationship with Western Europe—unless he also carried out far-reaching reforms inside the Soviet Union. "Gorbachev was coming to the realization that our success in foreign affairs—where things seemed to gain momentum—was correlated with our domestic situation," wrote his principal foreign-policy adviser, Anatoly S. Chernyaev.[3]

Gorbachev assumed that he could accomplish these reforms under the leadership of the Communist Party, and that doing so would not jeopardize either the party or the socialist system. The goal was to breathe new life into that system by relaxing the top-down, command approach to the economy, by opening the way for dissent, and by encouraging a freer flow of information. The policy of *glasnost* (openness) took hold in the months after the nuclear disaster at Chernobyl in April 1986, which demonstrated that Soviet officials had gone to great lengths, and in dangerous ways, to conceal information. Soviet media were encouraged to become more lively and to write about problems in the Soviet Union rather than pretend they didn't exist. Gorbachev pushed for major changes in personnel too. "Chernobyl showed to Gorbachev that there was a level of officials who cheated him, who didn't tell him the truth," recalled Anatoly Adamishin, a deputy foreign minister. "So he decided to change the upper middle levels [of government]."[4]

On December 16, 1986, to dramatize the new political climate, Gorbachev allowed the Soviet Union's leading dissident, Andrei Sakharov, to return to Moscow from seven years of internal exile in the closed city of Gorky. Sakharov, the physicist who once had been in charge of Soviet development of the hydrogen bomb, was for decades a staunch advocate for freedom of speech and for demilitarization of Soviet foreign policy. At the beginning of 1987, at a meeting of the Communist Party Central Committee, Gorbachev spoke openly, though vaguely, about the possibility of choosing officials through elections with secret ballots. "Democracy is not the opposite of order," he said in one speech that winter. "It is order of a greater degree, based not on implicit obedience, mindless execution of instructions, but on full-fledged active participation by all the community in all society's affairs."[5]

Gorbachev's domestic reforms were deeply unsettling to other Communist leaders in Eastern Europe. Their own power had long been based on maintaining the same control over dissent and political opposition as the Soviet Union had established. In Prague, where the Soviet Union had sent troops to crush a brief movement toward liberalization in 1968, a mordant joke began making the rounds that perhaps it was time for Czechoslovakia to send some "fraternal assistance" to the Soviet Union.[6]

The impact of the changes in the Soviet Union hit particularly hard in East Germany, where Honecker had remained atop the Communist Party hierarchy since 1971. Other Eastern European officials paid lip service to Gorbachev's policy of *glasnost*. "What is taking place in the Soviet Union is correct, completely correct, and must fully be supported," said Vasil Bilak, the hard-line ideologist for Czechoslovakia's Communist Party.[7] By contrast, Honecker and his aides made clear that they had no intention of following down the road of *glasnost*.

In the spring of 1987, Kurt Hager, the East German Communist official in charge of culture and ideology, was asked about Gorbachev's reforms. "If your neighbor decided to repaper the walls of his house, would you feel bound to repaper your home, too?" Hager retorted.[8] Honecker's regime moved to censor the coverage in the East German press of developments inside the Soviet Union. Frank Herold, who served from 1984 to 1988 as the Moscow

East German soldiers building the Berlin Wall in 1961. East German leader Erich Honecker, who had personally supervised its construction, predicted in early 1989 that it would still be standing "in 100 years."

(© Robert Lackenbach/Getty Images)

Richard Nixon and Ronald Reagan at the Rose Bowl on New Year's Day, 1969. Nixon had viewed Reagan as a rival for the Republican presidential nomination in 1968. Between them, the two men played leading roles in eight of the ten presidential elections from 1948 to 1984, the period at the heart of the Cold War. (© Bettmann/CORBIS)

Soviet leader Leonid Brezhnev at a party at Nixon's San Clemente home in 1973. Reagan, then governor of California, attended the party. It was the only time he met a top Soviet leader before he became president.

(© Wally McNamee/CORBIS)

Secretary of State Henry Kissinger with President Gerald Ford. Reagan had supported Nixon's foreign policy but when he ran against Ford for the Republican nomination in 1976, he promised to fire Kissinger.

(© Bettmann/CORBIS)

Reagan speaking to the National Association of Evangelicals in 1983. It was in this speech that Reagan branded the Soviet Union an "evil empire." He later said he gave the speech "with malice aforethought."

(Courtesy Ronald Reagan Library)

Reagan brought in Secretary of State George Shultz to replace Alexander Haig in 1982, and in Reagan's final years in office, Shultz became the dominant figure on Soviet policy. Richard Nixon belittled him, but Gorbachev fulsomely praised him as a statesman and an intellectual. (Courtesy Ronald Reagan Library)

Author Suzanne Massie with Ronald Reagan in the Oval Office. After meeting her in 1984, Reagan invited Massie back to the White House again and again to talk about life in the Soviet Union. She also quietly carried unofficial messages to and from Moscow. (Courtesy Ronald Reagan Library)

Radomir Bogdanov, a KGB veteran who served as deputy director of a leading policy institute in Moscow. He met regularly with Suzanne Massie on her visits to the Soviet Union. (© David Rubinger/Getty Images)

Ronald Reagan with his speechwriters. It was at this particular meeting, on May 18, 1987, that Reagan and his aides discussed what Reagan would say on his visit to Berlin. (Courtesy Ronald Reagan Library)

John Kornblum, the U.S. minister in West Berlin, who helped arrange for Reagan to speak at the Brandenburg Gate.

(© Scott J. Ferrell/Getty Images)

Rozanne Ridgway, the assistant secretary of state in charge of Soviet policy. She battled with the White House speechwriters over Reagan's Berlin Wall speech, arguing that it might undercut Gorbachev's position in the Soviet leadership. (© Terry Ashe/Getty Images)

Reagan and Nixon at their secret White House meeting on April 27, 1987. Reagan sought Nixon's support for his overtures to Gorbachev. Nixon refused to go along. (Courtesy Frank Carlucci)

Mikhail Gorbachev (center) with the Communist Party leaders of Eastern Europe at a 1987 Warsaw Pact meeting in East Berlin. From left to right: Gustáv Husák of Czechoslovakia; Todor Zhivkov of Bulgaria; Erich Honecker of East Germany; Gorbachev; Nicolae Ceauşescu of Romania; Wojciech Jaruzelski of Poland; and János Kádár of Hungary. (Bundesarchiv, Bild 183-1987-0529-029, Fotograf: Rainer Mittelstädt)

Ronald Reagan speaking at the Brandenburg Gate, June 12, 1987. (Courtesy Ronald Reagan Library)

East Germany's Communist Party leader Erich Honecker (center) with West German chancellor Helmut Kohl during Honecker's visit to Bonn in September 1987. (© Robert Maass/CORBIS)

Egon Krenz, Honecker's protégé, who succeeded him in October 1989, and was in charge on the night the Berlin Wall was opened.

(Courtesy Caroline Dexter)

Colin Powell was Reagan's sixth and final national security adviser. Powell served in that job during Reagan's summits with Gorbachev in Washington and in Moscow. (Courtesy Ronald Reagan Library)

Asked whether he was worried that Gorbachev was too charismatic and might upstage him, Reagan quipped, "Good Lord, I costarred with Errol Flynn once." (The movie was *Santa Fe Trail* in 1940.) (© Bettmann/CORBIS)

Reagan and Gorbachev at the summit in Washington, December 1987. (© Diana Walker/Getty Images)

At the time Reagan signed the Intermediate Nuclear Forces (INF) Treaty in 1987, most of the Democratic presidential candidates supported him, and most of the Republican candidates were opposed. In this cartoon, Reagan is surrounded by Democrats Richard Gephardt, Paul Simon, Jesse Jackson, Michael Dukakis, Al Gore, and Bruce Babbitt. (© Tribune Media Services, Inc. All Rights Reserved. Reprinted with permission.)

Reagan and Gorbachev in Red Square at the Moscow summit, May 1988. When asked whether he still considered the Soviet Union an evil empire, Reagan replied, "I was talking about another time and another era." (Courtesy Ronald Reagan Library)

George H. W. Bush with his vice-presidential nominee, Dan Quayle, at the 1988 Republican National Convention. Quayle had been among the conservative senators challenging Reagan's INF Treaty. That summer, Bush said he was worried about Reagan's sentimentality toward Gorbachev and complained that Reagan and Shultz were pushing too hard for further arms control with Moscow. (© Shepard Sherbell/CORBIS)

Tearing down the Berlin Wall, November 9–10, 1989. Krenz said that on the night it happened, he tried to call Gorbachev to ask what he should do, but he couldn't get the call through. (© Jacques Langevin/CORBIS)

correspondent for the East German Communist Party organ *Neues Deutschland*, later recalled that in his last two years there, he was barred from reporting about what was happening in political and intellectual life, because the subjects were too sensitive and too threatening to Honecker's regime. "I only covered science, sports and fine arts, no politics at all," Herold said.[9]

For ordinary East Germans, it was especially demoralizing to see that even the Soviet Union was opening up, while their own government was not. Even though they could not read about Gorbachev's reforms in East German newspapers, they could hear the reports about them from other sources, such as West German, British, and American radio stations. "Gorbachev had a very strong echo within the East German population," recalled Bettina Urbanski, who in 1987 was serving as the editor in charge of socialist countries for the East Berlin newspaper *Berliner Zeitung.* "The more he moved towards reform, the more restrictive the [East German] government became, both internally and externally in insisting on the wall."[10] Lothar de Maizière, the attorney and Lutheran Church leader who would briefly serve as East Germany's prime minister after the fall of the wall, said he felt that the turning point in East Germany's collapse came in 1986 and 1987. "It was clear Honecker was not going to follow Gorbachev," Maizière said. "At the time, I was active in the Protestant Church, and we were trying to keep people from leaving the country, telling them they could help bring about change. But people didn't believe it any more."[11]

At the meeting in East Berlin, Gorbachev unveiled another significant change to the Eastern European leaders. This one concerned not domestic policy but military doctrine. The Warsaw Pact, it was announced, would henceforth be considered a strictly defensive alliance. Its members would never start a war or strike first with nuclear weapons. They had no territorial ambitions in or out of Europe. Warsaw Pact nations "do not regard any individual government or group of people as their enemy," they declared in a written statement that was released on May 28, 1987.[12] For Eastern European leaders such as Honecker, this new doctrine meant that they were less able than in the past to justify repressive policies at home. How could they justify a hard line on the basis of an external threat if there was no longer an enemy?

The change in military doctrine was aimed at demonstrating to the world—above all, to Western Europe—that the Soviet Union should no longer be considered threatening. Gorbachev had decided to concentrate on Europe. "It's obvious that not a single issue can be decided without Europe," he had told his aides in the spring of 1987. "We even need it for our domestic affairs, for *perestroika* [his term for restructuring Soviet society]. And in foreign policy Europe is simply irreplaceable. Theirs is the strongest bourgeoisie, not only economically, but politically, too."[13]

These changes in the nature of the Warsaw Pact were made public at the time. Western officials and Soviet specialists quickly recognized their considerable significance. Yet Gorbachev didn't stop there. Behind closed doors in Berlin, he first broached the idea that the Soviet Union would not send its forces into Eastern Europe to preserve their fraternal Communist Party regimes, as it had in Hungary in 1956 and in Czechoslovakia in 1968. Leaders such as Honecker could no longer rely on Soviet military intervention to save them if they could not hold things together on their own. American intelligence agencies did not learn about this aspect of the Warsaw Pact gathering until several years later. It turned out to be an important step toward ending the Cold War.[14]

When Gorbachev had become Communist Party leader, Soviet military leaders had supported his drive for change, hoping that economic reforms could help upgrade military technology, which they realized had fallen further and further behind the West. But by 1987, Gorbachev had realized that he couldn't effect serious change in the Soviet Union if he left the military untouched. "Gorbachev's dilemma was that he could not avoid impinging on the military's prerogatives if he was to revitalize the economy, nor could he avoid a change in Soviet military doctrine if he was to relieve international tension so as to permit more attention to domestic reform," observed Jack Matlock, who spoke regularly to Gorbachev after arriving as the American ambassador to Moscow in 1987.[15]

Gorbachev began to clash with the generals and the defense ministry over such issues as military spending and his arms-control negotiations with the Reagan administration. "Our military command as well as some members of the political leadership were decidedly unhappy about Gorbachev's zeal in making deep concessions in order to achieve agreements with Washington," wrote Anatoly Dobrynin, the longtime Soviet ambassador to Washington, who had returned to Moscow in 1986.[16]

There were also signs that Soviet military leaders were displeased with the doctrinal change from an offensive to a defense military strategy. Less than two weeks before the new doctrine was announced in East Berlin, Soviet military leaders gave a preview of it to the military chiefs of staff of other Eastern European nations at a session in Moscow. While explaining what Gorbachev had decided, Soviet defense minister Sergei Sokolov was careful to add that "the only way to definitively crush an aggressor is by executing decisive attacks." Because NATO forces were continuing to modernize their forces and upgrade their technology, Sokolov said, "we cannot under any circumstances agree to unilateral reductions."[17] Those words seemed aimed at Gorbachev.

In the midst of the Warsaw Pact meeting, during Gorbachev's second day in East Berlin, he and the rest of the world were stunned by an event no one would have believed possible. A nineteen-year-old West German bank trainee named Mathias Rust, pursuing a vague, self-appointed mission for "world peace," flew a single-engine Cessna plane from Helsinki to Moscow, landed the plane on a bridge a short distance from Red Square, and then taxied to a stop between St. Basil's Cathedral and the Kremlin. Soviet air-defense forces had picked up the flight on radar but did not want to shoot it down for fear of another incident like the Korean Airlines disaster of 1983. Instead, they allowed the plane to fly unimpeded at low altitude for nearly five hours across four hundred miles of Soviet territory, never forcing it to land, never reaching a decision whether it might be a flock of birds or some sort of aircraft. Once in Moscow, Rust stepped out of the plane and asked to be taken to Gorbachev.[18]

The Soviet leader was furious at his generals. In East Berlin, he quickly briefed the Warsaw Pact, promising that he would take "severe measures against those who were responsible for the fiasco. This is even worse than Chernobyl," Gorbachev told them. "This is a major embarrassment." The Eastern European leaders were dismayed. "It is a very serious matter, if it is possible to fly that far without being seen or stopped," warned Honecker, who had built his career and, indeed, his entire regime on the ability to make sure that border guards were watchful and willing to shoot. "From the point of view of the system on duty, this is absolutely incredible!"[19]

Back in Moscow, Gorbachev seized upon the incident as reason to shake up his military command. The defense ministry and the generals were suddenly the subject of jokes and derision, undercutting their usual prestige in the Soviet Union. At a hastily called Politburo meeting, Gorbachev turned to Sergei Sokolov and said, "Under the present circumstances, I would resign at once." Sokolov did, and Gorbachev proceeded to replace about a hundred other generals and colonels, most of them conservative military leaders who had opposed his reforms.[20] "This will put an end to gossip about the military's opposition to Gorbachev, that he's afraid of them, and they're close to ousting him," Gorbachev told Anatoly Chernyaev, his foreign-policy adviser.[21]

Gorbachev's shakeups had profound implications not just for the Soviet Union but for Eastern Europe as well. His domestic reforms—his loosening of press controls and talk of elections—undermined the foundations of Communist Party rule. Gorbachev believed at the time that his own Soviet Communist Party could carry out democratization and still maintain control, but Eastern European leaders were under no such illusions. The new Warsaw Pact strategy based on defense rather than offense seemed to presage a more limited role for their armed forces. When Gorbachev replaced the top leaders of the Soviet military, he strengthened his own hand in pursuing arms-control negotiations and a new relaxation of tensions with the West. While Ronald Reagan's advisers were wrestling with how to call upon Mikhail Gorbachev to tear down the Berlin Wall, Gorbachev was beginning to create the relaxed climate in which the wall would eventually be torn down.

-10-

"I THINK WE'LL LEAVE IT IN"

Even after Ronald Reagan had discussed the Berlin Wall speech with Griscom and his speechwriters in the Oval Office, the foreign-policy team was still trying to keep the text away from the president. Fearing that Reagan would like and approve Robinson's draft, officials at the State Department and National Security Council resorted to delaying tactics. On May 27, Grant Green, an official at the NSC, wrote to one of Reagan's administrative aides:

> *We understand that consideration is being given to forwarding the Brandenburg Address to the President this evening or first thing tomorrow. . . .*
>
> *In reviewing the revised draft it is clear that serious differences still remain. We have only had a short time to review the revised draft. . . . We do not concur with the speech being forwarded to the President in its current form.*[1]

From the State Department, Rozanne Ridgway, the assistant secretary for Europe, continued to tell the White House she disliked the entire thrust of Robinson's Berlin Wall speech. In a memo to Colin Powell, the deputy national security adviser, Ridgway explained:

> *The draft emphasizes historical systemic conflicts and East-West differences. We prefer to be more forward-looking, emphasizing overcoming barriers, the tasks before us, and areas where progress might be made. The West Germans, who are working to develop a fragile dialogue with the East, have expressed concern to us on several occasions that the President's speech not condemn the East too harshly.*[2]

Powell assigned to an experienced NSC staff aide, Peter W. Rodman, the task of rewriting and contesting Robinson's speech line by line. During the Nixon and Ford administrations, Rodman had served as an aide to Henry Kissinger; the two men were sufficiently close that Rodman later helped write Kissinger's memoirs. He had thus been closely involved in the policy of détente with the Soviet Union that Reagan had opposed. Rodman nevertheless viewed himself as a conservative. He saw no contradiction in working first for Kissinger and then for Reagan. (He would later serve as a Pentagon official in the George W. Bush administration.)

In Rodman's view, the détente policies of Nixon and Kissinger had been designed to preserve America's position overseas and to outflank the political left amid the turmoil of the Vietnam War, at a time when a Democratic Congress was moving to bring American troops home. Rodman believed that in the changed political climate of the 1980s, Reagan, by virtue of his popularity, was able to succeed on some issues (such as, for example, Angola) where Kissinger had been unable to win public or congressional support.[3] Despite this effort to minimize the philosophical differences between realists and conservatives, however, Rodman tended to be skeptical of Reagan's young anti-Communist speechwriters, who knew less than he did about the details and history of various foreign-policy disputes.

Throughout late May of 1987, Rodman served as the point man for the National Security Council and State Department as they sought again and again to revise the Berlin Wall speech. State and the NSC had already been defeated in their attempt to throw out Robinson's draft in its entirety. They next tried to edit the speech, suggesting major changes in some passages and attempting to delete others.

The objections covered everything from broad policy to the most arcane details. On behalf of the State Department, Rodman tried to take out the allusion to Marlene Dietrich's song *"Ich hab' noch einen Koffer in Berlin"* ("I still have a suitcase in Berlin"), which Robinson had picked up at his dinner in West Berlin. Rodman said the line had "the wrong tone—nostalgia and abandonment, not commitment." State Department officials added that this was an old German song not particularly identified with Dietrich anyway. In a Solomonic compromise, the line stayed in, but not Dietrich: in his actual speech, Reagan attributed the song to its German composer, Paul Lincke.

Some of Rodman's suggestions were accepted. The early versions of the speech included the line "General Secretary Gorbachev, if you seek peace, come to Berlin." (Those words evoked John F. Kennedy's 1963 speech: "There are some who say, in Europe and elsewhere, we can work with the Communists. *Let them come to Berlin.*") But in his critique, Rodman argued that it would be silly for Reagan to utter these words, because by the time of the president's speech, Gorbachev would in fact have recently attended the Warsaw Pact meetings in Berlin and would have just departed. Was Reagan supposed to tell Gorbachev to come *back* to Berlin? This became too confusing, and the line vanished.[4]

Among the deletions Rodman sought was the line calling upon Gorbachev to tear down the Berlin Wall. In Rodman's editing of a draft of the speech dated May 27, 1987, the entire four-paragraph passage about demolishing the wall is crossed out with a big X.

Rodman had the support of senior officials. On June 1, Powell wrote a short note saying that "we (and the State Department) continue to have serious problems with this speech. . . . We still believe that some important thematic passages (e.g., pp. 6–7) are wrong." At the very top of page 6, the first sentence read: "Mr. Gorbachev, tear down this wall!"[5]

This was not merely a war of memos. In late May, the top officials of Ronald Reagan's foreign-policy team spent time on the phone and in meetings attempting to change the speech—in particular, to remove the words "Mr. Gorbachev, tear down this wall." At first, they directed their lobbying campaign at Thomas Griscom, the White House official responsible for overseeing the speechwriters. At one point, Robinson was summoned to Griscom's office, where he found Colin Powell waiting for him. Powell said he didn't like the tone of the speech.

Robinson defended what he had written, and Griscom supported his speechwriter. Reagan himself had already seen, recited, and felt comfortable with the line about tearing down the wall, Griscom pointed out. In an interview two decades later, Powell explained that he had merely been doing his job to pass along the objections of the State Department. The "fantastic" line about tearing down the Berlin Wall remained in the speech, Powell noted, "and the State Department said, 'Uh oh, this could be trouble.' I think the secretary of state had reservations that we might be putting our finger in Gorbachev's eye, while we were trying to build a relationship with him."[6]

A few days after the Powell meeting, the dispute was elevated to the very highest level of the Reagan administration. White House chief of staff Howard Baker called Griscom into his West Wing office for a session with Secretary of State George Shultz. The secretary said he had problems with the Berlin speech. He was concerned that if Reagan delivered the line urging Gorbachev to tear down the wall, it could set back the progress that had been made so far in improving relations between the United States and the Soviet Union. Indeed, such a speech might even jeopardize Gorbachev's position and the domestic reforms he was carrying out. (Shultz, in an interview for this book, said he did not recall making such an argument. "I can't imagine anyone objecting to him making that statement, 'Mr. Gorbachev, tear down that wall,'" Shultz said.)[7]

Griscom responded that "Mr. Gorbachev, tear down this wall" was the best line in the whole speech. "That is the sound bite that everyone is going to grab," he told Shultz and Baker. This would be one of the president's final trips to Europe, and the Berlin speech represented an opportunity for him to say something memorable, he argued. Moreover, Griscom pointed out, the line about the wall did not really represent any significant change in American foreign policy. The United States had always taken the position that the Berlin Wall should be torn down.

Baker was not persuaded. In the end, the decision went back to the president. Baker's deputy, Kenneth Duberstein, informed Reagan in the Oval Office that there had been a dispute within his administration over the words "Mr. Gorbachev, tear down this wall." Duberstein said that he thought it was a great line, but that the State Department strongly objected on grounds that it might be too inflammatory. Reagan asked Duberstein if he agreed. The White House aide gave no direct answer. You're the president, he said. You get to decide. Reagan looked down at his desk, looked back up, and said, "I think we'll leave it in."[8]

-11-

ROCK CONCERT

The battles over what Reagan would say in Berlin continued even as he departed for Europe. At 8:45 a.m. on June 3, 1987, the president and his wife left the White House by helicopter for Andrews Air Force Base, where they boarded Air Force One for Venice. Reagan was by then seventy-six years old and traveling less and less; this was the first time he had left the continental United States since the summit in Reykjavik nearly eight months earlier.

That same morning, officials at his National Security Council gathered in the Situation Room of the White House, the place where senior officials try to resolve foreign-policy crises. They were trying one more time to win approval for changes in Reagan's Berlin speech:

June 3, 1987

Memorandum For Colin L. Powell
From: Peter W. Rodman
Subject: Presidential Address: Brandenburg Gate

Attached is a redo of the Berlin speech, reflecting our meeting in the
Sit Room this morning. . . . You indicated you planned to call Tom
Griscom about it.[1]

This time, Reagan's foreign-policy advisers complained about several passages in the speech that depicted life in West Berlin. In the speechwriters'
draft, the president was supposed to praise the economic advances made there
in the four decades since World War II: "Where there was want, today there
is abundance—food, clothing, automobiles, the wonderful goods of the Ku-
damm [the Kurfurstensdamm, West Berlin's main shopping street]; even
home computers."

Rodman crossed out the words *food, clothing* and the rest of the sentence that
followed. "Patronizing as well as materialistic," he commented.

The foreign-policy team also attempted to cut a passage that asked residents of West Berlin why they continued to live in the city, despite its isolation inside East German surroundings, the history of the threatening Soviet
blockade, and the grim presence of the wall. "What keeps you here?" the
speech asked. It suggested that West Berliners had a way of life "that stub-
bornly refuses to abandon this good and proud city to a surrounding presence
that is merely brutish."

Officials at the State Department and the National Security Council
warned that Reagan should not ask the people of West Berlin why they stayed
there. Those words were too negative in tone, they argued. In fact, some
people lived in West Berlin for self-interested reasons: because it was among
the most subsidized cities in Europe, or because residence there won them
an exemption from the military draft to which other West Germans were
subject.

In another proposed revision, Rodman crossed out the passage asking
why people lived in West Berlin. The sentence referring to East Germany as
"merely brutish" was further highlighted. "This <u>must</u> come out," wrote Rodman. "West Germans do <u>not</u> want to see East Germans insulted."[2]

This last challenge by Reagan's foreign-policy team failed. The passage
about the food, clothing, and cars of West Berlin stayed in the speech. What
words could better have illustrated, to ordinary Berliners, the difference be-

tween the two economic systems? The line denouncing East Germany as "brutish" was not merely kept but strengthened. In the speech Reagan ultimately delivered, he referred to East Germany as "a surrounding totalitarian presence that refuses to release human energies or aspirations."

In short, Reagan's foreign-policy advisers wanted the speech to be about tangible diplomacy, not about political freedom. They wanted the speech to smooth over the differences between East and West. They were eager to do business with Gorbachev and afraid—far too concerned, as it turned out—that the Soviet leadership might react to Reagan's tough speech by refusing to negotiate with the United States. They failed to recognize how eager, if not desperate, Gorbachev was to work out agreements that would limit Soviet military spending. They did not see the extent to which the United States held an increasingly strong position in dealing with Moscow.

In addition, Reagan's foreign-policy team worried about the impact of the speech in West Germany and West Berlin. True, ordinary West Germans wanted no part of the East German system: its omnipresent Stasi security apparatus and stilted economy. Yet State Department and National Security Council officials did not want Reagan to deliver a confrontational speech at a time when the political and intellectual elites in West Berlin and in West Germany seemed eager to overcome the Cold War rhetoric of the past.

The very idea of a Reagan speech in front of the Brandenburg Gate made some West German officials extremely nervous. They didn't want the speech to be given—not there, not in front of the Berlin Wall. And so, in the weeks before Reagan's speech, there was one more test of wills over the speech—not in Washington but in West Berlin.

When Ronald Reagan's advance team had first decided in April that the president should speak in front of the Brandenburg Gate, officials in West Berlin objected. The site, they argued, was too sensitive: provocative and laden with emotion. It would be too difficult to protect the president. West Berlin mayor Eberhard Diepgen, then in the process of trying to reduce tensions with East Berlin and other West Berlin officials even worried aloud that the East Germans would somehow intervene to prevent Reagan from speaking in front of the wall.[3] They suggested that Reagan might instead speak at the Reichstag, which carried historical significance yet did not symbolize the Cold War in the same way as the Berlin Wall did. American officials, invoking their legal authority, decided to disregard the German complaints. Under the framework established after World War II, the United States, Britain, and France were still sovereign powers in their parts of the city.

In the final weeks before Reagan's visit, the uneasiness in West Germany about his speech, and the location for it, became so intense that the issue reached German chancellor Helmut Kohl. Foreign Minister Hans-Dietrich Genscher argued that the event could anger Gorbachev and create new tensions with the Soviet Union. "The general climate of opinion was, 'What a fool President Reagan is, he is making life miserable for us, he is alienating Mikhail Gorbachev,'" recalled Walter Ischinger, who was then serving in Bonn as an aide to Genscher. "1987 was a time when we were making bilateral efforts to improve relations with East Germany and with Honecker. So our attitude was, 'Oh, no, here comes Ronald Reagan with his hammer.'"[4]

Kohl was far more willing to support the American president than was his foreign minister. His own outlook was far closer to Reagan's. The German chancellor had himself called in public for the destruction of the Berlin Wall. On April 30, 1987, when the formal ceremonies opened in West Berlin for the celebration of the city's 750th anniversary, Kohl had told the audience, "There can be no talk of normality as long as a wall and barbed wire divide this city, our fatherland and thereby Europe."[5]

During the previous years, Reagan had gone out of his way to establish a personal relationship with Kohl and to do favors for him. On a visit to West Germany in May 1985, he had taken part with Kohl in ceremonies at the military cemetery at Bitburg, despite the revelation that it included the graves of members of the Waffen-SS, the military arm of Heinrich Himmler's Nazi police guard. The plan to visit Bitburg had touched off a wave of protests in the United States, and several of Reagan's top aides, including Secretary of State George Shultz, had urged him not to go. But the German chancellor had made an impassioned personal appeal, saying that "President Reagan could go to Bitburg, or he could cancel and see the Kohl government fall."[6]

Reagan had supported Kohl back then, and now, two years later, the German chancellor was willing to go along with a Reagan speech at the Brandenburg Gate. "We had a struggle within our government, because Genscher was a little concerned that this could be a kind of confrontation," recalled Horst

Teltschik, who was Kohl's principal adviser for foreign policy. "The problem was, is it the right time to do that. And well, in the end, the chancellor decided it was okay. I told the chancellor, 'Look, this is our strongest ally.'"[7]

West Berlin officials tried to forestall a speech at the Berlin Wall by raising new security problems. Reagan's White House planners had said they wanted an audience of roughly forty thousand people, but Diepgen's aides said it would not be feasible to have so large a crowd. There would of course have to be security checks on those who were coming to see the U.S. president, and the West Berlin government didn't have the time or personnel necessary to check so many people.

American officials once again overrode the objections from Diepgen's government. They decided to round up a crowd for Reagan on their own from the American community in West Berlin and from leading German employers. "We went to all the big companies here, and we said we want to invite all your people to see the president," said John Kornblum, the head of the U.S. diplomatic mission in West Berlin. "You give us your employment rolls, and we'll run them through the police computer." The United States and its allies retained direct control over the West Berlin police department. Over a period of several days, American officials took the lists of approximately sixty thousand workers at German companies and ran them one by one through computers inside the U.S. mission, checking their dates of birth and police records to make sure that no impostors or troublemakers were on the list. Everyone who was cleared was given a ticket and was told to bring a photo identification card to the event.[8]

When U.S. Secret Service officials arrived in West Berlin, they had their own security questions. What if someone in East Berlin—say, a representative of East Germany's Ministry of State Security, known as the Stasi—tried to take a shot at the American president? U.S. officials decided to erect a huge bulletproof screen behind the podium where Reagan would speak.

In the end, the Americans were so worried about security for Reagan that they resorted to an extraordinary measure, one tinged with irony. In order to lay the groundwork for Reagan's anti-Soviet speech, the United States sought the quiet help and cooperation of the Soviet Union.

On June 9, 1987, an American diplomat paid a visit to the spacious embassy of the Soviet Union along Unter den Linden in East Berlin, a few hundred yards from the Brandenburg Gate. He asked for Soviet cooperation in making sure that Reagan's trip went smoothly. According to Egon Krenz, the Politburo member then in charge of security for East Germany's Communist regime, this American official gave the Soviets all the detailed logistics for the American president's movements in West Berlin: Reagan would travel from Schloss Bellevue to the Reichstag, he would step out on the balcony of the Reichstag, and he would give a speech before the Brandenburg Gate that would be twenty minutes long. On the day before Reagan's arrival, the entire Tiergarten section of West Berlin near the site of the speech would be closed, while U.S. and West German security officials scoured the area, up close to the Berlin Wall, to look for weapons or explosives. During the event at the Reichstag and during Reagan's speech at the Brandenburg Gate, sharpshooters would be positioned on the roof of the Reichstag, armed with submachine guns, scanning the full 360-degree perimeter. U.S. officials also informed the Soviet embassy that loudspeakers would be used to amplify Reagan's speech at the Brandenburg Gate. It was possible, they said, that the speech might be audible on the East German side of the Wall.[9]

Soviets officials passed along these details to Krenz, ordering East German security officials to make sure there would be no problems during Reagan's visit. Krenz thought it was revealing that the United States had gone to the Soviet Union for help. It was just another sign that the Soviets were still in charge of East Berlin, just as the Americans, British, and French were the ultimate authorities in West Berlin.[10]

For East German officials, the meeting between the Americans and the Soviets raised another set of anxieties. Their regime, the German Democratic Republic, had no popular legitimacy; it depended on Soviet support and Soviet troops. What would happen if the Soviet Union altered course? That prospect no longer seemed so far-fetched. Gorbachev was not only easing controls on dissent at home, but he was also seeking to transform the Soviet Union's relationship with the West. He was even making changes in the Warsaw Pact, the military alliance on which East Germany depended for its security. Was it possible that the two superpowers could work out some deal, some accommodation, that would undermine the East German government of Erich Honecker?

Curiously, the conclusions Krenz reached in East Berlin ran parallel to some of the views of Germans on the other side of the Berlin Wall. Diepgen, West Berlin's mayor, was also extremely mistrustful of the two superpowers; he, too, feared that the United States and the Soviet Union might be working together, even conspiring, against the Germans.

Diepgen had been frustrated in his attempts to take part in ceremonies in East Berlin and to have Honecker cross through the wall to an event in the Western part of the city to commemorate the 750th birthday of the city of Berlin. The Reagan administration had made plain its opposition to Diepgen's going to East Berlin, and the Soviet Union rejected the idea of Honecker's going to West Berlin. "I have no proof, but it seemed as though the Russians and the United States didn't want this," reflected Diepgen two decades later.[11] Many others in West Germany had similar views. After Honecker had formally rejected Diepgen's invitation for an exchange of visits, the U.S. mission in West Berlin cabled Washington: "It seems likely to us that this episode will strengthen the belief of many here . . . that it is powerful foreigners, and not Germans, East or West, who call the shots on German soil."[12]

Diepgen and Krenz had different goals and interests. As West Berlin's mayor, Diepgen was seeking a reconciliation with the East Germans that could somehow overcome the divisions of the Berlin Wall. In the East, Krenz was attempting merely to preserve the tight control of the East German government on its own side of the wall. West German officials were hoping that Gorbachev represented the beginning of fundamental changes in Moscow. The East German leadership was hoping for the reverse, that Gorbachev would preserve the status quo.

Nevertheless, in their shared mistrust of collaboration between Washington and Moscow, both Diepgen and Krenz were reflecting a point of view, a submerged German nationalism, that was common in the mid- to late-1980s. Ronald Reagan viewed the Cold War as an economic and ideological conflict between the United States and the Soviet Union. Yet in Berlin, there were quite a few Germans who saw the Cold War also as a struggle against a world dominated by the two superpowers.

———

None of these leaders, whether in the West or in the East, anticipated what would happen in the streets of Berlin during the week before Ronald Reagan's arrival. Suddenly, politicians on both sides were presented by the uncomforting reality that pop culture operates with its own dynamics, its own diplomacy.

It was early June, the time of year when Berlin begins a run of glorious cool summer weather. On the evening of Saturday, June 6, 1987, tens of thousands of young residents of West Berlin thronged outside the Reichstag building, about two hundred yards from the Berlin Wall, to hear the first of three nights of open-air rock concerts with star British performers. The headliner for the first night was David Bowie; he was to be followed on Sunday night by the Eurythmics ("Sweet Dreams Are Made of This") and on Monday by Phil Collins and Genesis. RIAS (Radio in the American Sector), the West Berlin radio station started under the American occupation, had been promoting the Reichstag rock concerts for weeks, and these radio broadcasts could be heard in East Berlin. On the night of the first concert, the loudspeakers were turned toward the Berlin Wall, so that Bowie and his guitar could be heard on the other side.

In East Berlin, at least a thousand young people gathered near the Friedrichstrasse train station hoping to catch the sounds. About two hundred East German police appeared, put up a big metal fence blocking anyone from getting too close to the Berlin Wall, and told the crowds to go home. Shortly after midnight, the East German youths began throwing bottles and stones at the police.

On the second night, about three thousand East Germans gathered again on their side of the Berlin Wall to catch the sounds of the Eurythmics concert. Again, East German police put up a temporary metal fence to keep them away. This time, some of the East German youths tore through the fence and began skirmishing with the police. They began shouting slogans: "Down with the wall" and "The wall must go." Police chased them down Unter Den Linden, East Berlin's main boulevard, which ran down to the Brandenburg Gate and, behind it, the wall.

On the final night, the violence escalated. About a thousand East German police with batons charged into a crowd of about four thousand East

Germans who had gathered to hear the Genesis concert. Some protesters were beaten, dragged away, and put into police vans. By the third night, the East German protesters had a new series of songs and rallying cries. Some of them were singing "The Internationale," the Socialist anthem. Others chanted, "We want freedom." Still others gave voice to the most surprising and novel slogan of all: The young East Germans shouted, "Gorbachev! Gorbachev!"[13]

The demonstrations did not spread. They were not comparable to the massive uprising by workers that had threatened the East German regime in 1953. Yet there had been no unrest of any kind in East Germany for more than a decade. Witnesses said some of the youths at the rock concert seemed to be merely intoxicated. Nevertheless, the three nights of skirmishes over the rock concert demonstrated again the continuing, underlying discontent among ordinary East Germans with the Berlin Wall and with their own government. West German political leaders might be prepared to accept, for pragmatic reasons, the presence of the wall as an enduring if unpleasant fact of life in the city. Many East Germans were not.

In their chants of "Gorbachev, Gorbachev," the protesters gave voice to the hopes that the Soviet leader was inspiring in East Germany. They exposed the tensions between the Soviet Union and Honecker's East German regime, which was rejecting Gorbachev's drive for *glasnost*. The differences between the Soviet and East German governments were illustrated by their separate reactions to what had happened at the rock concert.

Soviet Foreign Ministry spokesman Boris Pyadyshev was asked about the nights of upheaval in East Berlin. "In shouting, 'Gorbachev, Gorbachev,' we're not in the least annoyed by that," he answered. "We can only be pleased with that." By contrast, East German officials at first denied there had been any incidents at all and later suggested they were the result of a "provocation" by West Germany.[14]

Because Reagan was to arrive in Berlin within days, the East German demonstrations were unsettling to American diplomats. Many of them recalled the disastrous events of 1956, when Radio Free Europe, the American radio station funded by the Central Intelligence Agency, broadcast encouragement for the Hungarian revolution. Hungarians taking to the streets were given the false impression that the Eisenhower administration might intervene on their behalf. Instead, the United States took no action as the rebellion was crushed.

Richard Burt, the U.S. ambassador to West Germany, sent a nervous cable to Secretary of State George Shultz and National Security Adviser Frank Carlucci, telling them the disturbances in East Berlin meant that "the speech will have even greater resonance than it might otherwise have had. It will be especially important to strike the right balance between inspiring hope and opposing totalitarianism, while making clear that [Reagan's] is a vision of change through peaceful means."

By this time, Burt knew it would be unwise to try on his own to reopen the acrimonious debate over whether the president should say, "Mr. Gorbachev, tear down this wall." That question had been decided—more or less.[15]

-12-

VENETIAN VILLA

During his final years in the White House, Ronald Reagan traveled abroad in a style that was both leisurely and regal. During his first trip to Europe as president in 1982, he had closed his eyes and dozed briefly during a meeting with Pope John Paul II at the end of a long day. Ever since, aides and his wife, Nancy, had made sure that he had plenty of time to rest overseas before he met with foreign leaders.

The president was scheduled to take part in the G7 summit, a gathering of the leaders of the world's seven leading economic powers that was to begin in Venice on Monday, June 8, 1987. The Reagans arrived nearly five days early, on the night of Wednesday, June 3, and went into seclusion eight miles outside the city at an eighteenth-century palazzo, the Villa Condulmer. The villa and its extensive gardens were being used as a hotel and golf course, but the entire complex was emptied out for the Reagans. White House stewards took over the cooking and service. Reagan's personal physician and Nancy Reagan's hairdresser also traveled in the presidential entourage.

A White House advance team had flown in a special bed from Portugal and installed it in the villa. The Reagans had slept in this king-sized bed during a state visit to Lisbon in May 1985, and had found it especially comfortable. White House aides were unable to explain to the press whether the beds in Villa Condulmer (or elsewhere in Italy) were too soft, too hard, or too small.[1] When the Reagans arrived at the villa near midnight, the president took a Dalmane sleeping pill and slept soundly until 8:45 a.m. He slipped off and had breakfast while Nancy Reagan slept until 10:00 a.m.[2]

They remained at the Villa for the following two days. Reagan's official schedule euphemistically called these days "Washington Work/Private Time," but the principal task was overcoming jet lag. Aides had brought videocassettes for the president, and the Reagans spent their first night in Italy watching a 1947 John Wayne movie called *Angel and the Badman*. On the second night, they chose Laurel and Hardy. One night at the villa, a White House aide gave the Reagans the tape of a more contemporary movie, *Shanghai Surprise*, starring Sean Penn and Madonna; the Reagans lasted only fifteen minutes before abandoning it.[3]

That Saturday, the Reagans flew to Rome for a visit to the Vatican. The president held an hour-long, one-on-one meeting with Pope John Paul II, who was preparing a visit to Poland the following week. One of the main subjects on the agenda was Mikhail Gorbachev; Reagan offered the pope his impressions of the Soviet leader and briefed him on U.S.-Soviet arms-control negotiations.

But as the pope was speaking, Reagan momentarily dozed off again, just as he had in 1982. The official White House photographer, Bill Fitzpatrick, noticed Reagan's eyes close and purposely dropped his camera, making a noise that woke up the president. On the plane ride back from Rome to Venice, Jim Kuhn, the president's personal assistant, offered the Reagans an explanation for his tendency to fall asleep during his meetings with the pope. "For some reason, the pope's voice has a hypnotic effect on the president," Kuhn told them. "It's not his fault. If he was to meet the pope again, the same circumstances would prevail. There's nothing you can do about it, Mr. President."[4]

The Reagans enjoyed one more day of rest at Villa Condulmer. The president was meeting with his top aides, preparing for the economic summit and for Berlin. One of the subjects the staff had to address, yet again, was the internal dispute within the administration over the speech Reagan was to give at the Brandenburg Gate. Secretary of State George Shultz, who joined the

Reagans in Venice, called Chief of Staff Howard Baker and Deputy Chief of Staff Kenneth Duberstein, explaining that the State Department continued to oppose some of the language in the speech. Shultz said he shared his department's objections and hoped that his views would be conveyed to the president.

The White House aides were meeting with Reagan daily at Villa Condulmer. Duberstein figured that Shultz's message was merely for the record, a formality that would enable him to tell subordinates in the State Department he had done his best. He knew that Shultz saw Reagan regularly and could get in to see him alone whenever he wanted. Duberstein reasoned that if the secretary of state still felt really strongly about the Berlin speech, he wouldn't have made his opposition known in a phone call to the White House staff; he would have asked for five minutes of time to see Reagan on his own.[5] As a result, Shultz's last protest was brushed aside. Once more, for the final time, the State Department lost the argument and the Berlin Wall speech remained intact.

By the first week in June, well before Reagan landed in West Berlin, anyone in the city who was paying attention would have known that the president's speech was going to urge that the Berlin Wall be torn down. Reagan administration officials made no effort to conceal that this would be a central theme of the speech.

The White House released the written text of an "interview" Reagan had given to the Deutsche Press-Agentur, West Germany's news service. In fact, this was once again not an interview in the usual meaning of the word, but written responses to written questions, issued in Reagan's name but prepared by his staff. It was the same sort of format used in the summer of 1986, when Reagan had said, "I would like to see the wall come down today, and I call upon those responsible to dismantle it."[6] This time, on June 2, 1987, Reagan said in the supposed interview: "In a word, we want the Berlin Wall to come down, so that the reintegration of all four sections of the city into one unit again becomes a reality." Shultz, meanwhile, offered a similar preview of the speech to another West German audience. Speaking to reporters in West Berlin, he called for removing "the dividing line in Europe, which includes the Berlin Wall." America would prefer to see Berlin as an open city without the wall, the secretary of state said.[7] Not surprisingly, these remarks were treated as major news in the West German press. Reagan: WE WANT THE WALL TO COME DOWN! said a front-page headline in the *Berliner Morgenpost* on June 4, eight days before Reagan's visit.[8]

In East Berlin, Erich Honecker got the message. East Germany's Communist Party leader gave his own interview to Dutch newspapers, saying he saw no basis for removing the Berlin Wall because the circumstances that had led to the building of the wall had not disappeared. On June 4, the East German Foreign Ministry called in the leading U.S. diplomat in East Berlin to protest Reagan's remarks in the interview about the Berlin Wall. The East German diplomat said that any questions regarding the "state border of the German Democratic Republic" were its own business. The United States should not interfere in East Germany's internal affairs, he said.[9]

These previews of Reagan's speech served the purpose of letting the German public know what was coming. The administration was making sure that no one in Berlin, on either side of the wall, would be caught off guard by Reagan's speech at the Brandenburg Gate. The words "tear down this wall" were meant to be a dramatic surprise primarily to Reagan's domestic audience, that is, to Americans back home who would not have noticed how many other times Reagan or other American officials had said similar things.

The previews also helped to preempt any last-minute appeals by West German officials that Reagan play down the importance of the wall in his speech. As a result, the last-minute battles between the West Germans and Americans were fought over the question of where Reagan should deliver his speech (should it be at the Brandenburg Gate?) and not over what he should say.

Although the advance interviews by Reagan and Shultz made it plain the president would call for the wall to be dismantled, they did not reveal that the president intended to call directly upon Gorbachev to dismantle it. That was, indeed, to be a surprise.

As Reagan left the United States, his aides were still trying to overcome the perceptions that had taken hold during the Iran-Contra scandal—above all, that he was a politically crippled president, a lame duck who would merely serve out inertly the remaining twenty months of his term in the White House. "It's not morning anymore, but it's not the twilight of the Reagan presidency, either," one senior White House official told the *Washington Post*.[10]

Yet Reagan's performance during the four-day economic summit in Venice seemed merely to reinforce these impressions of Ronald Reagan in decline. "The 76-year-old president is this week a shadow of his former self. . . . His leadership is compared unfavourably with that of Mr. Gorbachev," reported the *Guardian*. "Mr. Reagan resembles the old bull, wounded and stiff, defying a crowd which is waiting for the next act," said the *Financial Times*.[11]

At the end of the summit gathering, Reagan held a news conference at Venice's Hotel Cipriani in which he seemed to fumble several answers. The first three questions, and five of the first seven, were about Iran-Contra. National Security Adviser Frank Carlucci had instructed the president to deflect these questions by saying he was at an economic summit; Carlucci was thus dismayed to hear Reagan wade into the scandal once again, insisting he had no idea that his aides were organizing support for the Nicaraguan contras.[12] At one juncture, the president suggested that the United States might be willing to tolerate a lower value for the dollar against other currencies. Aides soon rushed to correct the record and make clear this was not the case. Talking about diplomacy at the United Nations, Reagan was unable to summon forth the words "Security Council"; after a moment's delay, he said, "committee."

He was asked about Mikhail Gorbachev. Why did Gorbachev have such a strong image in Europe as a man of peace? "Well, maybe because it's so unusual," Reagan replied. "This is the first Soviet leader, in my memory, that has ever advocated actually eliminating weapons already built and in place." The reporter persisted. "Do you trust him?" Reagan fell back on his standard answer, the familiar words given to him by Suzanne Massie. "Well, he's a personable gentleman, but I cited to him a Russian proverb . . . , *Doveryai no proveryai*. It means trust but verify."[13]

-13-

BRANDENBURG GATE

On June 12, 1987, Ronald Reagan landed at West Berlin's Tempelhof Airport after a ninety-minute flight on Air Force One from Venice. It was to be merely a day trip; it was not necessary to fly the Reagans' special European bed to Berlin. Indeed, Reagan's entire visit to Berlin lasted scarcely five hours.

He rode from the airport with West Berlin's mayor Eberhard Diepgen, the political leader who had tried for months to keep Reagan from speaking in front of the Berlin Wall. Diepgen was by now resigned to the inevitable, having concluded that the two superpowers would not permit him to carry out the exchange with East Germany that he had so eagerly sought.[1] Reagan and Diepgen sat down for talks with West Germany's president, Richard von Weizsäcker. The German president recalled years later that Reagan's visit had seemed mostly like a media event. Reagan did not tell von Weizsäcker what he planned to say in his speech.[2]

The American president went by motorcade to the Reichstag, which had housed the German parliament until the Nazi era. During the Cold War, it was used only for ceremonial functions, while the West German parliament met in Bonn. Reagan viewed an exhibition there commemorating the Marshall

Plan, and then stepped out onto a balcony so that he could look down from above at the Berlin Wall, a few hundred feet away. East Germany's Ministry of State Security, the infamous Stasi, operated a building on the eastern side of the wall, in a location that would enable it to hear as many conversations as possible in West Berlin. Ever attentive, the U.S. Secret Service had erected a large bulletproof glass shield around the balcony to protect Reagan from this Stasi outpost for the few minutes he would be on the balcony. John Kornblum, the U.S. minister in West Berlin, thought at the time that this particular precaution was a little silly, since it was unlikely the Stasi would try to take a shot at Reagan from inside its own building. As Reagan looked at the wall, a reporter asked him whether he thought it would ever be torn down. He responded with a biblical allusion. "Well, Jericho didn't last forever," Reagan replied.[3]

From there, it was only a three-minute car ride to the special platform that had been erected for Reagan's speech just on the west side of the Berlin Wall, with the Brandenburg Gate in East Berlin in the background. The crowd that had assembled for Reagan was, it turned out, far smaller than the forty thousand that U.S. officials had wanted and expected. Both Berlin police and internal U.S. government estimates put the figure at twenty thousand, and some thought the crowd was even smaller than that. The participants had been given American flags, which they waved from time to time.[4]

Aides had prepared for the president a special version of his speech in which all the non-English words were transliterated (for the German *Ich hab' noch einen Koffer in Berlin*, Reagan's text said, "Ish hob knock I-nen Coffer in Ber-leen." The German street *Ku'damm* became "Koo-damn," and German president *von Weizsäcker* was rendered as "Fun VITES-ecker." As usual, Reagan had marked up his version of the text with diagonal slashes so that he would pause at just the right places *("General Secretary Gorbachev, if you seek peace /// if you seek prosperity for the Soviet Union and Eastern Europe /// if you seek liberalization /// come here, to this gate").*[5]

West German chancellor Helmut Kohl and his wife, Hannelore, who had joined the Reagan party at the Reichstag, sat on the podium with him. First Diepgen and then Kohl welcomed the crowd. In introducing the American president, the German chancellor took note of the Berlin Wall behind him and said it could not be history's answer to the German problem. Finally,

Reagan, dressed in white shirt with a red tie, delivered effortlessly the speech over which his administration had been battling for weeks.

> *Thank you very much. Chancellor Kohl, Governing Mayor Diepgen, ladies and gentlemen: Twenty-four years ago, President John F. Kennedy visited Berlin, speaking to the people of this city and the world at the city hall. Well, since then two other presidents have come, each in his turn, to Berlin. And today I, myself, make my second visit to your city.*
>
> *We come to Berlin, we American Presidents, because it's our duty to speak, in this place, of freedom. But I must confess, we're drawn here by other things as well: by the feeling of history in this city, more than 500 years older than our own nation; by the beauty of the Grunewald and the Tiergarten; most of all, by your courage and determination. Perhaps the composer Paul Lincke understood something about American Presidents. You see, like so many Presidents before me, I come here today because wherever I go, whatever I do: "Ich hab' noch einen Koffer in Berlin." [I still have a suitcase in Berlin.]*
>
> *Our gathering today is being broadcast throughout Western Europe and North America. I understand that it is being seen and heard as well in the East. To those listening throughout Eastern Europe, I extend my warmest greetings and the goodwill of the American people. To those listening in East Berlin, a special word: Although I cannot be with you, I address my remarks to you just as surely as to those standing here before me. For I join you, as I join your fellow countrymen in the West, in this firm, this unalterable belief: Es gibt nur ein Berlin. [There is only one Berlin.]*
>
> *Behind me stands a wall that encircles the free sectors of this city, part of a vast system of barriers that divides the entire continent of Europe. From the Baltic, south, those barriers cut across Germany in a gash of barbed wire, concrete, dog runs, and guardtowers. Farther south, there may be no visible, no obvious wall. But there remain armed guards and checkpoints*

all the same—still a restriction on the right to travel, still an instrument to impose upon ordinary men and women the will of a totalitarian state. Yet it is here in Berlin where the wall emerges most clearly; here, cutting across your city, where the news photo and the television screen have imprinted this brutal division of a continent upon the mind of the world. Standing before the Brandenburg Gate, every man is a German, separated from his fellow men. Every man is a Berliner, forced to look upon a scar.

President von Weizsäcker has said: "The German question is open as long as the Brandenburg Gate is closed." Today I say: As long as this gate is closed, as long as this scar of a wall is permitted to stand, it is not the German question alone that remains open, but the question of freedom for all mankind. Yet I do not come here to lament. For I find in Berlin a message of hope, even in the shadow of this wall, a message of triumph.

In this season of spring in 1945, the people of Berlin emerged from their air raid shelters to find devastation. Thousands of miles away, the people of the United States reached out to help. And in 1947 Secretary of State—as you've been told— George Marshall announced the creation of what would become known as the Marshall plan. Speaking precisely 40 years ago this month, he said: "Our policy is directed not against any country or doctrine, but against hunger, poverty, desperation, and chaos."

In the Reichstag a few moments ago, I saw a display commemorating this 40th anniversary of the Marshall plan. I was struck by the sign on a burnt-out, gutted structure that was being rebuilt. I understand that Berliners of my own generation can remember seeing signs like it dotted throughout the Western sectors of the city. The sign read simply: "The Marshall plan is helping here to strengthen the free world." A strong, free world in the West, that dream became real. Japan rose from ruin to become an economic giant. Italy, France, Belgium—virtually every nation in Western Europe saw political and economic re-birth; the European Community was founded.

In West Germany and here in Berlin, there took place an economic miracle, the Wirtschaftswunder. *Adenauer, Erhard, Reuter, and other leaders understood the practical importance of liberty—that just as truth can flourish only when the journalist is given freedom of speech, so prosperity can come about only when the farmer and businessman enjoy economic freedom. The German leaders reduced tariffs, expanded free trade, lowered taxes. From 1950 to 1960 alone, the standard of living in West Germany and Berlin doubled.*

Where four decades ago there was rubble, today in West Berlin there is the greatest industrial output of any city in Germany—busy office blocks, fine homes and apartments, proud avenues, and the spreading lawns of park land. Where a city's culture seemed to have been destroyed, today there are two great universities, orchestras and an opera, countless theaters, and museums. Where there was want, today there's abundance— food, clothing, automobiles—the wonderful goods of the Ku'damm. From devastation, from utter ruin, you Berliners have, in freedom, rebuilt a city that once again ranks as one of the greatest on Earth. The Soviets may have had other plans. But, my friends, there were a few things the Soviets didn't count on: Berliner herz, Berliner humor, ja, und Berliner schnauze. *[Berliner heart, Berliner humor, yes, and a Berliner schnauze.]*

In the 1950's, Khrushchev predicted: "We will bury you." But in the West today, we see a free world that has achieved a level of prosperity and well-being unprecedented in all human history. In the Communist world, we see failure, technological backwardness, declining standards of health, even want of the most basic kind—too little food. Even today, the Soviet Union still cannot feed itself. After these four decades, then, there stands before the entire world one great and inescapable conclusion: Freedom leads to prosperity. Freedom replaces the ancient hatreds among the nations with comity and peace. Freedom is the victor.

And now the Soviets themselves may, in a limited way, be coming to understand the importance of freedom. We hear much from Moscow about a new policy of reform and openness. Some political prisoners have been released. Certain foreign news broadcasts are no longer being jammed. Some economic enterprises have been permitted to operate with greater freedom from state control. Are these the beginnings of profound changes in the Soviet state? Or are they token gestures, intended to raise false hopes in the West, or to strengthen the Soviet system without changing it? We welcome change and openness; for we believe that freedom and security go together, that the advance of human liberty can only strengthen the cause of world peace.

There is one sign the Soviets can make that would be unmistakable, that would advance dramatically the cause of freedom and peace. General Secretary Gorbachev, if you seek peace, if you seek prosperity for the Soviet Union and Eastern Europe, if you seek liberalization: Come here to this gate! Mr. Gorbachev, open this gate! Mr. Gorbachev, Mr. Gorbachev, tear down this wall!

I understand the fear of war and the pain of division that afflict this continent—and I pledge to you my country's efforts to help overcome these burdens. To be sure, we in the West must resist Soviet expansion. So we must maintain defenses of unassailable strength. Yet we seek peace; so we must strive to reduce arms on both sides. Beginning 10 years ago, the Soviets challenged the Western alliance with a grave new threat, hundreds of new and more deadly SS-20 nuclear missiles, capable of striking every capital in Europe. The Western alliance responded by committing itself to a counterdeployment unless the Soviets agreed to negotiate a better solution; namely, the elimination of such weapons on both sides. For many months, the Soviets refused to bargain in earnestness. As the alliance, in turn, prepared to go forward with its counterdeployment, there were difficult days—days of protests like those during my 1982 visit to this city—and the Soviets later walked away from the table. But through it all, the alliance held firm. And I invite those who protested then—I invite those who protest today—to mark this fact: Because we remained strong, the Soviets came back to the table. And because we remained strong, today we have within reach the possibility, not merely of limiting the growth of arms, but of eliminating, for the first time, an entire class of nuclear weapons from the face of the Earth. As I speak, NATO ministers are meeting in Iceland to review the progress of our proposals for eliminating these weapons. At the talks in Geneva, we have also proposed deep cuts in strategic offensive weapons. And the Western allies have likewise made far-reaching proposals to reduce the danger of conventional war and to place a total ban on chemical weapons.

While we pursue these arms reductions, I pledge to you that we will maintain the capacity to deter Soviet aggression at any level at which it might occur. And in cooperation with many of our allies, the United States is pursuing the Strategic Defense Initiative—research to base deterrence not on the threat of offensive retaliation, but on defenses that truly defend; on systems, in short, that will not target populations, but shield them. By these means we seek to increase the safety of Europe and all the world. But we must remember a crucial fact: East and West do not mistrust each other because we are armed; we are armed because we mistrust each other. And our differences are not about weapons but about liberty. When President Kennedy spoke at the City Hall those 24 years ago, freedom was encircled, Berlin was under siege. And today, despite all the pressures upon this city, Berlin stands secure in its liberty. And freedom itself is transforming the globe.

In the Philippines, in South and Central America, democracy has been given a rebirth. Throughout the Pacific, free markets are working miracle after miracle of economic growth. In the industrialized nations, a technological revolution is taking place—a revolution marked by rapid, dramatic advances in computers and telecommunications.

In Europe, only one nation and those it controls refuse to join the community of freedom. Yet in this age of redoubled economic growth, of information and innovation, the Soviet Union faces a choice: It must make fundamental changes, or it will become obsolete. Today thus represents a moment of hope. We in the West stand ready to cooperate with the East to promote true openness, to break down barriers that separate people, to create a safer, freer world.

And surely there is no better place than Berlin, the meeting place of East and West, to make a start. Free people of Berlin: Today, as in the past, the United States stands for the strict observance and full implementation of all parts of the Four Power Agreement of 1971. Let us use this occasion, the 750th anniversary of this city, to usher in a new era, to seek a still fuller, richer life for the Berlin of the future. Together, let us maintain and develop the ties between the Federal Republic and the Western sectors of Berlin, which is permitted by the 1971 agreement.

And I invite Mr. Gorbachev: Let us work to bring the Eastern and Western parts of the city closer together, so that all the inhabitants of all Berlin can enjoy the benefits that come with life in one of the great cities of the world. To open Berlin still further to all Europe, East and West, let us expand the vital air access to this city, finding ways of making commercial air service to Berlin more convenient, more comfortable, and more economical. We look to the day when West Berlin can become one of the chief aviation hubs in all central Europe.

With our French and British partners, the United States is prepared to help bring international meetings to Berlin. It would be only fitting for Berlin to serve as the site of United Nations meetings, or world conferences on human rights and arms control or other issues that call for international cooperation. There is no better way to establish hope for the future than to enlighten young minds, and we would be honored to sponsor summer youth exchanges, cultural events, and other programs for young Berliners from the East. Our French and British friends, I'm certain, will do the same. And it's my hope that an authority can be found in East Berlin to sponsor visits from young people of the Western sectors.

One final proposal, one close to my heart: Sport represents a source of enjoyment and ennoblement, and you may have noted that the Republic of Korea—South Korea—has offered to permit certain events of the 1988 Olympics to take place in the North. International sports competitions of all kinds could take place in both parts of this city. And what better way to demonstrate to the world the openness of this city than to offer in some future year to hold the Olympic games here in Berlin, East and West?

In these four decades, as I have said, you Berliners have built a great city. You've done so in spite of threats—the Soviet attempts to impose the East-mark, the blockade. Today the city thrives in spite of the challenges implicit in the very presence of this wall. What keeps you here? Certainly there's a great deal to be said for your fortitude, for your defiant courage. But I believe there's something deeper, something that involves Berlin's whole look and feel and way of life—not mere sentiment. No one could live long in Berlin without being completely disabused of illusions. Something, instead, that has seen the difficulties of life in Berlin but chose to accept them, that continues to build this good and proud city in contrast to a surrounding totalitarian presence that refuses to release human energies or aspirations. Something that speaks with a powerful voice of affirmation, that says yes to this city, yes to the future, yes to freedom. In a word, I would submit that what keeps you in Berlin is love— love both profound and abiding.

Perhaps this gets to the root of the matter, to the most fundamental distinction of all between East and West. The totalitarian world produces backwardness because it does such violence to the spirit, thwarting the human impulse to create, to *enjoy, to worship. The totalitarian world finds even symbols of love and of worship an affront. Years ago, before the East Germans began rebuilding their churches, they erected a secular structure: the television tower at Alexander Platz. Virtually ever since, the authorities have been working to correct what they view as the tower's one major flaw, treating the glass sphere at the top with paints and chemicals of every kind. Yet even today when the sun strikes that sphere—that sphere that towers over all Berlin—the light makes the sign of the cross. There in Berlin, like the city itself, symbols of love, symbols of worship, cannot be suppressed.*

As I looked out a moment ago from the Reichstag, that embodiment of German unity, I noticed words crudely spray-painted upon the wall, perhaps by a young Berliner, "This wall will fall. Beliefs become reality." Yes, across Europe, this wall will fall. For it cannot withstand faith; it cannot withstand truth. The wall cannot withstand freedom.

And I would like, before I close, to say one word. I have read, and I have been questioned since I've been here about certain demonstrations against my coming. And I would like to say just one thing, and to those who demonstrate so. I wonder if they have ever asked themselves that if they should have the kind of government they apparently seek, no one would ever be able to do what they're doing again. Thank you and God bless you all.

Reagan later wrote in his diary that "I got a tremendous reception—interrupted 28 times by cheers." Yet other witnesses reported that the audience seemed surprisingly low-keyed. Some of Reagan's top aides later that day voiced disappointment at the lukewarm turnout and reaction; throughout most of the speech, there was only polite, scattered applause. However, as Reagan said the words "Mr. Gorbachev, open this gate," the crowd applauded more strongly. Reagan, with his skilled sense of timing, then repeated the Soviet leader's name twice, to emphasize what was coming: "Mr. Gorbachev, Mr. Gorbachev, tear down this wall!" With those words, the crowd cheered lustily.[6]

As Reagan spoke, several hundred East Berlin residents gathered on the other side of the wall, trying to hear or at least see what was happening. They knew from West German television and radio that the American president would be speaking at 2 p.m. In the hour beforehand, they had strolled in groups down Unter den Linden, the main boulevard of East Berlin that runs to the Brandenburg Gate. When they reached Pariser Platz, the open square connecting the boulevard and the gate, they found that it had been sealed off. Many East Berliners congregated just to the east of this new barrier, listening to the music that preceded Reagan's speech. East German police, the Volkspolizei, arrived.

At 1:58 p.m. a loudspeaker warned, "You are asked to continue on your way. Do not remain standing." The message was repeated. Police officers wandered into the crowd, urging people to leave the area and, in one case, asking several young people for their papers. But most of the crowd stayed put; several people told the police officers they didn't understand why they had to leave.

The East German authorities were not eager for a confrontation. The crowd had assembled in virtually the same location where the clashes had broken out the previous weekend as East Berliners gathered to hear the rock concerts on the other side of the wall. Those earlier protests had attracted international press coverage, and Honecker's regime was reluctant to call attention to itself by cracking down once again. The police took no further action.

For the following hour, while Reagan was speaking, the East German crowd stood there, in a strange, silent tableau. They could not hear the speech; the barrier erected at Pariser Platz put them too far away. Through the arches of the Brandenburg Gate, they could see in the distance, from time to time, the American flags being waved during Reagan's speech. Some peered through binoculars toward the West, and others put children on their shoulders to see the flags. After an hour, as they saw the crowds in West Berlin beginning to disperse, the East Berlin onlookers began to wander off too.[7]

Some of the residents of West Berlin were not nearly as subdued. West Berlin officials put ten thousand policemen on the streets to help keep the city quiet during Reagan's visit. Nevertheless, both before Reagan's speech and in the hours after it, there were violent street battles between protesters and the police. Young West Berlin residents, wearing masks, threw paving stones at the police and smashed the windows of banks and department stores. Police cordoned off Kreuzberg, the area of the city where most of the demonstrations took place. The final words of Reagan's speech—"if they should have the kind of government they apparently seek, no one would ever be able to do what they're doing again"—were a hastily added reaction to the intensity of these West Berlin demonstrations.

Reagan left for Tempelhof Airport, where he took part in the event that had first prompted his visit to the city: an American-sponsored birthday party, complete with cake, in honor of the 750th anniversary of the founding of Berlin. He was following President François Mitterrand and Queen Elizabeth, who had already taken part in similar anniversary celebrations during the previous month. The American president viewed a display of the Berlin Airlift, shaking hands with three U.S. Air Force pilots who had taken part in the operation nearly four decades earlier.

The Reagans flew on Air Force One to Bonn, carrying Helmut Kohl and his wife along with them. The stopover was a formality: Bonn was the West German capital and the American president needed to put in an appearance there. It lasted only about ninety minutes, and Reagan did not leave the airport grounds. He stood with Kohl for the playing of national anthems, reviewed the troops, and talked with the German chancellor for about forty-five minutes in a room at the airport. Then he returned to his airplane for the long trip back across the Atlantic. At 9:47 p.m. Washington time, Reagan was back inside the White House. He was never to return to Berlin for the remainder of his presidency. He had said what he wanted to say.

-14-

WHY NOT "MR. HONECKER"?

Reagan's appeal to tear down the wall had little impact in East Germany, at least at the time. Quite a few East Germans knew what he had said—they had heard the speech on West German radio and television—but nobody thought it would lead to any change. "No one believed that the wall would come down any time soon," Bettina Urbanski, a journalist in East Berlin, remembered many years later. "Young people couldn't even remember the time before the wall existed."[1]

Ordinary East Germans were isolated. West Berlin, so close by, played no role in their lives. Even the television and radio broadcasts originating in West Berlin seemed as though they came from some distant place. "The weather reports for West Berlin were the same as for us, but the news was like the news from Brazil or Angola," recalled Maritta Adam-Tkalec, then a young newspaper editor. "I remember the Reagan speech. I thought, 'Crazy man.'"[2]

"I think I said, 'He's crazy,' " said Jörg Halthöfer, who was then a Communist Party official serving in East Germany's trade ministry. Halthöfer was by his own subsequent admission an opportunist, one who had joined the party to advance his own career, and he had learned enough to be cynical. "I knew *Neues Deutschland* [East Germany's Communist Party newspaper] was lying, so I assumed that the Western television was lying, too," he said. Halthöfer thought the idea of tearing down the Berlin Wall was unrealistic because he knew that East 'Germany's Communist regime couldn't survive without the wall. "Opening the gate was the same as ending the German Democratic Republic," he said. "It wasn't possible to make another system alongside the capitalist system without a wall."[3]

East Germany's news agency, also controlled by the Communist Party, reported that Ronald Reagan had called for destroying the "border security installations," its customary euphemism for the Berlin Wall. The American president's performance was aimed merely at "show effects," said the news agency. Reagan "could not hide his regret that the preponderance of Europe, which is socialist, wants no part of Western freedom, which is expressed particularly in the large army of the unemployed."[4]

At the highest levels of the East German leadership, there was less bravado. Egon Krenz, a Politburo member and Honecker's eventual successor, recalled many years later that Reagan's speech had taken the East German regime by surprise and had produced an internal debate. "The majority, including me, thought that President Reagan simply intended to provoke," Krenz said. "We thought that the U.S. authorities were testing the waters to see how far they could go with the new Soviet government, because Gorbachev had been in office for only two years."[5]

Honecker, however, took a more conspiratorial view. According to Krenz, Honecker suspected that the Berlin Wall speech was the result of secret collusion between the United States and the Soviet Union. The East German leader thought that Reagan's words, and his appearance in front of the Brandenburg Gate, reflected a larger strategic understanding with Gorbachev under which the Soviet Union seemed to be ready to give up East Germany, step by step. After Honecker fell from power in 1989, he believed even more strongly that the two superpowers had been collaborating with each other for several years, and that Reagan's visit to Berlin had been merely one part of the larger pattern.[6]

Recently declassified material shows that Honecker was especially unnerved by the key line in Reagan's speech. He was upset by the wording: the American president had urged *Mr. Gorbachev,* not *Mr. Honecker,* to tear down the wall. In a formal sense, it was East Germany's wall. Indeed, the East German authorities—Honecker and his boss, Communist Party leader Walter Ulbricht—had played the leading roles in building the wall in 1961, despite the Soviet Union's initial reluctance.[7] Yet Reagan, in addressing his appeal to Gorbachev, had succeeded in conveying the larger underlying reality: that East Germany would never have existed without Soviet support and Soviet troops. The American president had found a new way of reminding the world that Honecker was insignificant in the larger scheme of things, merely the leader of a satellite regime.

Declassified State Department cables show that on June 18, 1987, less than a week after Reagan returned from Berlin, an East German diplomat in Washington invited a State Department official to lunch and proceeded to ask the meaning of the speech at the Brandenburg Gate. "He asked plaintively whether Reagan's call to Gorbachev [rather than Honecker] to tear down the Wall was prompted by U.S. policy toward Berlin, or simply done to snub the GDR [East German] government," the official reported.

In short, Honecker wasn't willing to tear down the wall—but he would at least have liked to be asked.[8]

The idea of a Soviet-American conspiracy was entirely in Honecker's imagination. To be sure, by mid-1987, Gorbachev's foreign policy was beginning to change; the best evidence had been the defense-oriented military doctrine announced at the Warsaw Pact session two weeks before Reagan's visit. Gorbachev was also trying to forge a new relationship with West Germany as part of a larger effort to court Western Europe. Less than a month after Reagan's trip to Berlin, Gorbachev played host to Richard von Weizsäcker, the West German president, on a visit to Moscow.

Yet none of these developments in mid-1987 amounted to a Soviet-American conspiracy against the East German regime. When Ronald Reagan called for the destruction of the Berlin Wall, Soviet officials and the Soviet press promptly condemned his speech in the same fashion as the East German regime did, calling Reagan's words a return to the rhetoric of the Cold War. "West Berlin is a bad place for muscle-flexing," said Valentin Falin, a leading Soviet expert on Germany. *Pravda,* the Communist Party newspaper, accused Reagan of crying "crocodile tears" and said the Western allies had, through their own hostile actions, made it necessary for East Germany to build the Berlin Wall. *Izvestia*, the official Soviet newspaper, reminded its readers that a year earlier, Gorbachev had signed a guest book at the Brandenburg Gate praising the East German border guards.[9] Another *Izvestia* column warned that the existing division of Germany had helped to prevent military conflict between East and West. "While the German question remains open, the question of war in Europe also remains open," he said.[10] When von Weizsäcker visited Moscow, Gorbachev even refused to allow publication of the West German president's comments about the Berlin Wall or about a divided Germany. The Soviet leader wanted to be tough, not conciliatory. "The Germans have to be treated this way," Gorbachev told an aide. They respect firmness—*ordnung* [order]."[11]

Although the Soviet Union itself still lined up behind Honecker, some of its Eastern European neighbors did not. On June 14, two days after Reagan's speech, Hungarian television stations carried footage of the American president's appearance at the Brandenburg Gate, including his appeal to tear down the Berlin Wall. Hungarian TV had also shown, a few days earlier, a report about East German protests during the rock concerts in West Berlin. One Hungarian explained at the time that Gorbachev's policy of *glasnost* provided enough latitude for the government of Hungary to take occasional swipes at the aging leaders of East Germany and Czechoslovakia.[12] Reagan's Berlin speech wasn't the cause of these divisions within Eastern Europe, but by reminding everyone of the wall, it exacerbated the underlying tensions and helped to bring them into the open.

For West Germans, Reagan's speech was unsettling. German chancellor Helmut Kohl quickly endorsed Reagan's speech, but other West German officials were less enthusiastic. "At the time, people [in West Germany] thought that Reagan was not supporting Gorbachev as much as he should," asserted Karsten D. Voigt, a German specialist on the United States. "Americans all kept appealing to freedom, but we felt it'd be stronger if they had cooperated more with Gorbachev."[13]

"The subject of the wall was a taboo, in a sense," recalled Hans-Otto Bräutigam, West Germany's representative in East Berlin. "Everybody considered the wall unbearable, uncivilized—but you couldn't do anything about it. The subject was something one didn't want to touch, because it was so emotional. For West Berliners, Reagan's speech employed language they had really missed for some time. His words had a direct appeal. But in general, no one in Germany at that time believed there was a chance to open the wall in the near future."[14]

Hildegard Boucsein was sitting in one of the front rows during Ronald Reagan's speech, a privilege she enjoyed as an aide to the mayor of West Berlin. When Reagan called upon Mikhail Gorbachev to tear down the Berlin Wall, one German next to her muttered that he was a "nationalist dreamer" and another said he was indulging in fantasy.[15]

Back in the United States, Reagan's appeal to tear down the Berlin Wall was not taken particularly seriously. The focus of news coverage at the time was on the impending congressional hearings into Iran-Contra, not the Soviet Union or East Germany.

Within hours after Reagan's speech, Henry Kissinger appeared on television to deliver his gloomy, gravelly-voiced judgment. Asked whether it was realistic to hope the Soviet Union might ease its policies toward Berlin, Kissinger replied, "They might relax them to some extent, but they won't tear down the wall." Americans should in any event not become overly excited about Gorbachev's reforms, Kissinger told ABC's *Good Morning America*. "The purpose is to make the Soviet Union stronger."[16]

In an editorial a few days after Reagan returned from Europe, the *New York Times* compared Reagan to the Music Man, trying to replay the old tunes in River City. In the *Washington Post*, columnist Jim Hoagland wrote of Reagan's speech: "History is likely to record the challenge to tear down the wall as a meaningless taunt, delivered as a grand gesture that was not conceived of as part of a coherent policy."[17]

The State Department, which had for so long opposed the speech Reagan gave in Berlin, quickly sought to explain it away and to defuse its impact. State Department officials wrote what is called a "press guidance," a series of internal talking points for senior U.S. officials and press spokespersons to use in answering reporters' questions. On the day Reagan spoke at the Brandenburg Gate, the State Department instructed its officials to say: "The speech speaks for itself. We are consulting with our British, French and German allies." The press guidance explained that Reagan had "suggested possible steps to open up East-West contacts within Berlin to expand Berlin's role as a world meeting place." State Department officials were instructed to tell reporters that "we call on the other side to join with us in overcoming barriers and opening Berlin still further to all of Europe, East and West." Nowhere in the State Department's press guidance did the words *Berlin Wall* appear, or the phrase *tear down,* or the name *Gorbachev.*[18]

During the following months, State Department officials busied themselves with the task of pursuing the small, practical steps they called Reagan's Berlin Initiative. By this they meant not tearing down the wall, but the incremental steps concerning Berlin they had originally proposed should be at the heart of Reagan's speech.

American diplomats dutifully explored with other governments the possibilities for international conferences that could be held on both sides of the Berlin Wall. Could the Commission on Security and Cooperation in Europe (CSCE), an organization with members in both Western and Eastern Europe, meet at the same time in both West and East Berlin? "Embassy Berlin strongly supports . . . recommendation to propose Berlin both sides of the Wall for the next CSCE follow-up meeting," cabled a U.S. diplomat. The Soviets soon threw cold water on this proposal. How about having the Olympics in both sections of Berlin? That idea provided the fodder for diplomatic cables and meetings; it did not take hold either.[19]

If it had been up to the State Department, Reagan's exhortation, "Mr. Gorbachev, tear down this wall," would have been forgotten. But it was not. In the months after Reagan's visit, the words came up repeatedly in public discussions of Berlin and of the Cold War. On July 3, 1987, on a visit to West Berlin, French prime minister Jacques Chirac irked Soviet and East German officials by supporting what Reagan had said. Chirac deplored the fact that Berlin was divided by an "inhumane, absurd wall." The wall was "barbaric," he said, because it was erected to protect an ideology at the expense of freedom and human rights.[20]

Reagan himself was not inclined to drop the line either. During the following months, whenever the president spoke in public about the Soviet Union, he included a few words about tearing down the Berlin Wall. It became part of Reagan's repertoire. At a town hall meeting in Los Angeles that

August, he said he had asked "that the Soviets join us in alleviating the division of Berlin and begin with the dismantling of the Berlin Wall." In his regular Saturday radio speech three days later, he said that if Soviet officials wanted to improve relations with the United States, "they can get out of Afghanistan, they can tear down the Berlin Wall, they can allow free elections in Europe."[21]

-15-

ON HIS OWN

The prolonged struggle over the Berlin speech demonstrated once again the extent to which the Reagan administration's dealings with Mikhail Gorbachev represented the style and thinking of the president himself.

Reagan was often depicted as the instrument of larger forces and of the more assertive personalities around him. During his early years in the White House, Reagan's policy toward Moscow was often seen as a reflection of hawks in his administration such as William Casey, his CIA director, or Caspar Weinberger, his defense secretary. During Reagan's second term, as he proceeded to do business with Gorbachev, he was sometimes depicted as a figurehead for Secretary of State George Shultz, the real architect of America's extensive diplomacy with Moscow. "It is quite apparent that Shultz has sold his deal to both Reagan and [White House chief of staff Howard] Baker," Richard Nixon wrote in a note to himself after visiting the White House in the spring of 1987.[1]

Reagan's own behavior often contributed to these perceptions. The president rarely became involved in the details of whatever was being debated inside his administration; for weeks he would remain remote or inert in the face of a growing controversy. Yet in the end, it was Reagan himself who set the tone and made the decisions. Shultz managed the details of America's diplomacy with Moscow, but it was up to Reagan to provide the overall direction and to supply the ideas and rhetoric that would ensure there was support both in Congress and with the American public.

When it came to the Soviet Union, Reagan not infrequently seemed to move in several directions at the same time. He shifted direction with a canny sense of timing. Only nine months earlier, when faced with similarly intense divisions inside his administration about how to respond to the Soviet Union's jailing of American reporter Nicholas Daniloff, Reagan had sided with Shultz. He had infuriated conservatives by agreeing to negotiations and a package deal for Daniloff's release, in implicit exchange for the release of a Soviet spy in New York and the freeing of a leading Soviet dissident. This time, with Reagan's aides divided over Berlin, the president rejected Shultz's appeals. Instead, he chose to deliver a speech that reaffirmed the core value of political freedom and reminded Gorbachev the United States would not accept the continuing divisions in Europe.

Not only Shultz but many other foreign-policy officials had opposed the idea of having the president call upon Gorbachev to demolish the Berlin Wall. Soviet specialists at the State Department and the National Security Council had sought repeatedly to rewrite the speech. Colin Powell, the deputy national security adviser, coordinated and supported the bureaucratic opposition. Reagan's White House chief of staff, Howard Baker, was also dubious.

The issue raised by Shultz and others was quite simple: What would be the impact in Moscow of the words "Mr. Gorbachev, tear down this wall"? Would Gorbachev be so irritated that he would give up trying to deal with Reagan and lose interest in conciliatory policies toward the United States? Might the speech strengthen the hand of those who were seeking to limit the extent of his reforms? In short, was Gorbachev sufficiently eager to forge new ties with the United States and sufficiently secure in his leadership to be able to withstand Reagan's rhetoric?

In rejecting the State Department's warnings, Reagan was making his own judgment about Gorbachev. He was betting on the Soviet leader. This was based, at least partially, on Reagan's own perceptions. He had met Gorbachev twice at the summits in Geneva and in Reykjavik and had corresponded with him before and after those meetings. He had obtained a sense of how desperately Gorbachev wanted new agreements to ease the international climate and to limit Soviet military spending.

The dramatic exhortation to "tear down this wall" was in some ways a public-relations gimmick. Thomas Griscom, the White House communications director, acknowledged that he liked and approved the phrase because it was a perfect sound bite, one that helped get the president on television news shows in the United States. By itself, there was nothing new in Reagan's declaration that the Berlin Wall should come down. Reagan had said so before, and so had other American officials. True, the site of the speech—in front of the Brandenburg Gate—was novel, but that only underscored that this was a speech intended more for television than for international diplomacy.

The new element in the substance of Reagan's Berlin speech was not that the wall should come down, but that Gorbachev himself should take it down. This served a number of purposes. Reagan's words called attention to the fact that the Communist regimes of Eastern Europe still depended on the Soviet Union; Honecker, who had personally overseen the construction of the wall, would never have had his job without Moscow. Even more significant, the speech set out a standard by which Gorbachev should be judged: Would his reforms be limited in scope, or would they change the existing order in Europe? The speech reaffirmed Reagan's long-standing view that the ideological differences between the United States and the Soviet Union remained of fundamental importance. Finally, the speech buttressed Reagan's public and congressional support inside the United States as he was preparing for further diplomacy with Gorbachev. He was protecting his political flanks, particularly on the right.

Reagan never gave voice to such calculations, of course. He didn't talk about underlying strategy or tactics. The world saw only the simple façade: catching Reagan in some Machiavellian maneuver would have been akin to catching him dyeing his hair. As far as anyone could tell, he was an unreflective person, one who viewed events in simple terms. Indeed, it may well be that Reagan based his decisions largely on instinct. He may never have explained even to himself the considerations that lay behind changes in policy,

his reasons for sometimes standing on principle and then at other times setting those principles aside in favor of diplomacy or negotiation.

The Berlin speech had been largely the product of Reagan's speechwriters. The president no longer drafted his own speeches. Yet Reagan talked to
the writers, offered them ideas, and chose when and how to defend their work
in the face of objections from elsewhere in his administration. Within days
after Reagan returned from Berlin, he sent word to Anthony Dolan, the chief
White House speechwriter, saying how much he had liked the Berlin Wall
speech. The archives show that Dolan sent a gracious reply dated June 15,
1987, which said: "In view of all you told us about what you wanted in Berlin—including the outline and the killer lines you gave us—it was particularly generous of you."[2]

In Berlin, Reagan had set forth what he had long believed about the Soviet Union. He had acknowledged the possibility that Gorbachev might represent a change, but had also voiced skepticism about how far Gorbachev
would be willing to go. Having delivered his Berlin speech, Reagan was now
in position for his final eighteen months of diplomacy with Gorbachev.

PART IV
SUMMITS

-1-

"QUIT PRESSING"

Ronald Reagan had a favorite line to explain why he did not go to summit meetings with Soviet leaders during his first term. "They keep dying on me," he said.[1] That was literally true; Reagan was obliged to deal with four Soviet leaders during his first fifty months in the White House. But as usual, Reagan's quip was not the full story.

Reagan had written out by hand a letter to Soviet president Leonid Brezhnev in April 1981, during the period when he was recovering from the attempt by John W. Hinckley, Jr., to assassinate him. The president had also sent letters to Brezhnev's two successors, Yuri Andropov and Konstantin Chernenko. However, none of this correspondence included any proposal for a meeting. Throughout Reagan's first years in office, he had concentrated on rapidly increasing the U.S. arsenal of planes, warships, and other weaponry. In 1983, he asked his National Security Council for a detailed memo exploring the costs and benefits of a summit with Andropov, but many within his administration opposed such a meeting unless the Soviet Union would give something tangible in advance in exchange. Before the dispute could be resolved, the furor over the Soviet shooting of the Korean Airlines plane and Andropov's own illness scuttled any possibility of a summit.[2]

At the beginning of 1984, the lack of summitry became a political issue after Democratic presidential candidate Walter Mondale pointed out that Reagan might leave office as the first American president since Herbert Hoover to have failed to sit down with the leader of the Soviet Union. Reagan began thinking about the possibility of an election-year summit, seeking advice from everyone from Secretary of State George Shultz to his newly enlisted outside adviser, Suzanne Massie. "She reinforced my gut feeling that it's time for me to personally meet with Chernenko," Reagan recorded in his diary after talking with Massie.[3]

Instead of a summit, however, Reagan deflected Mondale's attacks in other ways. His speeches about the Soviet Union took on a more conciliatory tone. Reagan talked with Chinese leaders in Beijing. He met in Washington with Soviet foreign minister Andrei Gromyko. Even if Reagan had been willing to extend a summit invitation, the Soviets were in no mood to respond; they did not want to help him win a second term. Soviet leaders "would have liked to offer rhetorical assistance to the campaign of the Democratic candidate, Walter Mondale—not because they knew him, but because they preferred anybody to Reagan," Anatoly Dobrynin, the Soviet ambassador to Washington, recalled.[4]

Toward the end of the 1984 campaign, the Soviets recognized Reagan's political strength and shifted ground. That fall, a Soviet official approached Thomas Simons, one of the State Department officials responsible for Soviet affairs, and suggested that Moscow could help the president win reelection. But it was too late. "The president doesn't need your help," Simons replied. I know, said the Soviet official regretfully.[5]

After Reagan won reelection, summitry with the Soviet Union was on the agenda virtually from the start. Reagan had the political latitude of a president who would not have to run again and could focus on what he might accomplish before leaving office. For their part, Soviet leaders quickly recognized that Reagan would be in the White House for another four years, and that they would have to deal with him in some way.

The president was especially interested in high-profile summitry in Washington and Moscow. Reagan realized that a summit in which a Soviet leader came to the United States, or in which an American president traveled to the Soviet Union, carried political meaning well beyond any such meeting on neutral ground. Only two Soviet leaders had ever come to Washington: Nikita Khrushchev in 1959 and Leonid Brezhnev in 1973. Nixon had been the only American president to visit Moscow.

Reagan was also under increasing pressure from some of America's closest allies to start meeting face-to-face with Soviet leaders. West German chancellor Helmut Kohl was particularly eager. The acrimony between Washington and Moscow during Reagan's first term had prevented West Germany from developing the closer economic ties it sought with Eastern Europe. "Our main interest was to get the second Reagan administration back to a summit with the Soviets, because we had learned that [West] Germany's room for maneuver was dramatically restricted by this stalemate between the two superpowers," recalled Horst Teltschik, Kohl's foreign-policy adviser. "We felt that when they started the summits, we would get a new chance to develop our relations with the Central Europeans."[6]

Kohl was the first Western European leader to visit the White House after Reagan's reelection. On November 30, 1984, he persuaded Reagan to join with him in a statement that said the American president would be prepared for a summit with a Soviet leader at a "carefully prepared meeting."[7] The statement did not even mention the name of Chernenko, who by this time was terminally ill.

A few weeks later, Prime Minister Margaret Thatcher visited Camp David. She had just met in London with Gorbachev, then the rising star within the Politburo, who was already being viewed as a possible successor to Chernenko. During a speech in London, Gorbachev had talked about the possibility of reducing or even eliminating nuclear weapons. Thatcher had subsequently praised him in public, asserting that "we can do business together." At Camp David, she told Reagan she thought Gorbachev was eager for change in Soviet policies. Reagan's personal assistant, Jim Kuhn, later recalled that Thatcher's early impressions of Gorbachev made a big impact upon Reagan.[8]

When Chernenko died less than three months later and Gorbachev was chosen to succeed him, Reagan moved with surprising alacrity. On March 11,

1985, the same day the Politburo named Gorbachev as the next general secretary of the Communist Party, Reagan wrote him a private letter in which he
said: "I would like to invite you to visit me in Washington at your earliest
convenient opportunity. . . . I want you to know that I look forward to a
meeting that could yield results of benefit to both our countries and to the
international community as a whole."[9] This was, in a sense, merely a cordial
note to a new Soviet leader, but the significance could not be overstated: it
was also Reagan's first proposal for a summit, after more than four years in the
White House.

Gorbachev responded two weeks later saying he had a "positive attitude"
toward Reagan's suggestion for a meeting. Gorbachev refused, however, to
commit himself to a trip to Washington. When Secretary of State George
Shultz attempted a few weeks later to arrange a Washington summit, Soviet
foreign minister Andrei Gromyko replied, "Not possible. We can find a European city."[10]

Even Reagan's first two summits with Gorbachev, at Geneva in 1985 and
Reykjavik in 1986, were viewed, at the time, merely as the forerunners to
more important meetings in the United States and the Soviet Union. Indeed,
the main tangible result of Reagan's initial meeting with Gorbachev in Geneva was the announcement that the two leaders had formally agreed to a
summit in Washington and a subsequent one in Moscow. The press corps was
informed that Reagan had extended a formal invitation to Gorbachev to visit
Washington as the two men stood outside, without advisers, in a parking lot
near Lake Geneva; Gorbachev was said to have accepted on the spot, and in
return, invited Reagan to his own capital city. This version of events was
meant to convey to the world a sense of spontaneity and personal intimacy
between the two leaders. The reality was that Reagan had worked out the
plans for follow-on summits well in advance of Geneva through private negotiations in Washington with Dobrynin.[11]

After Geneva, Gorbachev had balked at setting a date for a Washington
summit. This time, it was the Soviets' turn to seek concessions in advance, in
the same way as the United States had done during Reagan's early years in the
White House. Gorbachev didn't want to travel to Washington until the two
sides had first settled on specific agreements on arms control that could be
signed while he was there.

The Reagan-Gorbachev meeting at Reykjavik in October 1986 is now considered the most significant and tumultuous of all the sessions between the two leaders, because it was there that they suddenly began to discuss the possibility of eliminating nuclear weapons and missiles. Yet at the time, Reykjavik wasn't even characterized as a full-blown summit; it was, rather, a hastily arranged business meeting whose purpose was merely to lay the groundwork for a summit in Washington. The meeting is "in no sense [a] substitute or surrogate for a summit," one National Security Council official wrote in a memo preparing for the meeting. Indeed, Reagan's desire for a Washington summit quickly became one part of the intense bargaining at Reykjavik.

"By the way, could we talk about the date for your visit? Are you going to give your suggestions, or should I name a date?" Reagan asked the Soviet leader during the opening morning of their talks there. Gorbachev avoided answering the question. "I will complete my thought," he said, returning to a discussion of arms control.[12]

Reykjavik had ended in disarray, and by early 1987 there was still no date for the Washington summit, even though such an event had been under discussion for nearly two years. Gorbachev was still eager to complete one or more arms-control agreements before he agreed to visit.

By the early months of 1987, Reagan and his wife, Nancy, were becoming increasingly impatient for a Gorbachev visit. Iran-Contra had shattered the president's popularity and threatened the collapse of his presidency. With the Democrats in control of Congress, Reagan had little hope of winning approval for any significant initiatives in domestic policy. One way of counteracting the devastating impact of Iran-Contra was to deliver ringing speeches, such as the one at the Berlin Wall. Yet the Reagans were also eager for something more tangible, some foreign-policy achievements that would extend beyond the realm of rhetoric. High-profile meetings with Gorbachev would serve this purpose.

Nancy Reagan had emerged alongside her husband as a strong and determined proponent of a summit with Gorbachev in the United States. Mrs. Reagan had been influential since the start of the administration. Inside the White House, Reagan referred to his wife as "Mommy," a nickname that let others know of her weighty but ambiguous role. World leaders paid unusually close attention to Nancy Reagan, scrutinizing her attitudes and her views. "Mrs. Reagan had a big problem with us Germans—she obviously harbored great suspicions because of the Nazis," reflected former West German chancellor Helmut Kohl two decades later. Kohl ascribed Nancy Reagan's suspicion of Germans to the influence of her Jewish friends in Hollywood (an implausible notion, since Ronald Reagan, whom Kohl found to be congenial to Germans, had the same Hollywood friends as his wife).[13]

Even during Reagan's first years in the White House, Nancy Reagan had made clear her desire for improved relations with the Soviet Union. "From the very beginning, she wanted him to be the 'president of peace,'" said Jack Matlock, the career diplomat and Soviet specialist who served as the Soviet specialist on Reagan's National Security Council and later as Reagan's ambassador to Moscow.[14]

In early 1982, as tensions between Washington and Moscow were nearing their peak, Nancy Reagan made a point of telling Dobrynin, the Soviet ambassador, that she would like to visit the Soviet Union, according to Dobrynin's subsequent account. Amid the Reagan administration's ceaseless factional disputes over Soviet policy, the first lady was from the outset one of the doves. "Nancy Reagan was troubled by her husband's reputation as a primitive cold warrior," wrote Richard Pipes, the Harvard professor who served as Reagan's adviser on Soviet affairs in the early years of the administration. Another of Reagan's more hawkish aides, Thomas C. Reed, complained that "once in the White House, Nancy preferred the comforts of détente to the conflicts of Soviet collapse."[15]

Mrs. Reagan made no attempt to hide what she thought. "With the world so dangerous, I felt it was ridiculous for these two heavily armed superpowers to be sitting there and not talking to each other," she wrote in her own memoir. "I encouraged Ronnie to meet with Gorbachev as soon as possible, especially when I realized that some people in the administration did not favor any real talks."[16]

Nancy Reagan's power was sometimes exaggerated. On many of the subjects that came before the president, she didn't voice any opinions at all, if indeed she had any. Even when she did seek to exert influence, she did not always get her way. In private, Reagan could often be stubborn, obstinately refusing to be swayed by his wife or aides. "At times, even Mrs. Reagan lost," said Kuhn.[17] In particular, foreign leaders found that once they succeeded in winning Ronald Reagan's loyalty, he would disregard his wife's advice.

In 1985, both Nancy Reagan and Secretary of State George Shultz vehemently opposed Reagan's planned visit to the German World War II cemetery at Bitburg. The issue was resolved in a phone call between Kohl in Bonn and Reagan at the White House. Kohl suspected that Nancy Reagan was listening in on the call. The West German chancellor said he was not willing to call off the event at Bitburg. If the American president wanted to cancel on his own because of the intense controversy it had engendered, so be it, Kohl said; but he, as chancellor, would not yield. After a long pause, Reagan had replied, "All right, Helmut, I'm coming."[18]

Over the course of Reagan's career, his wife had developed a fairly specific role for herself. "She was the personnel director," explained Stuart Spencer, the political consultant who served as a frequent adviser to Reagan from the 1960s through the 1980s. "She didn't have anything to do with policy. She'd say something every now and then, and he'd look at her and say, 'Hey, Mommy, that's my role.' She'd shut up. But when it came to who is the chief of staff, who is the political director, who is the press secretary, she had input, because he didn't like personnel decisions. . . . Over the years, she developed—she knew who fit best with her husband. She knew what his weaknesses were and his strengths."[19]

After Reagan became president, Nancy Reagan had assumed another job as well, a traditional one for the first lady. She was in charge of the ceremonial side of the White House: the social occasions and state dinners. It was a task she particularly relished; she sought from the outset to restore a sense of grandeur (and opulence) to White House occasions.

In early 1987, these two roles—chief of personnel and director of White House pageantry—combined to give Nancy Reagan more power than she had ever had before. At the beginning of the year, she had personally intervened to persuade her husband to fire Donald Regan as his White House chief of staff and replace him with Howard Baker. On the new White House staff, no one needed to be reminded of the risks of incurring the displeasure of the first lady. When Mrs. Reagan inquired about the possibility of a summit with Gorbachev in Washington, her words carried even more weight than they would have three years earlier.

Together, Ronald and Nancy Reagan became so persistent about a new summit that their efforts began to annoy Secretary of State George Shultz. During Reagan's first term, Shultz had been among the administration officials seeking to persuade the president to begin meeting with Soviet leaders, but Reagan had not yet been ready to do so. Now, the positions of the president and secretary of state were reversed. In late May 1987, Shultz later recalled: "[National Security Adviser] Frank Carlucci called. The president and Nancy, he told me, were talking about having Gorbachev come to the United States and visit their ranch at Thanksgiving. 'Oh, stop,' I said. 'Let the summit idea alone; quit pressing.' "[20]

-2-

AN ARMS DEAL AND ITS OPPONENTS

Reagan obtained the breakthrough he needed for a Washington summit when Gorbachev made a significant concession on arms control in early 1987.

The two leaders' turbulent meeting at Reykjavik the previous October had ended without agreement. Gorbachev had called for far-reaching reductions in missiles or nuclear warheads; he had also proposed that the United States and the Soviet Union eliminate their intermediate-range missiles in Europe. Reagan had responded with enthusiasm. It turned out, however, that all of the Soviet leader's proposals were contingent on American willingness to restrict spending and research for the Strategic Defense Initiative, the president's new missile-defense program. Reagan refused; Reykjavik came unglued.

On February 28, 1987, Gorbachev suddenly announced that the Soviet Union would drop the condition that a deal banning intermediate-range missiles in Europe would have to be part of a larger package. Instead, Gorbachev said, he was willing to go along with a separate deal on this issue "without delay," thus abandoning the effort to get Reagan to restrict work on missile defense beforehand. Soviet officials explained that Gorbachev and his aides wanted to finish at least a limited arms-control agreement while Reagan was in office. They did not want to wait another two years for a new American president; Gorbachev needed to ease tensions with the United States more quickly so that he could proceed with his reforms inside the Soviet Union.[1]

"We start from the assumption that as difficult as it is to conduct business with the United States, we are doomed to it. We have no choice," Gorbachev had told other Soviet leaders, according to the transcripts of a Politburo meeting two days earlier. "Our main problem is to remove the confrontation. That is the central tenet of our entire foreign policy."[2]

Gorbachev's announcement could not have come at a better time for Reagan. He had just replaced his White House chief of staff and was facing widespread skepticism that he could accomplish anything for the remainder of his term. Reagan had been avoiding the press since the beginning of the Iran-Contra scandal, but he rushed to the White House briefing room to praise Gorbachev's new offer.

On a visit to Moscow six weeks later, Shultz told Gorbachev that the Reagan administration was ready to move ahead with the treaty banning intermediate-range missiles in Europe. They began talking about the details, and Gorbachev suggested that he could sign the deal on a trip to the United States. Talking to Reagan over a secure phone from Moscow, the secretary of state reported happily on the prospects for a summit. "He talked about fall to the end of the year," Shultz told Reagan. When Shultz returned to the United States, he flew immediately to the Reagans' ranch house outside Santa Barbara to tell them firsthand about Moscow.[3]

However, at this point Reagan began to confront growing resistance to the prospect of a treaty, both inside the United States and in Europe.

The opposition in Washington was led by the veterans of America's Cold War diplomacy: Richard Nixon, Henry Kissinger, and Brent Scowcroft. These leading figures of the Republican foreign-policy hierarchy had been attacking the president with increasing intensity since he and Gorbachev had talked at Reykjavik about abolishing nuclear weapons. They didn't like what was being said about a treaty banning missiles in Europe. "If we strike the wrong kind of deal, we could create the most profound crisis of the NATO alliance in its 40-year history," wrote Nixon and Kissinger in the Sunday *Washington Post* less than two weeks after Shultz returned from Moscow. It was the grave risk of such a treaty, they said, that had caused them to join together on a public issue for the first time since Nixon's resignation.[4]

Two days after this article, Nixon made his secret visit to the White House. Reagan had invited him for talks about the prospects for a summit and an arms-control agreement. Nixon's memo to himself from that session shows that within minutes after he sat down with Reagan, he began to call into question the administration's negotiations with Gorbachev. Nixon challenged what he later called "the Reagan-Shultz position"—that is, their eagerness for an agreement limiting nuclear weapons.[5]

The thrust of Nixon's message was that Reagan should be more hawkish in dealing with Gorbachev. At one point, Nixon told Reagan that a deal with the Soviets would not really help Reagan's standing with the American public. After all, said Nixon, polls show that military action helps a president far more than diplomacy does. Recalling this part of the conversation in his private memo for his own records later that night, Nixon wrote: "I pointed out that many people felt my popularity had gone up because of my trip to China. In fact, it had improved only slightly. What really sent it up was the bombing and mining of Haiphong."[6]

Nixon argued that a summit in Washington should focus not on arms control but other issues, such as Afghanistan and Central America. He also criticized the details of the arms-control agreement that Reagan and Shultz were envisioning. Gorbachev had proposed a deal in which the two superpowers would remove all intermediate-range missiles from Europe but still keep one hundred of these missiles elsewhere. As a result, the Soviet Union would have maintained intermediate-range missiles in Asia. Nixon argued that Reagan should be able to persuade Gorbachev to give up the missiles in Asia too.

Nixon's broader complaint was that any agreement to remove these missiles from Europe would leave the Soviet Union with a large advantage in conventional military forces. Reagan pointed out that in his own face-to-face conversations with Gorbachev in Geneva and particularly Reykjavik, the Soviet leader had seemed sincere in his desire to reduce Soviet military power, including conventional forces. Gorbachev had said he didn't want to continue the unending arms race between the two superpowers. Nixon thought Reagan was naïve to believe in Gorbachev. He wrote in his subsequent memo that this part of his conversation with Reagan was "somewhat disturbing."[7]

Reagan's high-level critics were much more enthusiastic than he was about the value of nuclear weapons. American nuclear weapons were a key element to the American strategy of preventing Soviet aggression, and their supply should not be reduced, they argued. The principal exponent of this point of view was Brent Scowcroft, who had been Kissinger's aide and President Ford's national security adviser.

"It is not self-evident that fewer nuclear weapons *ipso facto* represent a better strategic situation," wrote Scowcroft in the spring of 1987. "We have for some 40 years relied on the threat of nuclear weapons to keep the Soviet hordes at bay." Scowcroft particularly opposed removing intermediate-range missiles from Europe. These missiles could deliver nuclear weapons deep into Soviet territory, Scowcroft argued, and their presence reassured Europe that the United States would come to its defense.[8]

In an interview nearly two decades later, Scowcroft continued to believe he had been correct. The American intermediate-range missiles in Europe "were what we relied on in case of an attack, to cut the Soviet front-line troops from their supplies," Scowcroft said. "What we needed to do was to cut the Soviet supply lines, to attenuate the force of any attack." The intermediate-range missiles gave the Americans that capacity, Scowcroft argued, and "it was wrong to negotiate them away."[9]

Reagan and Shultz pointed out that the United States would still be able to protect Europe with the many hundreds of nuclear weapons it could use from bombers or from American ships at sea. The treaty under discussion with Gorbachev would not affect those other nuclear weapons at all; it would merely cover the intermediate-range missiles in Europe. Still, the attacks on the proposed deal did not abate.

There was inescapable irony in the fact that the criticism of Reagan's conciliatory stance toward Gorbachev came from many of the same former officials who had, during the 1970s, been the proponents of détente with the Soviet Union.

To an extent, their reactions may have reflected their sense of alienation from the Reagan administration's diplomacy. For years, Nixon and Kissinger had been at the center of all conversations between the United States and the Soviet Union. Now they were on the outside. Not only were they not responsible for the proposed new arms agreement, but they had no public identification with it of any kind. Indeed, they were in position to gain considerably more public attention as opponents of the Reagan administration's diplomacy than as supporters of it.

During his talk with Reagan, Nixon privately acknowledged that Kissinger's motivations, in particular, might be suspect. The former president said he had heard that Shultz "was climbing the wall because he felt that Kissinger and I were attempting to sabotage his agreement." Nixon conceded it might have appeared that "if the agreement had been made by Kissinger itself [*sic*], he would have hailed it as a historic achievement." Nevertheless, the former president went on, while others might believe this about Kissinger, Nixon himself certainly did not.[10]

The condemnations from the foreign-policy elite also reflected a general disbelief that Ronald Reagan could be responsible for an improved relationship with the Soviet Union—or indeed, that any arms-control agreement negotiated under Reagan could be of genuine significance. After all, Reagan had been the leading opponent of détente in the 1970s. His early years in the White House had brought a period of Cold War tension unprecedented since the Cuban missile crisis. He had consistently rejected efforts at arms control during the initial years of his presidency. How, then, could these veterans of détente take seriously what Reagan was now attempting to negotiate? The former officials had grasped correctly the political dynamics underlying some of Reagan's diplomacy with Gorbachev—above all, Reagan's desire to regain stature and divert public attention away from Iran-Contra. Where they erred was in dismissing the long-term value and impact of the diplomacy itself.

Above all, the former officials reflected a static view not only of Reagan but of the Soviet Union. They refused to acknowledge the possibility of fundamental change in America's Cold War adversary. They argued repeatedly that Gorbachev was one more Soviet leader with the same foreign-policy goals, approaches, and assumptions as those who had preceded him. "Gorbachev has taken the first steps towards reform at home, but has not retreated one inch from Moscow's posture abroad," wrote Nixon and Kissinger in their commentary for the *Washington Post* in April 1987. "Indeed, his policy can be said to be a subtler implementation of historic Soviet patterns."[11]

In this, Nixon and Kissinger turned out to be wrong. Gorbachev was indeed in the midst of a profound transformation of Soviet foreign policy. In retrospect, there were early signs of this change in 1986, when Gorbachev began offering reductions in nuclear weaponry, and in early 1987, when he was so eager for an arms deal and a new summit with Reagan that he dropped his conditions. Critics such as Nixon and Kissinger tended to dismiss these efforts as cosmetic tactical maneuvers by Gorbachev on behalf of the same old Soviet foreign policy. But soon the changes of Soviet behavior would become undeniable. Only a month after the Nixon-Kissinger article was published, Gorbachev appeared in East Berlin to propound the new military doctrine under which the Warsaw Pact would henceforth be considered merely a "defensive" alliance that would no longer view the United States and its allies as enemies. That new doctrine undermined the Soviet-backed regimes in Eastern Europe—for if there was no threat from the West, then what was the justification for political repression, isolation, or economic deprivation?

In hindsight, it seems clear that Reagan and Shultz had understood Gorbachev better than Nixon and Kissinger. They intuited more quickly what his leadership of the Soviet Union might mean for American foreign policy. They seemed to comprehend, where the old hands did not, that even if Gorbachev was seeking to preserve the Communist Party's control at home, he was at the same time attempting to alter the Soviet Union's relationship to Europe and to the rest of the world. As a result, it was in America's interest to transact as much business with him as possible.

The traditional Washington outlook, exemplified by Nixon, Kissinger, and Scowcroft, was to view the Cold War as a matter of strategic calculations: troop deployments, military forces, overseas bases, nuclear weapons. Reagan and Shultz, by contrast, tended to view the Cold War as a contest of ideas and economic systems. Throughout his anti-Communist career, Reagan had always cared more about ideology than Nixon; now, this same interest in ideology made him instinctively more open to a Soviet leader whose words and ideas sounded different from those of his predecessors. When Nixon and Kissinger sought to minimize Gorbachev's impact by saying he had moved toward reform only at home and not abroad, they overlooked the fact that Gorbachev's domestic reforms had far-reaching consequences for Soviet foreign policy. Eastern European leaders such as Erich Honecker in East Germany were forced to explain why they could not allow *glasnost* too.

Finally, the critics of Reagan's 1987 diplomacy did not give the president credit for flexibility. By their logic, Reagan had been a hawk toward the Soviet Union; therefore, he would remain a hawk. If his actions during his second term seemed increasingly dovish, they should be discounted. But Reagan's zigzag approach to Soviet policy did not fit into such linear thinking. Indeed, Reagan's unusual blend of truculence toward the Soviet Union in his early years in the White House and eagerness for accommodation later on made sense as a negotiating tactic. It confused and unsettled his Soviet counterparts. It wasn't entirely deliberate, but it was effective.

Those who criticized Reagan's proposed deal with Gorbachev overlooked the larger political significance this diplomacy would carry inside both countries. Inside the Soviet Union, it gave Gorbachev the breathing room to proceed with his domestic reforms. It enabled him to fend off powerful constituencies such as the armed forces and the KGB, which could no longer argue that the Soviet Union should not risk domestic change in the face of an immediate external threat.

Reagan's conciliatory stance toward Gorbachev carried broad political implications inside the United States too. It helped foster the perception that the Cold War was winding down. Reagan had been the leader of the conservative wing of the Republican Party for more than two decades, ever since Barry Goldwater's defeat in 1964. His willingness to enter into an arms-control agreement with the Soviet Union carried considerably greater weight because of his own reputation and his unimpeachable credentials with the right wing of the Republican Party.

Jimmy Carter, Reagan's predecessor, had tried to win ratification of an arms-control agreement with the Soviet Union. He had been soundly defeated. A more moderate Republican would almost certainly have had similar difficulties. Jack Matlock, who served as the American ambassador to Moscow under both Reagan and President George H. W. Bush, believed that if Bush had been president instead of Reagan in 1987 and 1988, he would not have been able to win Senate approval of the proposed deal with Gorbachev.[12]

During a visit to Moscow in 1986, Nixon had suggested to Gorbachev that the Soviet Union try to conclude some sort of arms-control agreement with Reagan, rather than waiting until Reagan's successor came to the White House, because Reagan had a better chance of winning Senate approval of whatever deal he made. If the Soviets waited for a new American leader, Nixon argued, then Reagan, as an ex-president, could emerge as an incomparably powerful opponent. Nixon's assumption that Gorbachev was just another Soviet leader proved way off the mark, but he understood better than anyone else the political dynamics of the Cold War inside the United States.

Throughout the early months of 1987, Reagan and Shultz were obliged to defuse one other source of potential opposition to their agreement with Gorbachev: America's allies. Leaders in Western Europe had been rattled by the discussion between Reagan and Gorbachev at Reykjavik about cutting back or eliminating nuclear weapons and ballistic missiles. They feared Western Europe might be left more vulnerable to an attack by conventional forces, in which the Soviet Union and its Warsaw Pact allies held a considerable advantage.

The most important and most vulnerable of the European leaders was West German chancellor Helmut Kohl. During Reagan's first term in the White House, Kohl had confronted intense domestic opposition when he supported the deployment of American intermediate-range missiles on German soil. Now, only four years later, Reagan was talking about removing the same American missiles. To be sure, under the agreement under discussion, the Soviets would also remove their own missiles, the ones that had originally prompted the American deployment. Nevertheless, the Soviet-American deal seemed to leave Kohl in an awkward position.

In the spring of 1987, soon after his secretary of state returned from Moscow with the outlines of an agreement, Reagan went to work on Kohl. If the president could persuade him to go along with the deal, it would help deflect criticism not only in Western Europe but in Washington as well. Nixon, Kissinger, and Scowcroft based their objections in considerable part on the effect such an agreement would have on American relations with Western Europe. Kohl's approval would undercut them.

On May 6, the president agreed to take the lead in a concerted campaign to get the German chancellor to go along with the ban on American and

Soviet missiles in Europe. The following week, he called Kohl to lobby him. "I think he'll be cooperative," Reagan wrote in his diary.[13] Day after day, the National Security Council monitored every possible clue about what West Germany might do. Finally, in early June, Kohl endorsed the Reagan-Shultz proposal and won approval from the West German Bundestag for it.

The chancellor's decision was far from enthusiastic. He said the agreement contained "a very serious disadvantage for us Germans" because it would leave the Soviet Union with a "crushing superiority" in tactical nuclear weapons and a "clear superiority" in conventional forces.[14] He gave his assent to the Soviet-American agreement with one important qualification. West Germany's air force possessed seventy-two Pershing missiles, which carried American nuclear warheads. The agreement Shultz and Gorbachev had worked out covered only the missiles of the United States and the Soviet Union. Kohl said that while going along with the removal of the American Pershings, West Germany intended to keep its own.

Finally, in the summer of 1987, two closely related issues were settled to the Reagan administration's liking. In July, Gorbachev announced he had decided to support a worldwide ban on Soviet and American intermediate-range missiles, rather than simply the removal of such missiles from Europe. The Soviet Union dropped its insistence on keeping one hundred missiles in Asia—a change that was welcomed in China, Japan, and other Asian countries.

West Germany still had a problem, however, because Soviet officials insisted that any deal should also cover the seventy-two West German missiles with American warheads. Kohl came under further pressure at home to support the movement toward disarmament by the two superpowers. Both the opposition Social Democrats and Foreign Minister Hans-Dietrich Genscher urged him to give up on the West German missiles; but Kohl's own conservative supporters urged him to stand fast.

In public, Reagan supported Kohl's position, saying the United States couldn't presume to speak or negotiate for West Germany. Privately, Reagan appealed to the West German chancellor. "We made it clear to Kohl and Genscher that they weren't going to queer this agreement," recalled Matlock.

On August 26, the German chancellor yielded. He promised that after the United States and Soviet Union signed their deal and put it into effect, West Germany would dismantle its own Pershing missiles. The objections of the allies had been overcome. The outlines of a deal between Reagan and Gorbachev were complete.[15]

-3-

SHULTZ'S PITCH

The obvious question is why Mikhail Gorbachev should have been so accommodating. During the first nine months of 1987, Gorbachev made not one but several significant concessions to the Reagan administration. He dropped his insistence that the United States restrict research into strategic missile defense. He laid the groundwork for a far-reaching agreement to ban intermediate-range missiles. In the process of negotiating that agreement, he abandoned two previous Soviet positions: that the deal should apply only to Europe, and that the Soviet Union should be able to retain one hundred intermediate-range missiles in Asia.

What were the underlying causes for Gorbachev's behavior? To answer that, one must look to the Soviet economy and to the series of suggestions Gorbachev was getting in 1987 from American visitors about how the Soviet Union might transform itself. Secretary of State George Shultz in particular had developed a new set of themes to offer Gorbachev, ones that were well attuned both to the Soviet leader's interests and to his vulnerabilities at the time.

During Reagan's second term, Shultz began to weave into his speeches and congressional testimony some material that had little to do with the nitty-gritty of American foreign policy or diplomacy. He would frequently depart from current events for an abstract discussion of the future. He did this so often that reporters who had already heard earlier renditions would roll their eyes.

What Shultz was saying amounted to a version of the set of ideas that eventually became popularized as globalization. What the secretary of state was saying in the late 1980s was strikingly similar to what prominent proponents of globalization—such as, for example, President Bill Clinton or *New York Times* columnist Thomas Friedman—would assert in the following decade. Shultz spoke regularly about the information revolution, the impact of ever-faster computers and telecommunications, the speed with which money and capital flowed from one country to another, and the ways in which manufacturing could be transferred around the world. "With the advent of 'real time' transfers of information, an announcement made in the Rose Garden can be reflected two minutes later in the stock market in Singapore," Shultz declared in one speech. In another, he said, "The very process of production crosses national boundaries. . . . It is often difficult to identify what is 'national' and what is 'foreign.' "[1]

The talk about globalization dated to the late 1970s, when economists noticed that manufacturing companies were beginning to transfer production from one country to another. In 1983, a business school professor named Theodore Levitt wrote an article for the *Harvard Business Review* in which he argued that changes in technology allowed companies such as McDonald's and Coca-Cola to operate throughout the world. He pointed out that consumers everywhere were beginning to use the same standardized products and wear the same clothes, such as blue jeans. Levitt's article was titled "The Globalization of Markets."[2]

Shultz, an economist by training, had previously been the dean of the University of Chicago's business school and U.S. secretary of the treasury. He didn't use the word *globalization,* but simply talked about the information revolution and its impact. He got some of his information and ideas from his friend Walter Wriston, the former chairman of Citibank, who had described how easy it had become to move large sums of money around the world almost instantaneously. Wriston had also begun to talk and write about the larger political changes that would result from the advances in communications and information. A global marketplace meant that even democratic countries would have to adjust to "a wholly new definition of sovereignty," Wriston wrote. For Communist governments and other closed societies, the impact would be even greater: they would no longer be able to control what their own people saw and heard.

Shultz pushed the State Department to explore these ideas. In 1986, Richard D. Kauzlarich, a foreign-service officer and intelligence analyst who specialized in international economics, was assigned to gather materials on the implications of the information revolution for American foreign policy. Kauzlarich prepared charts on the increasing speed and declining costs of personal computers, on the replacement of old-style commodities such as copper by fiber optics. He found examples of how manufacturing was being moved from one country to another. One favorite was a shipping label for an American company that made integrated circuits. The label said: "Made in one or more of the following countries: Korea, Hong Kong, Malasia [sic], Singapore, Taiwan, Mauritius, Thailand, Indonesia, Mexico, Philippines. The exact country of origin is unknown." The memos that accompanied this research drew stark conclusions: "Increasingly," Kauzlarich wrote, "countries which cannot or will not compete in the global market place and interact with ideas from other societies will find themselves falling behind the advanced innovators and producers."[3]

Shultz introduced these themes into his meetings with several foreign ministers. He had a small audience for which this material was especially targeted: the top leaders of the Soviet Union, above all Gorbachev and his foreign minister, Eduard Shevardnadze. On a visit to Moscow in April 1987, after clearing with Reagan the details of what he would say, Shultz departed from the usual idiom of Soviet-American diplomacy. During a break in a long afternoon meeting about arms control, Shultz set up some of the graphs and charts that Kauzlarich and other aides had prepared. He told Gorbachev that the world's economy was changing rapidly, that financial markets and manufacturing were becoming international in scope, and that governments would have to learn to adapt to a new world where information was more important than minerals or heavy industry.

Shultz's implicit message was that if the Soviets didn't jump into the global marketplace fairly quickly, they would never catch up. Richard Solomon, then a senior State Department official, said in an interview two decades later that Shultz was engaged in "a kind of psychological warfare," aimed at telling Gorbachev that the Soviet system was failing. "Reagan and Shultz were trying to spook the Soviet leadership," recalled Solomon.[4]

Soviet leaders, particularly Gorbachev, did not need to be reminded of the country's economic difficulties. In the spring of 1987, Gorbachev had been in power for two years. He had been appointed general secretary in no small part because of the perception within the Soviet hierarchy that, since he was younger and more energetic than his predecessors, he might somehow find a way to reinvigorate the economy.

The Soviet economy had been slowly stagnating since the 1960s. The spike in oil prices produced by the OPEC cartel in the 1970s helped to divert attention away from these chronic problems; the Soviet Union was taking in huge new sums by exporting oil and was earning more by selling arms to Middle East countries awash in oil revenues. The Soviet Union used this revenue on a military buildup and on foreign adventures such as the invasion of Afghanistan. But by the mid-1980s the price of oil was declining, and so was Soviet oil production.[5]

The oil boom was over. The Soviets were left with an economy in which consumer goods were in desperately short supply, military spending was enormous, and technology remained at levels well behind the West's. Among those who worried about the country's inertia were leaders of the Soviet military, who feared that the backwardness of the Soviet economy undermined the capabilities of the armed forces. They watched with growing dismay in the late 1970s and early 1980s as the Pentagon developed new precision-guided weapons more advanced than anything the Soviet Union could produce. In June 1984, a senior Soviet military leader showed the staff of the Communist Party's Central Committee a documentary about the new American weaponry. Having watched it, one Soviet official wrote:

It was amazing: missiles homing in on their targets from hundreds and thousands of kilometers away; aircraft carriers, sub-

marines that could do anything, winged missiles that, like in a cartoon, could be guided through a canyon and hit a target 10 meters in diameter from 2,500 kilometers away. An incredible breakthrough of modern technology. And, of course, unthinkably expensive.[6]

When Gorbachev came to power in 1985, he focused on restoring discipline to the economy with campaigns against absenteeism and alcohol. Those efforts proved largely unsuccessful, and economic problems deepened in his first two years. The anti-alcohol campaign caused state revenues to plummet; the nuclear disaster at Chernobyl of April 26, 1986, sucked up billions in clean-up costs.[7] Soviet officials who traveled overseas were increasingly demoralized by the disparity between Communist and capitalist countries. "I compared the bustling capital of Thailand, with its vibrant economy and its people, who looked busy and dynamic, with the economic decline and people's apathy that was so obvious . . . , particularly in Vietnam," recalled Pavel Palazchenko, the Soviet official who became Gorbachev's interpreter, after a 1987 visit to Southeast Asia. "The contrast was dramatic. It could no longer be explained by the ravages of war."[8]

Increasingly, Gorbachev turned his attention to helping the economy through changes in Soviet foreign policy—by ending the Soviet war in Afghanistan and above all, by limiting the ever more expensive arms competition with the United States. In 1986, shortly before the meeting at Reykjavik with Reagan, Gorbachev told his aide Anatoly Chernyaev that his highest priority was to prevent being drawn further into the arms race. "We will lose, because right now we are already at the end of our tether," said Gorbachev.[9]

Throughout his career, Reagan had been in many respects the archetypical hawk. He had been in the vanguard in opposing Communist ideology and in supporting increases in American defense spending to combat the Soviet military threat. Yet for a conservative Republican, Reagan's views were also in a few ways unusual. Far from portraying the Soviet Union as all-powerful, he had from time to time expressed a cheery optimism that the Soviet system was fragile. During the mid-1970s, he asserted at one point that the Communist system was merely "a temporary aberration which will one day disappear from the earth because it is contrary to human nature." Ordinary citizens inside the Soviet Union wanted the same ordinary consumer goods and benefits as those in the West, and might eventually voice their discontent, Reagan argued. "Maybe we should drop a few million typical mail order catalogues on Minsk & Pinsk & Moscow to whet their appetites," Reagan said in one of his late-1970s radio addresses. After the Geneva summit, he wrote a friend that Gorbachev seemed to realize the Soviet economy was in shambles.[10]

It was one thing for Reagan and Shultz to be aware of Gorbachev's economic plight, however, and another to decide what they should tell him about it. Gorbachev would hardly be receptive to arguments that the Soviet system was fundamentally flawed. The Soviets were not prepared to abandon all at once the ideas and institutions they had developed over the previous seven decades. Nor were they going to listen to a lecture about the superiority of capitalism from representatives of the United States, their geopolitical adversary for forty years. Shultz's presentation to Gorbachev was aimed at circumventing these difficulties.

During one of Shultz's first meetings with Shevardnadze, he had spoken about the importance of human rights. The Soviet foreign minister cut him short. We may do some of the things you want, but we won't do them simply to please you, Shevardnadze said. We'll do them only if they serve our own interests. Shultz began looking for arguments for why it was to the Soviet Union's own advantage to change its policies.

Globalization and the information revolution offered Shultz a solution. He argued that the Soviet Union should alter its relationship with the rest of the world because doing so would make it economically stronger—and conversely, clinging to the status quo would enfeeble its international position. "The basic argument was that we're in an information age that demands openness, and it's going to happen all over the world," recalled Shultz in an interview. "And any country that closes itself off, or stays apart from it, that country is going to lose out."[11]

Shultz's presentation had the virtue of being phrased in terms of inevitable economic trends. He was not telling Gorbachev what he should do, but merely explaining how the international economy was being transformed. The presentation played down relations between the two superpowers and instead emphasized the larger context of what was happening elsewhere around the world. In fact, there was an implicit warning that the Soviet Union would be in danger of losing out to other rising powers if it concentrated too heavily on its military competition with the United States. Shultz specifically described to Gorbachev how other countries such as China, Singapore, South Korea, and Israel were rapidly advancing in technology. He did not have to mention the two other nations whose economic power was rising still more rapidly: Japan and West Germany, both of which had recovered from the destruction of World War II.

The collection of ideas that Shultz offered Gorbachev had some short-comings. Shultz was suggesting that Gorbachev reinvigorate the Soviet Union by integrating it into the international economy, but after seventy years of central planning, the Soviet Union was in no position to do so. Shultz's presentation emphasized the simple dichotomy of an open society versus a closed one: in his schema, as a result of the information revolution, open societies would succeed and closed ones would fail. He did not suggest the possibility of opening the economy while maintaining a tight control over dissent—the approach that China would later take, with extraordinary economic success.

Nevertheless, it seems clear Shultz's message was well crafted to appeal to the Soviet leader. "Gorbachev's fundamental failing was that he did not really understand economic problems and the policies to deal with them. He was always looking for advice," wrote former Soviet ambassador Anatoly Dobrynin, who returned from Washington to Moscow in 1986 and worked for the Politburo for the following three years.[12]

Talking to other Soviet leaders two days after his conversation with Shultz, Gorbachev seemed to embrace some of the secretary of state's ideas. "The world is interconnected, interdependent," he told the Politburo. In his memoirs, written nearly a decade later, Gorbachev described his meeting with Shultz in April 1987 to have been "a milestone. It was the first time that we touched on the philosophical aspects of the new policy, on the roles and responsibilities of our countries." He did not discuss the specifics of Shultz's lecture about the information revolution. But the Soviet leader said he had come to the conclusion during that meeting that in Shultz, he was dealing with "a serious man of sound political judgment . . . a statesman, an intellectual, a creative and at the same time a far-seeing person."[13]

While Shultz encouraged Gorbachev to dream about a revived Soviet economy, others in the Reagan administration had for several years been hoping to undermine that economy. Indeed, years later, some of Reagan's former aides and conservative admirers argued that the Soviet Union's collapse had resulted from a deliberate, if unstated, campaign by the administration to drive the country into bankruptcy.

"Nobody talked about it. Nobody articulated it," Jeane Kirkpatrick, Reagan's ambassador to the United Nations, said in an interview. "And I mean nobody, ever, articulated it. But I think that everybody understood it, that that was our goal, frankly, right there from the beginning." By "our" goal, Kirkpatrick acknowledged, she was speaking not necessarily of the entire U.S. government but of a small group within the administration during Reagan's early years in office: above all by the CIA director William Casey, Defense Secretary Caspar Weinberger, National Security Adviser William Clark; and herself. It was a goal, Kirkpatrick believed, that was shared by Reagan.[14]

By this interpretation of Reagan administration policy, the measures for subverting the Soviet regime were led by the Strategic Defense Initiative and the broader defense buildup, both of which might require high-cost Soviet responses. Other elements included cooperation with Saudi Arabia to drive down the price of oil; restrictions on high-technology exports to the Soviet Union; and covert support for the Solidarity movement in Poland and the mujahideen rebels in Afghanistan.[15] In addition, Casey's CIA is reported to have carried out a program of economic sabotage, including at one point an apparently successful attempt to explode a pipeline in Siberia.[16] Reagan's 1983 executive order, labeled NSDD-75, said vaguely that one strand of American policy was to create "internal pressure" on the Soviet regime.

There are, however, several problems with the idea that the Reagan administration won the Cold War by intentionally driving the Soviet Union over the brink.

The first is that there is no consensus among Reagan administration officials that such a strategy was ever the driving force behind the American policy. The strategy may have existed in Casey's mind, but others in the administration did not see it that way. During a series of discussions about Soviet policy among the administration's leading officials, "nobody argued that the United States should try to bring the Soviet Union down," recalled Jack Matlock, who served on the staff of Reagan's National Security Council.[17] Even Weinberger, the administration's most ardent hawk, did not believe Reagan's policies were aimed at toppling the Soviet Union. "There were some people who said that the whole thing was just an attempt to run the Soviet Union into bankruptcy. Actually, it was not, in my view," said Weinberger in one interview in 2002. "What he [Reagan] needed, what we needed and we were in full agreement on, was to restore our military deterrent capability—to get a capability that would make it quite clear to the Soviets that they couldn't win a war against us."[18]

The secret policy directive NSDD-75, which lies at the heart of claims that the Reagan administration sought to bring down the Soviet Union, was in fact watered down by Reagan himself before it was approved. By the subsequent account of Richard Pipes, the Soviet specialist on the National Security Council staff who drafted NSDD-75, the president personally intervened to delete provisions that would have authorized American efforts to block the Soviet Union's access to hard currency and would have sought to induce the Soviets to shift resources from defense industries to consumer goods. Pipes recalled that while signing this order, Reagan specifically emphasized the importance of compromise with the Soviet leadership.[19]

Even if there was a faction in the early Reagan administration that sought to bring the Soviet Union down, that group of officials increasingly lost out as time went on. "The old shoes were hopelessly outgunned; one by one, we drifted away," wrote Thomas Reed, who first worked for Reagan in California during the 1960s. Reed, who favored tough policies to confront the Soviet Union, had served as Air Force secretary during the Ford administration and worked on Reagan's National Security Council staff in the early years, before giving up.[20]

Reed's departure was merely part of the larger trend. Pipes left the NSC in 1983; Clark was replaced a few months later, Kirkpatrick left at the end of Reagan's first term. Casey stayed on but died in early 1987. Meanwhile, Reagan's own views evolved. In an interview for this book, Kirkpatrick said Reagan for years believed that Soviet leaders "weren't reliable people, that they were aggressive and expansionist and dangerous." She then added: "Those were his views, and he maintained those views, I think—until the Gorbachev era." Gorbachev, she said, changed Reagan's thinking.[21]

The fact that Reagan shifted course does not exclude the possibility that the policies of his first term had a long-term effect on the Soviet economy that might have eventually led to the country's disintegration. Yet there is little evidence that the American actions brought down the Soviet regime. To be sure, some of the Casey-led operations served the purpose of weakening the Soviet Union. Above all, there was the covert program in Afghanistan, which first prolonged the war there and then led to a Soviet withdrawal. Reagan's Strategic Defense Initiative had an impact only if one accepts Gorbachev's debatable assumption that the Soviet Union was obliged to stop it or match it.

The Soviet economy was foundering because of deep-seated and chronic problems that had little or nothing to do with the Reagan administration's policies. Although the Soviet system was in decline, it was not headed toward a collapse, and Reagan's first-term policies, including the defense buildup and the covert-action programs, did not cause the collapse. "Even though Soviet socialism had clearly lost the competition with the West, it was lethargically stable, and could have continued muddling on for quite some time," observed one scholar who studied the Soviet economy for this era.[22]

The Soviet leadership was overextended and would have had to retrench in one way or another, but it could have survived. Confronted by the new challenges from the United States, the Soviet Union might have sought to cut defense spending in the short term while slowly regaining strength over the long run, meanwhile maintaining the existing, repressive political order.[23] (In fact, the Washington critics of Reagan's second-term policies—not just the critics on the political right, but also "realist" Soviet specialists like Brent Scowcroft and Robert Gates—were concerned that Gorbachev's strategy was to rebuild Soviet power in this gradual fashion.)

Instead, the proximate cause of the Soviet collapse was Gorbachev. It was Gorbachev who made the historic decision not to intervene with force in Eastern Europe in 1989. It was Gorbachev who elected to reform the Soviet system in a way that left it partially opened and partially closed, partially democratized but with the Communist Party and the KGB still the country's most powerful institutions. This was the peculiar, unworkable hybrid arrangement that led, eventually, to the Soviet implosion.

The policies of Reagan's first term did not determine what Gorbachev would do. Rather, Reagan's willingness to do business with Gorbachev gave the Soviet leader the time and space he needed to demolish the Soviet system. The president and his secretary of state gave Gorbachev the clear though questionable message that if he reformed the economy, if he managed to integrate the Soviet system into a rapidly globalizing world, then that system might survive. Gorbachev unintentionally destroyed the Soviet system. Reagan gave him the help he needed to do it.

Those who dealt directly with Reagan during his second term did not believe he had ever sought to bring down the Soviet regime. "I don't think he ever thought of it in terms of bankrupting the Soviet Union or forcing it to collapse," said Frank Carlucci, who served as Reagan's national security adviser and defense secretary. "He just saw it as a lousy system, and if we could negotiate them into some common sense, they'd change their system."

Asked two decades later whether Reagan had intended to topple or bankrupt the Soviet regime, West German chancellor Helmut Kohl replied, "No, I don't think so. But he did think that the Soviet Union was simply living above its means."[24]

-4-

THE GRAND TOUR REJECTED

By early September 1987, the Reagan White House was already excitedly preparing for a summit in the United States, even though Mikhail Gorbachev had not yet agreed to one. White House documents show that officials weighed the options, sites, and logistics over and over again.

At times, the internal memos read as though the principal adversary of the White House was not the Soviet Union but the State Department. White House officials working for Chief of Staff Howard Baker and National Security Adviser Frank Carlucci wanted to make sure that they, not the diplomats, would be in charge of Gorbachev's still-unscheduled visit to America. One list of talking points prepared before a meeting between Baker and Secretary of State George Shultz pointed out that the "President's personal support operation" had been in charge of trips to the United States by Queen Elizabeth and Chinese premier Zhao Ziyang. The memo then set out the arguments for running a Gorbachev summit in the same fashion:

> *Previous meetings with Gorbachev (Geneva and Iceland) were result of coordination group chaired by Chief of*

Staff and NSC advisor and a working group of their designates. . . .

Overall control of schedule and events should rest with group representing all relevant agencies (State, White House, NSC, USIA, etc.); group to be co-chaired by Baker and Carlucci, as was done in past. [emphasis in original][1]

Reagan oversaw this planning. He made it clear to the staff that he desired as extensive a summit as possible. The Reagans wanted to invite the Gorbachevs to their home outside Santa Barbara. In addition, the president himself was eager to take the Soviet leader on a tour of the United States to display the wealth and prosperity of the country. "He wanted to take Gorbachev to car plants, he wanted to show him his beloved California and he wanted him on the ranch," recalled Colin Powell, then a young army officer serving as deputy national security adviser, who had been assigned by Carlucci the unenviable task of arranging the summit. "He was so confident of who we were and what we are that he wanted Gorbachev to see it."[2]

White House memos set forth the various scenarios. The most elaborate was called "The Grand Tour," a week-long extravaganza. After a couple of days in Washington, Gorbachev could be taken on a multistop westward excursion across the United States to California. White House officials proposed, for example, that Reagan could show Gorbachev a "City That Works"; the possibilities included Pittsburgh, Atlanta, and St. Louis. They also suggested taking the Soviet leader to a farm state and a national park.

A second, middle-ground scenario was a "Washington and California" summit. After Washington, Gorbachev might fly to Los Angeles for a foreign-policy speech at the World Affairs Council and some Hollywood event, before finally going up the Pacific Coast to the Reagan ranch. Even for the third and most limited option—called "Washington Only"—White House planners tried to satisfy Reagan's desire to show Gorbachev the United States through what they called an event "Outside the Beltway"—a reference to the suburban highway that encircles Washington. They listed a number of possibilities such as Harpers Ferry, West Virginia, and Gettysburg, Pennsylvania. The memos did not explore the tricky question of what lessons Gorbachev should be expected to draw from America's Civil War sites.[3]

In mid-September, Soviet Foreign Minister Eduard Shevardnadze landed in Washington carrying a letter from Gorbachev to Reagan. The Soviet leader made it clear he wanted to get past the talking stage and reach some concrete agreement with Reagan soon. "The question now is whether we will take that first step which the peoples of the world are so eagerly awaiting," Gorbachev wrote.[4]

The letter appealed to Reagan for further progress in a number of areas, including a treaty on long-range strategic weapons and limits on the president's Strategic Defense Initiative. On one issue, Gorbachev was specific: he was ready to conclude the deal banning Soviet and American intermediate-range missiles. Gorbachev also said he was prepared to talk about coming to the United States; he said he had authorized Shevardnadze to talk with Reagan and Shultz about "possible options for developing contacts at the summit level." Yet Gorbachev remained elusive—from the Reagans' perspective, distressingly so—about a date for a summit. In three days of talks in Washington, Shevardnadze refused to be pinned down. The Soviets seemed to be holding out to see if Reagan might make some concessions elsewhere in exchange for a summit.

Reagan and Shultz decided to play up the positive elements in Gorbachev's message. As Shevardnadze was leaving town, the United States and Soviet Union released a joint statement saying that they had reached an "agreement in principle" to conclude a treaty banning intermediate-range missiles. The statement said Shultz would go to Moscow the following month to work out a date for a summit later in the fall in which the treaty could be signed. At the White House, the president appeared before reporters and was asked how he would respond to complaints by conservatives that he was in too much of a hurry for the summit. "I don't know of anything in my life I waited over six years for," Reagan replied.[5]

Reagan's announcement of the impending treaty was too much for Henry Kissinger. He argued again that these missiles were essential to the close relationship between the United States and its allies. When Shultz phoned Kissinger to tell him about the agreement, Kissinger warned the secretary of state that it "undoes forty years of NATO." In public, Kissinger went further. He accused the Reagan administration of talking and behaving like the antinuclear activists who spearheaded the massive street demonstrations of the early 1980s. "The most conservative U.S. administration of the postwar era stigmatized nuclear weapons with arguments all but indistinguishable from the Committee for Nuclear Disarmament," Kissinger wrote in *Newsweek*. He claimed that the proposed agreement had produced "a crisis of confidence" between the United States and Western Europe. "Many Europeans are convinced a gap is being created that in time will enable the Soviet Union to threaten Europe while sparing the United States."[6] This was, overall, a profound misreading of where Gorbachev and the Soviet Union were headed.

Throughout the fall of 1987, there was a sense of impermanence in the air, a series of reminders that things do not always proceed in orderly fashion. In the United States, the stock market crashed, falling by 508 points (or more than 22 percent) on Black Monday, October 19. At the time, the Reagans were preoccupied with their own personal difficulties. Nancy Reagan was diagnosed with breast cancer and underwent a mastectomy. For several days, the president shuttled between the White House and his wife's room at Bethesda Naval Hospital. When one reporter asked whether the market crash might be "your fault," Reagan jibed, "Is it my fault? For what? Taking cookies to my wife?"[7] Four days after Nancy Reagan returned to the White House, her mother died, and the Reagans quickly left Washington for the funeral in Arizona. For most of October, official White House business was a secondary concern for the Reagans.

During that same month, there was a change in the senior ranks of the Reagan administration, another sign of the old order passing. In early October, Secretary of Defense Caspar Weinberger announced his resignation, explaining that his wife was in poor health. During Reagan's early years in the White House, Weinberger had been the cabinet's most powerful hawk, an ardent proponent of new weapons systems and defense spending. But in Reagan's second term, members of Congress had grown increasingly skeptical of his incessant pleas for more money and weaponry. Weinberger's former senior aides Richard Armitage and Colin Powell used to joke about Weinberger's proclivity for "taping"—offering Capitol Hill exactly the same answers in the same words and phrases he had used repeatedly in the past. "You have to change your answers a little bit, and Secretary Weinberger never did, so there were a lot more complaints from Capitol Hill," recalled Armitage.[8]

Weinberger's departure followed by only a few months the resignation of his own top Soviet specialist, Assistant Secretary of Defense Richard Perle, the neoconservative who had for years ardently opposed arms-control agreements with the Soviet Union. Perle left the Pentagon after he, too, found the climate on Capitol Hill increasingly inhospitable; he had clashed repeatedly with Senator Sam Nunn, the chairman of the Senate Armed Services Committee.[9]

Reagan appointed his national security adviser, Frank Carlucci, to replace Weinberger as defense secretary, and promoted Colin Powell, the deputy national adviser, to replace Carlucci. Earlier in the year, the president had named William Webster as CIA director, replacing William Casey, who had died of a brain tumor. During the previous years, Weinberger and Casey had been the secretary of state's principal bureaucratic adversaries. Now, for the first time, Shultz was the unchallenged leader of Reagan's foreign policy team. Where previously the Reagan administration had bogged down in fractious disputes over how to deal with the Soviet Union, the new team of Shultz, Carlucci, Powell, and Webster worked together in relative harmony.

Conservatives grew even more dismayed than they had been six months earlier when Reagan had chosen the moderate Howard Baker as his White House chief of staff. Howard Phillips, the chairman of the Conservative Caucus, wrote furiously that Reagan had become "the speech reader-in-chief for the pro-appeasement triumvirate of Howard H. Baker Jr., George P. Shultz and Frank C. Carlucci." Senator Steven Symms similarly suggested that Reagan had changed: "Peace and freedom are inseparable, as the president used to say. I'm concerned that we'll end up keeping the peace and losing the freedom." *New York Times* columnist William Safire, commenting on Weinberger's resignation, wrote, "The Russians . . . now understand the way to handle Mr. Reagan: Never murder a man who is committing suicide."[10]

In the late summer and early fall of 1987, Mikhail Gorbachev disappeared from sight for more than seven weeks. Rumors spread that he was ill, that he had suffered an attack of food poisoning, even that there had been an attempt to assassinate him. None of these reports was true. On September 29, Gorbachev reemerged at the Kremlin after an extended vacation, eager to revitalize the Communist Party leadership with a flurry of initiatives. He had been busy writing a book about *perestroika* for Western audiences and preparing a speech for the seventieth anniversary of the Communist revolution.[11]

But as Gorbachev soon found, Moscow was in flux too. The following month, at a meeting of the party's Central Committee, Gorbachev confronted opposition not merely from traditionalist Communist Party officials such as Yegor Ligachev, but also from a new source: Boris Yeltsin, the populist mayor of Moscow. Yeltsin excoriated the party for not moving far enough or fast enough; he also warned about the glorification of Gorbachev as party secretary, arguing that it was a form of personality cult and violated the principle of collective leadership. Ordinary people in the Soviet Union were beginning to lose faith in Gorbachev's reform program, said Yeltsin, who tendered his resignation as a candidate for the Politburo.

Gorbachev reacted bitterly, portraying Yeltsin as an opportunist. "Those who pointed to his overgrown ambition and lust for power were right," Gorbachev wrote many years later. "Time has only confirmed this evaluation." At the Central Committee session, Communist Party leaders took the podium, one after another, to denounce Yeltsin. The episode altered the political dynamics in Moscow, weakening Gorbachev's position. New battle lines were being drawn. It was no longer simply Gorbachev's reformers against the old guard of the Communist Party. From that point onward, the Soviet leader was forced to navigate between one group of party officials increasingly resistant to his proposals for change, and others who believed that the Soviet leader was too cautious. Gorbachev was obliged to worry about what he called "the extremists on either side."[12]

That fall, Erich Honecker, the East German Communist Party leader who had personally overseen the construction of the Berlin Wall, finally made a groundbreaking visit to West Germany, a trip he had sought for more than three years. Honecker flew to Bonn for talks with Chancellor Helmut Kohl and other West German officials.

The rapprochement between the two German governments had been delayed by the cool reactions in both Moscow and Washington, neither of which was eager for its own German ally to stray too far from the fold. The Soviet Union was worried that East Germany would become overly dependent on West German loans, while the Reagan administration was concerned that West Germans might come to accept the legitimacy of Honecker's government. The French and British had been even less enthusiastic about an event that might revive German nationalism.

Nevertheless, amid the sense of impending change in both the Soviet Union and the United States, no one could make a convincing argument against Honecker's excursion. In 1984, Soviet leaders had based their opposition on grounds that West Germany had allowed the Reagan administration to put Pershing missiles on West German soil. By mid-1987, the United States and the Soviet Union were moving toward an agreement to remove those missiles, and Gorbachev himself was talking about visiting Washington. Three years earlier, Honecker had sought Moscow's permission to meet with Kohl and failed to get it. But in 1987, when he was seventy-five years old, Honecker did not bother to ask Moscow in advance, according to Egon Krenz, who served under Honecker and later succeeded him as East Germany's Communist Party leader. Instead, Honecker arranged the meeting himself and only afterward asked Gorbachev for his assent.[13]

"It was, for Honecker, a very important journey," recalled Hans-Otto Bräutigam, then the West German representative to East Germany, who helped arrange the trip. "He felt much closer to the Federal Republic [West Germany] than to his major ally [the Soviet Union]." During the five-day visit, Honecker traveled to the town where he had been raised, Wiebelskirchen, and visited the graves of his parents. At a dinner in Honecker's honor, Kohl once again exhorted the East German leader to tear down the Berlin Wall, as he had the previous spring. Germans "suffer because of a wall that is literally in their way and repels them," he said. However, Kohl also cautioned that German reunification "is at present not on the agenda of world history."[14]

The larger trade-off underlying the visit was an implicit exchange of West German money for East German relaxation of travel restrictions. The West Germans extended a continuing series of loans to East Germany, plus further sums for the release of East German prisoners, and more than $500 million a year to help pay for postal delivery, transportation, and other services. During the first eight months of 1987, Honecker's regime allowed 867,000 East Germans to travel to the West for purposes such as short-term family visits—a number vastly more than the 100,000 allowed in the entire year of 1982, just before the West German cash began flowing. West Germany also raised the sum paid to each individual East German visitor from $33 in 1986 to $55 in 1987. "Our strategy was to intensify the contacts and the ties between East Germans and West Germans," Horst Teltschik, Kohl's principal foreign-policy adviser, explained two decades later. "It was not an easy decision for the chancellor to receive Honecker in Bonn, but the main reason was to deal with him to get more travel, what he called human relief."[15]

Honecker returned to East Berlin with a sense of triumph, hoping that the trip would revitalize his regime. He had obtained promises of new money and a false sense of legitimacy; the West Germans had flown the East German flag and played the national anthem. In fact, Kohl got the better of the bargain, because the greater contacts between East and West only further undermined Honecker's regime. "Honecker's visit to Bonn didn't work," said Bräutigam. "The East German leadership was too old to take risks, and the country was too weak. There was no money and no energy. The people were becoming restless. It was a boring place. People just wanted to get out."[16]

In late October, Shultz returned to Moscow to set a date for the Washington summit, bringing Carlucci (then still the national security adviser) with him. They did not expect the meetings to be contentious. The two governments had already announced the previous month that they had settled on the outlines of a treaty banning intermediate nuclear weapons, that Gorbachev would be coming to the United States in the fall, and that only the timing remained in doubt.

Gorbachev proceeded to astonish them by suddenly pressing for new concessions. Once again, as he had at Reykjavik a year earlier, the Soviet leader insisted that Reagan accept restrictions on the Strategic Defense Initiative. He also sought U.S. assent to at least the key provisions of a separate treaty on long-range strategic weapons.

Shultz tried to divert the conversation toward Gorbachev's visit to America. He proposed that the best time would be late November. "It would be very desirable for you to travel beyond Washington," he said, thus conveying

Reagan's eagerness to show off the American way of life. These efforts fell flat. Gorbachev suggested he might not be willing to meet Reagan or come to the United States at all if he couldn't obtain some new agreements. "People will not understand it if the two leaders keep meeting and have nothing to show for it," he said.[17]

The session became increasingly contentious. Gorbachev complained that the United States continued to portray the Soviet Union as an enemy. Shultz countered by bringing up the Soviet invasion of Afghanistan and its deadly attack on the Korean Airlines plane. Gorbachev, in turn, cited the U-2 incident of 1960, in which the American pilot Gary Francis Powers had been shot down while flying a reconnaissance plane over the Soviet Union. The atmosphere became so strained that Gorbachev's veteran interpreter Pavel Palazchenko recalled wanting to shout, "Stop! There's got to be a better way to do it. Why not take a break . . . ?"

This confrontation took place only days after the stormy meeting of the Communist Party leadership at which Gorbachev's own politics were called into question. "It could not but affect the atmosphere and Gorbachev's state of mind," reflected Palazchenko years later. "I think he felt, rightly, that the main danger was from the conservatives, who could use any concession to the Americans as a pretext to attack his foreign policy as too soft." At the same time, Gorbachev seemed to want to test whether Reagan might be so eager for a Washington summit in the wake of the Iran-Contra scandal that he would give more for it.

The secretary of state, however, yielded no ground. He suggested that if there were to be no summit in Washington, perhaps the nearly completed treaty on intermediate-range missiles could be signed by lower-ranking officials in some other location. The timing would have to be soon, however, for such a treaty to be ratified before Reagan left office. Those words played on Soviet fears that a new administration or a newly constituted U.S. Senate might decide to abandon whatever treaty the Reagan administration negotiated.

The meeting ended without agreement, and the secretary of state left for home without a summit. The following day, Reagan did some public bargaining of his own. During his weekly Saturday radio address, he reported on Shultz's trip. "No date was set for a summit meeting, but we're in no hurry,"

Reagan said. "And we certainly will not be pushed into sacrificing essential interests just to have a meeting."[18]

Gorbachev hurriedly shifted ground. A week later, Shevardnadze, the Soviet foreign minister, arrived in Washington carrying a letter from Gorbachev. The letter repeated Gorbachev's desire that at his next summit with Reagan, the two leaders should not only sign the treaty they had concluded on intermediate-range nuclear weapons, but also reach some sort of "agreement in principle" on long-range strategic weapons. Yet Gorbachev now made plain he would no longer hold up his visit to the United States to bargain for this separate agreement.

"If it suits your availability, then according to my schedule of events before the end of the year, the first ten days of December would be the most preferable period for my trip to Washington," Gorbachev told Reagan. He had finally dropped his preconditions and agreed to come.[19]

The Soviet leader was not, however, willing to do the American grand tour the Reagans had wanted. Gorbachev would not fly to California. He would not barnstorm the country the way Nikita Khrushchev had in 1959. He would not party with Hollywood stars as Leonid Brezhnev had in 1973. There were to be no national parks, no farm states, no visit to the Reagans' ranch, not even a trip to Camp David. Gorbachev made clear he would spend time only in Washington. In explanation, Gorbachev later laid some of the blame on the KGB's desire to protect him. "Security services (especially on our side) wanted to avoid complications and strongly recommended confining ourselves to Washington on this first trip," Gorbachev claimed in his memoirs.[20]

American officials came to a different conclusion. "Reagan wanted to take him to all these places, and Gorbachev was having none of it," recalled Colin Powell, who was in charge of arranging the trip for the National Security Council. "He came to do business. He didn't come to be a tourist. He also didn't want to be seen as, 'Oh gee, Mr. President, if I had only known [what the United States was like], I'd have given up communism.' He didn't want to be used by Reagan, even though Reagan wasn't trying to use him."[21]

-5-

OF DAN QUAYLE AND ERROL FLYNN

If any single member of Congress could be said to have embodied Ronald Reagan's conservative revolution, it would have been the junior senator from Indiana, a well-groomed, blond-haired, blue-eyed scion of a publishing family named J. Danforth "Dan" Quayle. In 1980, the year in which Reagan won the presidency, Dan Quayle had run for the U.S. Senate against the Democratic incumbent, Birch Bayh. At the time, Quayle had been a member of the House of Representatives for only four years, while Bayh had served for eighteen years in the Senate.

The dynamics of the American political system were changing. In the past Bayh had regularly defeated his opponents by attracting overwhelming margins in the industrial parts of Indiana. In 1980, however, amid rising unemployment and other economic problems, his blue-collar support declined. Quayle attracted a wave of money from what was then known as the New Right, a collection of groups around the country that contributed funds to conservative candidates. He went after the votes of working-class Democrats by raising social issues, such as opposition to abortion. The race was expected to be close, but on Election Day, with Reagan at the top of the Republican ticket, Quayle won easily. His was one of the changeover seats that gave the Senate to the Republicans.

Quayle took a seat on the Senate Armed Services Committee. He became a reliable vote for Reagan's defense buildup and in the process, landed some important defense contracts for Indiana. In 1986, the Republicans lost control of the Senate, but Quayle had no trouble winning reelection. He ran as a strong supporter of Ronald Reagan.

Then there was a remarkable shift. In the fall of 1987, as Mikhail Gorbachev was preparing to fly to Washington, Dan Quayle took a leading role in challenging Reagan's Soviet policy. The telegenic young senator repeatedly questioned the wisdom of the agreement that Reagan and Gorbachev were preparing to sign, known as the Intermediate Nuclear Forces (INF) treaty. Quayle put forward many of the arguments that others, such as Richard Nixon and Henry Kissinger, had earlier been making: that American nuclear weapons in Western Europe were necessary to preserve the close relationship between the United States and its allies, and that a prohibition on intermediate-range missiles would leave the Soviet Union with an advantage in conventional military forces.

America's Cold War adversary was not changing, Quayle maintained. "Let's have no illusions," he said. "We are dealing essentially with the same Soviet Union that we have for the past seventy years." Quayle proposed amendments to the treaty that would have had the effect of killing it. He suggested that some of the missiles be held back from destruction until after progress was made on a separate agreement limiting the Soviet Union's superiority in conventional weapons.[1]

At times, it seemed hard to believe Reagan was a Republican president. His treaty with Gorbachev met with more enthusiastic backing from the Democrats than from his own party. Those Democrats who had long favored curbing the arms race, such as Senator Alan Cranston and Senator Claiborne Pell, quickly endorsed the agreement. Proponents of arms control were delighted to hear Reagan and his aides endorse some of their own arguments. "Those are the kinds of statements I want Reagan's people to say, so I can quote them back for the next twenty years," said James Rubin, then a representative of the Arms Control Association (later a senior aide to Secretary of State Madeleine Albright). "We want Reagan's imprimatur on an arms control treaty." Reagan's stance caused conservative columnist George Will to inveigh against what he called "the cult of arms control." Will wrote that "the Soviets want victories; we want agreements. Or, as Jeane Kirkpatrick has said, they are playing to win and we want to get out of the game."[2]

During the fall of 1987, the only Republican presidential candidate to support Reagan's treaty was his own vice president, George Bush. Conservative Republicans Jack Kemp, Pat Robertson, and Pete du Pont were all against it. So was Alexander Haig, whose negative views about Reagan's treaty were similar to those of other Nixon administration veterans. One Republican candidate, Bob Dole, remained noncommittal. By contrast, all the Democratic candidates supported the treaty. A newspaper cartoon that fall depicted Reagan at his desk, surrounded by the Democratic candidates: Michael Dukakis giving a thumbs-up, Richard Gephardt patting Reagan on the back, Al Gore and Jesse Jackson smiling broadly. The caption said it showed the president with his "strongest supporters."[3]

The political alignments were similar for Gorbachev's visit: the reactions of Republicans and conservatives ranged from skeptical to hostile, while Democrats had few complaints. The early plans envisioned a speech by Gorbachev to a joint session of Congress, in exchange for a comparable address by Reagan later to a Soviet audience. To Gorbachev's dismay, that idea had to be scrapped, because of intense opposition from Senate Republicans. Jesse Helms threatened a filibuster to block any invitation to the Soviet leader. Dole, the Republican minority leader, warned that a speech by Gorbachev might cause "a rather ugly scene" on Capitol Hill.[4]

Bush, too, was nervous about the Gorbachev visit and the conflicts it generated among Republicans, particularly with the New Hampshire presidential primary less than three months away. As vice president, Bush could not distance himself from Reagan's INF treaty—even though some of his own friends, such as Scowcroft, had been doing so. Moreover, Bush stood to gain politically if the Reagan-Gorbachev summit was a success. Yet Bush also took care to show the public—and Republican voters—that he was willing to criticize the Soviets. When a surprisingly large crowd of more than two hundred thousand people assembled on the Mall in Washington for a demonstration on behalf of Jewish emigration from the Soviet Union, Bush appeared before television cameras promising he would raise the issue personally with Gorbachev and help make it a key issue at the summit. Marrying the language of the Old Testament with the syntax of Reagan's Berlin speech, Bush exclaimed: "Mr. Gorbachev, let these people go! Let them go!"[5]

Reagan and his advisers needed a public-relations strategy for the Gorbachev trip to deflect criticisms from the political right. They also realized that after the summit was over, they would have to win enough votes in the Senate to obtain ratification of the INF treaty, and this, too, became an essential part of the PR campaign.

In September 1987, Reagan's political strategists set up a focus group to explore Americans' attitudes toward a Washington summit with Gorbachev. They tried out various slogans and formulations: Should the theme be "first step for peace" or "moving towards the promise of peace" or "brightening the horizon for peace" or "first step in a new direction"? In an internal memo describing the focus group, Thomas Griscom, Reagan's director of communications, concluded that in talking about the summit, the administration should emphasize the key words that had tested well with the public: "movement" and "peace."[6]

The advisers concluded that one of the president's potential liabilities was the fear of Soviet conventional forces after a treaty was signed—precisely the issue that had been raised by critics, including Nixon and Kissinger. The solution was to have Reagan appear before an expanse of uniforms. Griscom explained in one memo that the president should "use the U.S. Military Academy as a backdrop to set the stage for the conventional weapons debate." On October 28, Reagan spoke at West Point, invoking the memories of General Douglas MacArthur and telling an anecdote about a young soldier named Sean Luketina who had murmured to his father on his deathbed, "God, honor, country." The president defended his Soviet policy and the impending treaty. "Now, some have argued that when the INF missiles have been removed, our commitment to Europe will have been weakened," he said. "Yet this is simply untrue. . . . In Europe itself, we will retain a large force of many types, including ground-based systems and aircraft and submarines capable of delivering nuclear weapons."[7]

The Reagan White House also knew how to play rough with its right-wing critics. One White House adviser, Tom Korologos, urged in a late-November memo that ". . . the president put all those on notice who oppose his treaty that he will fight for it and against them. This isn't a free ride. They have to pay a price for opposing the President."[8]

Reagan agreed. On December 3, the week before Gorbachev's arrival in Washington, the president granted an Oval Office interview to the anchormen for the four leading television networks: Peter Jennings of ABC, Dan Rather of CBS, Tom Brokaw of NBC, and Bernard Shaw of CNN. In it, he took direct aim at the critics of the INF treaty and the summit. "I think that some of the people who are objecting the most and just refusing even to accede to the idea of ever getting any understanding [with the Soviet Union], whether they realize it or not, those people basically down in their deepest thoughts have accepted that war is inevitable, and that there must come to be a war between the two superpowers," Reagan said.[9]

Conservative Republicans rose to this bait. Instead of ignoring the president's remarks, they reacted with outrage. Quayle took to the Senate floor the next day to say that he was "particularly appalled" by Reagan's comments, which Quayle said were "totally irresponsible." Thus, Reagan succeeded in cutting through the complexities of the treaty by portraying his opponents as warmongers and himself as a man of peace.

Most of the time, however, Reagan maintained public support not by being combative but by remaining genial and aloof, exhibiting the personality traits on which he had built his entire career. He knew how to defuse the continuing sensitivities of U.S.-Soviet relations by summoning forth a Hollywood analogy. When asked whether he was worried about being overshadowed by Gorbachev's charisma and dynamism, Reagan replied, "I don't resent his popularity or anything else. Good Lord, I co-starred with Errol Flynn once."[10]

It was Colin Powell's job as the new national security adviser to brief Reagan on the issues that would be on the summit's agenda. He realized that Gorbachev would know every nuance of the arms-control negotiations between the two countries, the ranges of various missiles, the history and conflicting interpretations of prior agreements. Reagan would not. "He hated the esoterica of arms control," recalled Frank Carlucci, Powell's predecessor. "He wasn't interested in the details. When I sent him a memo, it came back with his initials. It never had any comment."[11]

In advance of Gorbachev's arrival, Powell briefed Reagan on several occasions. He discovered that the president was thinking about what was to come, but not in the same way as his advisers. He was preoccupied with the ceremonial and personal aspects of the summit. From California friends, Reagan had obtained two sets of gold cuff links that showed men beating swords into plowshares, the traditional symbol of peace. He was planning to wear one pair and give the other to Gorbachev. "When do you think I ought to give him the cuff links?" Reagan asked his national security adviser. Powell tried to switch the conversation to what Gorbachev might say about Soviet SS-18 missiles, but Reagan talked about the cuff links again and again.[12] The president left it to his aides, especially Shultz, to negotiate the remaining details of the treaty. Reagan's subordinates and their Soviet counterparts were also working to draft a written statement that the two governments could issue after the summit.

It was Reagan's job to set overall direction for the administration and to win support for the policies he wanted. In doing that, he relied upon the catchwords, phrases, and formulas he felt would work with ordinary Americans. When discussing the Soviet Union, Reagan returned again and again to the Russian slogan he had been given by Suzanne Massie. In his interview with television anchormen just before the summit, Reagan said, as though it were a new idea, "I think I could sum up my own position on this with the recitation of a very brief Russian proverb: *Doveryai no proveryai*. It means, 'Trust, but verify.'"[13]

But what did "verify" mean? Reagan relied upon aides like Shultz, Powell, and Carlucci to decide. In meetings with Soviet officials shortly before the summit, the secretary of state worked out an elaborate system of cross-inspections by U.S. and Soviet officials of sites and weaponry to make sure that intermediate-range missiles would in fact be destroyed.

The bickering lasted until the eve of the summit. American officials delivered to their Soviet counterparts a photograph of a Pershing missile, the weapon that had been deployed in Europe and was to be destroyed under the agreement. Soviet officials were supposed to present their American hosts with a photograph of their counterpart, the SS-20 missile, but instead brought a picture of the missile inside a canister. Shultz said the United States would not sign the treaty if the Soviets were going to violate its terms before it was signed. Finally, Marshal Sergei Akhromeyev, the Soviet chief of general staff, who was in Gorbachev's delegation, asked aides in Moscow to send a picture of the missile by fax, and Soviet officials delivered it to the Americans the next morning and promised to turn over a real photograph soon. The last presummit business was cleared away.[14]

-6-

GORBACHEV IN WASHINGTON

Gorbachev arrived at the White House on the morning of December 8, 1987, for the beginning of three days of talks. By this time, after the summits in Geneva and Reykjavik, he and Reagan were accustomed to each other's idiosyncrasies. Gorbachev knew that Reagan would tell anti-Soviet jokes and repeat the same old arguments. Reagan knew that Gorbachev would defend the Soviet system by saying the United States had problems too.

The first session was between Reagan and Gorbachev themselves, without Shultz, Shevardnadze, or any other senior officials. Reagan presented Gorbachev with the cuff links. The two men sat in the Oval Office with translators at their backs and American and Soviet notetakers jotting down what the two leaders were saying. After welcoming Gorbachev, Reagan quickly brought up the question of human rights in the Soviet Union. In particular, Reagan wanted to know why Soviet authorities could not lift the continuing restrictions on Jewish emigration.

As Reagan continued to speak, Gorbachev turned to his translator and muttered, *"Ohn boltayet yeschchyo"* ("He's blathering on again"). When it was his turn, the Soviet leader pointed out that the United States maintained a well-guarded border with Mexico and had plans to build an extensive system of fences to make sure Mexicans did not cross. If it was acceptable for the United States to restrict immigration, Gorbachev asked, then why wasn't it permissible for the Soviet Union to impose limits on emigration?

As Gorbachev spoke, Reagan looked at the American notetaker, Fritz Ermarth, the Soviet specialist on the National Security Council. "He doesn't get it, does he?" Reagan whispered.[1] Then, turning to the Soviet leader, Reagan countered that there was a difference between a fence designed to keep people out of a country and one to keep them in. The Mexicans who sought to cross the border were attracted by the economic opportunities in the United States, Reagan said. That was not the same as holding people who wanted to leave inside a country.

The exchange over human rights was relatively brief. At one point, Gorbachev felt compelled to warn Reagan, "Mr. President, you are not a prosecutor and I am not on trial here." The two men had had these debates before, and expected to have them again. After a few minutes, they decided to move on to other subjects. Both agreed that they had made great progress in improving relations since their first meeting in Geneva—sometimes, Gorbachev noted, by "pounding their firsts on the table" in Washington and Moscow to keep their own bureaucrats in line.[2]

At their next session, Reagan performed so poorly that his own aides were taken aback. He and Gorbachev held afternoon talks in the Cabinet Room of the White House, surrounded by virtually all the American and Soviet officials involved in the summit: cabinet secretaries, ministers, national security aides—thirty-four people in all. Gorbachev opened with a broad overview of the situation inside the Soviet Union: what his economic reform program was trying to do and what he planned. He began to talk about the arms-control issues pending between the two countries; Shultz took the lead role in responding to him. Reagan remained quiet for a time, then finally seized the floor with a digression about the general importance of allowing people to run their own lives. He summoned forth one of his jokes about life in the Soviet Union: An American scholar about to fly from the United States to Moscow found that his cab driver to the airport was a student. He asked what the young man wanted to do after school. "I haven't decided yet," the driver replied. Upon landing in Moscow, the professor discovered that his Russian cab driver was also a student and asked the same question. "They haven't told me yet," said the Soviet cab driver.

The story fell flat. Powell, who was sitting next to the president, later wrote, "As Reagan finished the story, the Americans wanted to disappear under the table, while Gorbachev stared straight ahead, expressionless." The Soviet Union was a country rich in anecdotes, he told Reagan. Shultz broke in to say the working groups of American and Soviet experts were ready to start their talks.[3]

Reagan recorded in his diary that this large afternoon session was "not nearly as good a meeting as this morning's."[4] That was an understatement. His secretary of state and his national security adviser were so dismayed by Reagan's performance that both wrote about it in their memoirs. Powell blamed Shultz for having asked on short notice to enlarge the meeting and move it to the large Cabinet Room. "Sudden changes threw Ronald Reagan off his form," Powell explained.

After the session broke up, Shultz, Powell, and White House chief of staff Howard Baker went back to the Oval Office. "Mr. President, that was a disaster," the secretary of state told the president. "You can't just sit there telling jokes." Shultz agreed with Powell that there would be no more formal sessions in the Cabinet Room; Reagan would meet Gorbachev either in the Oval Office or in another smaller setting with fewer officials. Powell ordered his staff to stay up all night writing and rewriting talking points for the president to use in the next talks with Gorbachev the following morning.

On the second day, Reagan recovered. Before meeting Gorbachev, he spent a half hour carefully going over the talking points the National Security Council staff had drafted for him overnight. Sitting opposite Gorbachev in the Oval Office with Shultz, Powell, and Carlucci at his side, Reagan traced through the American positions. He and Gorbachev talked about how to follow up the treaty banning intermediate-range missiles in Europe with another sweeping agreement that would cut intercontinental missiles by half. The two leaders continued to disagree over Gorbachev's desire for limits on Reagan's Strategic Defense Initiative. They bickered over the terms for the Soviet Union's withdrawal of forces from Afghanistan. While most of this discussion was serious, the president also couldn't resist telling a few more jokes about the Soviet Union. (Reagan himself later wrote that Gorbachev "howled" at these jokes, although none of the other participants seem to remember this.) After two hours, Reagan and Gorbachev agreed that their aides would continue to negotiate, and the meeting broke up.[5]

American and Soviet teams met day and night to draft the joint statement the two governments planned to issue. The haggling went on until the last hours of the summit. Soviet officials were trying to win an American commitment to a ceiling of 5,100 ballistic missiles; the United States wanted 4,800. Finally, Carlucci proposed to Akhromeyev a figure of 4,900; the Soviet marshal agreed, and Gorbachev went along with the compromise. Soviet and American officials smoothed over their disagreements about the Strategic Defense Initiative with language that each side subsequently interpreted in a different way.[6]

The significance of this summit did not lie in the nuances of arms control. Indeed, Reagan and Gorbachev made less headway on those issues in their talks at the White House than they had in Reykjavik the previous year. Rather, the Washington summit was a milestone for its ceremony, symbolism, and public impact. The event dramatized to the American public, in a way that no other event had, that the Cold War was subsiding. American politicians recognized that the public's response to Gorbachev's visit was overwhelmingly positive. In all of this, Reagan led the way. When it came to shaping the public mood, particularly about the Cold War, he was the driving force for his own administration. He had pushed hard to have a summit with Gorbachev in Washington, recognizing that it would be more than simply another round of high-level diplomacy.

This was the first Reagan-Gorbachev summit held not on neutral ground, but in the capital city of one of the two superpowers. In Washington, it was treated as a state visit. When Gorbachev arrived at the White House, he was greeted with ceremonies on the South Lawn that included a twenty-one-gun salute. Outside the White House along Pennsylvania Avenue, American flags were hung side by side with those of the Soviet Union, each Soviet flag an expanse of bright red surrounding a yellow hammer and sickle.

The Reagans served as hosts at a state dinner with scores of prominent Americans, ranging from Henry Kissinger and David Rockefeller to novelist Saul Bellow and baseball star Joe DiMaggio. Gorbachev was seated at Nancy

Reagan's dinner table next to Richard Perle and a couple of seats away from Dick Cheney, then a member of Congress. During the dinner, Perle and Cheney, the two ardent proponents of American military power, clinked glasses with Gorbachev and tried to engage him in conversation on subjects such as the Soviet defense budget and the American Strategic Defense Initiative. Afterward, Perle told reporters, "I don't think either of us persuaded the other, but he is an intelligent man." At one point, pianist Van Cliburn played "Moscow Nights," and Gorbachev and the other Soviet officials rose to sing.[7]

The centerpiece of the summit was the signing of the treaty banning intermediate nuclear weapons. It required the Soviet Union to destroy about 1,500 nuclear warheads already deployed in Europe and the United States, about 350. This was the first time that the two countries had agreed to eliminate an entire class of nuclear weapons. The two leaders formally endorsed the long-negotiated agreement in ceremonies at the White House at 1:45 p.m., Tuesday, December 8, the opening day of the summit. Only a few White House staff members, including Powell, realized that the specific time for the signing had been set by a California astrologer, Joan Quigley. Nancy Reagan had been regularly asking the astrologer for propitious times for presidential activities ever since John Hinckley's assassination attempt on Reagan in 1981; her conversations with Quigley were a form of therapy, the first lady said.[8]

When Reagan offered a few remarks at the signing ceremony for the INF treaty, he quickly fell back upon his customary refrain: "We have listened to the wisdom in an old Russian maxim . . . *Doveryai no proveryai.* Trust but verify." The Soviet leader had by now heard this line too often. "You repeat that at every meeting," Gorbachev said, as the crowd tittered. "I like it," Reagan replied.

Gorbachev's activities were not limited to the White House. During his three days in Washington, he hosted receptions at the Soviet embassy for artists, writers, and scholars; he engaged in some verbal sparring with American publishers, broadcasters, and newspaper editors; he courted American business executives. He sat down for a talk with congressional leaders, a session that was offered as a substitute for the speech to Congress that Gorbachev had originally sought. The Americans who participated were able to dine out for months or years afterward with stories of what they had told Gorbachev or he had told them. At one point, en route from the Soviet embassy to the White House, Gorbachev ordered his car to stop along Connecticut Avenue. He got out and plunged into the crowds, shaking hands as though he were an American political candidate and in the process, setting back the White House schedule. "Mrs. Reagan was furious, because here was the president and everybody else in the White House waiting, and Gorbachev was out there doing what he had learned from observing us—working the crowd, controlling the agenda," recalled Griscom, the White House communications chief.[9]

Gorbachev was covered not merely on American network news shows each night, but throughout the day on cable television (where CNN was then the relatively new, unchallenged source of minute-by-minute news). The extensive coverage of the Soviet leader ranged from positive to neutral in tone. The images of Gorbachev did not match the stereotypes of an iron-fisted Soviet leader. He seemed clearly smarter than Brezhnev and more sophisticated than Khrushchev, the only other Soviet party secretaries to have visited the United States.

By the end of the three days of meetings, Gorbachev was trying to match Reagan anecdote for anecdote and joke for joke. At the end of a farewell lunch in the White House family dining room, the two leaders found themselves killing time while they waited for their aides to negotiate the last details of the joint statement that the two governments planned to release. Reagan told Gorbachev about the farmer who had developed a three-legged chicken. When asked how it tasted, the farmer replied, "I don't know, I've never been able to catch it."

Not to be denied, Gorbachev countered with a yarn about a Russian who was accused of driving a government car to a public bath. To defend himself, the man replied that he had not taken a bath for two years. Then the Soviet leader dropped the joke for a moment: "The same could be true of our governments," he said. "We would not want to be in the position of defending ourselves by saying we have done nothing—when we should have acted."[10]

When Gorbachev left for home, ABC News anchor Peter Jennings solemnly declared: "Look again at these good-byes this afternoon. Two men who really seemed determined that the adversarial relationship between the two countries not get out of control. Two men who say they will try harder to do better to keep the world away from war." An ABC poll taken that night showed that 76 percent of Americans believed that the United States and the Soviet Union were entering a new era.[11]

On the day following Gorbachev's departure, Richard Nixon scrawled one of his occasional private missives to Ronald Reagan. Such Nixon notes were usually complimentary, praising some Reagan speech or press conference. This particular note began in the same vein. The previous night, Reagan had given a televised address to the nation about the summit, and Nixon told the president it was "one of the most eloquent you have ever delivered."

But then Nixon went on to deliver a written warning to Reagan, one that was implicitly negative about the entire summit and its impact: "Just remember, Rome was not built in a day and it takes more than three days to civilize Moscow."[12] The note underscored how America's two veteran anti-Communist politicians had repositioned themselves. Reagan had welcomed the Soviet visitors; Nixon countered by saying they were still uncivilized. Nixon, once the architect of détente, was now skeptical about a visit by Gorbachev that had demonstrated unprecedented warmth between Washington and Moscow.

Henry Kissinger was even more negative. He was upset by the outpouring of American enthusiasm for the Washington summit. Kissinger didn't like Reagan's antinuclear views or his courtship of Gorbachev. In a lengthy, biting column in *Newsweek*, Kissinger denounced the "near rapture" of Gorbachev's American audiences, the mood of "euphoria" of the state dinner, and the "near ecstasy" of U.S. officials. He refused to take seriously the idea that Gorbachev might be seeking to wind down the Cold War. "He [Gorbachev] was in relentless pursuit of a strategic objective, to accelerate the loss of confidence in America's strategic power," Kissinger wrote. The Reagan administration was making a mistake if it tried to "help" Gorbachev, wrote Kissinger, because foreign relations do not depend upon "the fate of transitory personalities." Reagan himself "reflected a quintessential American dream: that history can be reversed by good will."[13]

Above all, Kissinger mourned Reagan's evident "preoccupation" with getting rid of nuclear weapons: "I could not shake a melancholy feeling as I watched the leaders of the country whose nuclear guarantee had protected free peoples for forty years embrace Gorbachev's evocation of a nuclear-free world—a goal put forward, if with less panache, by every Soviet leader since Stalin."[14]

Reagan's aides worried that the attacks by veterans of the national-security establishment would reinforce the separate denunciations from the political right. By this juncture, conservative leaders were heaping vituperation on their former hero. Several right-wing leaders held a press conference to announce the formation of an Anti-Appeasement Alliance aimed at defeating the new INF treaty. One of them, Howard Phillips of the Conservative Caucus, branded Reagan "a useful idiot for Soviet propaganda."[15]

Reagan was still courting the conservatives, attempting where possible to win them over. Even before Gorbachev had left Washington, Reagan granted an Oval Office interview to five conservative columnists. In it, Reagan contradicted Kissinger by arguing Gorbachev was different from previous Soviet leaders. Where Kissinger paid attention to geopolitics, Reagan's focus was on ideology. "In the past, Soviet leaders have openly expressed their acceptance of the Marxian theory of the one-world communist state," Reagan told the interviewers. "Gorbachev has never said that."[16] Reagan's view, it turned out, was considerably closer to the truth than Kissinger's: Gorbachev was not merely a "transitory personality," as Kissinger suggested. He was altering Soviet ideology in ways that were of transcendent importance for American foreign policy and for the balance-of-power considerations that preoccupied Kissinger.

Although the old hands, such as Nixon and Kissinger, had their qualms and the political right was infuriated by Reagan's Soviet policy, the American public clearly liked it. The polls showing the popularity of the Gorbachev visit were too clear for presidential candidates to ignore. Vice President Bush, who before the summit had been shown on television issuing admonitions to the Soviet leader, was back on news shows a few days later boasting, "I had three private meetings with Mr. Gorbachev!"

On the final day, Bush had a scheduled breakfast with Gorbachev at the Soviet embassy and was scheduled to ride with him to the White House. But Gorbachev was held back to talk with aides about the arms-control issues, and Bush was shuffled off into a small room. Soviet officials soon came to apologize for the delays and suggest Bush might go ahead on his own. "Oh,

I'll wait as long as it takes," Bush told them. He did not want to miss a chance to be seen with Gorbachev.[17]

Dole, Bush's principal rival for the Republican nomination, had for months refused to say what he would do when the Senate was asked to ratify the treaty banning intermediate-range missiles. Gorbachev held a brief private meeting in Washington with Dole, and one week later, Dole announced his unqualified support for the INF treaty. Reagan's summit with Gorbachev had altered the political climate inside the United States.

The Washington summit made an equally large impression upon Gorbachev himself. After arriving back in Moscow, Gorbachev began to sound a different tune. On December 17, less than a week after returning home, he delivered a report to the Politburo that described the Washington summit as a fundamental turning point:

> *In Washington, probably for the first time, we clearly realized how much the human factor means in international politics. Before . . . we treated such personal contacts as simply meetings between representatives of opposed and irreconcilable systems. Reagan for us was merely the spokesman of the most conservative part of American capitalism and its military industrial complex. But it turns out that politicians, including leaders of governments if they are really responsible people, represent purely human concerns, interests, and the hopes of ordinary people— people who vote for them in elections and who associate their leaders' names and personal abilities with the country's image and patriotism. These people are guided by the most natural human motives and feelings. . . . [And] now we've embraced the purely human factor in international politics. It is also a major component of the new thinking, which has borne fruit. And it was in Washington that we saw it so clearly for the first time.*[18]

The Soviet leader viewed the agreement he and Reagan had signed to ban intermediate-range missiles as one of historic significance. "The INF Treaty represented the first well-prepared step on our way out of the Cold War, the first harbinger of the new times," Gorbachev wrote in his memoir. "We had reached a new level of trust in our relations with the United States and initiated a genuine disarmament process, creating a security system that would be based on comprehensive cooperation instead of the threat of mutual destruction."[19]

By a curious dynamic, Gorbachev's deepening diplomacy with the Reagan administration helped to spur forward his domestic political reforms and to alter his view of the established order inside the Soviet Union itself. Increasingly, Gorbachev came to view the Cold War confrontation with the United States not merely as a foreign policy issue but as a domestic one: the Cold War supplied the rationale used by the Communist Party leadership to resist change and political liberalization at home.

"Paradoxically as it may seem, efforts towards disarmament and new relations with the West—originally meant 'to create favorable external conditions for *perestroika*'—in fact became its locomotive," said Gorbachev's adviser Anatoly Chernyaev. "To succeed with a new foreign policy, we had to demolish the myths and dogmas of a confrontational ideology. And this, through the general secretary's own ideas and those of the reformist press, immediately influenced society's intellectual life."[20]

Reagan and Shultz, ignoring the warnings of their critics, were happy to help Gorbachev open the Soviet political system. Reagan had one year left in the White House. He was becoming ever more detached from White House business, but he knew which foreign-policy issue deserved his attention.

-7-

MAKING A TREATY LOOK EASY

At the beginning of 1988, White House chief of staff Howard Baker sat down with Ronald Reagan to discuss ideas for foreign travel during Reagan's final year as president. Reagan had already agreed to visit Moscow in May, and he was committed to attend the annual economic summit of industrialized nations in Toronto in June. Beyond those two trips, Baker had a few others to recommend: How about Israel or India or Australia?

Reagan vetoed them all. He said he didn't want to travel to Israel because then he would have to choose which Arab countries to visit on the same trip, undoubtedly displeasing the ones he left out. He ruled out India because he'd already been there on a refueling stop during a trip to Asia seventeen years earlier. "It was the middle of the night, and I was asleep the entire time," he said. "But I was there, so I don't need to go to India." When Reagan's executive assistant, Jim Kuhn, supported the suggestion for a presidential visit to Australia, Reagan joked, "Well, you guys are all free to go to Australia—but you ain't taking me."[1]

By 1988, Ronald Reagan was not interested in new ventures or conquests. He was, in fact, increasingly removed from the daily routines of his own presidency. In February, Reagan reached the age of seventy-seven; he was the oldest president in American history. He was also the first in more than a quarter century to serve two full terms. After Dwight Eisenhower, five presidents had left the White House without lasting for eight years: one had been assassinated, one had resigned in midterm, one had decided not to seek re-election, and two had been defeated seeking additional terms.

A year earlier, at the peak of the Iran-Contra scandal, there had been some speculation that Reagan himself might go the way of Nixon. But he had survived, and by early 1988, had regained much of his earlier popularity. A New York Times/CBS poll showed that in the wake of Gorbachev's visit to Washington, Reagan's public-approval ratings had risen to 50 percent, unusually high for a president entering his last year.[2] In political terms, there was little reason to change course. As a result, Reagan's final year in office often took on the nature of a prolonged farewell. For each event on the presidential calendar—the State of the Union address, the presentation of the budget—reporters noted that it would be Reagan's last. White House aides encouraged a mood of continuing sentimentality.

The reality, which the public did not see, is that by 1988, Reagan was leaving much of the business of governing to his subordinates. When senior officials briefed him, he rarely asked questions or gave detailed responses. At one point, the CIA director, William Webster, expressed bewilderment to National Security Adviser Colin Powell. "I'm pretty good at reading people, but I like to get a report card," Webster said. "I can't tell whether I'm really helping him or not, because he listens, and I don't get a sense that he disagrees with me or agrees with me or what." Powell advised him not to take it personally. "Listen," he said, "I'm with him a dozen times a day, and I'm in the same boat."[3]

During Reagan's final year, his top three advisers tried to resolve many foreign-policy issues on their own. The idea had first been suggested by Secretary of State George Shultz. Each morning at 7 a.m., Shultz and Defense Secretary Frank Carlucci would gather in Powell's White House office. The aim was to reach consensus and avoid the sort of interagency disputes that would need to be brought to the president. Sometimes the secretary of defense gave way, and sometimes the secretary of state did. Shultz, in particular, was happy to put the years of bickering with Weinberger behind him. "We decided that the three of us had to agree on the day's events, the policy issues," recalled Carlucci. "Because if we agreed, that was it. Reagan was past the point where he could intervene in the system. We worked it that way for over a year."[4]

After the three men reached consensus, Powell carefully informed the president of the policies they had decided to pursue, giving him a chance to object if he chose. He rarely if ever did. "I would never, ever, characterize it as me, Frank and Shultz making the decisions, but we made it easier for him [Reagan] to make decisions," recalled Powell. "I would never usurp the authority of the president. I don't think we ever did anything that he did not agree with."[5] This pattern of decision making extended down from these top three officials to others within the senior ranks of the Reagan administration. The U.S. government's foreign-policy apparatus "kind of ran on automatic," said Richard Armitage, then an assistant secretary of defense. "We knew generally where Reagan wanted to go, where his red lines were."[6]

In retrospect, Reagan's behavior during the final year raises the question of whether he was in the earliest stages of Alzheimer's disease, which would disable him a half decade later. "The last year (in the White House), he was starting to have some trouble," said Powell, who as national security adviser spent more time with Reagan than anyone but his wife and personal staff. "I don't know that he had Alzheimer's. I don't know when Alzheimer's starts. But there were a few times in that last year when he looked like he wasn't quite as focused as he should be."[7]

Yet Powell also discovered that when crisis loomed or quick action was needed, Reagan would prove attentive and decisive. Once, when American ships were in the midst of a skirmish with Iranian gunboats in the Persian Gulf, the Pentagon told Powell the marines needed permission to enter Iran's territorial waters. Powell walked into the Oval Office and explained the situation. Reagan stopped everything and listened closely to the details. "Right, go ahead and do it," he said.[8]

The most acrimonious foreign-policy dispute within the Reagan administration in 1988 concerned Panamanian leader Manuel Noriega. In February, he had been indicted on drug charges in Miami, and soon afterward, the United States imposed economic sanctions against Panama. Over the following months, with Reagan's support, State Department officials negotiated a possible deal with Noriega under which the charges against him would be dropped and the sanctions would be lifted if he would leave the country. But Vice President George Bush determinedly argued against lifting the indictment against Noriega. He was joined by several other high-ranking officials, including Attorney General Ed Meese, Treasury Secretary James Baker, and White House chief of staff Howard Baker. The opponents maintained that a deal with Noriega would be immoral, diminish respect for law enforcement, and undermine American efforts to stop drug trafficking.

This was not a dispute that could be resolved at the morning meetings of Shultz, Powell, and Carlucci. It was, above all, a dispute between Reagan and Bush. For seven years, the vice president had consistently supported the administration's policy, but he was now running for president himself. He had survived the Republican primaries, defeating Dole and several conservative challengers, and he had by this point effectively won the Republican nomination. A deal with Noriega would have drawn criticism from the public in the midst of the election campaign.

Through the weeks of internal controversy, Reagan was by all accounts energetically involved. He was unyielding. He did not want to use American troops to remove Noriega from Panama. "I'm not giving in," he told Bush and the other opponents at one White House session in May. "This deal is better than going in and counting our dead. I just think you are wrong as hell on this. . . . What you guys are settling for is that we have to go in there with considerable loss of life, and how does that look to the rest of Latin America?"[9]

In the Panama dispute, Reagan emerged as the pragmatist and Bush, the moralist. The president overrode the objections and approved the deal. It soon fell apart in Panama. Noriega, who had originally accepted the agreement, told American officials that his own supporters in the Panamanian Defense Forces would not go along with the idea of his departure. In 1989, after Bush became president and after months of further upheaval in Panama, more than twenty thousand American troops were dispatched to oust Noriega from power.

On the morning of March 11, 1988, Suzanne Massie appeared at the White House to deliver an unusual plea directly to Reagan from one of Gorbachev's top advisers in Moscow. Powell, Chief of Staff Howard Baker, and Kenneth

Duberstein, Baker's deputy, gathered with Reagan in the Oval Office to hear Massie's message.

A memorandum of this conversation lies buried in the archives of the Reagan Library; its contents were not made public at the time or in the years since. According to the notes, "Mrs. Massie delivered an oral message to the president that she received in Moscow from Central Committee Secretary Anatoly Dobrynin."[10]

As Soviet ambassador to Washington for more than a quarter century, Dobrynin had been the master of back-channel communications between the Soviet leadership and American presidents since John F. Kennedy. Although he was called back to Moscow by Gorbachev in 1986, Dobrynin was still a key adviser for dealing with the United States. He had been part of Gorbachev's entourage both at Reykjavik and at the Washington summit. Massie said she understood that the message sent by Dobrynin originated "even higher," presumably from Gorbachev himself. That seems plausible, since during these same weeks, Dobrynin also relayed messages directly from Gorbachev to Jack Matlock, the U.S. ambassador to Moscow.[11] But it is also conceivable that Dobrynin was acting on his own.

The message was a plaintive one. Soviet officials believe "that the President still thinks of the USSR as an 'evil empire' whose social and political positions have placed it on the 'ash heap of history,'" Massie reported. These phrases were, of course, taken from Reagan's own past speeches. According to Dobrynin's message, despite the outpouring of goodwill at the Washington summit, Soviet officials were still worried "that the Administration's overall perception of Soviet international behavior has not changed." As a result, Soviet officials had a request, Massie said: if Reagan believed there had been changes in Soviet policy, "then it would be important for the President to state this prior to the Moscow summit. The Soviets ask what concrete steps they could take over the next few months to prompt such a statement by the President."

It was a demonstration of the impact that Reagan's condemnations of the Soviet Union had had upon the Communist Party hierarchy. Soviet officials were now, in effect, seeking to negotiate a change in what Reagan would say about them. They were suggesting a trade of their actions for American words—an alteration of Soviet policies in exchange for an easing of Reagan's rhetoric about the Soviet system. While he continued to praise Gorbachev as a leader, the president had still not retreated from the larger judgments of the Soviet Union that he had expressed during his early years in the White House. "I haven't changed from the time when I made a speech about an evil empire," Reagan had asserted in a television interview the previous December. That same month, when his old friend Nackey Loeb of the *Manchester Union Leader* wrote an editorial saying Reagan's INF agreement would "give communism the advantage," he wrote her a note which said, "Nackey, I'm still the Ronald Reagan I was and the evil empire is just that."[12]

During the early months of 1988, Gorbachev was especially sensitive to American criticism and eager for a few good words from Reagan. He was in the midst of the most far-reaching reversal of Soviet foreign policy since the beginning of the Cold War: a decision to withdraw Soviet troops from Afghanistan. On February 8, Gorbachev announced that the Afghan war was coming to an end; Soviet forces would be brought home over a ten-month period starting May 15, as long as certain conditions were met. American and Soviet officials continued to argue for several weeks over the terms, particularly whether the Americans would be allowed to continue to provide arms to the Afghan mujahideen. The Soviets ultimately yielded.

Inside the Soviet Union, the conservative opposition to Gorbachev's reforms burst into the open with the publication in March of a letter by a Leningrad teacher named Nina Andreyeva that defended Stalin and his principles. The Soviet leadership was splitting into factions, with one group under Gorbachev, headed by Alexander Yakovlev, pushing to speed up reforms and another, headed by Yegor Ligachev, resisting the changes. Recalling this opposition, Gorbachev wrote a few years later: "The top levels of the Party and state apparatus seemed to believe that there was no need to replace the existing system—God forbid—it only needed a bit of fine tuning."[13] He had called for a special party conference in June 1988 to determine the future direction and pace of his reform program; the meeting was to be held only four weeks after Reagan's visit to Moscow. An easing of Reagan's anti-Soviet rhetoric could be portrayed as a sign that Gorbachev's policies had succeeded in changing attitudes in the United States. By contrast, Gorbachev's conservative critics might seize upon continued rhetorical attacks from Washington as a demonstration that the Soviet leader was making too many concessions to the United States and getting little in return.

In advance of the Moscow summit, Dobrynin seemed to be searching for a way to open secret negotiations that would bypass the official channels of the State Department and Soviet Foreign Ministry. He suggested Massie as the message carrier. After raising the question of what "concrete steps" the Soviet Union could take, Dobrynin specified that the president could give his answer through Massie, who was planning to return to Moscow at the end of March. The former Soviet ambassador was seeking to put himself once again at the center of Soviet-American relations and to negotiate directly with the president of the United States.

Reagan spurned the offer. Initially, while Massie was in the Oval Office, the president began to reflect on the question of what, specifically, he might ask the Soviets to do. Should he ask that they cut back on arms supplies to Nicaragua, for example? But Reagan gave no immediate answer, and over the following days, the president decided to avoid doing business with Moscow in the way that Dobrynin had suggested. At the time, Shultz was talking regularly with Shevardnadze; the Soviet foreign minister had also just met with Reagan during a trip to Washington. When Massie checked back with the White House two weeks later before leaving again for the Soviet Union, she was given no response to Dobrynin's message.[14]

Reagan not only ignored the plea from Moscow, but also continued his rhetorical attacks on the Soviet Union. On April 21, 1988, appearing before a World Affairs Council meeting in Springfield, Massachusetts, Reagan said his own speeches about the Soviets of the previous few years had "made them understand the lack of illusions on our part about them or their system." He boasted he had been willing to talk about the Soviet Union in the plain, blunt terms that Soviet experts had long avoided in public discourse. "We rejected what Jeane Kirkpatrick called moral equivalency," the president asserted. "We said freedom was better than totalitarianism. We said communism was bad."[15]

Gorbachev was incensed. The president delivered this speech just as an American delegation headed by Shultz was arriving in Moscow to see Gorbachev and make arrangements for the summit. The following day, the Soviet leader vented his fury to Shultz, Powell, and the other American visitors. "The U.S. administration is not abandoning stereotypes," he complained. "So how am I to explain this? Is the summit going to be a catfight? Does he really intend to bring this ideological luggage to Moscow?"[16]

Shultz and Powell said later they had not seen Reagan's Springfield speech before it was delivered, and others in the delegation blamed the conservative White House speechwriters. "It was hard-hitting and insulting and all the rest," said Rozanne Ridgway, the assistant secretary of state for Europe. "It just struck us that every time we were going somewhere or were going to meet the Soviets, the speechwriters came out."[17]

Such remarks missed the larger point about Reagan's rhetoric. The president's job, interests, and priorities were not the same as those of the State Department. Reagan was the political leader; he needed to win public and congressional approval inside the United States for his foreign policy, and particularly for his diplomacy with Gorbachev. At the time of the Springfield speech and throughout the spring of 1988, Reagan was striving to obtain Senate ratification of the INF treaty he had signed the previous December. Reagan was aware that putting his signature onto that INF agreement, with Gorbachev, was not the final step in the process; after all, Reagan's own predecessor had failed to win Senate approval for the arms-control treaty he had negotiated with the Soviet Union. There would be time later on for Reagan to modify his "evil empire" rhetoric, but he would not do so while the INF treaty was still pending.

Although the president was increasingly disengaged from routine business, he had been paying fairly close attention to Soviet policy since the beginning of the year, particularly because he had just concluded one summit with Gorbachev and was approaching another. Reagan's diary shows his continuing interest. On New Year's Day, he read Gorbachev's year-end message to the American people. Four days later, he talked with aides about the tensions emerging in Moscow between Gorbachev and Ligachev. In mid-January, he spent a weekend at Camp David reading Gorbachev's new book, *Perestroika.*[18]

Above all, Reagan was preoccupied with getting the INF treaty through the Senate. The opponents of Reagan's Soviet policy continued to disparage the treaty. The *Wall Street Journal* mounted a campaign against it, with a series of editorials and columns. "The INF treaty doesn't address the real threat facing Europe, doesn't reduce the number of missiles aimed at the U.S. and doesn't destroy a single nuclear warhead," said a *Journal* editorial on January 29. "So what, exactly, is this treaty's relevance or point? What does it accomplish?" In early April, another *Journal* editorial branded Reagan a "utopian disarmer" and sought to link him to the left wing of the Democratic Party: "The administration that once decried the 'evil empire' now is pursuing radical arms reductions with a momentum that has even Jesse Jackson applauding," the newspaper said. Reagan's Springfield speech, delivered a few days later, was an attempt to respond to this critique.[19]

Richard Nixon once again challenged Reagan's beliefs about Gorbachev and the Soviet Union. Reviving the arguments he had made earlier, Nixon claimed that Gorbachev was merely another in a long line of Soviet leaders pushing for global predominance. "Under Gorbachev, the Soviet Union's foreign policy has been more skillful and subtle than ever. But it has been more aggressive, not less," wrote Nixon in the *New York Times Magazine* that March. "Like his predecessors, Gorbachev seeks to expand the influence and power of the Soviet Union."[20] It was hard to reconcile Nixon's words with Moscow realities that spring or with Gorbachev's actions, such as the withdrawal from Afghanistan. Nevertheless, Reagan administration officials worried that the former president would give further legitimacy to the political right.

Gorbachev, too, was concerned. He told American visitors that Nixon was clinging to old stereotypes about the Soviet Union. "The dead should not be allowed to take the living by the coattails and drag them back to the past," Gorbachev said.[21]

Reagan responded by courting and cajoling his adversaries. He kept in frequent touch with conservative leaders, even as they were denouncing the INF treaty. "He had a marvelous facility with the right wing," recalled Carlucci. "Periodically, he would invite them into the White House, into the Roosevelt Room, and he would come in and shake everybody's hand, and tell a joke or two, and leave the dirty work to the rest of us." William F. Buckley, Jr., complained to Reagan that after the Soviet Union destroyed its SS-20 missiles under the treaty, it might replace them with different missiles. Reagan consulted with his advisers and offered Buckley a simple reply: "We don't think that's something we can't handle."[22]

He treated the Nixon administration veterans with respect, despite their condemnation of his Soviet policy. He expressed disagreement with their views but avoided acrimony. He telephoned Nixon to wish him a happy birthday. He kept Henry Kissinger in mind for informal yet prestigious assignments. Reagan had earlier appointed Kissinger as chairman of a bipartisan commission on Central America. In early 1988, South Korea was to inaugurate a newly elected president, Roe Tae Woo, and the ceremonies required the presence of some prominent American. Vice President Bush, campaigning for president, was unavailable, as were Shultz and Carlucci. Reagan suggested Kissinger. (In the end, Treasury Secretary James Baker took on the assignment to represent the administration.)[23]

The result of these efforts was to defuse the opposition. Some of the conservatives continued to criticize Reagan's treaty, but without the passion or venom they were able to summon on other issues. Buckley wrote a column in *National Review* making the same points he had discussed with Reagan. But his column conveyed an air of inevitability to the treaty. It praised Jesse Helms, the leading Senate opponent of the INF treaty, but also portrayed Helms as quaintly out of touch with the times and with the romance between Reagan and Gorbachev: Buckley compared Helms to "the preacher who goes on and on with an endless sermon while the bride and groom are standing there, hands touching, in ardent desire to consummate their marriage."[24]

Meanwhile, the members of the old Nixon team could not quite bring themselves to come out in formal opposition to Reagan's INF treaty. The most striking example was Kissinger. Having argued the previous year that an INF treaty would lead to a crisis, Kissinger testified in early 1988 that the treaty should be approved, because if the Senate turned it down, that, too, would lead to a crisis. "Failure to ratify the treaty or insistence on amendments requiring renegotiation would not cure its defects," Kissinger said. "It would, on the contrary, vastly magnify all difficulties." He said Senate rejection of the treaty would "generate a crisis in the Atlantic alliance which would in the end almost certainly lead to the unilateral withdrawal of U.S. missiles from Europe and undermine the coherence of the alliance."[25]

Most of the Senate opposition came from Republicans. When Shultz testified before the Foreign Relations Committee, Helms greeted him with a series of accusations. Democrats rushed to the secretary of state's support. "He's here because we invited him," Senator Claiborne Pell, the committee chairman, admonished Helms. On the Armed Services Committee, Senator Dan Quayle led the charge, complaining that the administration had failed to address questions about how the treaty might apply to futuristic weapons, such as lasers.

The administration had some difficulties with a few Democrats too. David Boren, the chairman of the Senate Intelligence Committee, delayed action on the treaty to win a commitment from the administration for the funding of a new generation of surveillance satellites.[26] Senator Sam Nunn, the Armed Services Committee chairman, and Robert Byrd raised the constitutional issue of whether the administration's testimony about the treaty could be considered final and official; they did not want the Reagan administration to be able to "reinterpret" the treaty afterward, as it had with the 1972 Anti-Ballistic Missile treaty.

With Shultz taking the lead, the administration worked out understandings that would mollify several of the senators. The secretary of state assured Nunn that whatever administration officials told the Senate about the treaty would be authoritative. He overcame Quayle's objections by going back to the Soviets for a statement agreeing with the U.S. interpretation of how the treaty would apply to lasers, microwaves, and other futuristic weapons. Shultz finally grew impatient with Quayle, telling him: "Dan, you have to shut down. We can't have the president's achievement wrecked by Republicans."[27]

The opponents failed to kill or amend the treaty, but they delayed it. In the process, they achieved one not-inconsiderable success: the time and energy taken up by the Senate's consideration of the INF treaty forced the administration to slow down its other, even more ambitious efforts at arms control. At the Washington summit the previous December, Reagan and Gorbachev had said they hoped to settle on a separate treaty covering intercontinental missiles in time for the two leaders to sign it at the summit in Moscow. By the end of February, Reagan began to acknowledge that there might not be time to do this. Gradually, he and Gorbachev were forced to scale back their expectations. The Soviet leader told Shultz in late April that he hoped the Moscow summit could merely produce a statement that the two sides were making progress toward a treaty on long-range weapons.[28]

In early May, with the Moscow summit only weeks away, it was still unclear whether the INF treaty would be approved in time for the president's trip. By this juncture, administration officials and their Republican supporters in the Senate were virtually pleading for quick action. Failure to win Senate ratification would have been taken as a vote of no confidence in Reagan's policy toward Gorbachev. "It's our president who will be in Moscow next week, and he'd like to have this treaty," said Bob Dole, the Republican minority leader. "I say that as a Republican on behalf of a Republican president."[29]

In the end, the Republican opposition faded away. Conservatives forced a series of test votes on amending the treaty. All failed. Helms, for example, argued unsuccessfully that Gorbachev, as general secretary of the Communist Party, had no authority to sign a treaty for the Soviet Union. A number of Senate conservatives, including Quayle, decided that they would vote for the treaty. And most of the proposed amendments won the support of fifteen or fewer of the one hundred senators. "I am licked," Helms conceded.[30]

On May 27, 1988, two days after Reagan had flown to Helsinki to prepare for the Moscow summit, the Senate ratified the INF treaty by a vote of 93 to 5. It was the first arms-control treaty between the United States and the Soviet Union that had won Senate approval since 1972. And it was the first time since the beginning of the Cold War that the two governments had signed a genuine disarmament treaty—not merely reducing numbers of weapons, but eliminating them and agreeing to enforce the ban.

-8-

THE NOT-SO-EVIL EMPIRE

When Ronald Reagan departed for the Soviet Union in May 1988, he had scarcely traveled outside the United States for a year. Since his speech at the Berlin Wall the previous June, Reagan had ventured beyond America's borders only for a one-day stopover in Mexico and an obligatory visit to a NATO summit in Brussels. He and his advisers were long past the point of trying to conceal the president's chronic problems with sleep and jet lag. To prepare for Moscow, Reagan found it necessary to stop first for four nights of sleep and relaxation in Helsinki. While there, the president and his wife took turns having a massage by a Finnish masseuse George Shultz had recommended to them. As usual, they ventured forth rarely into the city they were visiting. Instead, they watched tapes specially brought to them of American network news shows. They retired early.[1]

As the president approached another summit, his old friends in the conservative movement shuddered. In a pair of columns, George Will acidly portrayed the president as having betrayed the cause of anticommunism. "Four years ago, many people considered Reagan a keeper of the Cold War flame. Time flies," Will wrote. "For conservatives, Ronald Reagan's foreign policy has produced much surprise but little delight. His fourth and, one prays, final summit is a suitable occasion for conservatives to look back with bewilderment and ahead with trepidation."[2]

The interlude in Helsinki gave the president a chance to start coping with the surveillance issues he would soon confront in Moscow. Reagan had never spent a night behind the Iron Curtain. His firsthand experience inside a Communist country had been confined to his fleeting afternoon drive into East Berlin a decade earlier and his 1984 visit to China (which Reagan had labeled a "so-called communist" country). In Helsinki, where American and Finnish officials were constantly mindful of the possibility of KGB spying, Reagan was obliged to converse with his advisers inside a secure room, "the box," in the American embassy.

One subject they discussed was Reagan's idea for a dramatic public demonstration of concern for Soviet Jews upon his arrival in Moscow. The wife of a Russian pianist who had emigrated to the United States let Nancy Reagan know about another Russian Jewish couple, Tatyana and Yuri Ziman, who were still living in Moscow and had been waiting for years for exit visas. Reagan's original plan was to make the Zimans' apartment his very first stop after arrival in the Soviet Union; the idea was for the president to visit the Jewish family even before his arrival ceremonies in the Kremlin. Gorbachev was furious when he learned what the Reagans wanted to do, according to U.S. Ambassador Jack Matlock. In Moscow, Deputy Foreign Minister Alexander Bessmertnykh was ordered to tell Matlock that if Reagan were to carry through on these plans, they would embarrass Gorbachev and could have disastrous consequences. Next, Bessmertnykh flew to Helsinki to protest directly to Assistant Secretary of State Rozanne Ridgway and the presidential entourage. The Zimans might never leave the Soviet Union if Reagan visited them, Bessmertnykh warned. If he didn't, the couple might be allowed to go soon.

It was the first contretemps of the summit, which hadn't even begun. Matlock rushed to Helsinki to confer with Powell and Chief of Staff Howard Baker. All of them spoke with the Reagans. The president decided to drop the Ziman event from his itinerary, and at the same time, to take Bessmertnykh's words as a promise to let the couple leave the country. "It was kind of am-

biguous, and we said, 'We're interpreting what you said as a commitment,'"
recalled Shultz. The Zimans were allowed to depart a few months later (but
only after Reagan, back in Washington, called the Soviet ambassador to in-
quire again about their exit visas).[3]

On Sunday, May 29, 1988, the president left Helsinki for Moscow. Peer-
ing out of the window of Air Force One onto Soviet territory, Reagan murmured to Powell, "Look, there's almost no traffic." He was accustomed to the
cars, houses, and opulence of the United States—the material well-being he
had dreamed of putting on display to Gorbachev during his visit to the United
States. Despite Reagan's three previous meetings with the Soviet leader, the
symbolism of the president's arrival in Moscow was lost on no one, including
the Reagans themselves. Over the previous quarter century, Reagan had
emerged as the most renowned anti-Communist in American political life;
now he was arriving at the headquarters of the Communist movement. "If
someone had told me when Ronnie and I were first married that we would
eventually travel to Moscow as president and first lady, and would be the
honored guests of the Soviet leadership, I would have suggested that he get his
head examined," Nancy Reagan admitted.[4]

Having canceled their visit to the Jewish family, the Reagans instead went
directly from the airport to the Kremlin. Inside, they had to walk up a long
staircase, covered by a red carpet. Mikhail and Raisa Gorbachev stood at the
top, waiting for them. Onlookers said Reagan seemed dazed and overwhelmed
by the moment. He started up the steps, stopped, and then took his wife's
hand before resuming the climb.[5]

After the arrival ceremonies, the president immediately sat down with
Gorbachev in St. Catherine's Hall at the Kremlin for their first talk. At each
of their summits, the two men held a couple of meetings that were labeled as
"one-on-one" sessions, in which Reagan and Gorbachev spoke to each other
outside the presence of top-level aides, such as Shultz and Eduard Shevardnadze, the Soviet foreign minister. (In fact, the two men were not completely
alone. Each brought a translator and two other officials to take notes.)

The texture of these one-on-one meetings was qualitatively different
from the larger meetings in which Reagan and Gorbachev were joined by

their advisers. They were more informal and unstructured, enabling the two leaders to demonstrate their priorities and personalities. The two leaders left the detailed policy discussion for the larger meetings.

It was during the first one-on-one session in Moscow that Reagan engaged in a bold but questionable endeavor well beyond his mandate as president of the United States. According to the transcripts of their meeting, which have now been declassified, Reagan secretly attempted to persuade Gorbachev of the existence of God.

The meeting opened with pleasantries. Both men agreed that they and their countries had come a long way since their first summit in Geneva three years earlier. Gorbachev then immediately turned to a surprise for which Reagan was not prepared: he read aloud and handed the president a written statement he wanted the two governments to sign during the summit that would commit the United States and the Soviet Union to "peaceful coexistence." Reagan said vaguely that he liked the idea and would talk it over with his advisers; he handed the piece of paper over to one of his notetakers, Thomas Simons. Gorbachev's proposal would become the subject of considerable acrimony over the following days.

The two men next revived their running debate about human rights. Reagan handed Gorbachev a list of names of Soviet citizens he believed were victims of repression in one fashion or another, starting with the Zimans and their eagerness to leave the country. As in the past, Gorbachev countered by arguing that America could be criticized for its own human rights abuses too.

Suddenly, Reagan switched the subject to religion. He told Gorbachev that what he was about to say would be considered entirely secret. According to the notetakers, Reagan told Gorbachev that "if word got out that this was even being discussed, the President would deny he had said anything about it." To emphasize this point, Reagan said again a few minutes later that "if there was anyone in the room who said he had given such advice [to Gorbachev about religion], he would say that person was lying, that he had never said it."[6]

In planning for the Moscow summit, Reagan had discussed with his aides the idea of focusing on freedom of religion. He had worked with aides on some talking points to use with the Soviet leader; he had honed these ideas during his stay in Helsinki.[7] Once he was alone with Gorbachev, the president began with a plea on behalf of religious tolerance in the Soviet Union. He praised Gorbachev for easing slightly the rules for the Russian Orthodox Church. According to the notes of the meeting: "The President asked Gorbachev what if he ruled that religious freedom was part of the people's rights, that people of any religion—whether Islam with its mosque, the Jewish faith, Protestants or the Ukrainian Church—could go to the church of their choice."

Gorbachev deflected this question. He insisted that religion was not a serious problem in the Soviet Union. According to the notes, Gorbachev told Reagan that "he, himself, had been baptized, but he was not now a believer, and that reflected a certain evolution of Soviet society." There might have been some "excesses" in repressing religion immediately after the Soviet revolution, Gorbachev said, but times had changed. His program of *perestroika* was designed to expand democratic procedures, and it would extend to religion.

Reagan then ventured further, taking a step that quite a few Americans would have found objectionable. The president switched from seeking to persuade Gorbachev of the value of religious tolerance to promoting a belief in God. Reagan did so by telling one of his trademark stories. According to the notes of their meeting:

> *The President said he had a letter from the widow of a young World War II soldier. He was lying in a shell hole at midnight, awaiting an order to attack. He had never been a believer, because he had been told God did not exist. But as he looked up at the stars he voiced a prayer hoping that, if he died in battle, God would accept him. That piece of paper was found on the body of a young Russian soldier who was killed in that battle.*[8]

Gorbachev tried to switch the subject. Perhaps the United States and the Soviet Union might open the way for greater cooperation in space, he told the president. But the president wasn't to be diverted. According to the transcript, Reagan told Gorbachev that space was in the direction of heaven, but not as close to heaven as some other things that they had been discussing.

As the meeting ended, Reagan became even more direct and personal. He noted that his own son Ron did not believe in God either. "The President concluded that there was one thing he had long yearned to do for his atheist son. He wanted to serve his son the perfect gourmet dinner, to have him enjoy the meal, and then to ask him if he believed there was a cook."

Of the two American notetakers who were present for this extraordinary conversation, one took Reagan's effort at face value. "Reagan thought he could convert Gorbachev, or make him see the light," said Rudolf Perina, who was then the director of Soviet affairs on the National Security Council. The second, Thomas Simons, the deputy assistant secretary of state, viewed Reagan's promotion of religion as, in part, a tactic to deflect Gorbachev away from discussion of other substantive issues.[9]

Reagan's proselytizing was extremely unusual for an American president, but not entirely unprecedented. Nine years earlier, Reagan's predecessor Jimmy Carter had stunned his aides when he asked the South Korean dictator Park Chung Hee about his religious beliefs and then told Park, "I would like you to know about Christ."[10] Religion had been a continuing theme underpinning Reagan's views of the Soviet Union. He had observed the impact of the Catholic Church in Poland, he had talked with Suzanne Massie about an upsurge in religious sentiment in the Soviet Union, he had speculated to Colin Powell that Gorbachev might be secretly devout. The secret one-on-one conversation in Moscow reflected Reagan's continuing belief that the Soviet system's repression of religion left it vulnerable to ideological challenge. It embodied his hope that Gorbachev was capable of changing the system.

The Reagans were determined to engage in some sort of seemingly spontaneous event with ordinary people on the streets of Moscow, comparable to Gorbachev's stroll along Connecticut Avenue in Washington. White House planners had recommended a walk in the shopping area known as the Arbat. The Secret Service objected to the risks, but the Reagans decided to go forward. They took a limo to the Arbat and shook hands with crowds of Russians for about ten minutes. When photographers complained that it was hard to get a good picture, Nancy Reagan found an old carriage and stood with her husband on it, framing the photo that they knew would be on newspaper front pages the next day. On the edges of the event, some KGB officials shoved away a couple of American onlookers, but the event was on the whole a success and served the purpose of showing that Reagan could do in Moscow what Gorbachev had done in Washington. "In my mind, the score with Gorbachev had been evened," wrote Jim Kuhn, Reagan's executive assistant.

The dispute over Reagan's walk in the Arbat exemplified the intense security that surrounded him throughout the stay in Moscow. The Reagans were staying at Spaso House, the residence attached to the U.S. embassy. The president was informed that the rooms might have bugs or cameras in them, and that any time he wanted to study a briefing paper or talk to an aide, he should move to a secure room in the building. Reagan balked, saying he wanted to be able to read his material in relaxed fashion without these cumbersome procedures. The issue was brought to Powell, who decreed that Reagan didn't have to go to the secure room for these routine preparations.[11]

The demands of American security irked Gorbachev. When the president and his wife were scheduled to accompany the Gorbachevs to the Bolshoi Ballet one evening, the show had to be delayed because of logistical problems. "It was reported to Gorbachev that they [the U.S. Secret Service] wanted to check all spectators themselves," recalled Gorbachev's interpreter, Pavel Palazchenko. "This was one of the few occasions that I ever saw Mikhail Gorbachev angry." Before eventually relenting, the Soviet leader talked with his aides about canceling an after-ballet dinner for the Reagans at his dacha.[12]

Despite the obsession with security, Reagan was able to attend several carefully orchestrated events aimed at demonstrating interest in several aspects of Soviet life. He visited the Danilov Monastery, where he declared that Americans shared "a hope for a new age of religious freedom in the Soviet Union." At a meeting with a group of Soviet writers and artists, Reagan voiced a hope that the works of exiled author Alexander Solzhenitsyn could be published inside the Soviet Union. He also reflected on his earlier career in film, saying that actors were often typecast and then added that "politics is a little like that, too." In the most politically sensitive event on the president's schedule, he met at Spaso House with nearly a hundred Soviet dissidents specially invited for the occasion. "You have the prayers and support of the American people, indeed of people throughout the world," Reagan told them. He spoke of the values of freedom of speech, religion, and travel. "I've come to Moscow with this human rights agenda because, as I've suggested, it is our belief that this is a moment of hope," he told the dissidents. "We hope that one freedom will lead to another and another."[13]

In a speech at Moscow State University, Reagan put forward many of the same ideas about globalization that, a year earlier, his secretary of state had offered in private to Gorbachev. "Linked by a network of satellites and fiber-optic cables, one individual with a desktop computer and a telephone commands resources unavailable to the largest governments just a few years ago," he said. "In the new economy, human invention increasingly makes physical resources obsolete." Reagan went on to draw a connection between these global changes, on the one hand, and economic freedom and individual liberty on the other. "Freedom is the right to question and change the established way of doing things," Reagan asserted. During a question-and-answer session, Reagan told the students he hoped they could look forward "to a day when there will be no more nuclear weapons in the world at all."[14] At the end, the students gave Reagan an ovation.

These events were staged, but they were not mere stunts. Through them, Reagan not only openly promoted political liberalization but also associated Gorbachev and his reforms with these ideals. The president was boosting the Soviet leader in the fashion that riled Reagan's critics back in the United States. At the same time, his remarks encouraged hopes and expectations inside the Soviet Union that the country was on the verge of political change.

The large formal meetings between the American and Soviet delegations, headed by Reagan and Gorbachev, made little headway. During the Moscow summit, there were two plenary sessions in which each leader was accompanied by six to eight other top officials. Reagan was joined by aides such as Shultz, Powell, Defense Secretary Frank Carlucci, and White House chief of staff Howard Baker; Gorbachev's side included Shevardnadze, Defense Minister Dmitri Yazov, former Foreign Minister Andrei Gromyko, and former ambassador Anatoly Dobrynin.

At the outset, the two leaders congratulated each other over the completion of the INF treaty. According to the declassified notes of this meeting, Reagan said he and his aides had "shed a lot of blood" to win approval for the treaty. Gorbachev joked that the 93-to-5 vote for Senate ratification was impressive, but "the Soviet side had done better—with 100 percent of the votes in favor."[15]

The two sides were still committed to completing the more sweeping START treaty covering strategic weapons during Reagan's final six months in office. But at the summit, they repeated old arguments and did little to narrow their differences. At one awkward moment, Reagan, seeking to emphasize a point with a hand gesture, spilled a glass of water onto the table and apologized. "Never mind," Gorbachev told him. "A careless move with a glass of water is no big deal. If it had happened with missiles. . . ."[16]

During the second of the two large meetings, Soviet officials brought up the proposed joint statement on "peaceful coexistence," which Gorbachev had given to Reagan three days earlier. It would have committed both sides to a summit communiqué that said:

> The two leaders believe that no problem in dispute can be resolved, nor should be resolved, by military means. They regard peaceful coexistence as a universal principle of international relations. Equality of all states, non-interference in internal affairs and freedom of socio-political choice must be recognized as the inalienable and mandatory standards of international relations.[17]

Gorbachev pointed out that Reagan had not voiced any objections when the statement was first read to him, merely noting that his aides should study it. When the advisers saw the language, they were horrified. It may have seemed on the surface to be an anodyne commitment to avoid the use of force, but the statement contained a series of words and phrases with a long history and hidden political content. "Peaceful coexistence" was a phrase that Soviet officials had used since the 1920s to describe the relationship they envisioned between the socialist and capitalist systems. In the Soviet lexicon, the terminology did not cover relationships among the socialist countries themselves, such as, for example, the use of Soviet troops in Hungary or Czechoslovakia. Similarly, the vague phrase "freedom of socio-political choice" could have been interpreted as formal American acceptance of Soviet predominance in the Communist systems that had been imposed in Eastern Europe and the Baltic states.

"This was Cold War rhetoric that sent all kinds of signals, but if you weren't steeped in the lore, you wouldn't recognize it," said Carlucci.[18] To make matters worse, Reagan's aides noted that after the Nixon administration went along with comparable language as part of the process of détente; the Soviet Union felt no compunction about sending its troops into Afghanistan.

Assistant Secretary of State Rozanne Ridgway, who was in charge of negotiating the formal postsummit statements with her Soviet counterpart, had rejected the language Gorbachev proposed. At the second meeting between the full Soviet and American delegations, however, Gorbachev revived the issue and pushed hard, concentrating directly on Reagan. He insisted that by saying once vaguely that he liked the sound of the statement, the American president had already given his assent. Ridgway passed a note to others in the American delegation, saying it was crucial to stop Gorbachev from obtaining Reagan's approval. Shultz and Carlucci began to break into the discussion to voice their own objections.

As the officials of both governments looked on, Gorbachev appealed to Reagan to exercise his authority as president. "Should we record that the Americans would not agree to the paragraph because of George Shultz or Frank Carlucci?" Gorbachev asked. "Are they the intransigent parties? . . . . Perhaps Ambassador Matlock or Assistant Secretary Ridgway?"[19] The president seemed to be wavering, eager to accommodate Gorbachev but unwilling to override his subordinates. "Reagan looked uncomfortable—which he was in improvised situations," recalled Powell.[20]

The president told Gorbachev he didn't want to be "the skunk at the picnic." Finally, Gorbachev suggested the two sides should take a break at which the American delegation could review the statement he had been urging upon Reagan. The Americans huddled together and Reagan's aides repeated their objections. According to Powell, Reagan accepted their complaints with a "disappointed shrug." He told Gorbachev, who briefly and angrily tried to argue further. "Gorbachev blew up. He had a temper," said Carlucci. After a few moments, Gorbachev gave up and once again became amicable as the meeting ended.

Several of Reagan's advisers felt that Gorbachev had mounted this campaign at the behest of traditionalist forces in the Communist Party leadership. Sitting alongside Gorbachev at these meetings were Gromyko and Dobrynin, veterans of Soviet-American diplomacy dating back to the earliest days of the Cold War. "We had the impression that this was showtime for Gorbachev," recalled Ridgway. "If he could get American approval of 'peaceful coexistence' for all these guys sitting around him like Dobrynin, he would. And if not, he would show them that it wasn't possible. This all came up, I'm convinced, only because Gorbachev was still struggling inside the Politburo with a lot of people who were skeptical of where things were heading."[21]

The episode represented an ironic reversal of roles between Reagan and his own foreign-policy team. The underlying issue was the recurrent one of how much the United States should accept the divisions of the Cold War. When it came to public rhetoric, such as Reagan's call in Berlin for Gorbachev to "tear down this wall," the president was willing to play the hawk, while Shultz, Powell, and Ridgway were much more cautious. But on matters of formal diplomatic language, such as a commitment to "peaceful coexistence," they switched sides. Reagan was willing to try to placate Gorbachev, while his advisers became the hawks.

The contrast was striking. Reagan paid attention to the larger ideas and principles underlying the Cold War. He was the dominant force in his administration on questions of American politics and the mood of the public. His foreign-policy advisers thought of public speeches as a hazardous or frivolous diversion, but they cared about the lasting implications of a written statement. Reagan was largely indifferent to the nuances of a formal communiqué. To Reagan, the Berlin Wall was concrete. "Peaceful coexistence" was merely an abstraction.

Mikhail Gorbachev went out of his way to let the world know that he and Ronald Reagan liked each other. The relationship served important purposes for his foreign policy and for his personal standing as Soviet leader. The private reality was more complicated.

Sitting in a meeting with Reagan required patience—sometimes more patience than Gorbachev possessed. Reagan told anecdote after anecdote. He quoted from letters he claimed to have received. He repeated the same phrases and lines over and over again, never going beyond them or explaining their particular relevance to the point at hand. Gorbachev was a debater, a specialist in argument and refutation. Reagan was a storyteller. If he had a debating style at all, it was akin to Mohammed Ali's "rope-a-dope" in boxing: let your opponent punch himself out until he is exhausted. After a session with Reagan, interlocutors would often find that they had engaged in pleasant and superficial banter but had achieved nothing. They would be left wondering whether Reagan had cleverly deflected them away from their purpose, or whether it had just turned out that way.

For Gorbachev, this process was exasperating. Rudolf Perina, the National Security Council aide who served as official notetaker for Reagan's one-on-one sessions with Gorbachev in Moscow, described the tenor of the conversations. "In general, Gorbachev thought he was clearly smarter than Reagan. There was an element of condescension," Perina said. "Sometimes, when Gorbachev made a clever point, he would look around the room, in the vain hope there would be some audience there to recognize his superior intelligence. But these were one-on-one meetings, and there was no one there but the notetakers, who would avert their eyes and go back to their notes."[22]

When Reagan arrived at Gorbachev's Kremlin office for their final one-on-one session, the Soviet leader expressed some apparent uneasiness at the prospect of being left alone once again with the American president. The notes show that as the session started, the Soviet leader invited White House chief of staff Howard Baker, who had accompanied the president to the meeting, to stay. Baker demurred, saying he wasn't scheduled to participate and would instead wait outside.[23]

Reagan entered bearing a gift. He had brought Gorbachev a denim jacket. It was, he said, an example of the American wardrobe, a gift from a friend in the American West. Gorbachev seems to have been momentarily bewildered. He asked Reagan whether the jacket was in his size (perhaps wondering whether the CIA had somehow been covertly measuring his chest and waist). Reagan said he didn't know. Gorbachev tactfully called the jacket "a marvelous souvenir. This was one he would keep at home." He reciprocated by giving Reagan a scale model of the Kremlin.

By now, Gorbachev was prepared to deal with Reagan on Reagan's terms.

The Soviet leader escorted the president over to his desk and displayed some of the letters he said he had been receiving. He read excerpts from the letters; the Soviet leader was imitating Reagan's style. Here was a letter from the city of Grodno in Byelorussia by a man who had named his son Ronald and wanted the American president to be the godfather, Gorbachev reported. Here was another letter from someone in Togliatti on the Volga, who had just named his newborn daughter Nancy in honor of the president's wife. And here was another from Ivanovo in the Ukraine, from a woman who urged Reagan and Gorbachev to eliminate all nuclear weapons.[24]

This time, it was Reagan's turn to switch the conversation back to substantive issues. He said he had read Gorbachev's book *Perestroika* and asked the Soviet leader what steps he would be taking next. Gorbachev gave an overview of the political reforms he expected to put forward at the party conference a few weeks later. The main thrust was greater democratization, Gorbachev told Reagan. He said the Communist Party of the Soviet Union "had to give up some of the functions it should not properly have." Still, Gorbachev warned, these changes would all be carried out within the context of developing the socialist system.

It was not long before Reagan was telling stories again. This time, the Soviet leader could not hide his irritation. Reagan said there were examples in the United States of the kinds of economic opportunities that Gorbachev was trying to open up with his program of *perestroika*. Why, said Reagan, he had met an American woman, a professional pianist who had developed arthritis and could no longer play. She was at home with nothing to do. Her aunt reminded her that she baked the best brownies anyone had ever tasted. (Here, one of Reagan's notetakers, Thomas Simons, had to explain to the Russian interpreter that brownies were small square-shaped chocolate cakes.[25]) The woman had begun selling her brownies to grocery stores.

"That was three or four years ago," Reagan went on, but before he could complete his story, Gorbachev interrupted. "I predict that she now has a prosperous business," he said sarcastically, knowing exactly where Reagan's anecdotes were invariably headed. Exactly right, Reagan said: the woman now employed more than thirty-five people, sold to the airlines and restaurants, and earned more than a million dollars a year.

Nevertheless, the tone of cordiality prevailed. The meeting was largely confined to generalities, but Reagan placed himself squarely on the side of those who wanted to improve relations with the Soviet Union. He told Gorbachev that he observed "one simple rule: you don't get in trouble by talking *to* each other, and not just *about* each other." Gorbachev complained that there were some people in America who asked, "Why help the Soviet Union expand? Wouldn't it be better for it to be weak?" Reagan replied that he did not feel that way at all. Let us keep on building trust with each other, he said.

What followed, as it turned out, was the principal event of the summit.

After their talk, the two leaders strolled out of the Kremlin onto Red Square. They stopped to talk with small groups of people. Picking up a small boy in his arms, Gorbachev said, "Shake hands with Grandfather Reagan." The president repeated in public the line he had used with Gorbachev a few minutes earlier: "We decided to talk to each other, instead of about each other."

As the two men were walking back toward the Kremlin, Reagan was confronted with the same question he had been asked repeatedly over the past couple of years. Reporters brought up Reagan's famous epithet about the Soviet Union five years earlier. "Do you still think you're in an evil empire, Mr. President?" asked ABC correspondent Sam Donaldson.

Reagan didn't hesitate. "No," he answered. "I was talking about another time and another era."

The reply appeared to be casual and spontaneous. Yet this was, in fact, precisely the issue that had been under discussion between Moscow and Washington at least since the previous March, when Dobrynin sent a message to Reagan asking him to renounce his past rhetoric about the Soviet Union. The president had stuck with the "evil empire" phraseology at the time of the Washington summit a half year earlier and throughout the Senate campaign to win ratification of the INF treaty. Now, Reagan moved to cut loose from the "evil empire" label.

A day later, at a press conference just before leaving Moscow, Reagan again rejected the "evil empire" wording. and elaborated further, this time emphasizing Gorbachev's personal role. Asked what had changed in the half decade since he had branded the Soviet Union an "evil empire," Reagan replied, "I think that a great deal of it is due to the General Secretary, who I have found different than previous Soviet leaders. . . . A large part of it is Mr. Gorbachev as leader." The president said he had read Gorbachev's book *Perestroika* and found much in it with which he could agree. There had been a "profound change" in the Soviet government, Reagan said, and while there were fundamental differences between the United States and the Soviet Union, these differences "continue to recede."[26]

Those words were of singular importance for Gorbachev. Reagan was conferring a sense of recognition both on the Soviet leader himself and on the reforms he was carrying out. For years, the opponents of political liberalization within the Soviet Communist Party had pointed to the external threat from the United States as a primary reason for resisting change at home. Now, Reagan was undermining this rationale for preserving the status quo.

For Gorbachev, the timing of Reagan's words could not have been better. The Soviet leader was just weeks away from the special party conference at which he would press for further political changes, including greater openness in the press and new limits on the power of the Communist Party. Once again, reformers within the party would do battle with conservative forces. Eventually, over the following years, the reformers would move beyond Gorbachev. But during this crucial period, Reagan was helping to strengthen Gorbachev's hand, giving him the time and breathing room he needed to open up the Soviet political system.

Indeed, Reagan's decision to jettison the phrase "evil empire" carried weight with several different audiences. For the American public, it signified a winding down of the Cold War. In Moscow, it helped Gorbachev within the Communist Party leadership, particularly with orthodox elements of the Soviet hierarchy and with veteran officials such as Dobrynin. Gorbachev was unable to obtain American approval for a formal diplomatic statement in support of "peaceful coexistence," but he could claim to have succeeded in changing Reagan's rhetoric.

Reagan's abandonment of the phrase "evil empire" had an impact upon a larger Soviet audience too. It served to reinforce the notion that political life in the Soviet Union was indeed opening up. If Ronald Reagan, the most determined and most prominent of all anti-Communists, accepted that Gorbachev's reforms were a sign of fundamental change, then others would be considerably less skeptical. The Russian poet Andrei Voznesensky remarked after Reagan's visit that the president's words had emboldened reformers throughout the Soviet Union.[27]

Gorbachev himself recognized the significance of what Reagan had said. "It meant that he [Reagan] had finally convinced himself that he had been right to believe, back in Reykjavik, that you could 'do business' with the changing Soviet Union," wrote Gorbachev in his memoirs. "In my view, the 40th president of the United States will go down in history for his rare perception."[28]

Reagan's words were not merely for public consumption, but reflected his own views. Upon returning to Washington, he offered essentially the same positive views of the Soviet Union to conservative friends. Responding to a letter from George Murphy, the former actor and U.S. senator, Reagan wrote a few weeks after his visit to Moscow: "Murph, for the first time, I believe there could be a stirring of the people that would make the bureaucrats pay attention. . . . If *glasnost* was just showboating, they may have to keep at least some of the promises, or face a public they've never seen before."[29]

It seems unlikely that Reagan, in such a short and carefully restricted trip, had sufficient basis for such broad conclusions about the changes in the Soviet Union. But there could be no denying the political impact of his words or his judgments about Gorbachev.

-9-

BUSH V. REAGAN

Within a week of Reagan's return to Washington, his positive views of Gorbachev and of the Soviet Union were disputed by an unusual source: his own vice president, George H. W. Bush.

In the midst of his campaign for the presidency, Bush made clear that he disagreed with what Reagan had been saying in Moscow. On June 7, while appearing before a group of television executives in Los Angeles, Bush was asked about Reagan's assertion that a profound change was under way in the Soviet Union. He replied: "I don't agree that we know enough to say that there is that kind of fundamental change." The vice president acknowledged that Gorbachev was "stylistically different, obviously generationally different" from previous Soviet leaders, but he said that when it came to Gorbachev's intentions, "my view is, the jury is still out." He did not believe that the Soviets were less threatening to the United States than they had been in the past. Asked directly by columnist George Will whether he disagreed with Reagan on Soviet policy, Bush carefully replied in the affirmative: "Maybe there's a difference there."[1]

America was in the early stages of a political transition. Reagan would be leaving office in a half year, giving way to a new president with new policies. Now that they had become comfortable with Reagan, the Soviets were worried about his departure. Reagan had assured Gorbachev at the end of their last private talk in Moscow that he would do everything he could to make sure that the next president maintained a relationship of trust with Gorbachev and preserved continuity in American policy toward the Soviet Union. At one of the Moscow dinners, Gorbachev pleased Nancy Reagan by telling her, "I wish your husband could stay on for another four years."

Yet Gorbachev also displayed an undertone of ambivalence about the prospective changes in Washington. When Reagan brought up the subject of human rights abuses in the Soviet Union, Gorbachev argued that the United States had its own problems; it just failed to acknowledge them. According to the notes of their conversation, "Gorbachev said he thought the President's successors would be more self-critical than he was. . . ." Nervous as he was about Reagan's successor, Gorbachev was happy with the prospect of dealing with a new president who might not be so cheerily optimistic and might not take up the time of summit meetings with diversionary stories.[2]

By mid-June 1988, the presidential primaries were over. Bush had clinched the Republican nomination, and he was preparing to run against Michael Dukakis, the Democratic governor of Massachusetts, in the general election. Reagan had told Gorbachev that he was hoping and praying for Bush. The vice president, after all, had steadfastly supported Reagan for most of the previous eight years, until Bush was in the midst of his own 1988 presidential campaign.

Bush had first set himself apart from the president's foreign policy earlier that spring, when he had pushed Reagan aggressively but unsuccessfully for a much more hawkish policy toward Manuel Noriega in Panama. That had at first seemed to be a one-shot affair arising from the political issue of drugs rather than larger questions of foreign policy. By June, however, Bush was beginning to distance himself from the Reagan administration on the central issues of Soviet policy too.

Bush had a political interest in staking out a tough-sounding public view of Gorbachev. He was hoping to emphasize national-security issues in his fall campaign against Dukakis, aiming to win over the support of the Republican

right and to portray his opponent as a liberal in the tradition of George Mc-
Govern. Bush's campaign manager, Lee Atwater, called Dukakis "a balloon
ready to be punctured."[3]

Over the following months, with Atwater at the helm, the Bush campaign would unleash a series of attacks on Dukakis for vetoing a bill that
would have required students to recite the Pledge of Allegiance in class and
for granting a furlough to a convicted murderer named Willie Horton. Reagan's negotiations with and endorsement of Gorbachev had aroused intense
opposition from Republican conservatives. As a matter of electoral tactics,
then, it was not surprising that during the 1988 campaign, Bush took a position well to the right of Reagan on Soviet policy.

Nevertheless, Bush's campaign statements about the Soviets were not
merely an election tactic. They also represented genuine disagreements with
Reagan about Gorbachev and the Soviet Union. Over the course of the previous eight years, Bush had moved in the opposite direction from Reagan, becoming more hard-nosed toward Moscow as the president was becoming
more conciliatory.

During Reagan's first term, amid the defense buildup and the "evil empire" rhetoric, Bush had let it be known repeatedly in private that he believed
the president was too combative toward the Soviet Union. In one conversation, he confided to Soviet ambassador Anatoly Dobrynin that Reagan's views
of the Soviet Union had been dominated by Hollywood clichés and by deep-
seated stereotypes. "Well, he's hard, very hard indeed," Bush had said in 1983.
Two years later, before Reagan's first summit with Gorbachev, the vice president told Dobrynin that he personally wished for a better atmosphere between the United States and the Soviet Union.[4]

Things began to change after Reagan and Gorbachev talked in Reykjavik
about eliminating nuclear weapons. The vice president had a more traditional
view about the value of these weapons, and he was also more skeptical than
Reagan and Shultz that the Gorbachev approach represented something dramatically new for Soviet foreign policy. Bush was closer in outlook to Nixon,
Kissinger, and Scowcroft. During the 1988 campaign, then, polite though he
was, the vice president became the highest-ranking critic of Reagan's diplomacy with Gorbachev.

During the Moscow summit, Reagan, Gorbachev, and their delegations had agreed to try to reach agreement before the end of the year on a treaty that would reduce strategic weaponry. But over the following months, Reagan administration officials found that it wasn't possible. One reason was the opposition of the Bush campaign.

"At the end of the Moscow summit, the whole relationship [between Washington and Moscow] just went into limbo," recalled Rozanne Ridgway, the assistant secretary of state for European affairs. "We were working on the treaty, but a large cadre of naysayers, like Brent Scowcroft and James Baker and all these guys, were saying that George Shultz had pushed the president too far and that we should put the thing on hold. Their argument was that we have only six months left, and we can't get anything done."[5]

Jack Matlock, who was then serving as Reagan's ambassador to the Soviet Union and eventually stayed on as Bush's ambassador, came to the same conclusion: Bush wanted the Reagan administration to go no further with Gorbachev. "He knew that he would have to indulge in some hard-line rhetoric to pacify the Republican Party's right wing, and it would be difficult to fight for ratification of a major arms reduction agreement at the same time," Matlock wrote. "Besides, he did not want his administration to look like a continuation of the Reagan administration."

For his own part, Bush, during the summer of 1988, complained privately that he was disturbed by Reagan's "sentimentality" toward Gorbachev. He worried that Reagan and Shultz were "crashing too hard" toward a final agreement with the Soviet leader in the last months of the Reagan administration.[6]

When Soviet foreign minister Eduard Shevardnadze visited Washington in late September, he and Shultz tried once more to see if they could conclude a treaty on reducing strategic weapons. They failed; there was too little time left. The Reagan White House was reluctant to make a deal for which the Bush team had no enthusiasm.

Gorbachev was not disposed to sit on his hands and wait for the results of the American election. In late October 1988, while Bush and Dukakis were in the closing days of their campaigns, the Soviet leader served as host for a groundbreaking visit to Moscow by West German chancellor Helmut Kohl, one that would pave the way for a reordering of the diplomacy and the political alignments throughout Europe.

Over the previous few years, the relations between the two men had been icy. Kohl had paid a courtesy call upon Gorbachev in the Kremlin just after Gorbachev was appointed party secretary in March 1985. At the time, with Foreign Minister Andrei Gromyko at his side, Gorbachev had invoked the memory of the twenty million Soviets who had died during World War II. Anyone who talked about German unity was a warmonger, Gromyko had declared. Kohl had responded by asking Gorbachev to imagine a wall along the Moscow River, dividing parts of the city from one another. "Suppose you're on this side, and your mother and your sister were living on the other side, and you were trying to get from here to there—are you a warmonger then?" he asked.[7]

Gorbachev's initial impression was that Kohl was merely an agent of the Americans. "The government in Bonn followed President Reagan's course with German precision," he wrote. Relations became further strained in 1986, when Kohl used an analogy from the Nazi era to characterize Gorbachev. The chancellor was arguing that Gorbachev's efforts at change were merely cosmetic in nature, meant more to beguile the West than to change the Soviet Union. American skeptics had been making similar points, but the wording Kohl chose had been unique. "He is a modern communist leader who understands public-relations," the German chancellor said in an interview with *Newsweek*. "Goebbels, who was one of those responsible for the crimes of the Hitler era, was an expert in public relations, too."[8]

Gorbachev, infuriated, froze all contacts with Kohl, whose advisers quickly concluded that the chancellor had made a serious mistake. Kohl's foreign-policy adviser, Horst Teltschik, was reduced to begging friendly officials in Hungary and Czechoslovakia to pass on tidbits of information about what was happening in the Kremlin. The chancellor wrote a letter of apology to Gorbachev, claiming his remarks had been taken out of context.

Two years later, as West Germany's economy continued to thrive and as it developed ever-deeper ties with its central European neighbors, Gorbachev and his aides decided to try to do business with Kohl. "In 1988, there was a growing awareness on Gorbachev's part that he needed Western help," recalled Kohl. "He told me that he had to find a suitable partner. It was not to be expected that the Americans would help him. The Europeans might, and the strongest role among the Europeans was played by the Germans."[9]

This time, on October 28, 1988, the Soviet and West German leaders established a close personal rapport and working relationship. Kohl spoke to Gorbachev about the horrors of World War II, about his own family and the need for peace. Gorbachev chose not to challenge Kohl when he referred at one point to the hope for a unified Germany. "We witnessed an amazing metamorphosis that day," said Gorbachev's foreign-policy adviser, Anatoly Chernyaev, who, together with Teltschik, sat in on the session in Moscow. "In any case, as a result of that meeting, the trust between Gorbachev and Kohl began growing rapidly, trust that soon turned into a real, informal friendship."[10] Along with the new personal warmth came West German credits of $1.6 billion and a series of trade deals for West German companies in the Soviet Union.

Kohl's visit to Moscow was particularly disquieting to East German Communist Party leader Erich Honecker, who judged correctly that Gorbachev was gradually changing his attitudes toward the two German governments. According to Egon Krenz, Honecker's aide, East German officials noticed how Gorbachev and Soviet foreign minister Eduard Shevardnadze stopped raising German issues in discussions with the Reagan administration. The East Germans believed Gorbachev was gradually abandoning them. Honecker's paranoia was increased all the more by his difficulty in obtaining a full account from Soviet leaders of the Kohl-Gorbachev meeting. Chernyaev had advised Gorbachev not to give the East German leader the transcripts. "It is not necessary that he be aware of everything, especially not the atmosphere of the talks," he wrote in one memo. "Honecker could draw some sort of 'ideological' conclusions that we can absolutely do without. . . . We determine our policy, which is by no means identical to Honecker's."

The talks with Kohl were merely prologue. By the fall of 1988, Gorbachev was already preparing a much bolder initiative, aimed at transforming the Soviet Union's relationship with Western Europe.

———

Presidencies do not end all at once. Ronald Reagan began to yield some of the powers of his presidency in the summer and fall of 1988. The abandonment of efforts at a treaty on strategic weaponry was merely one part of a much broader trend. As cabinet officials resigned from his administration, Reagan allowed Vice President Bush to recommend their successors. When Ed Meese resigned as attorney general, Bush recommended the appointment of Richard Thornburgh, the former governor of Pennsylvania, to take his place. Reagan approved. When James Baker stepped down as treasury secretary to run Bush's campaign, the vice president suggested Nicholas Brady to succeed Baker. Reagan went along with that appointment too, and it was the same for a new secretary of education. All of the new cabinet members stayed on in the next administration.

During the election campaign, Reagan spent his time on routine business and ceremonies, while following the polls on the Bush-Dukakis race. At one point, Dan Quayle was ushered into the Oval Office for advice on how to handle himself before his televised vice presidential debate with Lloyd Bentsen. In his diary, Reagan pronounced Quayle to be "a fine person," but the tutelage didn't work; Quayle was devastated by Bentsen's quip "You're no Jack Kennedy."[11] Late in the fall, Reagan made a few campaign stops for Bush in California, Wisconsin, and Ohio—enough to say that he had helped his vice president, but not enough to qualify as an impassioned effort.

Bush didn't need much help. The political coalition that Reagan had assembled for the Republican Party in 1980 remained largely intact. The fact that Reagan had dramatically shifted course in his approach to the Soviet Union made little difference in the fall campaign. In the debates, Bush at one point alluded vaguely to the intense debates in Washington about Gorbachev. "I think the jury is still out on the Soviet experiment," he said.[12] Having successfully fended off challenges from conservatives in the Republican primaries, Bush proceeded to attack Dukakis and the Democrats as weak on national security in the general election. The strategy worked; Bush won with 54 percent of the vote.

Throughout that fall, Gorbachev had been pressing for political changes in Moscow that would reduce the power of the Communist Party and at the same time, strengthen his own position in the leadership. After the summit with Reagan in Moscow and the Communist Party conference that followed, Gorbachev's leading opponent within the party, Yegor Ligachev, challenged Gorbachev's ideas again by arguing that Soviet foreign policy should continue to reflect "the class character of international relations." Gorbachev countered with a reorganization of the leadership. Ligachev was ousted from his position in charge of party ideology and instead placed in charge of agriculture; Andrei Gromyko, who had guided Soviet foreign policy since the early years of the Cold War, was forced to retire. While remaining Communist Party secretary, Gorbachev also took over Gromyko's title as chairman of the presidium of the Supreme Soviet—the Soviet president, or head of state.

Although the Reagan administration was in its last months, the Washington debates about Gorbachev intensified. On October 14, 1988, Robert Gates, deputy CIA director, delivered a speech in Washington in which he once again called into question Gorbachev's reforms and his foreign policy. Gates asserted that the Soviet leader was pursuing a strategy to make the Soviet Union a stronger, more competitive adversary to the United States. Soviet military programs and troop deployments had not changed, Gates said. Most of these claims about Gorbachev would soon prove to be wrong. There was another theme in Gates's speech that, in retrospect, had some validity: he argued that Gorbachev's economic reforms were failing and raised the prospect that he might not be able to maintain control as the Soviet leader.

Gates's speech infuriated the secretary of state. Shultz had been at odds with Gates for several years, both over Gorbachev's significance and also over what Shultz saw, more generally, as improper attempts by the CIA to use intelligence analysis to influence policy. Even though the administration was in its final months, Shultz tried to have Gates fired. He argued to National Security Adviser Colin Powell and Secretary of Defense Frank Carlucci at their daily breakfast meeting that Gates had intruded on administration policy. Shultz pursued the same request with Reagan, to no avail. The president had spent most of the previous eight years breezily avoiding the disputes within his administration, and his operating style was hardly going to change in his final months in the White House.[13]

Within weeks, it was clear that Gates, not Shultz, reflected the views of the incoming Bush administration. Two weeks after Election Day, Bush appointed Scowcroft, one of the principal critics of the Reagan administration's policies toward Gorbachev and arms control, to be his national security adviser. The president-elect announced that Scowcroft would reevaluate the policies toward the Soviet Union pursued by Reagan and Shultz.

Soon afterward, Scowcroft in turn announced the choice of his own deputy national security adviser: the CIA's senior Soviet expert, Robert M. Gates. There could have been no clearer signal that the Soviet policies of Reagan's last years in office were being called into question and that the new Bush administration intended to take a more skeptical, hardheaded stance toward Gorbachev.

-10-

THE WALL WILL STAND FOR "100 YEARS"

On the weekend after Election Day, Yuri Dubinin, the Soviet ambassador to Washington, gave Secretary of State George Shultz an urgent message: Mikhail Gorbachev wanted to sit down with Ronald Reagan one more time. The Soviet leader was planning to visit New York for a speech to the United Nations General Assembly and hoped he could see the president while there. Gorbachev was eager for Bush to be at the meeting too. Reagan's aides were dismayed; they feared Gorbachev might be planning to unveil some new proposal for which they would not be prepared. Bush was uneasy too. He was nervous that Gorbachev was trying to inveigle him into making some sort of commitments or into giving an overview of his policies before he had been sworn in as president.[1]

Gorbachev was in fact eager to scrutinize Bush, but this was merely a secondary reason for his trip to New York. His main purpose was to speak to the United Nations. Since the summer, Gorbachev had been preparing an address that would demonstrate to the world a dramatically new Soviet foreign policy, including both new ideas and concrete steps to accompany them. Ever ambitious, Gorbachev envisioned this address as "the exact opposite of

Winston Churchill's famous Fulton speech" in 1946, in which Churchill had used the image of an "iron curtain" descending across Europe. Churchill's words had symbolized the beginning of the Cold War; Gorbachev wanted to signify that it was coming to an end. Gorbachev also believed that a triumph abroad and further recognition of his role as a statesman would help to increase his standing at home, in much the same fashion that the summit with Reagan in Moscow had benefited Gorbachev politically a few months earlier. "I will not deny that I also hoped that a positive international response to my programme would strengthen my position and help overcome the growing resistance to change inside the Soviet Union," Gorbachev later reflected.[2]

The speech, as finally delivered, was breathtaking in scope. As a tangible demonstration of change, Gorbachev announced that the Soviet Union would cut the size of its military by half a million troops. It would also withdraw six armored divisions from East Germany, Czechoslovakia, and Hungary, and disband them; in all, Soviet forces in these three countries would be reduced by fifty thousand men and five thousand tanks. On the conceptual level, Gorbachev made it plain that the Soviet Union was abandoning many of the tenets that had guided its foreign policy for decades. He asserted that relations between nations should be free of ideology—thereby rejecting the idea that Soviet foreign policy should be based on questions of class or on the conflict between socialism and capitalism. Gorbachev also spoke of the importance of "freedom of choice" for all countries. "Interference in [a country's] internal processes with the aim of altering them according to someone else's prescription would be all the more destructive for the emergence of a peaceful order," he said. In that single sentence, he formally abandoned the Brezhnev doctrine, which had been used to justify the Soviet invasion of Czechoslovakia and, more generally, the preservation of the existing order in Eastern Europe.

More generally, the Soviet leader emphasized that nations, particularly the leading powers, should not use force in settling disputes and should rely instead on the rule of law and the United Nations. "All of us, and first of all the strongest of us, have to practice self-restraint and renounce the use of force in the international arena," he maintained. He spoke of a new international order. He praised the Universal Declaration of Human Rights as a benchmark for the Soviet Union and the rest of the world. Finally, Gorbachev's address also embraced many of the ideas about a globalizing world that Shultz had been putting forward to him during the previous two years. It was impossible for any state to preserve a closed society when communications, information, and transportation were increasing contact so rapidly, Gorbachev said. He announced that the Soviet Union would end its jamming of radio broadcasts; the programs of the Voice of America, Radio Free Europe, and the BBC would all be allowed freely into the country. "The world is becoming a single organism, outside of which not a single state can develop normally, whatever social system it belongs to or whatever economic level it has reached," said Gorbachev.[3]

Gorbachev's watershed speech marked the furthest he had ever gone toward embrace of a liberal international order. Only a few weeks earlier, Gates had portrayed the Soviet leader as interested in rebuilding Soviet power in order to become a more formidable adversary to the United States. The United Nations address—especially its troop cutbacks—contradicted that interpretation. Reagan had repeatedly maintained that Gorbachev was fundamentally different from his predecessors and that his foreign policy represented a break with the past. For several years, critics had charged that Reagan was being overly optimistic or credulous. But the skeptics were wrong about Gorbachev, and Reagan was right.

Gorbachev's meeting with Reagan and Bush that same day turned out to be an afterthought, an event of far lesser consequence than the Reagan-Gorbachev summits of the past or the speech Gorbachev had just delivered. The session was held on Governors Island in New York Harbor, a location dictated above all by security considerations; Shultz had originally proposed the Metropolitan Museum, but the Secret Service objected. The site also offered the advantage of a superb photo opportunity—Reagan, Gorbachev, and Bush with the Statue of Liberty in the background. The leaders were happy to oblige.

Powell and other Reagan advisers had already made clear that the meeting should not be considered a summit at all. There should be no proposals of substance, because it was too late for the Reagan administration to do anything. Bush, meanwhile, emphasized both before and during the meeting that he was attending only as vice president of the Reagan administration, not as the president-elect; Reagan was still in charge, and Bush intended to say as little as possible. For his own part, Gorbachev was distracted; he had been informed shortly beforehand of a major earthquake in Armenia, one that would require him to curtail his trip and return home as soon as possible.

On Governors Island, Gorbachev directed his attention to Bush, seeking to persuade him to say he would continue Reagan's policies. Gorbachev told the president-elect that his foreign-policy initiatives were not designed merely for show; they were not mere gambits aimed at surprising or undermining American policy. "He was trying to convince Bush to sign on to everything Reagan had agreed to, and Bush wouldn't do it, that was the gravamen of the meeting," recalled Thomas Simons, the deputy assistant secretary of state. "Gorbachev's message was that 'the president and I have made progress, we think that's a basis for the future, and I hope you agree.' But Bush kept being evasive. He said, 'I'm going to have to do a review, I'm going to look at things.' "[4]

Afterward, Reagan recorded in his diary that the meeting was "a tremendous success." Gorbachev "sounded as if he saw us as partners making a better world," Reagan said.[5] Yet by now, when it came to Soviet policy, Reagan had been consigned to history. The Reagan administration had already stopped proposing new policies. Gorbachev knew (and later wrote) that Reagan had become a lame duck.[6]

The transition from the Reagan administration to the Bush administration was unusually antagonistic. In theory, this was merely a change from one Republican administration to another, from a president to the vice president who was succeeding him. It should not have been as difficult as the transition from the Ford administration to the Carter administration, or from Carter to Reagan. In fact, career officials found that the Reagan-to-Bush handover was, if anything, more rancorous than one involving a change of parties. Bush's team was determined to take control of the new administration, to install its own personnel throughout the federal bureaucracy and to dispel perceptions of continuity with the Reagan era. Designated transition teams met rarely, if at all. Officials who had held jobs under Reagan were sometimes told to vacate their offices on a day's notice.

At the State Department, those who had been part of the Reagan-Shultz diplomacy with Gorbachev were shunted aside. The incoming secretary of state, James Baker, brought in his own small network of aides; the new team was openly disdainful of those who had been involved in the summits or the negotiations of the previous four years. "Jim Baker called me in about a week after he was named secretary of state," recalled Rozanne Ridgway, who had been in charge of European policy under Shultz. "He said, 'Tell me, Roz, don't you think that you all went too fast?' I said, 'No, sir.'"[7]

The Nixon-Kissinger foreign-policy network reasserted itself. Reagan and Shultz were on the way out, and so, too, were the approaches they had embraced: the emphases on economics, ideas, and rhetoric as key components of American policy toward the Soviet Union. American strategy was to be redirected toward the more traditional issues of geopolitics and the balance of power.

Henry Kissinger quickly sought to place himself at the center of American policy once again. In December 1988, a month before the start of the new administration, Kissinger visited the White House to talk with the president-elect, Scowcroft, and Baker in Bush's vice presidential office. He argued that they should allow him try to open up a secret channel to Gorbachev on behalf of the new administration. In particular, Kissinger was interested in arranging a quiet deal or understanding with Gorbachev about the future of Eastern Europe. The Soviet leader would be asked to agree that the Soviet Union would not intervene with force in Eastern Europe to stop political reforms or liberalization. In exchange, the Bush administration would recognize Soviet security interests in Eastern Europe and agree not to try to entice countries such as Poland, Hungary, and Czechoslovakia away from their Warsaw Pact alliance with the Soviets.[8]

Kissinger's idea seemed to assume that Gorbachev's U.N. speech was not to be taken seriously. In it, Gorbachev had already renounced the idea of military intervention. State Department officials in charge of Europe and Soviet policy thought Kissinger's idea was a lousy one. "We thought, 'Don't talk to the Soviets about Eastern Europe, period,'" recalled Thomas Simons. Developments in Eastern Europe were moving in the right direction anyway, and the United States should not "buy what it can get for free," Simons argued. He and others at the State Department dubbed Kissinger's idea

"Yalta-2"—a biting reference to the Yalta conference of 1945 that had paved the way for the division of Europe after World War II.[9]

On January 19, 1989, Reagan's last full day as president, East German leader Erich Honecker offered a defiant prediction aimed above all at Reagan and his outgoing administration. He said that the Berlin Wall "will still exist in 50 and even 100 years."[10]

The previous day, Shultz, attending a conference in Vienna on his last trip to Europe as secretary of state, had called once again for the Berlin Wall to be torn down, echoing Reagan's frequent refrain. British foreign secretary Geoffrey Howe had joined in by branding the wall a "grisly anachronism." From East Berlin, Honecker retorted with his usual defenses of the wall, which as usual he called the "anti-fascist protective barrier." The wall was necessary to safeguard East Germany and to preserve peace and stability, he said. It protected East Germans from "the machinations of the West's society of drugs" and from being "plundered" by the currency exchange rates of one West German mark for every seven East German marks. "The Wall will remain for as long as the reasons for its presence have not been eliminated," Honecker concluded.

East Germany's situation was becoming increasingly bleak. In 1988, approximately 9,700 East Germans had fled, more than in any year since 1961, when the wall was built. "We saw that people were leaving the country. They felt that East Germany had no future," recalled Lothar de Maizière, the East German lawyer who in 1990 served as his country's final prime minister before reunification. "At that time, I was active in the Protestant Church. We were trying to keep people here, telling them that they could help to bring about change. But people didn't believe it."[11]

Honecker, as the East German official in charge of security, had supervised construction of the wall; a decade later, he had become general secretary of the East German Communist Party. In early 1989, at the age of seventy-six, he spoke in the same style, with the same stilted language and about the same central-planning targets as in the past. The highlight of his New Year's Day speech to East German citizens had been the pledge that "212,200 apartments will be either newly built or modernized in 1989." He did not mention the problem that even if the numerical goal was met, the apartments would be as ugly and lifeless as all the others.

In the same New Year's speech, Honecker boasted as usual of "the unshakeable friendship and firm solidarity" between the leaders of East Germany and the Soviet Union. "We will continue to raise the level of our fraternal relations, which are exemplary in intensity and diversity," Honecker said.[12] Yet in the wake of Gorbachev's speech to the United Nations, the signs of change were unmistakable. In January 1989, Hungary announced that a Soviet tank division would leave the country within six months and several other units by the end of the year. A few days later, Poland disclosed that some of the Soviet units on its soil would soon leave. Honecker himself, seeking to show that he was conforming to the spirit of Gorbachev's speech, said East Germany would scale back its armed forces by ten thousand troops, a modest reduction.[13]

These troop cutbacks in Eastern Europe were important for their own sake, but they also further undermined Honecker's public justifications for the Berlin Wall. For decades, one primary reason advanced for the wall had been to preserve the peace and to protect East Germany from an aggressive NATO alliance. The troop reductions throughout Eastern Europe in 1989 reflected—indeed, were based upon—the idea that the military threat from the West had lessened.

Still, Honecker remained confident that any changes in the existing order would be relatively minor. He was hardly alone in that belief. In 1989, during a visit to Munich, John McLaughlin, an American intelligence official who later rose to the top of the CIA, asked the head of West Germany's intelligence service, the Bundesnachrichtendienst (BND), about the prospects for German reunification. "Not in my lifetime," replied the official.[14]

As it turned out, Honecker would have been wrong about the Berlin Wall even if he had predicted that it would last for only one more year.

Ronald Reagan had believed that his last day on the job would be January 19. His advisers felt compelled to remind him that he would still be president until noon on Inauguration Day and would need to demonstrate that fact. "Symbolically, Mr. President, you need to come to the office on the morning of the 20th," White House chief of staff Kenneth Duberstein told the president. Reagan agreed. Duberstein authorized White House spokesman Marlin Fitzwater to make public the fact that Reagan would be at work on the morning of Inauguration Day. That turned out to be a mistake. Throughout the night of January 19 and into the early-morning hours of January 20, Duberstein and other White House officials were besieged with phone calls seeking last-minute favors from Reagan. In particular, members of Congress argued repeatedly that it was not too late for Reagan to pardon Oliver North, who had been indicted and was awaiting trial for his role in the Iran-Contra scandal. This campaign failed.[15]

Reagan, often detached from the daily business of the presidency, had become ever more so since Election Day. Two weeks after the election, he had flown to California to buy a house in Bel Air and to take part in the groundbreaking for his presidential library in Simi Valley. Back in Washington, he had begun to pack up his papers. On December 6, the White House physician brought to the Oval Office a doctor who had set up a team in Los Angeles to take care of Reagan's medical needs after he left the White House. In an apparent coincidence, Reagan's diary shows that immediately afterward, he met with representatives of the Alzheimer's Association, who gave him a plaque for his support.[16]

On the morning of January 20, Reagan appeared in the Oval Office, which had been stripped of all decorations. His aides, gathering to say goodbye, had to stand because there were no chairs in the empty office. They went through the formalities of briefing the president. As national security adviser, Colin Powell informed Reagan that the world was quiet.

Reagan reached into his pocket and pulled out his nuclear code card—the card with authentication codes that verify presidential authorization for the launch of nuclear weapons. "Colin, what do I do about this?" Reagan asked, trying to hand over the card. Powell wouldn't take it. Reagan's executive assistant, Jim Kuhn, told him he had to keep it for two more hours. "You're still the president, sir," Kuhn said. The plan that had been worked out with national-security officials called for Reagan to give the card to a military aide just as he was leaving the White House for Bush's inauguration. Finally, just before noon, Reagan handed over the nuclear card, relieving himself of the responsibility he didn't want.[17]

Within days, Bush's new team began to call into question the assumptions of the Reagan administration and to put forward a more negative view of Gorbachev and the Soviet Union. "I think the Cold War is not over," Brent Scowcroft, the new national security adviser, said on television the weekend after the inauguration. Scowcroft offered, once again, a dark interpretation of Gorbachev's motivations. "He's interested in making trouble within the Western alliance, and I think he believes the best way to do it is a peace offensive, rather than to bluster the way some of his predecessors have."[18]

Scowcroft also had a mistrustful view of Gorbachev's address to the United Nations. "It was rhetoric," he said. "Our mantra was that we need facts on the ground. The time for speechifying was over." Scowcroft asked the CIA to watch closely and see whether the Soviet Union was really changing its policies and troop deployments.[19]

What followed, in Bush's early months in office, was essentially a freeze on diplomacy with Gorbachev. The new administration was not interested in high-level meetings or in negotiations left over from the Reagan administration on issues such as arms control. This early Bush period later became known as the pause, but that word reflects a historical perspective that no one had at the time. In fact, Gorbachev and other Soviet leaders were increasingly distressed that the relationship they had forged with the Reagan administration was being abandoned. "Weeks and months passed," observed Gorbachev. "What were they waiting for? Some of the signals we were receiving were quite alarming." Gorbachev's foreign-policy adviser, Anatoly Chernyaev, recalled that Gorbachev grew angry in early 1989 as he complained that Bush "wasn't drawing the proper conclusions from his U.N. speech and even has in mind a Western effort to undermine the Soviet Union's international initiatives."[20]

Ridgway, the Shultz aide who stayed on as assistant secretary of state for the first few months of the Bush administration, argued many years later that the freeze on diplomacy with Gorbachev was risky and could have had lasting, harmful effects. "I mean to tell you, they [the Bush team] damn near lost it," said Ridgway. "Their view on stopping everything and looking again—maybe it was prudent, but the fact of the matter is the process had a rhythm to it, and had been moving right along. I give Reagan a fair amount of credit for rolling things down the hill towards the point where it was almost unstoppable."[21]

That was not how the members of the new Bush administration saw it. They felt Reagan and Shultz were overly enamored of Gorbachev. They believed that his position as Soviet leader was shaky and that he could be replaced at any time with someone in the mold of Brezhnev or even Stalin. They also believed that Reagan and Shultz had been pursuing the wrong priorities. "Our notion was that the Cold War was not about ballistic missiles but basically about Eastern Europe," explained Scowcroft in an interview. "So we turned away from arms control and focused on getting Soviet troops out of Eastern Europe."[22]

The new Bush team decided not to pursue Henry Kissinger's offer to work out an understanding with Gorbachev on the future of Eastern Europe. Although Scowcroft was interested, Bush was leery. Meanwhile, Baker, the new secretary of state, was especially unenthusiastic not merely about the substance of the idea but also about handing a central role in American diplomacy back to Kissinger. Instead, the new administration conducted a series of reviews of Soviet policy, with one of the main studies concentrating on Eastern Europe. This review was led by a young Soviet specialist from Stanford University whom Scowcroft had brought to the staff of the National Security Council, Condoleezza Rice.

In the early spring of 1989, Rice produced a memo arguing that American policy should move beyond the Cold War strategy of containment, crafted by George Kennan four decades earlier to stop Soviet expansion in Europe. Instead, Rice argued, the new strategy should be to try to integrate the Soviet Union into the institutions of the West. It was difficult to understand how this new Bush approach differed much from the ideas that had been pursued first by Shultz in his talk with Gorbachev in 1987 and then by Reagan in his speech at Moscow State University the following year. However, Bush liked the phrase "beyond containment" so much that it served as the basis for his first speech on Soviet policy.[23]

By the spring, Bush and his advisers had decided to concentrate on talking to the Western allies first, before dealing directly with Gorbachev. In late May, Bush made his first trip to Europe, and while there he delivered a speech in West Germany outlining his ideas for an integrated Europe. The goal, said Bush, was a Europe "whole and free."[24]

Bush's speech that day was noteworthy for what it also included: an exhortation to tear down the Berlin Wall. Among his foreign-policy advisers, there had been reluctance to do this. Scowcroft in particular had urged Bush not to revive Reagan's rhetoric about the wall.[25]

Scowcroft lost the debate. Bush, speaking in Mainz, West Germany, reminded his audience of the division of Europe, and then drew specific attention to Berlin. "Nowhere is the division between East and West seen more clearly than in Berlin," Bush declared. "There, a brutal wall cuts neighbor from neighbor and brother from brother," the new president said. "That wall stands as a monument to the failure of communism. It must come down!"

Bush's next words were unmistakably directed not to Erich Honecker but to Gorbachev, to the leader of the Soviet Union. "*Glasnost* may be a Russian word," he said, "but 'openness' is a Western concept. . . . Bring *glasnost* to East Berlin!" The Reagan legacy had proved not so easy to discard.

EPILOGUE

In the spring of 1989, life inside East Germany showed every outward sign of proceeding as usual. On May 7, 1989, the people of East Germany "voted" in local elections. Erich Honecker and his aides proclaimed the standard triumph. According to the official figures, Communist Party candidates won 98.85 percent of the votes. Those candidates ran without opposition. East Germany's election laws did not permit a no vote; the only way to avoid voting for the approved candidates was to cross out all their names. Almost all of the 12.4 million registered voters in the country were said to have participated.[1]

Three months earlier, on the night of February 5–6, Chris Gueffroy, a twenty-year-old waiter in East Berlin, attempted to flee with a friend to West Berlin by crossing a canal and dashing across a section of the Berlin Wall. Gueffroy guessed that since Cold War tensions were easing, the shoot-to-kill order issued to East German border guards would no longer be enforced. He was wrong. The border guards shot him ten times, and he died immediately. The friend was also shot, but survived; he was arrested and jailed.

The East German authorities, however, could not so easily control events in the neighboring countries of Eastern Europe. Throughout the spring and summer of 1989, spurred on by Gorbachev's encouragement of "freedom of choice" for the Soviet Union's allies, Hungary and Poland embarked upon political and social changes so far-reaching that they called into question the fundamental arrangements that had prevailed in Europe since the beginning of the Cold War.

In May, Hungary took the first step by opening up its border with Austria, removing the fences and barbed wire that blocked free exit from its territory. "Hungarian glasnost has many faces, and one of them is the world passport which moved Hungary closer to Western Europe," explained Andras Koevari, Hungary's interior minister. Hungarian officials said the new travel freedom would legally apply only to Hungarians, not to residents of other Eastern European countries. However, each year more than a million East Germans were allowed to spend their vacations in Hungary, more than in any other country. In the summer of 1989, many of these East Germans made one-way trips across Czechoslovakia to Hungary and crossed, without permission, through the woods or open fields into Austria. Some made it. Others stayed on in Hungary or in Czechoslovakia, hoping to find some other way to make the final step—in some cases squatting in West Germany's embassies in Budapest or Prague.

On June 4, Poland's government held open parliamentary elections, the first of their kind in more than four decades. The goal was to win public support for a program of economic reforms that might be supported not just by Wojciech Jaruzelski's Communist Party but by Lech Walesa's opposition Solidarity movement, which, it was thought, might gain a minority of seats in the legislature. Instead, surpassing all predictions, the Solidarity candidates won virtually everything, including ninety-nine out of one hundred seats in the Senate.

Ronald Reagan, in the unaccustomed role of ex-president, quickly seized upon these changes in Hungary and Poland, urging the new Bush administration to stop being so aloof toward Mikhail Gorbachev. "Amazing things are afoot in the world this spring," said Reagan, speaking in London nine days after the vote in Poland. "It is true that the West could stand pat while this is happening. . . . But it is exactly when you are strong and comfortable that you should take risks." In particular, said Reagan, the United States and its allies should "take the risk that the Soviets are serious in their efforts to reach genuine arms reductions with the West."

As he had in the White House, Reagan emphasized the significance of

Gorbachev's personal role as Soviet leader, repeating the arguments he had made while in the White House. Senior officials of the new George H. W. Bush administration, such as Defense Secretary Dick Cheney and Deputy National Security Adviser Robert Gates, had been arguing that American policy should not be centered on Gorbachev. Reagan argued precisely to the contrary. "I believe Mikhail Gorbachev is the Soviets' best and probably only hope to turn things around," Reagan said.[2]

Gorbachev and Eastern European leaders gathered for a summit meeting of the Warsaw Pact in early July. The Soviet leader made it clear he would do nothing to reverse the political changes in Hungary and Poland, and that other Communist leaders could not rely on the Soviet Union to send in troops. Gorbachev's rhetoric was lofty. "We are talking about the end of a period that has lasted over forty years, about the beginning of a transition to a new international order," Gorbachev said. In a response, Honecker was less sanguine. "Looking at the state of international affairs, we cannot say that there has been a fundamental change for the better," he told Gorbachev and the assembled Communist Party leaders. (A few weeks earlier, Honecker's wife, Margot, had been overheard wondering aloud: "Who would ever have dreamed that the counterrevolution would come at us from the Soviet Union?")[3]

In late August, Poland formed a new coalition government led by Solidarity. Throughout the summer, Poland's Communist Party leaders had resisted, but Gorbachev had finally helped persuade them to give way for the first non-Communist government in the Warsaw Pact. Within days, Hungary dropped the next shoe: its government announced that starting on September 11, it would lift restrictions on travel by East Germans to Austria. As a result, the exodus of East Germans became larger and more frenetic. In Czechoslovakia the crowds of East Germans at the West German embassy in Prague were swelling out of control. Each day, new entrants climbed the walls into the building and squatted inside, begging for beds, water, and bathrooms.

By September 1989, the sense of change was exhilarating. "The Poles toppled their Communist government. And in Hungary, you could just feel it, that the Communists were changing in the leadership," recalled Helmut Kohl, then West Germany's chancellor, in an interview many years later. West

Germany was quietly granting credits and other financial benefits to encourage the reforms. "We had a simple strategy, that we have to support the Poles, we have to support the Hungarians, that means economic support, political support, whatever they want," said Kohl's principal foreign-policy adviser, Horst Teltschik. Born in the Sudetenland, the western part of Czechoslovakia, Teltschik played the leading role in West Germany's relations with Eastern Europe. In August, Teltschik arranged for Hungary's President Miklos Nemeth to meet secretly in West Germany with Kohl. At the end of September, shortly after dropping its travel restrictions, Hungary obtained loan credits of 500 million marks (about $250 million) from the West German government.[4]

East Germany was a more complicated problem. Kohl's government was cautious: eager to use its financial leverage, but reluctant to do anything that would create turmoil or a counterreaction. In late September, West German Foreign Minister Hans-Dietrich Genscher negotiated a delicate agreement with Honecker's government: several thousand East Germans camped out in Prague would be permitted to leave for West Germany, but only in special locked trains that would pass through East German territory. That arrangement allowed Honecker to save some face by claiming that those who were leaving his country had been expelled.

The refugees in Prague had been reluctant to get on the trains, afraid that they were being deceived and would be detained during the crossing through East Germany. As a result, West Germany agreed to place its own officials on the trains as guarantors of the agreement and the refugees' safety. Walter Ischinger, then a young official of the German Foreign Ministry, was sent to Prague to ride one of the trains. It was unheated and damp, with no food. When the train passed through East Germany, other East Germans had to be blocked from trying to jump on. In the predawn hours, the train finally crossed into the West German town of Hof in Bavaria. The East German passengers, starving and cold, began to shout, *"Freiheit, freiheit* ('Freedom, freedom')."[5]

Their success prompted other East Germans to leave or at least think about leaving. Freedom to travel had been the single preoccupying political issue in East Germany. Restricting emigration lay at the core of Honecker's repressive apparatus; it was, after all, the reason for the Berlin Wall. "If there was one mass grievance [among East Germans], it was the inability to go abroad," wrote the historian Charles S. Maier. Now, thanks to East Germany's neighbors, the system of controls on travel was unraveling.

No dissident leader had emerged in East Germany of a stature comparable to Walesa in Poland or to Vaclav Havel in Czechoslovakia. In the spring of 1989, the early stirrings of a movement could be detected in Leipzig, where a series of Monday-night prayer meetings began to attract hundreds of protesters. In late September, amid the crisis over the East German refugees, these previously modest Leipzig demonstrations attracted five thousand people. The next Monday night the numbers grew to twenty thousand and on October 9, more than seventy thousand. By then, the protests were spreading to East Berlin and throughout East Germany.

Honecker was losing control not only over the country but the Communist Party leadership. For months, he had been planning a gala celebration on October 7, the fortieth anniversary of the creation of the East German state, with a huge parade and a reviewing stand of visiting Communist Party leaders. Indeed, one reason for Honecker's decision to allow the East German refugees to leave Prague had been the desire to avoid embarrassment on the eve of October 7.

Instead, the anniversary gala accelerated Honecker's downfall. It was accompanied by protest demonstrations that day, both in East Berlin and elsewhere. Gorbachev flew in for the ceremonies, but his presence served only to underline the unpopularity of Honecker's regime. On the streets, ordinary people, ignoring their own leader, shouted "Gorbachev! Gorbachev!" Even an officially organized torchlight procession of young East Germans, composed mostly of Communist Party members and their families, produced chants of "Gorbachev! *Perestroika!* Help us!"[6]

During the previous four years, Gorbachev had met Honecker several times and urged him to proceed with reforms. "It was as if I had been speaking to a brick wall," Gorbachev later wrote. During his visit to East Berlin in October 1989, the Soviet leader thought Honecker seemed as if he were in a trance. When the two men met privately for three hours, Honecker simply denounced the protests and listed the successes of his own regime. Afterward, in a session with other East German Communist Party leaders, Gorbachev issued a vaguely worded warning: "History punishes those who come too late."[7]

Before the October 9 demonstrations in Leipzig, East German authorities put thousands of armed police into formation and were considering the use of force. The city's illustrious orchestra conductor Kurt Masur and local Communist Party officials broadcast an appeal for dialogue and restraint. That succeeded in avoiding bloodshed, but not in stopping the demonstrations. On the following Monday, October 16, more than 150,000 protesters assembled in Leipzig.

Two days later, after a Politburo meeting, Honecker resigned from the job of party secretary, which he had held for eighteen years. East Germany's other Communist Party leaders had been secretly talking for weeks about the need for someone new at the top. Their choice, Egon Krenz, was fifty-two years old, a quarter century younger than Honecker, but he hardly represented far-reaching change. Groomed as Honecker's protégé, he had risen through the same career path as his predecessor, starting in the Free German Youth, the Communist youth organization, and eventually becoming the Politburo member in charge of the security apparatus. Krenz immediately set out to craft some new program with a semblance of reforms that might defuse the unending demonstrations. Over the next three weeks, however, the protests grew to hundreds of thousands of people on the streets of Leipzig and East Berlin.

Krenz also tried one other tack: to enlist new support from the Soviet Union. He had the right credentials. At the beginning of his career, he had spent three years in Moscow attending the party school of the Communist Party Central Committee. He spoke fluent Russian. He had met with Gorbachev on several occasions, first on the day after Gorbachev had become Soviet leader in 1985 and again at the Warsaw Pact sessions where Gorbachev reported to Eastern European leaders on his meetings with Reagan.

Krenz flew to Moscow and on November 1, 1989, sat down for a four-hour conversation with Gorbachev. In it, he made a plaintive appeal, using a crude familial metaphor. "Mikhail Sergeyevich, do you still stand by your paternity?" Krenz asked. Gorbachev, baffled, said he didn't understand the question. "You [Soviets] are basically the father of the German Democratic

Republic [East Germany]," Krenz continued. "The German Democratic Republic is a child born out of the victory of the Soviet army over German fascism. Do you still stand by your paternity?"[8]

"Egon, how can you ask such a question?" replied Gorbachev. He told Krenz that the Soviet Union still supported East Germany. In fact, said Gorbachev, he had spoken with George Bush, British prime minister Margaret Thatcher, and French president François Mitterrand—all had assured him that German reunification was not on the agenda. Krenz left the meeting convinced that Gorbachev was a friend and ally who wanted only the best for the East German regime. In an interview many years later, Krenz said of Gorbachev bitterly, "My mistake was that I trusted him."[9]

Back in East Berlin, however, the unrest continued, and Krenz failed in several increasingly desperate attempts to stop it. At the beginning of November, he announced a package of reforms, including an end to compulsory military service and tolerance of dissent. His initiative had little impact. On November 4, close to 500,000 demonstrators turned out in East Berlin's Alexanderplatz, carrying signs that called for free elections and reassignment of the Stasi, the East German secret police, into production work. Two days later, 750,000 people took part in demonstrations throughout East Germany. On November 7, the East German cabinet resigned, and within twenty-four hours, the Politburo members also stepped down. As he appointed some replacements, Krenz also told the country vaguely that there would be free democratic elections in the future.[10]

With continuing tumult in the streets and uncertainty over the changes in the leadership, it was virtually inevitable that the weakened East German regime would make a mistake. It did. On the afternoon of November 9, the Communist Party Central Committee, again seeking to regain at least a modicum of public support, decided on a far-reaching reform of the travel rules. The idea was to allow East Germans to travel directly to West Germany, without going through third countries such as Czechoslovakia. What Krenz and his aides envisioned was an orderly process. The rules were aimed at allowing emigration, not necessarily to open the border for day trips, tourism, or other unfettered back-and-forth. The border guards would have required East Germans to show passports, and while they would have been vastly more permissive than in the past, they would still have regulated the outflow. "It was supposed to happen in a very Prussian way, a very exact way," maintained Krenz many years later.

The new rules were supposed to take effect the following day, on November 10. At the end of the afternoon, however, Krenz handed over the new rules to another senior Communist Party official, Günter Schabowski; Krenz said Schabowski could tell the news media about the new development but did not brief him carefully about the details. Schabowski still hadn't read the new rules closely when the press conference began. The written announcement for the press, dated November 10, said the change would then go into effect "immediately." But when reporters asked Schabowski when the rules would take effect, he looked quickly at his papers, missed the November 10 starting date, and answered, "Immediately."

His answer was broadcast on East and West German television stations and elsewhere around the world. He left the impression that there would be no more restrictions on passage through the Berlin Wall from that moment forward. Immediately, huge crowds of East Berliners rushed to the checkpoints at the Berlin Wall. In the vacuum of leadership, the border guards didn't know their instructions and, for hours, were unable to get any guidance. Gradually, they let more and more East Germans pass through. At first, the border guards stamped each person's identity papers; within a short time, they stopped doing even that. Their confusion and the East German government's indecision were decisive. After twenty-eight years, the Berlin Wall was open.

Krenz didn't know what to do. He did not want to resort to force; he had issued an order a few days earlier instructing border guards not to use weapons against demonstrators. "I tried to call Gorbachev that same evening, but I couldn't get through," said Krenz in an interview for this book. The following day, a distraught Vyacheslav Kochemasov, the Soviet ambassador in East Berlin, called Krenz, demanding to know what he had done and why. The Soviet Union had always taken the position that East Germany was not the ultimate legal authority over the borders between East and West Berlin because the city was still under the four-power agreement of the Soviets, Americans, British, and French. Krenz told the Soviet ambassador that once the outflow started, he had decided not to do anything that could jeopardize human life. Kochemasov asked him to write a telegram to Gorbachev immediately explaining what had happened. Krenz did. Two hours later Koche-masov called back. "Comrade Egon" he declared, "in the name of Mikhail Sergeyevich Gorbachev, I would like to congratulate you on the courageous step you have taken."[11]

Once again, Gorbachev's role had proved decisive to the outcome. The Soviet Union might have intervened. It didn't. Gorbachev had paved the way for the epochal change, first by setting the Soviet Union's overall foreign policy on a new course, then by accepting the far-reaching political changes in Poland and Hungary, and finally, in the most dramatic flourish of all, by allowing the Berlin Wall to be torn down.

There are indications that Gorbachev did not foresee the implications of what he was doing. He believed that permitting East Germans to leave the country would help to reestablish a new equilibrium in which the two German governments would continue to coexist in some fashion or another. On November 17, a delegation of French and West German legislators visited Moscow, the first European officials to talk with Gorbachev after the fall of the wall. Walter Ischinger, the West German diplomat accompanying the delegation, was astonished to find the Soviet leader unperturbed. He sought to minimize the significance of what had happened.

The legislators asked Gorbachev about the long lines of East German cars at the borders seeking to cross into West Germany. "I'm not worried about this. This is normal," Gorbachev told them. "You see, the East German government made some dumb decisions that led to the fact that the situation in East Germany was like a pressure cooker. They didn't let people travel. And now we've taken the lid off the pressure cooker. You can be assured that by next week or in a couple of weeks, they'll all be back and life will go on."[12]

Life did not go on, at least not in the way Gorbachev meant. The consequences of the events of November of 1989 proved impossible to contain. Within hours after the Berlin Wall came down, even Willy Brandt, the former West German chancellor who had led the way in improving relations with Eastern Europe, talked vaguely about East and West Germans' joining together. Within weeks, Kohl made a formal proposal to accomplish that goal; and within a year, the two Germanies were reunited. Within two years of the fall of the Berlin Wall, Gorbachev's own Communist Party collapsed too, and with it the empire the Soviet Union had constructed.

The Cold War was over. For years, many of America's political leaders and most established foreign-policy experts, such as Richard Nixon and Henry Kissinger, had spoken of the conflict between the two superpowers as an enduring stalemate. Ronald Reagan, by contrast, had grasped the possibility that the Cold War might come to an end. On this, it turned out that Reagan was right. He had not "won" the Cold War in the fashion that American conservatives later claimed. Rather Gorbachev had abandoned the field. Yet Reagan had supported Gorbachev at just the right time. He had undercut the Soviet perceptions of the United States as an enemy, thereby helping to give Gorbachev the recognition and breathing room that he needed to proceed with domestic reforms that proved to be irreversible. Whereas Nixon had repeatedly depicted Gorbachev as yet another tough Soviet leader, a man of steel eager to reassert Soviet power, Reagan had come to a more accurate reading.

Reagan's successors eventually came around to his view of Gorbachev's significance. After an initial "pause" of more than six months, President George H. W. Bush and his senior advisers, Brent Scowcroft and James Baker, decided to proceed toward their own summitry with Gorbachev. Bush announced at the end of October that he would meet soon with the Soviet leader in Malta. Ten days later, before the two leaders met, East Germans began rushing through the Berlin Wall. Bush was guarded in his public comments, unable to summon forth the rhetoric Reagan might have used and unwilling to say anything that might embarrass Gorbachev. "I'm not going to dance on the wall," Bush quipped. Scowcroft told reporters East Germany would probably remain a separate state within the Soviet sphere of influence.[13]

Within two years, Bush's Soviet policy was tied as closely to Gorbachev as Reagan's had been, even though Gorbachev was losing support at home. "They complain that we put too much emphasis on Gorbachev, but we're getting good deals from him all over the world," remarked Baker in the summer of 1991.[14] Gorbachev and his Communist Party fell from power following a failed coup attempt in August. But before the tumult, on July 31, Bush and Gorbachev signed a new treaty to cut back on long-range ballistic missiles and nuclear weapons—a step toward the goal Reagan and Gorbachev had pursued at Reykjavik of reducing or eliminating nuclear weapons.

As the Soviet empire began to crumble, Richard Nixon did another about-face. During the late 1980s, Nixon had aligned himself with the right-wing criticisms of Reagan's Soviet policy; he had repeatedly suggested that Reagan was too enamored of Gorbachev and too willing to reduce America's nuclear arsenal. By the early 1990s, however, Nixon repositioned himself on the political left, this time urging more conciliatory policies toward Moscow and greater support for democracy in Russia.

In particular, Nixon criticized the George H. W. Bush administration for not providing greater economic aid to Russia. In early 1992, soon after the breakup of the Soviet Union, Nixon denounced the Bush administration's "pathetically" insufficient economic support for the new government of Boris Yeltsin. "The stakes are high, and we are playing as if it were a penny-ante game," Nixon wrote in a memo that was leaked to the *New York Times*. Nixon's words put the Bush administration on the defensive; officials rushed to defend the administration against the charge that it might somehow be "losing" Russia by not providing enough money.

Watching from retirement in California, George Shultz was astonished. Nixon's recommendation caused a lot of damage, Shultz believed, because it helped foster in Russia the notion that the route to economic prosperity was through aid from abroad. Above all, Shultz wondered what had happened to Nixon, whom Shultz had come to view during the Reagan years as a hawk. "He flipped from over here to over here," Shultz said, gesturing with his hands to show the move from one end of the political spectrum to the other.[15] One explanation for Nixon's behavior may have been supplied by the *New York Times* story itself. Its account of Nixon's memo said that this was "the latest of many public policy pronouncements that have helped to refurbish the image of the former President, who resigned in disgrace in 1974 over the Watergate scandal."[16]

Nixon's push for aid to Russia attracted support from the Democratic presidential candidate, Bill Clinton. A few weeks after he was inaugurated, Clinton asked Nixon to come to the White House to talk about Russia. Nixon had mounted an intensive campaign to obtain the invitation from Clinton, enlisting the help of Republican political consultant Roger Stone and Clinton's adviser Dick Morris. This time there was no secrecy of the sort that had prevailed when Nixon visited the Reagan White House six years earlier. The Nixon-Clinton meeting was made public, to Nixon's considerable satisfaction. "In twelve years, neither Reagan nor Bush *ever* put me on the White House schedule or put a picture out," Nixon told one of his aides.[17]

In September 1990, Ronald and Nancy Reagan made their first trip to the Soviet Union since leaving the White House. In St. Petersburg (then called Leningrad), they met Reagan's old friend, adviser, and unofficial intermediary, Suzanne Massie. Her son, Robert, had survived, despite his hemophilia; he would go on to work as an Episcopal priest and social activist. Massie herself eventually divorced, remarried, and moved to Maine while still continuing to visit Russia.

Massie never regained the influence she had wielded with Ronald Reagan during the period from 1984 to 1986, when the president's views of the Soviet Union were changing. She was an outsider, not a diplomat; she had failed in her campaign to become Reagan's ambassador to Moscow; and after the Iran-Contra scandal, Reagan's newly constituted National Security Council harbored a healthy mistrust of informal go-betweens and message carriers. When Anatoly Dobrynin had sent a message directly to Reagan through Massie in early 1988, the president and his aides decided not to respond. Massie asked to be included in the delegation for Reagan's visit to Moscow, but the president rejected her request (along with similar appeals from other more prominent Americans such as Armand Hammer and Paul Laxalt).[18]

To the end of Reagan's term, Massie was still permitted to visit the president several times a year, but she could no longer succeed, as she had before, in bypassing his aides and advisers. In the summer of 1988, after setting up a lunch in the White House residence with the president and Nancy Reagan, she sent Reagan a private handwritten note. "I very much hope that we will be alone, just the three of us, to talk as openly and informally as we have on past occasions in that setting," she said. Instead, Colin Powell and Kenneth Duberstein, then the national security adviser and White House chief of staff, joined the lunch and monitored the conversation. By this juncture, Reagan, having visited the Soviet Union himself, had concluded that Massie had little new to say. The lunch was "strange," he recorded in his diary. Massie had usually imparted inside information or insights, but this time, what Massie offered was "almost like a travelogue."[19]

As an ex-president in St. Petersburg in 1990, Reagan was more content to get a travelogue. Massie gave the Reagans a tour of the Pavlovsk Palace outside St. Petersburg; it was Massie's books about Russian culture and about St. Petersburg that had first brought her to Reagan's attention six years earlier. Reagan went to church services, laid flowers at the graves of Dostoyevsky and Tchaikovsky, and praised the movement toward political liberalization in the Soviet Union.

During this trip, Reagan also went out of his way to lend a hand to Gorbachev, supporting his efforts to prevent a breakup of the Soviet Union. Delivering a speech in Moscow, Reagan warned that the fifteen Soviet republics should not let their eagerness for independence go too far. "Differences can be resolved in ways that are fair to all, but reason must prevail over passion if there is to be a climate conducive to the settlement of disagreements," Reagan said. (When Reagan's successor George H. W. Bush offered similar views during a visit to Ukraine the following year, critics in the United States denounced what they called the Chicken Kiev speech. What Reagan had said was not strikingly different.)[20]

During Reagan's 1990 trip, Massie noticed one thing that seemed unusual. Nancy Reagan was holding tightly her husband's hand, never letting him walk too far away.[21]

Reagan's old friends began to notice the changes in the early 1990s. In the summer of 1991, Richard Allen, Ed Meese, and Martin Anderson—three of Reagan's earliest conservative supporters, each of whom had known him since the 1960s–walked up to Reagan at the Bohemian Grove in California. "He was startled," recalled Allen. "I could see he had no idea who we were."[22]

Reagan's aides insisted until 1994 that everything was fine. Early that year, Reagan flew to the East Coast, and when he arrived in New York, he seemed "a slight bit out of sync," recalled Frederick J. Ryan, Jr., who was then serving as chief of staff in charge of Reagan's office and his activities as a former president. "It just seemed like he was having a really bad case of jet lag."

From New York, Reagan flew to the nation's capital to deliver the keynote speech at a black-tie Republican fund-raising event, cast as a celebration of Reagan's eighty-third birthday. In the Washington hotel, Ryan noticed that Reagan seemed still more disoriented. At the ceremonies, with luminaries such as Margaret Thatcher looking on, Reagan started his speech at a painstakingly slow pace, one word at a time. Something is wrong, Ryan thought. Finally, Reagan noticed the TelePrompTer and proceeded to read his speech without further difficulties.[23]

Reagan had been secretly flying once a year to the Mayo Clinic for an extensive two-day checkup. During the late summer of 1994, the doctors there said they had discovered memory loss that went beyond that of normal aging. The clinic dispatched a doctor to Los Angeles to spend a few days with Reagan and observe him. The doctor concluded that Reagan had Alzheimer's disease.

Reagan's staff aides thought about keeping the disease secret; they might have said only that the former president had decided to do no more public appearances and had retired to his ranch. Yet several of the Reagans' other medical problems—the president's colon cancer, his use of a hearing aid, his wife's mastectomy—had been made public. In several instances, Ronald or Nancy Reagan had received letters from ordinary people who had gone for testing or who were otherwise grateful for the public discussion of the medical problems. The Reagans decided to disclose the Alzheimer's disease as well. On November 5, 1994, Reagan's office in Los Angeles released a handwritten letter to the American people, saying that he was in the early stages of Alzheimer's disease. "I now begin the journey that will lead me into the sunset of my life," he said.

Gradually, Reagan's presidency and the last years of the Cold War faded away. At one point, George Shultz paid a visit to the Reagan home. While he was there, the former president got up, went outside, and approached one of his Secret Service aides. "Now, who is that man in there?" the former president quietly asked, referring to his former secretary of state. "I know he's very important, but I don't know his name."[24]

CONCLUSION

Nancy Reagan was sitting on the mostly empty patio of the Bel Air Hotel in Los Angeles, one of her favorite haunts, wearing a light-green suit, her eyes shaded with sunglasses. She was endeavoring to answer a writer's questions about her husband. It was a quiet, pleasant midweek afternoon, June 29, 2005.

She had recently visited Washington for the first time since her husband's death more than a year earlier. While visiting the White House as a guest of George W. Bush, she had suddenly been confronted with the new atmosphere since she had lived there two decades earlier. In the middle of the day, as she was watching a television news show, Secret Service agents suddenly rushed in and, overcoming her attempts to ignore them, swept her away to the secure bunker deep underneath the White House.

The reason, it turned out, was that a small Cessna plane had flown off course from rural Pennsylvania into restricted air space over Washington. Air force F-16s were scrambled to intercept the plane and came close to shooting it down before the plane, run by a confused pilot, finally turned away. The incident was a reminder of how the White House was more edgy from day to day after the events of September 11, 2001, than it had been at the peak of the Cold War. The Soviet Union had vastly more firepower than any terrorist group, but was also considerably more predictable. In fact, during the eight years in which she lived in the White House, Nancy Reagan had never once seen the bunker beneath it—and had not even known of its existence. "Maybe they showed it to Ronnie," she mused.[1]

By 2005, Mrs. Reagan, not surprisingly, had few new stories she was willing to tell. In talking about her husband's second term and the final years of the Cold War, she returned to the familiar ground she had trod many times before. She dwelled on the episodes in which she had played a central role, such as the firing of White House chief of staff Donald Regan in early 1987 and her continuing feuds with Mikhail Gorbachev's wife, Raisa. She offered characterizations of her husband that fit with the reigning images. "He was absolutely without guile, Ronnie," Nancy Reagan asserted. "He just assumed that other people were that way too."

Absolutely without guile. This is the interpretation of Reagan that has endured, both with conservatives who yearn to see him as a man of uncomplicated virtues, and among liberals who cling to the belief he was a dunce. It is the version of Reagan that many took from his television appearances, where his answers to questions were often formulaic; from the meetings where he deflected visitors and confrontation with stories and jokes; even from his diaries, where he recorded the events of the day (most of them, anyway) in a sanitized fashion and with a few brief impressions. It is the view of Reagan put forward by his wife, who devoted most of her life to protecting his image, with guile when necessary. Indeed, this may even have been the way Reagan perceived himself.

Yet any examination of Reagan's policies in the last years of the Cold War will show that he acted with what certainly looks like guile—or if not guile, then crafty instincts. His actions sometimes did not fit with his rhetoric—and it is the blend of the two, of his words and his actions, by which Reagan should be judged. Ringing anti-Soviet speeches served to marshal support for conciliatory policies. Conversely, the continuing diplomacy made it easier for Reagan to give speeches reaffirming a belief in democratic principles without raising the hackles of Gorbachev and other Soviet leaders. Visitors found Reagan virtually impossible to pin down, and often that was the point. "He had a facility for charming people while he was not budging an inch," observed Frank Carlucci, his national security adviser.[2]

To be sure, Reagan's personal operating style sometimes seemed strange or even, occasionally, embarrassing. He chose to sign an important arms-control treaty with Gorbachev at a date and time set by his wife's astrologer. He used the valuable time of a summit meeting to tell jokes that made his own advisers cringe. He was so detached from daily events by his final year in office that his top subordinates made many decisions on their own without telling him.

Nevertheless, the judgments on which he based his policy toward the Soviet Union during this period usually turned out to be correct—even when, in retrospect, other prominent American political leaders and foreign-policy experts were wrong. Reagan guessed that Gorbachev represented significant change—that he was not just another in a line of leaders eager to reassert Soviet power around the globe, despite what both conservatives and old hands like Richard Nixon and Henry Kissinger were arguing. He sensed that the Soviet economy was in desperate shape. He figured, rightly, that the Soviet Union would eventually be willing to enter into arms-control deals without the series of conditions it had previously set. He decided that Gorbachev would not react strongly to his speech at the Berlin Wall, despite what the State Department and the National Security Council were saying. Above all, Reagan recognized that the Cold War was not a permanent state of affairs; that it could, one day or another, draw to a close.

It seems fair to ask: How much of this was attributable to Reagan himself? Or to put it another way, was Reagan merely a tool or vehicle used by other people, other interests? Such questions are raised not merely by Reagan's veneer of guilelessness, but also by his often-passive approach to decision making. An examination of the record, however, shows that no one person or group "owned" Reagan.

One frequent claim, most prevalent during Reagan's early years in the White House, was that he was merely the instrument of conservative forces—of right-wing groups in the U.S. heartland and of military hawks in Washington. But during Reagan's eight years in office, this interpretation became increasingly implausible, and by his final three years in office, it was demonstrably false. If Reagan had been merely a puppet of the American right, there would have been no embrace of Gorbachev, no drive to reduce America's supplies of nuclear weapons and missiles, no treaty to ban intermediate-range missiles in Europe, no negotiated deals for the release of the imprisoned journalist Nicholas Daniloff, no abandonment of the "evil empire" label. If Reagan had heeded the wishes of conservatives, then George Shultz would have been replaced as secretary of state by someone like Jeane Kirkpatrick.

During Reagan's final three years as president, frustrated American conservatives regularly offered a contrary theory: that he had become the tool of a cabal of "moderates" inside his administration. They complained that the president, in his policy toward the Soviet Union, was carrying out the agenda of a group of officials including Shultz, Frank Carlucci, Colin Powell, and Howard Baker, with Nancy Reagan lurking in the background. The conservatives kept crying, "Let Reagan be Reagan," a slogan implying that Reagan was who they thought he was or wished him to be.

In fact, this supposed "moderate" faction did not own Reagan either. Shultz and others at the State Department and National Security Council tried repeatedly but in vain to persuade Reagan to change the Berlin Wall speech and to remove its core sentence, "Mr. Gorbachev, tear down this wall." In 1988, Shultz and others were eager for Reagan to conclude a second major arms-control treaty with Gorbachev to limit intercontinental missiles. But the decision was up to Reagan, not Shultz, and in the end, the administration decided to hold off.

The impact of Reagan's second-term policies—his summit meetings with Gorbachev, his arms control treaty, his declaration that there was no more evil empire—could be felt both inside the United States and in the Soviet Union.

At home, Reagan gradually brought the American public toward an awareness that the Soviet Union was changing and the Cold War subsiding. He overcame the resistance of the political right, effectively marginalizing it. In the fall of 1987, not only the leading conservative columnists but all the Republican presidential candidates except for Vice President George H. W. Bush attacked Reagan for his nonconfrontational approach to Gorbachev. In the Senate, Republican conservatives such as Dan Quayle determinedly challenged Reagan's arms-control treaty. But in the end, the opposition melted away; Reagan's treaty won more than ninety votes. After all, Reagan had been the political leader and indeed, the symbol of American conservatism for two decades. In this end-of-Cold-War drama, he succeeded in defusing opposition at home where other American leaders might well have failed. Gorbachev and his aides recognized Reagan's political significance. "His big plus was his authority inside the country," said Anatoly Adamishin, the Soviet deputy foreign minister. "Other leaders, like [Vice President George H. W.] Bush, had to cater to political forces. But Ronald Reagan could overcome the resistance of the hawks."[3]

In the Soviet Union, the impact of Reagan's second-term policies was less direct, but arguably even more significant. Reagan's policies gave Gorbachev enough time, latitude, and prestige to proceed with his reforms, to the point where they could no longer be undone. Gorbachev was hardly radical in his domestic policies; he was opening up the Soviet system, but always with the goal of maintaining the leadership of the Communist Party. Yet Gorbachev's foreign policy was, in fact, a break with the past. During this period, he progressively reduced the role of the Soviet military—bringing troops home, forswearing the use of force, allowing the Soviet Union's Eastern European allies to go their own way. These foreign and domestic policies were interconnected: his glowing reviews overseas helped Gorbachev to fend off domestic opposition for several critical years. Reagan and Shultz grasped Gorbachev's importance and these underlying dynamics in a way that Reagan's critics in Washington did not. They helped give the Soviet leader the breathing room he required. They also offered Gorbachev the underlying economic rationalization he needed for his changing approach to the world—that the Soviet Union had to accommodate to the inevitable trends of globalization.

The triumphal interpretation of Reagan says that he "won" the Cold War through the confrontational policies of his first term—above all, by increasing spending for the military in a big way and by launching the Strategic Defense Initiative. But no matter how one judges the impact of the American defense buildup, it did not bring the Cold War to an end. By itself, it could at best have led to a prolonged stalemate during which the Soviet leadership, while unable to match American military spending, clung to power. There was nothing in Reagan's first-term policies that could induce Mikhail Gorbachev to abandon the Brezhnev doctrine's assertion of the Soviet Union's right to intervene with force in Eastern Europe. The "Star Wars" program did not persuade Gorbachev to sit passively by in 1989 while the Berlin Wall was torn down.

It was Reagan's second-term policies, his decision to do business with

Gorbachev, that set the course for the end of the Cold War. If Reagan had not been responsive, then events might have taken a different course during the crucial period from 1985 to 1989. Gorbachev's critics at home could have succeeded in resisting change by warning that American policy remained a continuing danger and that Gorbachev was failing to obtain any alteration of the Soviet Union's relationship with the United States.

Gorbachev himself might have tried to freeze the degree of change in the Soviet political system. Or alternatively, traditionalists in the Soviet leadership might have attempted to overthrow Gorbachev—as, indeed, they tried to do in the abortive coup d'etat of August 1991. Instead, Gorbachev proceeded to open up the Soviet system, and by the time the old guard in the Soviet leadership finally mobilized against him, it was too late. The changes of the previous six years turned out to be irreversible.

Gorbachev occasionally joked that through his actions, he was depriving the United States of an enemy. The reverse was also true: Reagan, through his policies, deprived the Soviet Union of the intensely adversarial relationship with the United States that had, over the decades, repeatedly served as Moscow's justification for preserving its enormous military and security apparatus. In order to proceed at home, Gorbachev had to show that he was moving toward a different role in the world. As Gorbachev later acknowledged, he needed American and international recognition of his foreign policy to shore up his position in Moscow and overcome resistance within the Soviet leadership. By treating Gorbachev as fundamentally different from his predecessors, Reagan's policies gave the Soviet leader what he required.

In the end, the Cold War sputtered out without any large-scale violent upheavals or explosions. It was not inevitable that the climax should have been so anticlimactic. Unquestionably, Gorbachev played the leading role in bringing the four-decade-old conflict to a close. Yet Reagan, overcoming considerable opposition of his own at home, played a crucial role by buttressing Gorbachev's political position. It was in this sense that Ronald Reagan helped ensure the Cold War ended in the tranquil fashion that it did. Reagan didn't win the Cold War; Gorbachev abandoned it. By recognizing Gorbachev's significance, when many others in the United States did not, Reagan helped create the climate in which the Cold War could end.

ACKNOWLEDGMENTS

By far the most significant institution for me in writing this book was the Johns Hopkins University's Paul H. Nitze School of Advanced International Studies. SAIS, as it is commonly known, provided a home for me from the time I started this book in 2004. Its dean, Jessica Einhorn, has been supportive of my work and, in general, of books about America's relations with the world. I am also grateful to other SAIS administrators, including Thomas Keaney and Ted Baker of the Foreign Policy Institute. I am thankful to the SAIS Library, particularly Linda Carlson, for handling so professionally my many requests for materials and information. A talented and knowledgeable SAIS graduate student, David A. Beffert, provided important assistance with research and translation.

There were two other institutions that provided invaluable help to me as an author. The first was the American Academy in Berlin, where I lived for four months in the fall of 2005. It was through the help of the American Academy that I was able to conduct book interviews in Germany. I am grateful to Gary Smith, the executive director, and to several others who helped so much in the research and the interviews in Berlin, including Ingrid Mueller, Thomas Rid, Marie Unger, Maria Lueck, and Tessa Fanelsa.

The second institution was the Rockefeller Foundation's Bellagio Center, which enabled me to spend four weeks reading, thinking about, and organizing the book just as I was getting started on the project.

The professional archivists at the Ronald Reagan Presidential Library in Simi Valley tolerated my visits and many requests for material; I am particularly grateful to Shelly Williams for her help there. The Richard Nixon Library was responsive and helpful to my queries; John H. Taylor and Greg Cumming deserve special mention. The National Security Archive in Washington proved, as always, to be the principal and most accessible source of declassified materials, providing information that extends well beyond the collections of the presidential libraries; Thomas Blanton and William Burr provided special help and insight. Several collections of oral interviews were invaluable for the Reagan years: above all, those of the University of Virginia's Miller Center of Public Affairs and the oral interviews that were conducted jointly by the Hoover Institution and by the Gorbachev Foundation.

The research also included approximately one hundred of my own interviews with participants in the events of the final years of the Cold War. I am always astonished to discover how interviews produce more information, more details, and more insight than is on the historical record. Among those who were kind enough to be interviewed, at least once and sometimes more than once: Morton Abramowitz, Anatoly Adamishin, Richard Allen, Martin Anderson, Richard Armitage, Egon Bahr, Dennis Blair, Thomas Blanton, Hildegard Boucsein, Hans-Otto Bräutigam, Zbigniew Brzezinski, Richard Burt, Frank Carlucci, William Cohen, Lothar de Maizière, Eberhard Diepgen, Anthony Dolan, Kenneth Duberstein, Dieter and Ingeborg Elz, Fritz Ermarth, Francis Fukuyama, Thomas Griscom, Helga Haftendorn, Jörg Halthöfer, Frank Herold, Fred Ikle, Walter Ischinger, Richard Kauzlarich, Jeane Kirkpatrick, Helmut Kohl, John Kornblum, Egon Krenz, Nelson Ledsky, Jon Lellenberg, Barry Lowenkron, Robert McFarlane, John McLaughlin, Andrew Marshall, Suzanne Massie, Jack Matlock, Edwin Meese, Don Oberdorfer, William Odom, Rudolf Perina, Michael Pillsbury, Colin Powell, Nancy Reagan, Rozanne Ridgway, Peter Robinson, Peter Rodman, Dana Rohrabacher, Brent Scowcroft, George Shultz, Thomas Simons, Richard Solomon, Helmut Sonnenfeldt, John Taylor, Horst Teltschik, Maritta Tkalec, Bettina Urbanski, Karsten Voigt, Richard von Weizsäcker, George Will, and Vladimir Zubok.

I am fortunate to have had the remarkable help of Joel Havemann, a former colleague from the *Los Angeles Times* who has been, over the years, one of the best and most careful editors in the country. His contribution to the book was immeasurable. Joel read through the entire manuscript, offering suggestions and queries, finding the sentences that needed fixing and the thoughts that needed elaboration. Meanwhile, as I was writing the book, Warren I. Cohen and Nancy Bernkopf Tucker, two of America's leading historians, read chapters and offered their insightful comments and reactions. Their friendship and encouragement have meant much to me over the years. Another fine *Los Angeles Times* colleague, Tyler Marshall, was kind enough to read the German chapters of the book and provide thoughtful commentary on them.

I am once again grateful to have had the help and support of Adrian Zackheim, my editor at Viking, who remained patient and supportive through the long time it takes to produce a book. My agent, Rafe Sagalyn, provided sagacious advice, as he regularly does. Above all, I am thankful to my ever-supportive wife, Caroline Dexter, who knows all too well what it's like to live with someone trying to write a book.

NOTES

Part I: Two Anti-Communists

Chapter 1: Clandestine Visit
1.   The details in this section are based upon an interview with Frank Carlucci, January 19, 2005, and an extensive private memorandum Nixon wrote to himself: Richard M. Nixon Memorandum to the File, April 28, 1987, obtained from the Richard Nixon Library.
2.   Richard Nixon, *RN: The Memoirs of Richard Nixon* (New York: Grosset & Dunlap, 1978), 1088.
3.   Author interview with John Taylor, Nixon Library, August 3, 2006.
4.   Nixon memorandum.

Chapter 2: "It's Time to Stroke Ronnie"
1.   For Reagan and Nixon in 1960, see Ronald Reagan, *An American Life* (New York: Simon & Schuster, 1990), 133–36.
2.   Stuart Spencer, oral interview, Miller Center of Public Affairs, University of Virginia, November 15, 2001.
3.   Richard Nixon, *RN: The Memiors of Richard Nixon* (New York: Grosset & Dunlap, 1978), 285–86.
4.   Lyn Nofziger, oral interview, Miller Center, March 6, 2003.
5.   William Safire, *Before the Fall* (Garden City: Doubleday & Co., 1975), 53; Reagan, *American Life*, 178.
6.   Author interview with Brent Scowcroft, May 26, 2005.
7.   Wallace Turner, "Reagan Urges Nixon to See Congress, *New York Times*, August 7, 1974, 18.

8.   Julie Nixon Eisenhower memorandum, Richard Nixon Library, October 30,1974.
9.   Nixon letter to Reagan, August 20, 1976; Reagan letter to Nixon, August 20, 1976, in postpresidential correspondence, Richard Nixon Library.
10. Richard V. Allen, oral interview, Miller Center, May 28, 2002.
11. Memo to President-elect Ronald Reagan from Richard Nixon, November 17, 1980, Richard Nixon Library.
12. Allen oral interview, Miller Center.
13. Nixon letters to Ronald Reagan (Mark Felt, April 16, 1981; Reggie Jackson, October 31, 1981; Lech Walesa, December 31, 1981; political advice, October 1, 1982), Richard Nixon Library, postpresidential correspondence.

Chapter 3: Two Schools of Thought
1.   Author interview with Richard Allen, November 2, 2004.
2.   Stephen E. Ambrose, *Nixon: The Triumph of a Politician 1962–72* (New York: Simon & Schuster, 1989), 20.
3.   H. R. Haldeman, *The Haldeman Diaries* (New York: G. P. Putnam's Sons, 1994), 424.
4.   Reagan letter to Hugh Hefner, July 4, 1960, in *Reagan: A Life in Letters* (New York: Free Press, 2004), 147–48.
5.   Stuart Spencer, oral interview, Miller Center of Public Affairs, University of Virginia, November 15, 2001, 9, 14, 66.
6.   Kenneth Adelman, oral interview, Miller Center, September 30, 2003, 48.
7.   Associated Press, "Watergate Depriving Nixon of Acclaim Due Him, Reagan Says," *Los Angeles Times*, June 27, 1973, A3.
8.   Lou Cannon, *Governor Reagan: His Rise to Power* (New York, Public Affairs, 2003), 396–97.
9.   Jerry F. Hough, "The Soviet System—Petrification or Pluralism?" in *Problems of Communism* 21 (1972): 25–45.
10. Henry Kissinger, *Years of Renewal* (New York, Simon & Schuster, 1999), 99.
11. Wayne King, "Reagan for Economic Slowdown as a Method of Curing Inflation," *New York Times*, January 29, 1976, 21; James Naughton, "Ford-Reagan Race: Similarity of Views," *New York Times*, March 26, 1976, 16; Richard Bergholz, "Reagan Attacks Kissinger and Ford's Foreign Policy," *Los Angeles Times*, February 11, 1976, B1; Ronald Reagan, "Tactics for Détente," from speech at Philips Exeter Academy, February 10, 1976, as excerpted in *Wall Street Journal*, February 13, 1976, 8.
12. Nofziger oral interview, Miller Center, 15–16; R. W. Apple, "Reagan Tops Ford in North Carolina," *New York Times*, March 24, 1976, A1.
13. Republican platform, "Morality in Foreign Policy," proceedings of the 1976 Republican National Convention.
14. Kiron K. Skinner, Annelise Anderson, and Martin Anderson, eds., *Reagan: In His Own Hand* (New York: Touchstone/Simon & Schuster, 2001), 12–15.

15. Skinner et al., *Reagan In His Own Hand*, 12.
16. Author interview with George Shultz, February 16, 2005.

Chapter 4: Evil Empire

1. Richard Nixon, *The Real War* (New York: Warner Books, 1980), 314.
2. Bernard Gwertzman, "Reagan Advisers Ponder Kissinger Foreign Policy Role," *New York Times*, October 31, 1980, A-17; Anatoly Dobrynin, *In Confidence* (New York: Times Books, 1995), 464.
3. A. James Reichley interview with Richard Allen, Gerald R. Ford Library; Richard Allen "Memo For Governor Reagan Re Strategy for Peace," August 25, 1978, obtained by author from Allen and on file in Hoover Institution archives.
4. William C. Wohlforth, ed., *Witnesses to the End of the Cold War* (Baltimore: Johns Hopkins University Press, 1996), 106.
5. Anatoly Dobrynin, *In Confidence* (New York: Times Books, 1995), 471–72.
6. Text of the President's News Conference, January 29, 1981, Ronald Reagan Presidential Library.
7. Author interview with Richard Allen, November 2, 2004.
8. Dobrynin, *In Confidence*, 490–91.
9. Author interview with Dennis Blair, March 25, 2005.
10. Ronald Reagan, Address to Members of the British Parliament, June 8, 1982.
11. Ronald Reagan Presidential Library, White House Staff and Office Files, Anthony Dolan, Box 19, speech drafts.
12. Ronald Reagan, Address of National Association of Evangelicals, March 8, 1983.
13. Stuart Spencer, oral interview, Miller Center of Public Affairs, University of Virginia, November 15, 2001, 119; Ronald Reagan, *An American Life*, 568–70.
14. The text of NSDD-75 was declassified and published in Robert C. McFarlane, *Special Trust*, (New York, Cadell & Davies, 1994), 372–80.
15. Richard Pipes, *Vixi: Memoirs of a Non-Believer* (New Haven, Yale University Press, 2003), 198; Thomas C. Reed, *At the Abyss* (New York: Ballantine Books, 2005), 240.
16. Pipes, *Vixi Memoirs*, pp. 201–2.
17. Jack F. Matlock, Jr., *Reagan and Gorbachev* (New York: Random House, 2004), 24–25.
18. Author interview with Peter Rodman, April 25, 2005.
19. Dobrynin, *In Confidence*, 554.

Chapter 5: Nixon Detects Gorbachev's "Steel Fist"

1. Henry A. Kissinger, "Reagan Must Seize the Middle Ground," *Los Angeles Times*, November 18, 1984, E-1.
2. Michael Dobbs, *Down With Big Brother* (New York: Alfred A. Knopf, 1997), 26.

3.   Richard Nixon, "Meeting the Russians at the Summit," *New York Times*, September 1, 1985, sect. 4, 13.

4.   Memorandum on conversation with General Secretary Gorbachev at the Kremlin, July 18, 1986, Ronald Reagan postpresidential correspondence, Richard Nixon Library.

5.   Ibid.

6.   Anatoly S. Chernyaev, *My Six Years With Gorbachev* (University Park: Pennsylvania State University Press, 2000), 76–77.

Chapter 6: Abolition

1.   Kenneth Adelman, oral interview, Miller Center of Public Affairs, University of Virginia, September 30, 2003.

2.   The fullest exposition of Reagan's antinuclear views is in Paul Lettow, *Ronald Reagan and His Quest to Abolish Nuclear Weapons* (New York: Random House, 2005). For accounts of the 1976 speech, see Lettow, 30–31, and Jim Kuhn, *Ronald Reagan in Private* (New York: Sentinel, 2004), 19–20.

3.   Hoover Institution/Gorbachev Foundation Oral History Project, Interview with Michael Deaver, June 6, 2000. See also "Reagan Says U.S. Should Have Acted," (unsigned), *Los Angeles Times*, January 27, 1968, 8.

4.   Thomas C. Reed, *At the Abyss: An Insider's History of the Cold War* (New York: Ballantine Books, 2005), 241–46.

5.   Ronald Reagan, *An American Life* (New York: Simon & Schuster, 1990), 585–86.

6.   Ronald Reagan, *The Reagan Diaries*, (New York: HarperCollins, 2007), 199. For an extensive examination of the events of this period, see Beth A. Fischer, *The Reagan Reversal* (Columbia: University of Missouri Press, 1997), 112–40.

7.   "Excerpts from the President's Speech in Tokyo," *New York Times*, November 11, 1983, A-7; George P. Shultz, *Turmoil and Triumph* (New York: Charles Scribner's Sons, 1993), 466.

8.   Author interview with Frank Carlucci, January 19, 2005; Lettow, *Ronald Reagan and His Quest*, 234–35.

9.   Author interview with Thomas Simons, May 17, 2006. Actually, Reagan won forty-nine states in 1984, losing only Minnesota and the District of Columbia.

10.   James Kuhn, oral interview, Miller Center, March 7, 2003.

11.   Ronald Reagan letter to George Murphy, December 19, 1985, in Ronald Reagan Presidential Library.

12.   Anatoly S. Chernyaev, *My Six Years with Gorbachev* (University Park: Pennsylvania State University Press, 2000), 52–53.

13.   Anatoly Dobrynin, *In Confidence* (New York: Times Books, 1995), 603; Jack F. Matlock, Jr., *Reagan and Gorbachev* (New York: Random House, 2004), 176–78.

14.   Chernyaev, *My Six Years*, 59.

15. Mikhail Gorbachev, *Memoirs* (New York: Doubleday, 1995), 414; Chernyaev, *My Six Years*, 78–79.
16. Henry Kissinger, "Danger at the Summit," *Newsweek*, October 13, 1986, 38.
17. Memorandum of Conversation, October 12, 1986, 3:25 p.m.–6 p.m., Hofdi House, Reykjavik, in Ronald Reagan Presidential Library; George P. Shultz, *Turmoil and Triumph* (New York: Charles Scribner's Sons, 1993), 772.
18. Kuhn oral interview, Miller Center, 46–47.
19. William C. Wohlforth, ed., *Witnesses to the End of the Cold War* (Baltimore: Johns Hopkins University Press, 1996), 175.
20. "Memorandum for the President from John M. Poindexter, Nov. 1, 1986, "Guidance for Post-Reykjavik Follow-up Activities," and "Dec. 18, 1986: Meeting with the Joint Chiefs of Staff," in National Security Archive collection, The Reykjavik File: http://www.gwu.edu/~nsarchiv/NSAEBB/NSAEBB203/index.htm
21. "Session of the Politburo, Oct. 14, 1986," in National Security Archive; Chernyaev, *My Six Years*, 5.

Chapter 7: Conservative Uproar
1. Author interview with Brent Scowcroft, May 26, 2006.
2. Author interview with Nelson Ledsky, March 3, 2005; George P. Shultz, *Turmoil and Triumph* (New York: Charles Scribner's Sons, 1993), 776.
3. Author interview with Fritz W. Ermarth, January 25, 2005.
4. Richard Nixon and Henry Kissinger, "A Real Peace," *National Review*, May 22, 1987, 32–34. For relationship of Nixon and Kissinger, see Henry A. Kissinger, *Years of Renewal* (New York: Simon & Schuster, 1999), 87.
5. "An Interview with Richard Nixon," *Time* magazine, May 4, 1987, 23.
6. Henry A. Kissinger, "Kissinger: How to Deal with Gorbachev," *Newsweek*, March 2, 1987.
7. "An Interview with Richard Nixon," *Time*; "Kissinger: How to Deal with Gorbachev," *Newsweek*.
8. Kuhn oral interview, 231–32.
9. Author interview with George Will, April 12, 2005; George F. Will, "The Opiate of Arms Control," *Newsweek*, April 27, 1987, 86; Charles Krauthammer, "Gorbachev's Iron Smile," *Washington Post*, April 24, 1987, A27.
10. Hoover Institution/Gorbachev Foundation oral interview with Lyn Nofziger, June 5, 2000, 27–28.

Chapter 8: The Conversation
1. Author interview with Frank Carlucci, January 19, 2005.
2. Richard Nixon, "Memorandum to the File, Meeting with President Reagan at the White House, 5 p.m., April 28, 1987."
3. Ibid.

Chapter 9: Reversal of Roles

1.   Unsigned editorial, "The Proposed Treaty," *National Review*, May 22, 1987, 13–14; Robert M. Gates, *From the Shadows* (New York: Simon & Schuster, 1996), 404.
2.   Author's Carlucci interview, January 19, 2005.
3.   See National Security Decision Directive Number 250, "Post-Reykjavik Follow-Up," November 4, 1986, obtained from "The Reykjavik File," National Security Archive; Jack C. Matlock, Jr., *Reagan and Gorbachev* (New York: Random House, 2004), 246.
4.   Author's Ermarth interview, January. 25, 2005; author interview with William Odom, March 23, 2005.

PART II: INFORMAL ADVISER

Chapter 1: A New Friend

1.   This account is based upon appointment calendars at the Ronald Reagan Presidential Library, records of the Massie-Reagan correspondence at the Ronald Reagan Presidential Library, and interviews with Suzanne Massie, March 21, 2005, and Robert McFarlane, April 28, 2005.
2.   Hoover Institution/Gorbachev Foundation oral interview with Donald Regan, June 17, 2000. Regan's assertion is too sweeping. The Reagan archives demonstrate that some of Massie's meetings with Reagan were in the Oval Office, and that advisers such as McFarlane and his successors John Poindexter, Frank Carlucci, and Colin Powell took part in some of the sessions.
3.   Ronald Reagan Presidential Library: Letter to Samuel Robert Massie, August 5, 1987, WHORM ME001, case file 509807; Scheduling Note, Dona to Wilma, Aug. 6, 1985, WHORM PR007-01, Box 16, 273288 and following.
4.   Suzanne Massie letter to Ronald Reagan, March 12, 1986, Ronald Reagan Presidential Library.
5.   Interview with Nancy Reagan, June 29, 2005; interview with Suzanne Massie, March 25, 2005.
6.   Don Oberdorfer, *The Turn* (New York: Poseidon Press, 1991), 143; John Leonard book review, "Land of the Firebird," *New York Times*, October 8, 1980, C-25.
7.   Nancy Reagan, *My Turn* (New York: Random House, 1989), 289.

Chapter 2: Banned from the Land of the Firebird

1.   This section is taken from interviews with Suzanne Massie, March 21, 2005, and February 16, 2008, and from Robert and Suzanne Massie, *Journey* (New York: Alfred A. Knopf, 1973), 1–9, 196–98.
2.   Massie and Massie, *Journey*, 154–55.
3.   Ibid., 214–21.
4.   Ibid., 163–64.

5. Author's Massie interviews, March 21, 2005, and February 16, 2008.
6. Suzanne Massie, *Land of the Firebird: The Beauty of Old Russia* (New York: Simon & Schuster, 1980), 13–14. John Leonard, "Books of The Times," *New York Times*, October 8, 1980, C-25.
7. Author's Massie interview, February 16, 2008.

Chapter 3: War Scare
1. Author's Massie interview, March 21, 2005; William Drozdiak, "Pilots Begin Soviet Boycott," *Washington Post*, September 15, 1983, A15.
2. John F. Burns, "Andropov Attacks U.S. Missile Plan as Unacceptable," *New York Times*, September 29, 1983, A1; John M. Goshko, "20 Soviet Scholars Recalled from U.S.," *Washington Post*, September 17, 1983, A10.
3. Author's interview with Vladimir Zubok, September 10, 2007.
4. Christopher Andrew and Oleg Gordievsky, *KGB: The Inside Story* (New York: HarperPerennial, 1990), 502–3, 644.
5. David Remnick, *Lenin's Tomb* (New York: Random House, 1993), 445.
6. Author's Massie interview, March 21, 2005.
7. "Life In Russia: Pattern of Subtle Change," *U.S. News and World Report*, February 1, 1982, 33; Strobe Talbott, "Trying to Influence Moscow," *Time*, November 22, 1982.
8. Andrew and Gordievsky, *KGB: The Inside Story*, 593, 599–600. For other accounts of Able Archer, see John Prados, "The War Scare of 1983," in Robert Cowley, ed., *The Cold War: A Military History* (New York: Random House, 2006), 438–54; Robert M. Gates, *From the Shadows* (New York: Simon & Schuster, 2006), 270–73; Don Oberdorfer, *The Turn* (New York: Poseidon Press, 1991), 64–68.
9. Author interview with Robert McFarlane, April 28, 2005.
10. Author interview with Fritz Ermarth, January 25, 2005.
11. Special National Intelligence Estimate 11–10-84/JX, May 18, 1984, "Implications of Recent Soviet Military-Political Activities, declassified and published by Center for the Study of Intelligence; Gates, *From the Shadows*, pp. 272–73.
12. Ronald Reagan, *An American Life* (New York: Simon & Schuster, 1990), 588–89.
13. Author's McFarlane interview; interview with George Shultz, February 16, 2005; George P. Shultz, *Turmoil and Triumph* (New York: Charles Scribner's Sons, 1993), 464–65.
14. Bernard Weinraub, "Risk of War Rises, Mondale Asserts," *New York Times*, January 4, 1984, A-7.
15. Ronald Reagan, "Address to the Nation and Other Countries on United States–Soviet Relations," January 16, 1984, Ronald Reagan Presidential Library.
16. Jack F. Matlock, Jr., *Reagan and Gorbachev* (New York: Random House, 2004), 80–87.

17.   Ibid., p. 83.
18.   Anatoly Dobrynin, *In Confidence* (New York: Times Books, 1995), 551.

Chapter 4: Improbable Emissary
1.   This section is based upon interviews with Jack Matlock, Robert McFarlane, and Suzanne Massie.
2.   Jack F. Matlock, Jr., *Reagan and Gorbachev* (New York: Random House, 2004), 93–94; George P. Shultz, *Turmoil and Triumph* (New York: Charles Scribner's Sons, 1993), 903.
3.   Author interview with Brent Scowcroft, May 26, 2006.
4.   This section is based upon interviews with McFarlane and Massie.
5.   Author interview with George Shultz, February 16, 2005; Anatoly Dobrynin, *In Confidence* (New York: Times Books, 1995), 600.

Chapter 5: Hunger for Religion
1.   Ronald Reagan letter to Suzanne Massie, February 15, 1984, Ronald Reagan Presidential Library, Presidential Handwriting File, Box 008, folder 116.
2.   Ronald Reagan letter to John O. Koehler, in Kiron K. Skinner, Annelise Anderson, and Martin Anderson, eds., *Reagan: A Life in Letters* (New York: Free Press, 2003), 375.
3.   Author interview with Colin Powell, November 2, 2006; Stuart Spencer, oral interview, Miller Center of Public Affairs, University of Virgina, November 15, 2001.
4.   Robert and Suzanne Massie, *Journey* (New York: Alfred A. Knopf, 1973), 164–65; Suzanne Massie, "The Importance of the Russian Culture and the Russian Church: A Personal Testimony," speech to Holy Trinity Orthodox Seminary, June 7, 1981, republished at suzannemassie.com.
5.   Suzanne Massie letters to Ronald Reagan, January 20, 1984, and March 8, 1984, Presidential Handwriting File, Ronald Reagan Presidential Library.
6.   Author interview with Suzanne Massie, March 21, 2005; Suzanne Massie, "The New Russian Spirit," speech given to Smithsonian Institution, May 1, 1986.
7.   Ibid.
8.   Massie quote from interview, March 21, 2005. Nancy Reagan quote from Nancy Reagan, *My Turn* (New York: Random House, 1989), 89.
9.   Robert F. Gates, *From the Shadows* (New York: Simon & Schuster, 1996), 344.
10.   Author interview with Rozanne Ridgway, June 20, 2005.
11.   Jack F. Matlock, Jr., *Reagan and Gorbachev* (New York: Random House, 2004), 143–44.
12.   Anatoly Dobrynin, *In Confidence* (New York: Times Books, 1995), 584.
13.   Reagan's appointment calendars from Ronald Reagan Presidential Library.
14.   Suzanne Massie letter to Ronald Reagan, October 27, 1985; Ronald Reagan

letter to Suzanne Massie, November 15, 1985, Presidential Handwriting File Box 14, Folder 209, Ronald Reagan Presidential Library.

15.   Ronald Reagan letters to Elsa Sandstrom and Alan Brown, in Skinner et al., *Reagan: A Life*, 414–15.

16.   Author interview with Colin Powell, November 2, 2006.

Chapter 6: An Arrest and Its Consequences

1.   Daily diaries of President Reagan and memo, Jack F. Matlock to John Poindexter, September 22, 1986, in Ronald Reagan Presidential Library.

2.   George Shultz, *Turmoil and Triumph* (New York: Charles Scribner's Sons, 1993), 724. See also Serge Schmemann, "Chernobyl Fallout: Apocalyptic Tale and Fear," *New York Times*, July 26, 1986, 1.

3.   Author interview with Suzanne Massie, March 21, 2005.

4.   Mikhail Gorbachev letter to Ronald Reagan, October 12, 1985; Ronald Reagan letter to Mikhail Gorbachev, November 1, 1985, in White House Staff and Office Files, Head of State, Box 2940, Ronald Reagan Presidential Library.

5.   Ronald Reagan, *An American Life* (New York: Simon and Schuster, 1990), 667.

6.   For the general facts of the Daniloff case, see Jack F. Matlock, Jr., *Reagan and Gorbachev* (New York: Random House, 2004), 197–214, and Shultz, *Turmoil and Triumph*, 728–50.

7.   Shultz, *Turmoil and Triumph*, 746.

8.   George F. Will, "Reagan Botched the Daniloff Affair," *Washington Post*, September 18, 1986, A25; George F. Will, "Reeling Toward Reykjavik," *Washington Post*, October 3, 1986, A23.

9.   Author interview with Frank Carlucci, January 19, 2005.

10.   Anatoly S. Chernyaev, *My Six Years with Gorbachev* (University Park: Pennsylvania State University Press, 2000), 84.

11.   Barrett Seaman, "Has Reagan Gone Soft?" *Time*, October 13, 1986, 38.

12.   Reagan's memory as an actor: William H. Webster, oral interview, Miller Center of Public Affairs, University of Virginia, August 21, 2002, 26; David Remnick, "Reagan to Gorbachev, 'Rodilsya, Ne Toropilsya,'" *Washington Post*, May 29, 1988, A20.

13.   Chernyaev, *My Six Years*, 51.

14.   Robert M. Gates, *From the Shadows* (New York: Simon & Schuster, 1996), 377.

Chapter 7: Keep Her Away

1.   William S. Cohen and John Heinz, letter to The Honorable Ronald W. Reagan, June 3, 1986, Ronald Reagan Presidential Library, WHORM files PE002, casefile 404941.

2.   Suzanne Massie letter to Ronald Reagan, January 4, 1987, Ronald Reagan Presidential Library.

3.   Ronald Reagan letter to Suzanne Massie, January 13, 1987, Ronald Reagan
      Presidential Library.
4.   James Mann, *Rise of the Vulcans* (New York: Viking, 2004), 157.
5.   President's Daily Diary, February 3, 1987, Ronald Reagan Presidential Li-
      brary; George Shultz, *Turmoil and Triumph* (New York: Charles Scribner's
      Sons, 1993), 872–73.
6.   Author interview with Suzanne Massie, February 16, 2008; Shultz, *Turmoil
      and Triumph.*
7.   Author interview with Frank Carlucci, January 19, 2005.
8.   Author interview with Nelson Ledsky, March 2, 2005.
9.   Steven Engelberg, "Marines Say Two Guards Allowed Russians to Roam
      U.S. Embassy," *New York Times*, March 28, 1987, 1.
10.   The former NSC official passed on the information on the understanding
      that it would not be attributed to him.
11.   Pete Early, "Spy Fiasco," *Washington Post Magazine*, February 7, 1988,
      W20.
12.   Shultz, *Turmoil and Triumph*, 880–85, 900.
13.   Memorandum for Frank C. Carlucci from Fritz W. Ermarth (and attached
      letter to Massie for the president's signature), April 23, 1987, Ronald Rea-
      gan Presidential Library.
14.   Memorandum for the President from Frank C. Carlucci, April 30, 1987,
      Ronald Reagan Presidential Library.

Chapter 8: Carlucci's Notes
1.   Handwritten notes of Massie meeting of February 25, 1987, and Memo-
      randum for the President from Frank C. Carlucci, April 30, 1987, Ronald
      Reagan Presidential Library.
2.   Ibid.
3.   Message to be mailed to Suzanne Massie, March 2, 1989, Ronald Reagan
      Presidential Library.
4.   Author interview with Suzanne Massie, February 16, 2008.

PART III: BERLIN

Chapter 1: The Speech
1.   Interview with Dana Rohrabacher, May 5, 2005.
2.   Philip Zelikow and Condoleezza Rice, *Germany United and Europe Trans-
      formed* (Cambridge, Harvard University Press, 1995), 20.
3.   Author interview with Brent Scowcroft, May 26, 2006.

Chapter 2: Twenty-fifth Anniversary
1.   For details of the anniversary celebrations, see Rupert Cornwell, "German
      Views Collide Across Berlin Wall," *The Guardian*, August 14, 1986, 2;

Kevin Costelloe, "Berlin Wall Turns 25," Associated Press, August 13, 1986.

2. Robert J. McCartney, "Berlin Wall At 25," *Washington Post*, August 13, 1986, A19.

3. Terence Hunt, "Reagan Says East Germany Should Tear Down Wall," Associated Press, August 11, 1986.

4. Ronald Reagan News Conference, August 12, 1986, in Ronald Reagan Presidential Library.

5. Author interview with Barry Lowenkron, May 18, 2005.

6. John Lewis Gaddis, *Now We Know* (Oxford: Oxford University Press, 1997), 140 and passim.

7. Hope M. Harrison, *Driving the Soviets Up the Wall* (Princeton: Princeton University Press, 2003), 158.

8. Gaddis, *Now We Know*, 146.

9. Harrison, *Driving the Soviets*, 180–81.

10. David Binder, "Revival of the Berlin Wall Debate: If West Had Knocked It Down," *New York Times*, August 14, 1986, A-16.

11. Arthur M. Schlesinger, Jr., *A Thousand Days* (London: Mayflower-Dell, 1967), 681–82.

12. Author interview with Egon Bahr, December 20, 2005.

13. Author interview with Eberhard Diepgen, October 12, 2005.

Chapter 3: Day Visit of a Presidential Candidate

1. Kiron K. Skinner, Annelise Anderson, and Martin Anderson, eds., *Reagan: A Life in Letters* (New York: Free Press, 2003), 536.

2. Memorandum for Governor Reagan from Dick Allen re "The Strategy for Peace Theme," August 25, 1978.

3. Oral interview of Peter Hannaford to Hoover Institution and Gorbachev Foundation, June 5, 2000.

4. Author interview with Helmut Kohl, September 27, 2007.

5. Peter Hannaford, "Listening and Learning: Ronald Reagan's first visit to Berlin, 1978," article for *Tear Down This Wall*, museum publication of the Allied Museum in Berlin, 2007.

6. Author interview with Richard Allen, November 2, 2004; Hannaford oral interview.

7. Friedhelm Kemna, "Reagan schliesst neue Kandidatur bei den Republicanern nicht aus," *Die Welt*, December 2, 1978.

8. Lou Cannon, "Reagan Urges Deterrence Through Strength," *Washington Post*, June 10, 1982, A1.

9. Leslie Colitt, "Go Back to Hollywood, 60,000 Berliners Tell Reagan," *Financial Times*, June 11, 1982, 3; John Tagliabue, "Thousands of Anti-Reagan Protesters Clash with the Police in West Berlin," *New York Times*, June 12, 1982, 8.

10. Ronald Reagan, "Remarks to the People of Berlin," June 11, 1982, Ronald Reagan Presidential Library.
11. Ronald Reagan, "Remarks on Arrival in Berlin," June 11, 1982, Ronald Reagan Presidential Library.
12. Steven R. Weisman, "Reagan, in Berlin, Bids Soviet Work for a Safe Europe," *New York Times*, June 12, 1982, 1.
13. Ronald Reagan, "Remarks on Arrival in Berlin."
14. Author interview with Barry Lowenkron, May 18, 2005.
15. Author interview with Richard von Weizsäcker, November 23, 2005.
16. Transcript of Honecker-Chernenko Meeting in Moscow, August 17, 1984, in Vojtech Mastny and Malcolm Byrne, eds., *A Cardboard Castle? An Inside History of the Warsaw Pact 1955–1991* (Budapest: Central European University Press, 2005), 496.
17. Author interview with Egon Krenz, November 17, 2005.
18. William Drozdiak, "Soviet Campaign Against W. Germany Seen as Aimed at Unity of East Bloc," *Washington Post*, June 28, 1984, A-17.
19. Author interview with Egon Bahr, December 20, 2005.
20. Author interview with Eberhard Diepgen, October 12, 2005.
21. Author interview with Helmut Kohl, September 27, 2007.
22. John Kornblum, "Reagan's Brandenburg Concerto," *The American Interest*, Summer (May/June) 2007, 28.
23. Author interview with Nelson Ledsky, March 2, 2005; author interview with John Kornblum, September 20, 2005.
24. Author interview with Richard Burt, May 4, 2005.

Chapter 4: "He Blew It"
1. Author interview with Nancy Reagan, June 29, 2005,
2. Author interview with George Shultz, Feb. 16, 2005.
3. Jim Kuhn, *Ronald Reagan in Private*, (New York: Sentinel, 2004), 203.
4. George J. Church, "Can Reagan Recover?" *Time*, March 9, 1987, pp. 20–24.
5. Author interview with Ken Duberstein, July 11, 2002.
6. Author interview with Thomas Griscom, April 12, 2005.

Chapter 5: Anti-Soviet Jokes
1. Agriculture joke: Jim Kuhn, *Ronald Reagan in Private* (New York: Sentinel, 2004), 115. Car salesman joke: author interview with Rudolf Perina, May 18, 2005. Brezhnev joke: Richard Pipes, *Vixi* (New Haven: Yale University Press, 2003), 166.
2. Author interview with Eberhard Diepgen, October 12, 2005; author interview with Hildegard Boucsein, October 10, 2005.
3. George P. Shultz, *Turmoil and Triumph* (New York: Charles Scribner's Sons, 1993), 875.
4. Eberhart Diepgen, Zwischen den Mächten: *Von dem Besetzten Stadt zur Hauptstadt* (Berlin: im.be.bre Verlag, 2004), 58.

5. These quotes are taken from "Presidential June 12 Berlin Speech," and accompanying "Draft Presidential Speech, Berlin, June 12, 1987," dated March 6, 1987, obtained from the State Department under the Freedom of Information Act.

6. Ibid., 1, 2, 22.

7. Ibid., cover letter, 2.

8. John C. Kornblum, "Reagan's Brandenburg Concerto," *The American Interest*, May/June 2007, 31.

9. Peter Robinson, *How Ronald Reagan Changed My Life* (New York: HarperCollins, 2003), 96.

Chapter 6: The Orator and His Writers

1. Lou Cannon, *Governor Reagan: His Rise to Power* (New York: Public Affairs, 2003), 116.

2. George P. Shultz, oral interview, Miller Center of Public Affairs, University of Virginia, December 18, 2002, 33.

3. Donald Regan, oral interview, Hoover Institution, June 7, 2000, 37.

4. Jim Kuhn. *Ronald Reagan in Private* (New York: Sentinel, 2004), 139.

5. Richard Allen, oral interview, Miller Center, May 28, 2002.

6. Jack F. Matlock, *Reagan and Gorbachev* (New York: Random House, 1984), 87.

7. Frederick K. J. Ryan, Jr., oral interview, Miller Center, May 25, 2004, 7.

8. Ronald Reagan State of the Union address, January 26, 1982.

9. Kiron K. Skinner, Annelise Anderson, and Martin Anderson, eds., *Reagan: In His Own Hand* (New York: Simon & Schuster, 2001).

10. Edwin Meese, oral history with Hoover Institution, January 22, 2001, 55.

11. Author interview with Dana Rohrabacher, May 5, 2005.

12. Aram Bakshian, oral interview, Miller Center, January 14, 2002.

13. Author interviews with Anthony Dolan, June 21, 2006, and April 23, 2007.

14. Author interview with Thomas Simons, May 17, 2006.

Chapter 7: One Night Free in West Berlin

1. This account is taken from interviews with John C. Kornblum on September 26, 2005, and June 6, 2006, as well as from Kornblum's own published account. See John C. Kornblum, "Reagan's Brandenburg Concerto," *The American Interest*, Summer (May/June) 2007, 25–32.

2. Author interview with Thomas Griscom, April 12, 2005.

3. Peter Robinson, *How Ronald Reagan Changed My Life* (New York: Regan-Books, 2003), 9–12.

4. Author interviews with Peter Robinson, February 16, 2005, and November 1, 2006.

5. Berlin Initiative, office files of Nelson Ledsky, Ronald Reagan Presidential

Library; see, for example, "Berlin Mayor Diepgen and Soviet Ambassador Kochemassov Discuss April 30 Festamt," Cable 161547Z, April 1987.

6. Robinson, *How Ronald Reagan*, 96.
7. "Presidential June 12 Berlin Speech," March 6, 1987.
8. Author interview with Dieter and Ingeborg Elz, September 29, 2007.
9. Notes of dinner in West Berlin provided to author by Peter Robinson.
10. Dimitri K. Simes, "Tearing Down the Berlin Wall," *Washington Post*, March 1, 1987, D-5.
11. Robinson notebook.
12. Author interview with Eberhard Diepgen, October 12, 2005.
13. Author interview with John Kornblum, September 20, 2005.

Chapter 8: Competing Drafts
1. Author interviews with Anthony Dolan, June 21, 2006, and Peter Robinson, November 1, 2005.
2. These documents are taken from Peter Robinson drafts in Ronald Reagan Presidential Library: Berlin (undated); Brandenburg II (undated); May 20, 1987 draft of Presidential Address at Brandenburg Gate.
3. Author interviews with Thomas Simons, May 17, 2006, and Rozanne Ridgway, June 20, 2005.
4. State Department cable E.O. 12356, May 20, 1987, "Presidential Initiative on Berlin," in Nelson Ledsky Files, Box 92169, Ronald Reagan Presidential Library.
5. Memo from Grant S. Green, Jr., "Presidential Initiative on Berlin," May 8, 1987, in files of Colin Powell, Ronald Reagan Presidential Library.
6. Author interview with John Kornblum, June 6, 2006.
7. Richard A. Viguerie, "Hello Baker, Bye-bye Reagan: In the End, the Washington Establishment Always Wins," *Washington Post*, March 15, 1987, C-5.
8. Author interview with Thomas Griscom, April 12, 2005.
9. Ibid.
10. Author interview with Dana Rohrabacher, May 5, 2005.
11. Author interview with Peter Robinson, November 1, 2006; Peter Robinson, *How Ronald Reagan Changed My Life* (New York: ReganBooks, 2003), 99–100.
12. Author interview with Frank Carlucci, January 19, 2005.
13. Colin Powell, *My American Journey* (New York: Ballantine Books, 1995), 321–22.
14. "NSC Comments on Berlin Speech (5/21/87-12:00 noon draft)," Ronald Reagan Presidential Library, WHORM files SP1140, 501964.
15. "26 May to Amb. Ridgway," White House Staff and Office Files of Colin Powell, Box 92476 (5), Ronald Reagan Presidential Library.

Chapter 9: Warsaw Pact

1.   Front-page photos, *Berliner Zeitung*, May 28 and 29, 1987.
2.   Author interview with Egon Krenz, November 17, 2005.
3.   Anatoly S. Chernyaev, *My Six Years With Gorbachev* (University Park: Pennsylvania State University Press, 2000), 87.
4.   Author interview with Anatoly Adamishin, April 10, 2008.
5.   Jack F. Matlock, Jr., *Autopsy on an Empire* (New York: Random House, 1995), 61–66; Celestine Bohlen, "Gorbachev Says Democracy Will Strengthen Nation," *Washington Post*, February 26, 1987, A32.
6.   Michael T. Kaufman, "Glasnost Upsetting to Soviet Allies," *New York Times*, April 5, 1987, Section 4, 4.
7.   Ibid.
8.   Charles S. Maier, *Dissolution: The Crisis of Communism and the End of East Germany* (Princeton: Princeton University Press, 1997), 155; "E. Germany Won't Copy Gorbachev," *Journal of Commerce*, April 10, 1987, 4A.
9.   Author interview with Frank Herold, November 14, 2005.
10. Author interview with Bettina Urbanski, November 14, 2005.
11. Author interview with Lothar de Maizière, October 18, 2005.
12. Voitech Mastny and Malcolm Byrne, eds., *A Cardboard Castle? An Inside History of the Warsaw Pact, 1955–1991* (Budapest: Central European University Press, 2005), 563–64.
13. Chernyaev, *My Six Years*, 105.
14. Robert M. Gates, *From the Shadows* (New York: Simon & Schuster, 1996), 423.
15. Matlock, *Autopsy on an Empire*, 139.
16. Anatoly Dobrynin, *In Confidence* (New York: Times Books, 1995), 631.
17. Mastny and Byrne, *A Cardboard Castle?* 559–60.
18. An excellent account of Rust's trip is in Michael Dobbs, *Down With Big Brother* (New York: Alfred A. Knopf, 1997), 179–82.
19. Stenographic record of the meeting of party secretaries, May 29, 1987, in Mastny and Byrne, *A Cardboard Castle?* 566–67.
20. Dobrynin, *In Confidence*, 632.
21. Chernyaev, *My Six Years*, 119.

Chapter 10: "I Think We'll Leave It In"

1.   "May 27, 1989, Memorandum to Rhett Dawson From Grant Green," WHORM Files SP 1150, 501694, Ronald Reagan Presidential Library.
2.   Memo, May 27, 1987, from Rozanne L. Ridgway to Colin Powell, "President's Berlin Speech," obtained from State Department under Freedom of Information Act.
3.   Author interview with Peter Rodman, April 25, 2005.
4.   "NSC Changes to Robinson Draft of May 29, 1987, 9:00 a.m.," Speechwriting Records, Office Records OA 18094-18100, Ronald Reagan Presidential Library.

5. "NSC Changes Recommended to Robinson Draft of May 27, 1987, 1:30 p.m." and Colin L. Powell Memorandum for Tom Griscom, June 1, 1987, WHORM files SP1150, Ronald Reagan Presidential Library.

6. Author interviews with Peter Robinson, November 1, 2006; Thomas Griscom, April 12, 2005; and Colin Powell, November 2, 2006.

7. Griscom interview; author interview with George Shultz, February 16, 2005.

8. Author interviews with Kenneth Duberstein, July 11, 2002, and June 24, 2005.

Chapter 11: Rock Concert

1. Rodman memo to Powell, June 3, 1987, WHORM files SP 1150, Ronald Reagan Presidential Library.

2. Ibid.

3. Author interview with Hildegard Boucsein, former assistant to Eberhard Diepgen, October 10, 2005; author interview with Eberhard Diepgen, October 12, 2005.

4. Author interview with Walter Ischinger, June 15, 2005.

5. Robert J. McCartney, "Kohl Calls on East Germans to Tear Down Wall," *Washington Post*, May 1, 1987, A10.

6. George P. Shultz, *Turmoil and Triumph* (New York: Charles Scribner's Sons, 1993), 550.

7. Author interview with Horst Teltschik, October 5, 2005.

8. Author interviews with John Kornblum, September 20, 2005, and June 6, 2006.

9. Author interview with Egon Krenz, November 17, 2005.

10. Krenz interview.

11. Diepgen interview.

12. State Department cable "The Inner-German Merry-Go-Round," May 12, 1987, in Nelson Ledsky Files, Ronald Reagan Presidential Library.

13. "East German Rock-Music Fans Throw Stones at Police," Associated Press, June 7, 1987; Ingomar Schwelz, "Police Battle with East Berlin Rock Fans Near Berlin Wall," Associated Press, June 8, 1987; Robert J. McCartney, "East German Rock Fans, Police Clash," *Washington Post*, June 9, 1987, A1.

14. Anna Christensen, "East German Authorities Deny Police Clashed With Youths," Associated Press, June 9, 1987.

15. State Department Cable, "The East Berlin Disturbances and the President's Brandenburg Gate Speech," June 10, 1987, obtained from State Department under Freedom of Information Act.

Chapter 12: Venetian Villa

1. Donnie Radcliffe, "Bed to Go: In Venice, the Rest Is Reagan," *Washington Post*, June 3, 1987, D-1.

2.   Ronald Reagan, *The Reagan Diaries* (New York: HarperCollins, 2007), 503.

3.   Radcliffe, "Bed to Go"; Reagan, *The Reagan Diaries*, 504; Jim Kuhn, *Ronald Reagan in Private* (New York: Sentinel, 2005), 230.

4.   Kuhn, *Reagan in Private*, 102.

5.   Author interview with Kenneth Duberstein, July 11, 2002, and June 24, 2005.

6.   Terence Hunt, "Reagan Says East Germany Should Tear Down Wall," Associated Press, August 11, 1986.

7.   Text, "Written Responses to Questions Submitted by Deutsche Press-Agentur of the Federal Republic of Germany," June 2, 1987, Ronald Reagan Presidential Library; State Department cable 031038Z June 1987, obtained through Freedom of Information Act.

8.   State Department cable 041107Z June 1987, obtained through Freedom of Information Act.

9.   State Department cables 031038Z and 051458Z, June 1987, obtained through Freedom of Information Act.

10.   Lou Cannon, "Reagan Hopes Summit Will Boost Image," *Washington Post*, June 5, 1987, A-22.

11.   Alex Brummer, "Reagan Leaves the Talking at Venice to his Aides," *The Guardian*, June 9, 1987; Lionel Barber, "The Old Reagan Magic Fails as Americans Await the Next Act," *Financial Times*, June 17, 1987, 4; Lou Cannon, "Aides Repair Gaffe by Reagan on Dollar," *Washington Post*, June 12, 1987, A-19.

12.   Interview with Frank Carlucci, January 19, 2005.

13.   Transcript of the President's News Conference, June 11, 1987; Lou Cannon, "Aides Repair Gaffe."

Chapter 13: Brandenburg Gate

1.   Author interview with Eberhard Diepgen, October 12, 2005.

2.   Author interview with Richard von Weizsäcker, November 23, 2005.

3.   Author interview with John Kornblum, September 20, 2005.

4.   Gerald M. Boyd, "Raze Berlin Wall, Reagan Urges Soviet," *New York Times*, June 13, 1987, 3; State Department cable 15155Z June 1987, obtained under Freedom of Information Act.

5.   Ronald Reagan transliteration copy of Berlin Wall speech, at Ronald Reagan Presidential Library, WHORM file, SP1150, 501964 (box 5 of 9).

6.   Videotape of Berlin Wall address; Lou Cannon, "Reagan Challenges Soviets to Dismantle Berlin Wall," *Washington Post*, June 13, 1987, A1; Edmund Morris, *Dutch*, p. 624.

7.   This description of the East German crowd is taken from an eyewitness account filed by an American diplomat in East Berlin: State Department cable 121341Z June 1987, obtained under Freedom of Information Act.

Chapter 14: Why Not "Mr. Honecker"?

1. Author interview with Bettina Urbanski, November 14, 2005.
2. Author interview with Maritta Adam-Tkalec, November 14, 2005.
3. Author interview with Jörg Halthöfer, December 15, 2005.
4. "Reagan-Rede als militant bezeichnet," *Frankfurter Allgemeine*, June 15, 1987, 2. State Department cable130758Z, obtained under Freedom of Information Act.
5. Author interview with Egon Krenz, November 17, 2005.
6. Ibid.
7. Hope Harrison, *Driving the Soviets Up the Wall* (Princeton: Princeton University Press, 2003), 139–234.
8. State Department cable 218719Z, obtained under Freedom of Information Act.
9. "Pravda: Reagan's Berlin Speech Laden with 'Crocodile Tears," Associated Press, June 13, 1987; State Department cable 151233Z, June 1987, obtained under Freedom of Information Act. Reuters News Service, "Reagan Talk 'War-Mongering,' Soviets Say," *Toronto Star*, June 13, 1987, A3.
10. Aleksandr Bovin, "Moscow Distrusts Tears," commentary in *Izvestia*, June 18, 1987, contained in Nelson Ledsky files, Box 921679, Berlin Initiatives, Ronald Reagan Presidential Library.
11. Anatoly S. Chernyaev, *My Years with Gorbachev* (University Park: Pennsylvania State University Press, 2000), 116.
12. State Department cable 161511Z June 1987, obtained under Freedom of Information Act.
13. Author interview with Karsten D. Voigt, November 11, 2005.
14. Author interview with Hans-Otto Bräutigam, October 11, 2005.
15. Author interview with Hildegard Boucsein, October 10, 2005.
16. Kissinger comments as reported in State Department cable 121501Z June 1987.
17. Editorial, "Reagan's Greatest Hits," *New York Times*, June 17, 1987; Jim Hoagland, "The Pope's Politics," *Washington Post*, June 19, 1987, A-2.
18. EUR Press Guidance, "Berlin: President's Speech," June 12, 1987, obtained from State Department under Freedom of Information Act.
19. "Berlin as site for CSCE Follow-Up Meeting," State Department cable 071649Z, July 1987, Nelson Ledsky Files Box 92169, Berlin Initiative, Ronald Reagan Presidential Library.
20. Foreign News Briefs, United Press International, July 3, 1987.
21. Ronald Reagan Remarks on Soviet-United States Relations at the Town Hall of California Meeting in Los Angeles, August 26, 1987; Radio Address to the Nation on Soviet-United States Relations, August 29, 1987, Ronald Reagan Presidential Library.

Chapter 15: On His Own
1. Richard M. Nixon Memorandum to the File, April 28, 1987, Richard Nixon Library.
2. Memorandum for the President from Anthony R. Dolan, June 15, 1987, WHORM files SP1150, Box 501963, Ronald Reagan Presidential Library.

PART IV: SUMMITS

Chapter 1: "Quit Pressing"
1. See, for example, Ronald W. Reagan, *An American Life* (New York: Simon & Schuster, 1990), 611.
2. Jack F. Matlock, Jr., *Reagan and Gorbachev* (New York: Random House, 2004), 64–66.
3. Ronald Reagan, *The Reagan Diaries* (New York: HarperCollins, 2007), 222 (March 1, 1984).
4. Anatoly Dobrynin, *In Confidence* (New York: Times Books, 1995), 560.
5. Author interview with Thomas Simons, May 17, 2006.
6. Author interviews with Horst Teltschik, October 5, 2005, and December 7, 2005.
7. Joint Statement of President Reagan and Chancellor Helmut Kohl, November 30, 1984.
8. James F. Kuhn, oral interview, Miller Center of Public Affairs, University of Virginia, March 7, 2003, 71.
9. President Reagan letter to Mikhail Gorbachev, March 11, 1985, in White House Staff and Office Files, Head of State Correspondence, Box 3940, Ronald Reagan Presidential Library.
10. Mikhail Gorbachev letter to Ronald Reagan, March 24, 1985, ibid.; George P. Shultz, *Turmoil and Triumph* (New York: Charles Scribner's Sons, 1993), 564–65.
11. Matlock, *Reagan and Gorbachev*, 159; Dobrynin, *In Confidence*, 595.
12. Memorandum, October 3, 1986, from Rodney B. McDaniel to Tony Dolan, "Iceland Themes," White House Staff and Office Files, National Security Council, European and Soviet Division, Box 3, Ronald Reagan Presidential Library. Reagan quote from Soviet transcript of Reykjavik meeting of October 11, 1986, published in United States by Foreign Broadcasting Information Service, May 17, 1993, 3.
13. Author interview with Helmut Kohl, September 27, 2007.
14. Author interview with Jack Matlock, September 18, 2007.
15. Dobrynin, *In Confidence*, 509; Richard Pipes, *Vixi* (New Haven: Yale University Press, 2003), 163; Thomas C. Reed, *At the Abyss* (New York: Ballantine Books, 2005), 258.
16. Nancy Reagan, *My Turn* (New York: Random House, 1989), 288–89.
17. Kuhn, oral interview, Miller Center, 152.
18. Author's Kohl interview.

19. Stuart Spencer, oral interview, Miller Center, November 15–16, 2001, 12–13.
20. Shultz, *Turmoil and Triumph*, 904.

Chapter 2: An Arms Deal and Its Opponents

1. Don Oberdorfer, *The Turn* (New York: Poseidon Press, 1991), 217.
2. Politburo meeting, February 26, 1987, INF document collection, National Security Archive.
3. George P. Shultz, *Turmoil and Triumph*, (New York: Charles Scribner's Sons, 1993), 896–99.
4. Richard M. Nixon and Henry A. Kissinger, "An Arms Agreement—on Two Conditions," *Washington Post*, April 26, 1987, D-7.
5. Richard M. Nixon, Memorandum to the File, April 28, 1987, Richard Nixon Library.
6. Ibid.
7. Ibid.
8. Brent Scowcroft, "Fewer Is Not Better," *Washington Post*, April 20, 1987, A-15.
9. Author interview with Brent Scowcroft, May 26, 2006.
10. Nixon memorandum, April 28, 1987.
11. Nixon and Kissinger, "An Arms Agreement."
12. Author interview with Jack Matlock, September 18, 2007.
13. Ronald Reagan, *The Reagan Diaries* (New York: HarperCollins, 2007), 495.
14. Serge Schmemann, "West German Parliament Backs Plan on Medium-Range Missiles," *New York Times*, June 5, 1987, A-2.
15. Author's Matlock interview; Ronald Reagan, *An American Life* (New York: Simon & Schuster, 1990), 686; Robert J. McCartney, "Bonn Pledges to Scrap Missiles if U.S., Soviets Agree on Treaty," *Washington Post*, August 26, 1987, A-1.

Chapter 3: Shultz's Pitch

1. George Shultz, "The Shape, Scope and Consequences of the Age of Information," speech delivered in Paris, March 21, 1986; Shultz, "Western Leadership and the Global Economy," speech delivered in Washington, D.C., April 28, 1988, from U.S. Department of State.
2. Michael Lang, "Globalization and Its History," *The Journal of Modern History* 78 (December 2006), 903.
3. This account is based upon interviews with George Shultz, February 16, 2005, and Richard D. Kauzlarich, June 21, 2005, as well as memos and charts supplied by Mr. Kauzlarich. See also George P. Shultz, *Turmoil and Triumph* (New York: Charles Scribner's Sons, 1993), 891–93,
4. Author interview with Richard Solomon, April 18, 2005.

5.   Stephen Kotkin, *Armageddon Averted: The Soviet Collapse 1970–2000* (New York: Oxford University Press, 2001), 15–16.

6.   Anatoly S. Chernyaev, *My Six Years with Gorbachev* (University Park: Pennsylvania State University Press, 2000), 9.

7.   Vladislav M. Zubok, *A Failed Empire* (Chapel Hill: University of North Carolina Press, 2007), 288–91.

8.   Pavel Palazchenko, *My Years with Gorbachev and Shevardnadze* (University Park: Pennsylvania State University Press, 1997), 64.

9.   Chernyaev, *My Six Years*, 84.

10. Kiron K. Skinner, Annelise Anderson, and Martin Anderson, eds., *Reagan: In His Own Hand* (New York, Touchstone/Simon & Schuster, 2001), 12, 147; Reagan letter to George Murphy, December 19, 1985, White House correspondence files, Ronald Reagan Presidential Library.

11. Author's Shultz interview.

12. Anatoly Dobrynin, *In Confidence* (New York: Times Books, 1995), 644.

13. Politburo meeting, April 16, 1987, INF document collection, National Security Archive; Mikhail Gorbachev, *Memoirs* (New York: Doubleday, 1996), 440.

14. Author interview with Jeane Kirkpatrick, March 3, 2005.

15. Peter Schweizer, *Victory* (New York: Atlantic Monthly Press, 1994), passim.

16. Thomas C. Reed, *At the Abyss* (New York: Ballantine Books, 2004), 266–69. The phrase "old shoes" had been originally used by William Safire.

17. Jack C. Matlock, *Reagan and Gorbachev* (New York: Random House, 2004), 75.

18. Caspar Weinberger, oral interview, Miller Center of Public Affairs, University of Virginia, November 19, 2002.

19. Richard Pipes, *Vixi: Memoirs of a Non-Belonger* (New Haven: Yale University Press, 2003), 201–2.

20. Reed, *At the Abyss*, 271.

21. Author's Kirkpatrick interview.

22. Steven Kotkin, *Armageddon Averted: The Soviet Collapse 1970–2000* (New York: Oxford University Press, 2001), 2.

23. For an extended version of this argument, see Zubok, *A Failed Empire*, 305–6.

24. Author interview with Frank Carlucci, January 19, 2005; interview with Helmut Kohl, September 27, 2007.

Chapter 4: The Grand Tour Rejected

1.   "Talking Points for Senator Baker, Conversation with Secretary Shultz," September 8, 1987, White House Staff and Office Files, Howard Baker, Series I, Subject Box 2, Ronald Reagan Presidential Library.

2.   Author interview with Colin Powell, November 2, 2006.

3. Memo, "Options for Gorbachev's Visit," September 23, 1987, White House Staff and Office Files, Files of Kenneth Duberstein, Subject File Index, Box 1, Ronald Reagan Presidential Library.

4. Mikhail Gorbachev letter to Ronald Reagan, September 15, 1987, at Ronald Reagan Presidential Library.

5. White House documents, "Remarks on the Outcome of the Soviet-United States Diplomatic Talks," September 18, 1987, Ronald Reagan Presidential Library.

6. George P. Shultz, *Turmoil and Triumph* (New York: Charles Scribner's Sons, 1993), 988. Henry A. Kissinger, "A New Era for NATO," *Newsweek*, October 12, 1987, 57.

7. "Informal Exchange with Reporters, October 19, 1987," Ronald Reagan Presidential Library.

8. Author interview with Richard Armitage, July 13, 2006.

9. Jay Winik, *On the Brink* (New York: Simon & Schuster, 1996), 488, 583–84.

10. William Safire, "Secrets of the Summit," *New York Times*, December 6, 1987, Section 4, 31; Lou Cannon, "Reagan's Arms Control Dream Is Nightmare for Conservatives," *Washington Post*, October 30, 1987, A-1; Howard Phillips, "The Treaty: Another Sellout," *New York Times*, December 11, 1987, A-39.

11. Philip Taubman, "After 52 Days and Many Rumors, Gorbachev Reappears at Kremlin," *New York Times*, September 30, 1987, A-1.

12. Mikhail Gorbachev, *Memoirs*, Doubleday, New York, 1995, pp. 242–4.

13. Author interview with Egon Krenz, Nov. 17, 1995.

14. Author interview with Hans-Otto Bräutigam, Oct. 11, 2005; Serge Schmemann, "Honecker Visit to West Stirs More Curiosity Than Passion," *New York Times*, Sept. 13, 1987; Robert J. McCartney, "Bonn Receives E. German Leader," *Washington Post*, Sept. 8, 1987, A-13.

15. Schmemann, *op. cit.,* interview with Horst Teltschik, Dec. 7, 2005.

16. Author interview with Hans-Otto Bräutigam, Elizabeth Pond, "German Leaders Agree to Disagree," *Christian Science Monitor*, September 9, 1987.

17. The most extensive accounts of this meeting are in Shultz, *Turmoil and Triumph*, 995–1002; Don Oberdorfer, *The Turn* (New York: Poseidon Press, 1991), 246–57; and Pavel Palazchenko, *My Years With Gorbachev and Shevardnadze* (University Park: Pennsylvania State University Press, 1997), 70–76.

18. "Radio Address to the Nation on the Economy and Soviet–United States Relations," October 24, 1987, Ronald Reagan Presidential Library.

19. Gorbachev letter to Reagan, October 28, 1987, INF document collection, National Security Archive.

20. Gorbachev, *Memoirs*, 446.

21. Author's Powell interview.

Chapter 5: Of Dan Quayle and Errol Flynn

1. Pat Towell, "Before the Ink Is Dry," *Congressional Quarterly*, December 5, 1987, http://library.cqpress.com/cqweekly/WR100402273. Norman D. Sandler, "Summit Ends, Salesmanship Begins," United Press International, December 11, 1987.

2. Tim Ahern, "Lawmakers Sharpen Arms-Control Rhetoric," Associated Press, December 4, 1987; Pat Towell, "Waiting for the INF Treaty: Political Jockeying," *Congressional Quarterly*, September 5, 1987, http://library .cqpress.com/cqweekly/WR100401692; George F. Will, "The Cult of Arms Control," *Washington Post*, December 6, 1987, D-7.

3. Cartoon: Oman, *The Oregonian*, reprinted in *Time* magazine, December 14, 1987, 32.

4. Russell Watson, "The Right Wing Opens Fire," *Newsweek*, November 30, 1987, 36.

5. ABC News Transcripts, "World News Tonight," December 6, 1987; Saundra Saperstein Torry and John Mintz, "Free Jews, Thousands Demand," *Washington Post*, December 7, 1987, A1.

6. Tom Griscom, "Memorandum on Summit Activities," October, 14, 1987, in Files of Kenneth Duberstein, Subject File Index, Box 2, Ronald Reagan Presidential Library.

7. Griscom, ibid.; Ronald Reagan, "Remarks at the United States Military Academy," October 28, 1987, Ronald Reagan Presidential Library.

8. Tom C. Korologos memo, "Summit," November 17, 1987, in Files of Kenneth Duberstein, Subject File Index, Box 2, Ronald Reagan Presidential Library.

9. Ronald Reagan, "Interview With Television Network Broadcasters," December 3, 1987, Ronald Reagan Presidential Library.

10. ABC News Transcripts, "World News Tonight," December 6, 1987.

11. Author interview with Frank Carlucci, January 19, 2005.

12. Author interview with Colin Powell, November 2, 2006; Colin Powell, *My American Journey* (New York: Ballantine Books, 1995), 347–48.

13. Reagan interview with broadcasters.

14. George P. Shultz, *Turmoil and Triumph* (New York: Charles Scribner's Sons, 1993), 1006–9; Pavel Palazchenko, *My Years With Gorbachev and Shevardnadze* (University Park: Pennsylvania State University Press, 1997), 77.

Chapter 6: Gorbachev in Washington

1. Author interview with Fritz Ermarth, January 25, 2005.

2. Memorandum of Conversation, 10:45 a.m., December 8, 1987; Ronald Reagan, *An American Life* (New York: Simon & Schuster, 1990), 698; Mikhail Gorbachev, *Memoirs* (New York: Doubleday, 1995), 447.

3. Memorandum of Conversation, 2:30 pm., December 8, 1987; Colin Powell, *My American Journey* (New York: Ballantine Books, 1995), 350–51;

George P. Shultz, *Turmoil and Triumph* (New York: Charles Scribner's Sons, 1993), 1010–11.

4. Ronald Reagan (Douglas Brinkley, ed.), *The Reagan Diaries* (New York: HarperCollins, 2007), 555.

5. Powell, *My American Journey*, 353–54; *Reagan Diaries*, 557; *An American Life*, 700–701.

6. Shultz, *Turmoil and Triumph*, 1014; Jack F. Matlock, Jr., *Reagan and Gorbachev* (New York: Random House, 2004), 279–80.

7. Elizabeth Kastor and Donnie Radcliffe, "The Night of the Peacemakers," *Washington Post*, December 9, 1987, B1.

8. Shultz, *Turmoil and Triumph*, 1005–6; Nancy Reagan, *My Turn* (New York: Random House, 1989), 38–42.

9. Author interview with Thomas Griscom, April 12, 2005.

10. Memorandum of Conversation, Working Lunch, December 10, 1987.

11. ABC News transcripts, Dec. 10 and 11, 1987.

12. Nixon letter "Dear Ron," December 10, 1987, in Presidential Handwriting File, Series IV, Presidential Telephone Calls Box 10, 700604, Ronald Reagan Presidential Library.

13. Henry A. Kissinger, "The Dangers Ahead," *Newsweek*, December 21, 1987, 34.

14. Ibid.

15. Jacob V. Lamar, "An Offer They Can Refuse," *Time* magazine, December 14, 1987, 32.

16. R. Emmett Tyrell, Jr., "Why a Renowned Hawk Is Mellow," *The Washington Post*, December 11, 1987, A-27.

17. Palazchenko, 78.

18. Gorbachev report quoted in Anatoly S. Chernyaev, *My Six Years with Gorbachev* (University Park: Pennsylvania University Press, 2000), 142–43.

19. Gorbachev, *Memoirs*, 443, 445.

20. Chernyaev, *My Six Years*, 144.

Chapter 7: Making a Treaty Look Easy

1. Jim Kuhn, *Ronald Reagan in Private* (New York: Sentinel Books, 2004), 251–52.

2. Steven V. Roberts, "Waning Days Cast New Glow Over White House," *New York Times*, January 29, 1988, A-14.

3. Interview with William H. Webster, Miller Center for Public Affairs, University of Virginia, August 21, 2002.

4. Author interview with Frank Carlucci, January 19, 2005.

5. Author interview with Colin Powell, November 2, 2006.

6. Author interview with Richard Armitage, July 13, 2006.

7. Author's Powell interview.

8. Ibid.

9. George P. Shultz, *Turmoil and Triumph* (New York: Charles Scribner's Sons, 1993), 1052, 1074.

10. "Memorandum of Conversation, March 11, 1988," attachment to Memorandum for Colin L. Powell from Fritz W. Ermarth, March 31, 1988, in Powell files, Ronald Reagan Presidential Library.

11. Shultz, *Turmoil and Triumph*, 1089.

12. Reagan Interview with Television Network Broadcasters, December 3, 1987; Kiron K. Skinner, Annelise Anderson, and Martin Anderson, eds., *Reagan: A Life in Letters* (New York: Free Press, 2003), 384.

13. Mikhail Gorbachev, *Memoirs* (New York: Doubleday, 1995), 250.

14. Memos of March 11 and March 31, 1988, to Powell.

15. Ronald Reagan speech, "Remarks to the World Affairs Council of Western Massachusetts in Springfield," April 21, 1988.

16. Gorbachev, *Memoirs*, 452; Shultz, *Turmoil and Triumph*, 1097.

17. Author interview with Rozanne Ridgway, June 20, 2005.

18. Ronald Reagan, *The Reagan Diaries* (New York: Harper Collins, 2007), 564–65, 568.

19. "INF's Blue Horizon," *Wall Street Journal*, January 29, 1988, 18, "Mad Momentum," *Wall Street Journal*, April 13, 1988, 28.

20. Richard Nixon, "Dealing With Gorbachev," *New York Times Magazine*, 26, March 13, 1988.

21. Colin Powell, *An American Journey* (New York: Ballantine Books, 1995), 362.

22. Author interview with Frank Carlucci, January 19, 2005; *Reagan Diaries*, 570.

23. *Reagan Diaries*, 566, 574.

24. William F. Buckley, Jr., "Senator Helms Is Luckily in the Way," *National Review*, vol. 40, no. 4 (March 4, 1988), 60.

25. Helen Dewar, "Kissinger Backs Pact, with Misgivings," *The Washington Post*, February 24, 1988, A4.

26. Eloise Salholz, "INF: The Politics of Ratification," *Newsweek*, May 16, 1988, 22.

27. Shultz, *Turmoil and Triumph*, 1084.

28. Don Oberdorfer, *The Turn* (New York: Poseidon Press), 289–90; Lou Cannon, "Reagan: No Pact by Moscow Summit," *Washington Post*, February 26, 1988, A1.

29. Pat Towell, "With Summit Near, Senate Debates INF Treaty," *Congressional Quarterly*, May 21, 1988, 1357.

30. Janet Hook, "Just in Time for Moscow Summit: Senate Votes 93–5 to Approve Ratification of the INF Treaty," *Congressional Quarterly*, May 28, 1988, 1431.

Chapter 8: The Not-So-Evil Empire

1. Ronald Reagan, *The Reagan Diaries* (New York: HarperCollins, 2007), 612–13.

2. George Will, "Détente, Reagan Style," *Washington Post*, May 26, 1988, A-21; George Will, "Foreign Policy That Bewilders," *Washington Post*, May 29, 1988, C-7.

3. Author interview with George Shultz, February 16, 2005; Jack F. Matlock, Jr., *Reagan and Gorbachev* (New York: Random House, 2004), 296–7.

4. Colin Powell, *My American Journey* (New York: Ballantine Books, 1995), 365; Nancy Reagan, *My Turn* (New York: Random House, 1989), 301.

5. Author interview with Rudolf Perina, May 18, 2005; author interview with Richard Solomon, January 21, 2005.

6. Memorandum of Conversation, The President's First One-on-One Meeting with General Secretary Gorbachev, May 29, 1988, in White House Staff and Office Files, Fritz Ermarth, Boxes 92084–5, Ronald Reagan Presidential Library.

7. Author's Perina interview; *Reagan Diaries*, 612.

8. Memorandum of Conversation, May 29, 1988.

9. Author's Perina interview; author interview with Thomas Simons, May 17, 2006, and e-mail exchange, December 7, 2007.

10. Don Oberdorfer, *The Two Koreas* (New York: Basic Books, 2001), 107.

11. Jim Kuhn, *Ronald Reagan in Private* (New York: Sentinel Books, 2004), 240–42.

12. Pavel Palazchenko, *My Years with Gorbachev and Shevardnadze* (University Park: Pennsylvania State University Press, 1997), 92–93.

13. Transcripts of Reagan remarks at Danilov Monastery, May 30, 1988; at luncheon hosted by artists May 31, 1988; and at Spaso House, May 30, 1988, Ronald Reagan Presidential Library.

14. Transcript of Reagan remarks at Moscow State University, May 31, 1988.

15. Memorandum of Conversation, First Plenary Meeting, May 30, 1988, Ronald Reagan Presidential Library.

16. Mikhail Gorbachev, *Memoirs* (New York: Doubleday, 1995), 454.

17. Memorandum of Conversation, Second Plenary Meeting, June 1, 1988, Ronald Reagan Presidential Library.

18. Author interview with Frank Carlucci, January 19, 2005.

19. Memorandum of Conversation, Second Plenary Meeting.

20. Powell, *My American Journey*, 367.

21. Author interview with Rozanne Ridgway, June 20, 2005; author's Carlucci interview.

22. Author's Perina interview.

23. Memorandum of Conversation, President's Second One-on-One Meeting with General Secretary Gorbachev, May 31, 1988.

24. Ibid.

25. Author's Thomas Simons interview.

26. ABC News Transcript, *World News Tonight*, May 31, 1988; Transcript of President's News Conference, June 2, 1988.

27. Jack F. Matlock, Jr., *Autopsy on an Empire*, (New York: Random House, 1995), 124–25.

28. Gorbachev, *Memoirs*, 457.

29. Kiron K. Skinner, Annelise Anderson, and Martin Anderson, eds, *Reagan: A Life in Letters* (New York: Free Press, 2004), 387.

Chapter 9: Bush v. Reagan

1. David Hoffman, "Bush Denies Soviets Have Changed," *Washington Post*, June 8, 1988, A9.

2. Memoranda of Conversations, First and Second One-on-One Meetings with General Secretary Gorbachev, May 29 and 31, 1988, in Ronald Reagan Presidential Library.

3. David S. Broder, "Nomination Is Won, Dukakis Declares," *Washington Post*, June 8, 1988, A1.

4. Anatoly Dobrynin, *In Confidence*, (New York: Times Books, 1995), 535–36, 586–87.

5. Author interview with Rozanne Ridgway, June 20, 2005.

6. Jack F. Matlock, Jr., *Reagan and Gorbachev* (New York: Random House, 2004), 306; Michael R. Beschloss and Strobe Talbott, *At the Highest Levels* (Boston: Little, Brown and Company, 1993), 9.

7. Author interview with Helmut Kohl, September 27, 2007.

8. Mikhail Gorbachev, *Memoirs* (New York: Doubleday, 1995), 518; Maynard Parker, "Kohl to Reagan: Ron, Be Patient," *Newsweek*, October 27, 1986, 25.

9. Author's Kohl interview; author's interview with Horst Teltschik, October 5, 2005.

10. Anatoly S. Chernyaev, *My Six Years With Gorbachev* (University Park: Pennsylvania State University Press, 2000), 199–200; Gorbachev, *Memoirs*, pp. 518–20.

11. Ronald Reagan, *The Reagan Diaries* (New York: HarperCollins, 2007), 653.

12. Transcript of First Bush-Dukakis Presidential Debate, September 25, 1988, Commission on Presidential Debates.

13. Robert M. Gates, *From the Shadows* (New York: Simon & Schuster, 1996), 443–47; Michael Gordon, "CIA Aide Sees Soviet Economy Failing to Gain," *New York Times*, October 15, 1988, A-1.

Chapter 10: The Wall Will Stand for "100 Years"

1. Colin Powell, *An American Journey* (New York: Ballantine Books, 1995), 377–78; George Bush and Brent Scowcroft, *A World Transformed* (New York: Alfred A. Knopf, 1998), 3.

2. Mikhail Gorbachev, *Memoirs* (New York: Doubleday, 1995), 459–60.

3. Text of Mikhail Gorbachev Speech to the United Nations, December 7, 1988, in *Vital Speeches of the Day*, vol. 55, February 1, 1989, 229–36.

4.   Author interview with Thomas Simons, May 17, 2006.
5.   *The Ronald Reagan Diaries*, (New York: HarperCollins, 2007), 675.
6.   Gorbachev, *Memoirs*, p. 463.
7.   Author interview with Rozanne Ridgway, June 20, 2005.
8.   For a full account of this episode, see Michael R. Beschloss and Strobe Talbott, *At the Highest Levels* (Boston: Little, Brown and Company, 1993), 13–15, 19–20. See also Bush and Scowcroft, 16–18.
9.   Author's Simons interview.
10.   ADN news agency transcript of speech by Erich Honecker to Thomas Muenster Committee, BBC Summary of World Broadcasts, January 19, 1989.
11.   Leslie Colitt, "More Flee From East Germany," *Financial Times*, January 6, 1989, 2.
12.   ADN news agency text, New Year's Address by Erich Honecker, BBC Summary of World Broadcasts, January 4, 1989.
13.   "Hungarians Confirm Tank Withdrawal," *Financial Times*, Jan. 26, 1989, 2; Robert J. McCartney, "East Germany to Reduce Its Armed Forces," *Washington Post*, January 24, 1989, A1.
14.   Author interview with John McLaughlin, March 8, 2005.
15.   Interviews with Kenneth Duberstein, July 11, 2002, and June 24, 2005. North was subsequently convicted, but his conviction was overturned on appeal and the charges against him were dismissed.
16.   *Reagan Diaries*, 675.
17.   Duberstein interview; Powell, *An American Journey*, p. 382; Jim Kuhn, *Ronald Reagan in Private* (New York: Sentinel, 2004), 268.
18.   NBC News Transcripts, January 22, 1989.
19.   Author interview with Brent Scowcroft, May 26, 2006.
20.   Gorbachev *Memoirs*, 496–97; Anately S. Chernyaev, *My Six Years with Gorbachev* (University Park: Pennsylvania State University Press, 2000), 215.
21.   Author's Ridgway interview.
22.   Author's Scowcroft interview, May 26, 2006; Derek H. Chollet and James M. Goldgeier, "Once Burned, Twice Shy? The Pause of 1989," in William C. Wohlforth, *Cold War Endgame* (University Park: Pennsylvania State University Press, 2003), 147–51.
23.   Don Oberdorfer, *The Turn* (New York: Poseidon Press, 1991), 347.
24.   Transcript of Speech by President Bush, May 31, 1989, Federal News Service.
25.   Philip Zelikow and Condoleezza Rice, *Germany United and Europe Transformed* (Cambridge: Harvard University Press, 1995), 20; Author's Scowcroft interview.

Epilogue
1.   "Unopposed Candidates Elected in East Germany," United Press International, May 8, 1989.

2. Maureen Johnson, "Reagan Says West Must Take 'Risks' With Gorbachev," Associated Press, June 13, 1989.

3. Vojtech Mastny and Malcolm Byrne, eds., *A Cardboard Castle?* (Budapest: Central European University Press, 2005), 644–46; Jonathan Greenwald, *Berlin Witness*, (University Park: Pennsylvania State University Press, 1993), 40.

4. Author interview with Helmut Kohl, September 27, 2007; author interview with Horst Teltschik, October 5, 2005; Charles S. Maier, *Dissolution* (Princeton: Princeton University Press, 1997), 129.

5. Author interview with Walter Ischinger, June 15, 2005.

6. Mikhail Gorbachev, *Memoirs* (New York: Doubleday, 1995), 522–25.

7. The Gorbachev quote is also sometimes translated as, "Life Punishes Him Who Comes Too Late." See Elizabeth Pond, "A Wall Destroyed," *International Security*, vol. 15, no. 2 (Autumn 1990), 42.

8. Author interview with Egon Krenz, November 17, 2005.

9. Ibid.

10. Pond, *op. cit.*, 45–48.

11. Author's Krenz interview.

12. Author's Ischinger interview.

13. Michael R. Beschloss and Strobe Talbott, *At the Highest Levels* (Boston: Little Brown and Company, 1993), 136.

14. James Baker conversation with author, July 29, 1991.

15. Author interview with George Shultz, February 16, 2005.

16. Thomas L. Friedman, "Nixon Scoffs at Level of Support for Russian Democracy by Bush," *New York Times*, March 10, 1992, A-1.

17. Marvin Kalb, *The Nixon Memo* (Chicago: University of Chicago Press, 1994), 144–66; Monica Crowley, *Nixon Off the Record* (New York: Random House, 1996), 168.

18. Ronald Reagan, *The Reagan Diaries* (New York: HarperCollins, 2007), 590.

19. Ronald Reagan correspondence with Suzanne Massie, WHORM 5003, case file 588091, Ronald Reagan Presidential Library; *Reagan Diaries* (New York: HarperCollins, 2007), 636.

20. Leslie Shepherd, "Reagan Urges Soviet Republics to Let Reason Prevail Over Passion," Associated Press, September 17, 1990.

21. Author interview with Suzanne Massie, March 21, 2005.

22. Richard Allen, oral interview, Miller Center of Public Affairs, University of Virginia, May 28, 2002.

23. Frederick B. Ryan, Jr., oral interview, Miller Center, May 25, 2004.

24. William H. Webster, oral interview, Miller Center, August 21, 2002.

Conclusion

1. Author interview with Nancy Reagan, June 29, 2005.

2. Author interview with Frank Carlucci, January 26, 2007.

3. Author interview with Anatoly Adamishin, April 10, 2008.

INDEX